A Critical Introduction to European Law

2nd Edition

Ian Ward
Professor of Law
University of Newcastle

Members of the LexisNexis Group worldwide

United Kingdom	LexisNexis Butterworths Tolley, a Division of Reed Elsevier (UK) Ltd, Halsbury House, 35 Chancery Lane, London, WC2A 1EL, and 4 Hill Street, EDINBURGH EH2 3JZ
Argentina	LexisNexis Argentina, BUENOS AIRES
Australia	LexisNexis Butterworths, CHATSWOOD, New South Wales
Austria	LexisNexis Verlag ARD Orac GmbH & Co KG, VIENNA
Canada	LexisNexis Butterworths, MARKHAM, Ontario
Chile	LexisNexis Chile Ltda, SANTIAGO DE CHILE
Czech Republic	Nakladatelství Orac sro, PRAGUE
France	Editions du Juris-Classeur SA, PARIS
Hong Kong	LexisNexis Butterworths, HONG KONG
Hungary	HVG-Orac, BUDAPEST
India	LexisNexis Butterworths, NEW DELHI
Ireland	Butterworths (Ireland) Ltd, DUBLIN
Italy	Giuffrè Editore, MILAN
Malaysia	Malayan Law Journal Sdn Bhd, KUALA LUMPUR
New Zealand	LexisNexis Butterworths, WELLINGTON
Poland	Wydawnictwo Prawnicze LexisNexis, WARSAW
Singapore	LexisNexis Butterworths, SINGAPORE
South Africa	LexisNexis Butterworths, DURBAN
Switzerland	Stämpfli Verlag AG, BERNE
USA	LexisNexis, DAYTON, Ohio

© Reed Elsevier (UK) Ltd 2003

A CIP Catalogue record for this book is available from the British Library.

First edition 1996

ISBN 0 406 95810 6

Typeset by M Rules, London
Printed and bound in Great Britain by William Clowes Limited, Beccles and London

Visit Butterworths LexisNexis *direct* at www.butterworths.com

To my parents

Preface

I have found the idea of writing a second edition of *A Critical Introduction to European Law* rather daunting, and have tended to evade the responsibility with whatever vaguely credible excuse has come to mind. However, time has taken its toll, and it has become ever harder to refute the accusation that the first edition has become rather dated. So much in European law changes so rapidly. Seven years ago, the 'new' Union was indeed new. It is not new now. But it is certainly different, not just from that devised in 1992, but from that of which we were all trying to make sense of back in 1995 when I was drafting the first edition of this book. I try to chart these developments in a new chapter 2. The introduction of this chapter, effectively splitting the 'historical' introduction across the first two chapters, is one of a number of structural, as well as substantive, alterations in this second edition. The material on European 'public' law, originally confined to one chapter, has also been broadened so that chapter 3 now concentrates solely on the general principles of European public law, whilst chapter 4 is focused on the reception of these principles in the member states, and primarily in the United Kingdom.

The following two chapters address what is sometimes termed the 'private' or the substantive law of the Community. In doing so, they follow the same structural division that was adopted in the first edition. Chapter 5 examines the law of the market, including the free movement of goods and services, the Common Agricultural Policy and the legal regime that seeks to regulate competition. There are also new sections on the single currency, on the completion of the market and on the European consumer. Chapter 6, meanwhile, investigates the other side of the same coin, those provisions that describe the relationship between the market and the people who seek to work and to move in it. Accordingly, it takes a look at the social law and policy of the Union, as well as the supposed rights of free movement, and it also investigates more recent attempts to address the various forms of discrimination that continue to scar the Community and Union.

The final two chapters then seek to stretch the context still wider, moving away from the 'internal' law of the Community and Union, and towards the deeper questions that arise from the situation of the 'new' Europe in the 'new' world order. They address two particular challenges. Chapter 7 concentrates on external relations, and the external profile, of the Union. Aside from a commentary on the Community's external trading competence, this new chapter addresses Union policy in the related areas of defence, security, enlargement and migration. The need to address these latter challenges will become ever more important during the first decades of the twenty-first century. The final chapter addresses the second challenge, revisiting the same aspiration that was addressed in the final chapter of the first edition. The need for a 'European' public philosophy has become ever more widely accepted, and the weight of scholarship that has emerged in this area during the last seven years is striking. Regardless of its economic efficacy, the 'new' Europe remains bereft of a coherent or compelling public philosophy. It is short on human and civil rights, shorter still on democracy and social justice. It need not be this way, and it should not be this way. The 'peoples' of Europe deserve better.

The structure, and the substance, of the book have then changed. But the critical aspiration has not. I still hold firm to the original premise that lay behind the first edition of this book, that European law, like indeed any other area of law, 'warrants the most rigorously critical examination'. Moreover, such a critique remains both 'internal', in its desire to uncover inconsistencies and injustices, and 'external', in its deployment of broader critical and sceptical commentaries from beyond the narrow confines of legal scholarship. The role of the sceptic remains one that should be constructive, and such a role must be interdisciplinary and contextual. Few now argue against the assertion that the idea of a 'discrete' legal system is as absurd as it is arcane. Law can only be understood as an expression of history, politics, philosophy and a multitude of other disciplines and discourses. European law presents a vivid affirmation of this truth.

The need to acknowledge the assistance of so many friends and colleagues remains just as strong, and those debts acknowledged in 1996 remain just as valid. More recently, I must express my particular gratitude to the University of Alberta Law School for inviting me to take up the Bowker Visiting Professorship, something which impelled me towards developing my ideas on Europe's deeper role within a changing world. Similar more recent debts of gratitude are owed to the Department of Cultural Studies at the University of Turku, as well as the law faculties at Helsinki University, at Montpellier University, at Stanford University and at the Independent University in Lisbon. More generally, I must express my particular gratitude to William Twining for his consistent support for the idea behind this book, as well as his various intellectual interventions over the years. Finally, perhaps the deepest debts are owed to Clare, and to Ross, whose recent arrival has seemed to make the future shape of the world, and Europe's bit of it, all the more important.

Ian Ward
January 2003

Contents

Table of EC Legislation

Table of UK Legislation

Table of cases

PAGE

PAGE

PAGE

PAGE

PAGE

PAGE

**Decisions of the European Court of Justice are listed below numerically.
These decisions are also included in the preceding alphabetical list.**

PAGE

PAGE

PAGE

PAGE

PAGE

Chapter 1

Building Rome

Europe has a long history, even if the history of the European Community is rather shorter, and the history of the European Union shorter still. The purpose of these first two chapters is to explore this history. We cannot hope to understand the present state of Europe if we do not understand its history. In due course we will concentrate upon the political, economic and social aspects of Europe and European law. It will make little sense if we have no notion of where the present idea of Europe and European integration came from. There is one overriding paradox about the 'new' Europe. Whilst its present form might, in some ways, seem to be 'new' indeed, in other ways, it is quite the opposite. The dream of some kind of European community or union has been with us for countless centuries. Moreover, and this is no coincidence, the pervasive semiotic has always been that of Rome. From the Roman Empire to the Holy Roman Empire to the Treaty of Rome, Europe has always been trying to 'build' Rome. And it has not been built in a day. On the contrary, it has taken us two thousand years to get where we are.

The idea of Europe

The European 'idea' is in fact centuries old, twenty-five centuries at least. Down these centuries, various kings and priests, politicians and philosophers have argued the case for some kind of united Europe.

Some, indeed many, have gone to war in order to prove their case. It might indeed be said that only the countervailing idea of the modern nation state, an idea that has come to the fore during the last three of these centuries, has distracted us from this deeper historical truth. There is a very obvious irony in the fact that the European Community was founded by a Treaty of Rome. Scholars invariably cite the Roman Empire as the first concerted attempt to forge a united Europe. The claim is, of course, perfectly credible. The very place, as we have just seen, has acquired a particular symbolic import in European cultural history.

The idea of Europe is 'embedded in Christendom'. The Papacy was the first institution to use the concept of Europe as a political identifier. It symbolised the geopolitical, as well as the cultural, boundaries of the *respublica Christiana* (Delanty, 1995, pp 16–64). Within these boundaries could be found the Christian sequestration of the Aristotelian tradition, the political and legal philosophy articulated by the likes of St Augustine and St Thomas Aquinas, a philosophy geared to images of reason and truth and obedience to both divine and civil authority. Beyond these boundaries could be found the barbarian and the infidel. It was essential that these barbarians should either be kept out or made to conform to European social and cultural norms. The medieval French lawyer Pierre Dubois advocated the despatching of nubile European women in order to seduce and convert the heathens who resided beyond the *respublica* (Heater, 1992, p 11) Sadly the image of 'fortress' Europe remains a dominant one.

A list of those who, over the intervening centuries, have sought to confirm this image of a united Europe includes many of the most famous names in medieval and modern European history; from the Holy Roman Empire of Charlemagne to the Christian Commonwealth of Henry IV of France to the altogether more secular empires envisaged by Napoleon and Hitler. Seminal figures in European intellectual history, such as Gottfried Leibniz, Immanuel Kant and Friedrich Nietzsche, have all projected the idea of some kind of European 'community' as an ultimate political good. For each there were very different motivations, and their prophesies were accordingly rather different.

For Leibniz, writing in the early eighteenth century and amidst the carnage of Europe's seemingly endless religious wars, the idea of a united Europe was very much the idea of a reunited Europe. Leibniz dreamt of 'an age of gold', of what many of his contemporaries termed a 'perpetual peace'. The key to making such a dream a reality, Leibniz affirmed in his *Codex Juris Gentium*, lay in reinstituting a 'universal jurisprudence', by which he meant a pan-European public philosophy (Riley, 1996, pp 236, 243; Ward, 2001, pp 24, 32–37). In simple terms, Leibniz looked back in time in order to perceive the future. Written within the same context, but perhaps in a rather more prophetic tone, Callieres's classic study of diplomacy *On the Manner of Negotiating with Princes* suggested that:

> We must think of the states of which Europe is composed as being joined together by all kinds of necessary commerce, in such a way that they may be regarded as members of one Republic, and that no considerable change can take place in any one of them without affecting the condition of disturbing the peace of all the others. (Held, 1995, p 19.)

Towards the end of the same century, another German philosopher, Immanuel Kant, took up the challenge of devising a 'perpetual peace', writing a series of essays on precisely this theme. Inspired by successive revolutions in America and France, Kant was convinced that the Enlightenment would usher in a new world order based on the fundamental principles of liberty and equality. The French revolution of 1789 in particular proved the 'moral tendency of the human race' (Reiss, 1991, p 182). Whilst approving the idea of a Europe of independent nation states, Kant was convinced that 'perpetual peace' could only be secured if these individual political communities were tied together by a system of 'cosmopolitan right'. In his essay *Perpetual Peace*, he affirmed that:

> This right, since it has to do with the possible union of all nations with a view to certain universal laws for their possible commerce, can be called cosmopolitan right (*ius cosmopoliticum*). (Reiss, 1991, p 158.)

For Kant, as for Leibniz, everything depended upon the institution of a common European public philosophy, and most importantly, a common European jurisprudence. Citizens across the continent, he affirmed, must be encouraged to think 'of the whole of Europe as a single confederated state' (Reiss, 1991, p 156). We shall return to both Kant and Leibniz in due course.

Kant's idea of 'cosmopolitan right', of a 'confederated state', was conceptually quite distinct from the kind of federal order which would, in due course, emerge in the United States and elsewhere. The critical difference lies in the fact that a confederal polity, in Kant's words, 'merely signifies a voluntary gathering of various states', with the possibility of some kind of overarching jurisprudence, perhaps of human rights or international trade, whilst a federal polity 'is based on a political constitution and is therefore indissoluble'. In the parlance of modern international relations, this difference is cast as one between intergovernmental polities and supranational polities. The distinguishing feature here is the presence of a range of supervening political and legal institutions, and very probably a far more intensive and substantive legal system, in a supranational polity. The 'new' Europe, as we shall see in due course, is rather peculiar in that it is partly intergovernmental and partly supranational. Whilst the Community is clearly supranational in form, the shape of Union is rather more ambiguous. Kant would have been confused. Most of our fellow Europeans certainly are.

For the final of our three prophets, Friedrich Nietzsche, writing a century later, the prospect of a united Europe was an inevitable function of a modernity that threatened to crush humanity. He wrote:

> What matters is One Europe, and I see it being prepared slowly and hesitantly. All the vast and profound minds of this century were engaged in the work of preparing, working out and anticipating a new synthesis: the Europe of the future . . . the small states of Europe – I mean our present empires and states – will become economically untenable, within a short time, by reason of the absolute tendency of industry and commerce to become bigger and bigger, crossing natural boundaries and becoming worldwide. (Heater, 1992, p 123.)

If the latter-day Eurosceptic craves an intellectual authority, then Nietzsche offers himself as the supreme harbinger of a seemingly appropriate doom. A 'new' Europe will merely presage the advance of a 'new world order'. It will be the final realisation of the promise of Enlightenment, the kind of promise so enthusiastically savoured by Kant. Everything will be as one, a moral, political and cultural totality. We shall revisit this thesis, just as we will revisit Kant's, in the final chapter of this book. We are still trying to work out which vision, the hopeful or the despairing, is the more apposite; not just for the new Europe, but also for the new world in which we live.

Visions of Europe

It is generally assumed that the present idea of a 'new' Europe sprung up after the end of the 1939–45 war. This is erroneous. It was, in fact, the 1914–18 war that convinced everyone that the Bismarckian balance between nation states could not itself guarantee indefinite peace. At the same time, as Nietzsche had prophesied, it was equally apparent that the new technological world possessed an enormous and frightening capacity to alienate the increasingly disorientated individual. It was during the 1914–18 war, and in the years immediately following it, that it became obvious that the modern world was in a state of crisis, and that a rather more unsettling post-modern one beckoned. The old world order was breaking up, and with it were going all the old certitudes, political, social and philosophical (Eksteins, 1989). The European Union is the most recent, and so far most successful, attempt to reassert some kind of political order amidst this broader mood of pervasive intellectual uncertainty. Again, we will investigate this critical tension, between the modern and post-modern visions of the 'new' world order, in the final chapter of this book.

One of the greater ironies is the fact that the idea of some kind of European community was most significantly developed in one of those countries which has, over time, seemed least comfortable with its conception, the United Kingdom (Wistrich, 1994, p 22). In the years following 1918, the British Federal Union Research Institute vigorously pushed the case for a newly mapped, and distinctively federal, Europe (Ransome, 1991). The origins of this campaign can be traced to Lord Milner's Round Table movement established in 1910. Its ideas were taken up with renewed vigour following the end of the war, and it was Lord Lothian who wedded together the two, the Union Research Institute and Lord Milner's movement, and formed one unified pressure group, the Federal Union movement. Amongst the leaders of Lothian's Federal Union could be found a number of the most influential of early twentieth century British economists, including Lionel Robbins and William Beveridge. From the very beginning it was always assumed that the single most pressing reason for a European community would be economic. The idealism of a Leibniz or a Kant was long gone.

The rise of fascism during the 1920s and 1930s added a further impulse to debates surrounding the possibility of a European federation. A popular federal movement was established in the United Kingdom in 1938. According to Clement Attlee, the choice was clear, 'Europe must federate or perish'. Commenting in 1940, Prime Minister Winston Churchill likewise asserted that there was an 'indissoluble' union between the United Kingdom and France. It was not mere rhetoric, but rather the product of a mindset that had been established by two decades of federal debate at the centre of British political life (Ransome, 1991, pp 1–40; Wistrich, 1994, p 23). The idea of a modern union of European states is quintessentially British. Jean Monnet, who, as we shall see, played the key role in fashioning the European Community during the late 1950s, admitted that many of his ideas were borrowed from the Federal Union. Another of the founding fathers of the Community, Altiero Spinelli, made the same acknowledgment.

What is perhaps most significant about the papers of the Federal Institute and Union, and this is something that is emphasised by the 'constitutional' document which was presented to the 1939 Union Conference, is the determination to effect and maintain a future European Union through the rule of law. Although the intellectual fuel of the Union was largely provided by economists, it was always envisaged that the people who would make it work would be lawyers (Ransome, 1991, pp 118–157). This was the Federal Union's particular intellectual bequest. Not only should there be a Union, but it should be shaped by lawyers and run by lawyers. It is one of the central themes of this book that the particular nature of the new Europe, both its strengths and its weaknesses, are rooted in the fact that it is so peculiarly reliant on the dynamics of legal 'integration'.

At the same time, it would, of course, be a mistake to think that the United Kingdom was the only country in which federal ideas were being explored. In the wake of the Versailles Treaty, a number of individuals in various countries across Europe gravitated towards the idea of some sort of federal union. Two Italians, Giovanni Agnelli, the founder of Fiat, and Attilio Cabiati, an economist, published a paper advocating a strongly centralised European alternative to what they already appreciated was an essentially toothless League of Nations (Weigall and Stirk, 1992, pp 6–7). In 1923, Richard Coudenhove-Kalergi founded the Pan-European Movement, the principal ambition of which was to reassert European autonomy, and thereby reduce both American and Russian influence. In direct contrast, just a few months later, Leon Trotsky advocated a 'United Socialist States of Europe', with the precise intention of spreading Soviet propaganda into the heart of the continent. Meanwhile, any number of economists were busy devising all kinds of European customs unions. Perhaps the most influential was Aristide Briand's 'Regime of a European Federal Union', one of the most interesting facets of which was the idea that the legitimacy of a customs union might be enhanced by appeal to certain common 'moral' principles along with a series of political institutions. Such a structure would, Briand affirmed, provide for something more than the 'simple pact of economic solidarity' (Weigall and Stirk, 1992, pp 8–19; Heater, 1992, pp 124–143; Murphy, 1980, pp 319–330).

Of course, the most fervent advocates of European union during the 1930s were the fascists. Hitler was a particular enthusiast. Moreover, fascist ideology could be found scattered around a number of other influential documents of the time, including Briand's Idealised Union which was founded on certain shared 'racial affinities' (Heater, 1992, p 135; Delanty, 1995, pp112–114). In the end, however, it was as a reaction against the experience of fascism that the new Europe was formed. During the early 1940s, as Churchill mused on the possibility of some kind of British–French union, the federal idea had taken strong root amongst the various socialist resistance movements (Urwin, 1995, pp 7–8). The French resistance produced an influential blueprint through the pen of Leon Blum, whilst Spinelli and Ernesto Rossi penned the famous Ventotene Manifesto on behalf of the Italian communist resistance. The pervasive fear of the resistance movements was a post-war return to the political system of bourgeoisie nation states. The Ventotene manifesto stated:

> The most privileged classes in the old national systems will attempt, by underhand or violent methods, to dampen the wave of internationalist feelings and passions and will ostentatiously begin to reconstruct the old State institutions.

Accordingly:

> The question which must be resolved first, failing which
> progress is no more than mere appearance, is the definitive abo-
> lition of the division of Europe into national sovereign states.
> (Weigall and Stirk, 1992, pp 29–32.)

Of course, the extent to which the fears expressed by Spinelli and
Rossi have come to pass remains a matter of debate. Is today's Europe
anything more than a collection of nation states?

Well before Soviet troops entered Berlin in 1945, Europe's political
leaders had divided into two broad camps. On the one hand were those
like Churchill and the pending President of France, Charles de Gaulle,
who clung rigidly to the idea that the building blocks of Europe would
be its nation states. On the other were those, such as Spinelli and his
fellow socialists, who saw these same nation states as more like stum-
bling blocks than building blocks. This basic perceptual dichotomy
remains, today cast in terms of Europhiles and Eurosceptics.

In the immediate context of the end of the 1939–45 war, a third critical force entered the equation, the United States. Having effectively
won the war that the European allied forces had managed to save, the
United States clearly felt that it should have a say in how the future of
Europe would be determined. The primary concern was to limit the
extent of American financial involvement in Europe's reconstruction
through the Marshall plan. Successive American governments
favoured some kind of federal model, a United States of Europe mod-
elled on a United States of America. This latter idea has enjoyed huge
intellectual currency for half a century or more. One of the most strident supporters of this idea was President Franklin Delano Roosevelt.
Along with Churchill, Roosevelt made it a centrepiece of the
'Declaration on liberated Europe', which was published following the
Yalta Conference. The Declaration is of particular interest, not just
because it confirmed American support for a federal Europe, but
because it also signalled that whilst the United States, and indeed the
United Kingdom, favoured such a model, neither intended to get too
involved with it. A federal Europe would be supported, even funded.
But it would be left to direct itself. This sense was reinforced by one of
the key conditions of the Marshall Plan, which laid down that there
should be the establishment of a 'European economic foundation', so
that, in due course, Europe would be able to reconstruct itself.

It was further reinforced in Churchill's famous speech given in Zurich in 1946:

> We must build a kind of United States of Europe. In this way only will hundreds of millions of toilers be able to regain the simple joys and hopes which make life worth living . . . I am now going to say something that will astonish you. The first step in the recreation of the European family must be a partnership between France and Germany. In this way only can France recover the usual leadership of Europe. There can be no revival of Europe without a spiritually great France and a spiritually great Germany . . . The structure of the United States of Europe, if well and truly built, will be such as to make the material strength of a single state less important . . . Our constant aim must be to build and fortify the strength of the United Nations. Under and within that world concept we must recreate the European family in a regional structure called, it may be, the United States of Europe . . . In all this urgent work, France and Germany must take the lead together. Great Britain, the British Commonwealth of Nations, mighty America, and I trust Soviet Russia . . . must be friends and sponsors of the new Europe and must champion its right to live and shine. (Weigall and Stirk, 1992, pp 40–41.)

Churchill was not much of a political theorist, but his were ideas that were listened to, and it was clear that he envisaged a Europe that would govern itself. Friendship and sponsorship would only go so far. At the same time, it was equally clear that the United Kingdom did not intend to be part of any new European union and, moreover, the reduction of nation state power would only apply to certain nation states, most obviously Germany.

In the years immediately following 1945, the problem of Germany was pivotal. It was not so much a problem of guarding against any resurgent German nationalism, but of engineering German economic reconstruction, and then channelling it for the wider service of Europe. Indeed, the whole future of Europe in 1945 was largely dependent on the regeneration of the European economy (Milward, 1992, p 119). Thus, whilst visionaries might muse upon the idylls of a reunited *respublica*, whether or not it be socialist in tone, the pragmatic arguments oscillated around the potential economic benefits of some kind of dramatically remodelled European 'family'. As one commentator noted, 'it was a question of trying to transform a gaggle of bickering second rate powers into one superpower' (Walters, 1992, p 24). European integration appeared to make sense, not because it was a laudable ideal, but because the gradual and careful implementation of non-tariff based liberal economic policy seemed likely to be the quickest way towards relieving the financial burden of reconstructing Europe; a burden which lay immediately upon the US Treasury.[1] The niceties of nation state sovereignty in Europe were costing millions of US dollars.

To a certain extent it seemed that both sides wanted the same resolution. The United States wanted to relieve its own commitment to Europe, and Europe wanted to reassert its own political and economic autonomy. The cry for European integration and for the establishment of some kind of supranational organisation came to represent a means of moving beyond US hegemony (Laurent, 1989, pp 90–95). The European Union of Federalists, established in 1946 in Paris, stressed these political aspirations in the 1947 Montreux resolutions. It suggested that:

> To start our efforts at unification in the West of Europe means for the West escaping the risk of becoming the victim of power politics, restoring to Europe, at any rate partially, her pride in her legitimate independence . . . Federalists must declare firmly and without compromise that it is absolute sovereignty that must be abated, that a part of that sovereignty must be entrusted to a federal authority. (Weigall and Stirk, 1992, p 42.)

If Europe was going to reassert itself, then its constituent nation states would have to acknowledge that there were sacrifices to be made. The extent to which national sovereignty would have to be limited emerged as a burning question. The republication of Harold Laski's *Liberty in the Modern State* recatalysed theoretical debate. Laski noted that the events of 1939–1945 bore out prewar suspicions that the 'principle of national sovereignty has exhausted its usefulness'. At the same time, however, Laski understood that political sentiment in the various capitals of Europe would not accept the simple abandonment

---

[1]   It has become common postwar historiography to suggest that developments in Europe, and elsewhere in the world, were dictated by the desire of the US to restabilise the international economy (Laurent, 1989, pp 90–91).

of the nation state. So instead he advocated a 'functional' as opposed to 'territorial' federalism, based upon supranational control of economic production (Lasok and Bridge, 1994, pp 4–5).

Meanwhile the familiar intergovernmental and supranational alternatives were beginning to line up, attracting familiar centre-right and left-wing political affiliations. It was in Germany, the state governed by the most recognisably socialist government, that integrationist and federal idealism was most apparent. Not only, of course, was Germany the most socialist of western European states, but so too was it was the one that stood to gain most from the economic reconstruction which integration promised. Carlo Schmid, the prominent social democrat ideologue who played a major role in drafting the German Basic Law, argued strongly that only supranational bodies could effectively check the nation state (Weigall and Stirk, 1992, pp 48–49). Likewise, only a strong supranational economic organisation could effect a rapid reconstruction of Germany.

Whilst being much more conservative than their German counterparts, the British Labour Party similarly spoke of the need for a 'spiritual' Union in Europe, although Ernest Bevin, in his plan for a Western Union, remained firmly intergovernmental, warning against any 'rigid' political 'thesis'. Emphasising the ambivalence in British socialism and, given his own earlier enthusiasm for a federal Europe, in his own mind, the now Prime Minister Clement Attlee went further still in declaring that the idea of European federation actually threatened the countervailing idea of international socialism. Such confusion has been the hallmark, not just of the British Labour Party, but of Britain itself since the very inception of the European idea (Weigall and Stirk, 1992, p 46; Urwin, 1995, pp 29–34, 46; George, 1994, p 20).

A coming together

Ideological rhetoric, thus, vied with economic pragmatism. If the currency of debate during the 1930s and 1940s was rather more visionary, by the 1950s the pragmatic argument had become ascendant. As Robert Schuman, another of the 'fathers' of the new Europe, emphasised, the case for European integration was driven by economic necessity (Laurent, 1989, p 100). It was a view that chimed with wider developments in global trade. In the immediate post-war years a number of intergovernmental economic organisations were established, including the IMF, the Havana Charter, the General Agreement on Tariffs and Trade (GATT), the Marshall Plan, which established the OEEC, NATO, the Council of Europe and the Benelux Union. The latter Union, which operated as a customs union between Holland, Belgium and Luxembourg, can perhaps be seen as being more supranational in spirit, and accordingly as something of a dry run for future European integration. At the same time, however, in the eyes of many, including Jean Monnet, who like Schuman is commonly regarded as one of the founding figures of the European Community, such firmly intergovernmental organisations as the OEEC or the Council, were precisely the 'opposite of the Community spirit' (Monnet, 1978, p 273). The establishment of the Council of Europe, a body entirely devoid of real supranational governance, described the kind of Europe that the more nostalgic nation states preferred to imagine.

The first substantive plan, which, though still very much intergovernmental in its conception, again expressed a certain supranational sentiment, was the establishment of the ECSC, or European Coal and Steel Corporation (Heater, 1992, p175; Milward, 1992, pp 134–167). The immediate impetus for the ECSC came from the Schuman Declaration. And whilst the presence of both Schuman and Monnet in the drafting of the Declaration, as well as the establishment of the ECSC, might suggest the triumph of integrationist idealism, in reality it was an acknowledgment that the primary dynamics were still very much economic. Political integration, if there was to be any, would follow in the slipstream of economic necessity.

The idea, that economic integration would be a first step, and that future political, social, even cultural, integration might follow in due course, has become known as incrementalism. The Schuman Declaration provided an unambiguous testament to the efficacy of this approach:

> Europe will not be made all at once or according to a single plan. It will be built through concrete achievements which first create a *de facto* solidarity. The coming together of the nations of Europe requires elimination of the age-old opposition of France and Germany. Any action which must be taken in the first place

must concern these two countries . . . The pooling of coal and steel production should immediately provide for the setting up of common foundations for economic development as a first step in the federation of Europe. (Weigall and Stirk, 1992, pp 58–59.)

European integration, then, was to be led by France and Germany. The ECSC offered something to both. For Germany it offered a route to the restoration of international respectability, as well as the prospective recovery of the Saarland. Moreover, according to Chancellor Adenauer, it also provided an image for the future development of Europe itself:

> I believe that for the first time in history, certainly in the history of the last two centuries, countries want to renounce part of their sovereignty, voluntarily and without compulsion, in order to transfer the sovereignty to a supranational structure. (Weigall and Stirk, 1992, p 67.)

What was good enough for Germany and France, provided it worked, should be good enough for the rest of the continent. For France, meanwhile, the benefit of the ECSC was very simple. It provided a means by which to control the German economy, whilst providing a ready, accessible and cheap market for French coal. More than anyone perhaps, France remained sensitive to the German problem, and there was much to be said for joint control of those industries which built German tanks and planes. As Monnet admitted in his correspondence with Schuman, the great virtue of the ECSC lay in its benefit to the French national interest (Weigall and Stirk, 1992, pp 57–58).

As such, then, the ECSC, rather than being an expression of liberal free trade, in fact sealed a series of enhanced non-tariff barriers in order to protect the French economy. German coal and steel industries had far outstripped projected capacity, and the need to bind them 'in place' was becoming ever more urgent. As Alan Milward has emphasised, the post-war reconstruction of Europe, including the ECSC and the subsequent Treaty of Rome, was geared not by an integrationist ideology, but by a determination to preserve the nation state. The partial surrender of sovereignty in certain areas, primarily economic, was the necessary price for the survival of the European nation state. The nation states were fully aware that their survival depended purely and simply upon the rapidity and extent of their economic reconstruction. It might be a 'paradox' that both the nation state and the idea of European integration benefited from the same economic growth, but it was certainly not a chance happening. Moreover, socialist demands for labour rights and the welfare state, which were becoming ever louder as the process of unionisation progressed, were best accommodated and funded by integrated economies (Milward, 1992, pp 1–43, 121–167.)

The ECSC was formally enacted in the Treaty of Paris in 1951. In article 1 it declared itself to be 'founded upon a common market, common objectives and common institutions'. That the common market was founded upon, first, the 'free' trade principles enshrined in article 4, and second, a complementary series of governing institutions, is worthy of particular note given the subsequent development of the European Community around precisely these two constructs. The presence of a Court of Justice, established in article 7, again served notice of a determination to use law as a primary tool of integration. It also ensured that the evolution of a European common market would be supranational, at least in ambition.

Although there was certainly an element of supranationalism in much of what was being said during the two decades before the Treaty of Rome, the rhetoric of integration was always compromised by the harder realities of the nation state and the immediate utility of intergovernmentalism. Despite Schuman's rhetoric, therefore, and the presence of putatively supranational institutions, the essence of the ECSC remained intergovernmental precisely because it was established to serve the best interests of two nation states, France and Germany. Again, the fate of the projected European Defence Community, as spectacular in its demise as the ECSC was successful, further revealed that where there was no immediate tangible economic benefit to be had, there was little enthusiasm amongst the nation states for anything which threatened established intergovernmental mechanisms, most pertinently in this case, NATO. The United Kingdom was vociferously opposed to the idea of a common defence policy, and when the French Assembly, preoccupied by events in Korea, recoiled from approving what seemed to be an unnecessary relinquishment of sovereignty, the idea was dead in the water. The fate of the projected Defence Community served to emphasise that there was nothing inevitable about European integration. It is striking that, half a century later, the European Union is still wrestling with precisely the same problem: the extent to which it should exercise a military capacity separate from that of NATO.

For the first half of the 1950s it was far from clear that the process of European integration would gather pace. Yet, these years turned out to be of huge importance as the economic success of the ECSC became ever more apparent. The idea of sacrificing a bit of sovereignty for a lot of wealth seemed to be more and more attractive. The two became six, when Italy and the Benelux countries joined. Indeed, to a certain extent, the subsequent enactment of the wider Community merely formalised a whole series of existing preferential trading arrangements between the six countries. For the federalists, this enlargement seemed to be vindication of the restrained strategy of incrementalism, or 'spillover'.

In 1956, Monnet resigned his Presidency of the ECSC and founded an 'Action Committee for the United States of Europe', comprising a number of likeminded intellectuals and politicians from the six member states. Ideology poked its head up and over the parapet once again. The recommendation of the Committee was that mere intergovernmentalism was not enough. Power must be delegated to supranational bodies (Mayne, 1966, pp 368–370). Alan Milward famously referred to a Europe devised by 'saints', by which he meant a few key personnel, including Schumann, Spinelli and, above all Monnet, who shared the same acutely federal vision. To a certain extent, all the 'saints', Monnet included, were caught between the drive to promote supranational integration and a residual desire to reinforce their respective nation states (Monnet, 1978, p 392; Mayne, 1966; Burgess, 1989, p 32; Holland, 1994, pp 5–21). The ambiguity was well captured by another of the 'saints', Van Zeeland:

> It is up to us to revise our superannuated conception of sovereignty. Certainly I remain a partisan of the sovereignty of the nation state; it is a necessary notion; patriotism is a mighty lever, legitimate and precious . . . In this conception the nation state remains live, autonomous, master of its destinies; by using its rights and accepting its obligations it delegates certain powers to organisations of which it is an integral part and which fulfil tasks from which it will itself benefit . . . In this compromise between two profound tendencies I see the best defence of small

countries; it is there that their real chance of remaining what they are is to be found, masters of their destiny. (Milward, 1992, pp 342–343.)

Running alongside Monnet's Action Committee, the ECSC established its own committee, at Messina, under the direction of the Belgian Foreign Minister, Paul-Henri Spaak. Its brief was to investigate the possibilities of a wider common market. Ideas are no use without power, and it is striking that the idea of European integration started to gather pace as its most fervent supporters attained high political office within their respective nation states. Spaak, Schuman and of course Monnet, all attained high office during the early 1950s.

At the same time nothing breeds confidence like success, and the ECSC had continued to prosper as the decade wore on. Unsurprisingly, the Spaak Report reinforced this sense of destiny, and recommended that:

> The object of a European common market should be to create a vast area with a common political economy which will form a powerful productive unit and permit a steady expansion, an increase in stability, a more rapid increase in the standard of living, and the development of harmonious relations between member states.

These very sentiments, and phrases, were about to be written into the constitutional heart of a new European Community.

A common market

On 27 March 1957, six countries, France, Germany, Italy and the Benelux nations, Belgium, Luxembourg, and the Netherlands, signed the Treaty of Rome, and in doing so gave birth to the European Economic Community, or common market as it quickly became known, and the Euratom, or European atomic agency. The pervasive influence of the Spaak Report could be found in the key 'mission statement' of the Treaty, article 2, which expressed the desire to:

> promote throughout the Community a harmonious development of economic activities, a continuous and balanced expansion, an increased stability, an accelerated raising of the standard of living and closer relations between its Member States.

A number of points can be gleaned from this article. The first is perhaps the most obvious. The Community was created in order to make money. As the Preamble to the Treaty rather grandiloquently implied, the creation of economic wealth, the 'pooling of resources', was the best way 'to preserve and strengthen peace and liberty' in Europe. A second point is that the Community will deal in terms of 'member' states. It will be three decades before anyone realises that a progressive Europe might prefer to think in terms of its citizenry. The third point is this idea of progression. The Rome Treaty did not establish a European Community fully formed. It merely laid the foundations upon which a common market might be secured.

These foundations were then laid out in the following 246 articles, all of which were drafted in 'titles' or sets of articles relating to particular aspects of the market. Amongst the most important were those which defined the principles of free movement. Articles 9–11 set up the principle of the free movement of goods, whilst articles 12–29 set up a common customs tariff and articles 30–37 eliminated quantitative restrictions in inter-member state trade. Articles 48–51, meanwhile, established the principle of the free movement of workers, whilst articles 59–66 and 67–73 did likewise for the free movement of services and capital respectively.[2] Of considerable collateral importance were articles 85–90 which established the basic principles of competition law.[3] The essential provisions for a complementary social policy were concentrated in the eighth 'Title', articles 117–122.[4]

The most common, and most obvious, criticism of the Rome Treaty is that it was a 'negative' treaty, rather more concerned with preventing things than with creating positive obligations or promoting alternatives. To a certain extent this kind of minimalism is endemic to free trade ideology (A Williams, 1991, pp 25–27). Above all, the Treaty neglected to provide any complementary public philosophy. The reason for this is simple. Whilst the more idealistic, such as Walter Hallstein, the first President of the Commission, might have seen the Community's role as one of the 'integrating politics', of 'jointly building a new and bigger house', the immediate truth was

---

[2] We shall investigate these principles further in chapters 5 and 6.
[3] We shall investigate these principles further in chapter 5.
[4] This policy will be investigated further in chapter 6.

rather more prosaic. The drafters of the Treaty saw themselves as devising a vast customs union, rather than any substantive political association. The Rome Treaty did not establish the framework for a federal Europe, or at least not wittingly. Only in time would it become clear that the foundations might equally well support a political 'Union'.

In 1958, however, there was no clear sense of a deeper political aspiration, or at least few were prepared to articulate one. The European Community was created to preserve the nation state, not to threaten it. For each of the six signatories the Treaty offered either economic survival or international respectability, or both. For the Benelux countries it presented a whole new market. As Milward has revealed in his study of the Belgian coal industry, the economic viability of the Belgian state was increasingly dependent upon securing access to new European markets. Thus, rather than embracing any spirit of free trade, the Belgian coal industry was desperate to find sanctuary within the protected markets described by the new Community (Milward, 1992, pp 46–118). Likewise, it is no coincidence that the most vigorous proponent of a wider common market in the years immediately before 1958 was the Netherlands, the country with comfortably the worst trade deficit in western Europe. For Germany and Italy, meanwhile, admission to the Community represented a major step towards regaining international respectability, whilst also securing a voice in the redevelopment of Europe. For France, for whom the German problem remained the essential problem, joining the Community was essential if these voices were to remain firmly muzzled.

Not everyone was so convinced. Denmark decided not to pursue an application for membership (Sorensen, 1993, pp 89–100). Britain, too, remained studiously aloof, preferring the more obviously intergovernmental institutions such as NATO. The post-war Attlee government remained riven with uncertainty regarding a prospective Community. Deploying a suitably confused metaphor, Ernest Bevin famously commented, 'I don't like it. I don't like it. When you open a Pandora's Box you'll find it full of Trojan horses' (Greenwood, 1992, p 30). Fellow cabinet minister John Strachey echoed Attlee's expressed view that the idea of European integration was a dastardly plot designed to overthrow international socialism. Herbert Morrison declared that joining the ECSC was impossible because the 'Durham miners won't wear it' (Young, 1993, pp 33–34). The assumption was as pompous as it was bizarre; if the Durham miners would not wear it, then neither would the British government, and so inevitably the entire European project would have to be abandoned. It was not. There are no mines left in Durham. There are, however, plenty left in Belgium.

The Churchill administration, which followed Attlee's government, was even less enthusiastic. Foreign Secretary Antony Eden despised 'pushy' foreigners. Joining a European Community, he declared, was 'something which we know in our bones we cannot do'. He was, he informed Chancellor Butler, 'bored' with Europe. Butler's Treasury, meanwhile, was merrily circulating a series of memoranda accusing the French government of nurturing a plot to 'dominate' Europe. Another government minister, Selwyn Lloyd, was rather less troubled, airily dismissing the idea of a European community as 'much ado about nothing' (Greenwood, 1992, pp 42–43, 64–67, 76–77). Eden's eventual replacement at the Foreign Office, Harold Macmillan, was no more enthusiastic, declining to accept an invitation to attend the Messina conference and declaring to all and sundry that the idea of European integration was one put about by 'the Jews, the planners, and the old cosmopolitan element' (Milward, 1992, p 432; Young, 1993, pp 29–44).

A trend, bred of little more than petty-minded xenophobia, was set. Britain has consistently failed to take the experience of European integration seriously, and it has consistently paid the price. It was not that the six signatories were any less suspicious of one another. It was just that they were more perceptive, first in recognising that the overriding economic imperative necessitated their joining the Community, and second in appreciating that the Community, as it had been cast in the Rome Treaty, represented little immediate threat to the integrity of the sovereign nation state. Even if some did suspect that the threat might emerge in due course, the former imperative was anyway irresistible.

The nature of this potential, if distant, threat was noted by the Moscow Institute of World Economics and International Relations, which addressed the emergence of a European Community in its *Seventeen Theses* Report. It stated:

> The promoters and signatories of the Treaties of Rome, instructed by the unhappy experience of the failure of the EDC, have to pretend that these Treaties do not have a supranational

character and that they contain nothing which could threaten the sovereign rights of any state. But the language of facts tells otherwise. The Treaties establishing the EEC and Euratom provide for the setting up of various controlling organs. The transference to these institutions of certain important competences in the economic, political and military fields will result in the curtailment of the sovereignty of the weaker states; it will inevitably limit the rights of Parliaments of these countries to make important social and national decisions.

Moreover, it added, the Community was essentially established by certain social and intellectual elites with the immediate purpose of bolstering the flagging fortunes of the capitalist nation state (Weigall and Stirk, 1992, pp 109–111). The thesis might seem to be overstated, and perhaps a little outdated. But it was correct.

Merits and demerits

Article 8 of the Rome Treaty laid down that the market should be 'progressively established in the course of a transitional period of twelve years'. Twelve years later, the Community had barely progressed at all. The 1960s were a decade of acute disappointment. The 1970s were little better. Something was wrong. The reasons for the apparent demise of the Community during the 1960s are various. Some are external. Whereas the 1950s had been a decade of relative international economic prosperity, the 1960s were a decade of economic crisis. When global recession began to bite, each member state looked to itself. As President de Gaulle caustically observed in 1962, 'at present there is and can be no Europe other than a Europe of the states – except, of course, for myths, fictions and pageants' (Holland, 1994, p 9). De Gaulle had always favoured a firmly intergovernmental Europe of nation states, and it increasingly appeared that his model was altogether more likely than the more visionary aspirations articulated by the likes of Monnet and Spaak a few years earlier.

At the same time, the primary reasons for the Community's difficulties during what Weiler terms its 'foundational' period are internal (Weiler, 1991a). In simple terms, the common market had been constructed in order to preserve the interests of its nation states. Moreover, the relationship between the two had barely been addressed, still less properly defined. As Spinelli famously, if rather gnomically, declared, in this matter, as in many others, Monnet had 'the great merit of having built Europe and the great responsibility to have built it badly' (Burgess, 1989, pp 55–56).

The pressing nature of the problem quickly became apparent in two particular instances. The first relates to the Common Agricultural Policy, or CAP. Nothing more readily illustrates the problem of trying to pursue the completion of a genuine free market whilst accommodating the interests of particular nation states, in this case France. French agriculture was, and is, hopelessly uncompetitive. Agriculture across the Community could not, and again cannot, survive in an open global marketplace. The CAP, described in articles 32–38, was intended to protect it. The problem is not merely one of principle, that there should be a special regime which exists outwith the free market, but also one of finance. During the 1960s and 1970s, the CAP took up 80 per cent of the administrative effort, and 70 per cent of the budget of the Community. Moreover, an elaborate series of trade and price controls led inevitably to vast surpluses, the notorious wine lakes and butter mountains, the venting of which was cripplingly expensive. The subsidising of wheat and sugar beet in France alone, for example, cost a third of the entire agricultural export income of the Community (Milward, 1992, pp 224–284). As we shall see in chapter 5, there have been various attempts to reform the CAP, all of which have run up against the protectionist impulses of certain member states. At the same time, the myth of the 'blooming peasant' has always been aligned with the European idea, at least in the original conception of Monnet and his fellow 'saints'. If the European farmer were to become extinct, the prophecy seems to run, then Rome will surely fall.

The second problem, equally revealing and equally enduring, is that of governance. Whilst it was keen to play down its political aspect, the Community could not avoid the collateral issues generated by the presence of supranational institutions, and the necessary tension which these institutions created in relation to countervailing intergovernmental sentiments. Monnet had placed great faith in institutions, for 'only institutions grow wiser; they accumulate experience' (Monnet, 1978, p 373). They were intended to be the gears that would drive the process of integration.

The institutional framework of the new Community was described in article 4, which stated that there would be a Parliament, a Council, a Commission, and a Court of Justice. The institutions were spread across the Community, with a Parliament in Strasbourg, a Court in Luxembourg, a Commission in Brussels and a peripatetic Council which is intended to rove around the Community, periodically setting up in different member states, but which has, increasingly, also based itself in Brussels. Back in 1958, national sensitivities precluded the idea of centralisation. No one was prepared to allow anyone else to play host to the 'capital city' of the new Europe. Accordingly, European politicians and bureaucrats are left to scamper merrily around the Community, racking up their expense accounts, resembling nothing so much as a latter-day medieval royal progress (Urwin, 1995, p 137). In a very real sense the political history of the Community, and more recently the Union, can be constructed around the respective fates of these various institutions and their various internecine struggles.

The constitution and responsibilities of the Council were described in articles 145–154, four of which are of particular importance. Article 145 described particular responsibilities to 'ensure that the objectives' of the Treaty were realised, to coordinate the 'economic policies of the Member States', to take 'decisions' and to 'confer' on the Commission 'powers for the implementation of the rules which the Council lays down'. It also reserved for the Council the right 'in specific cases' to 'exercise directly implementing powers itself'. Article 146 confirmed that there would be one Council representative from each member state, the Presidency of which would revolve on a six-monthly basis, whilst article 148 provided for a system of qualified majority voting, with a voting ratio roughly proportionate to the size of each member state. This latter provision, as we shall see, has remained a constant source of inter-member state bickering. Finally article 152 laid down that the Council 'may request' the Commission to 'undertake any studies' that were deemed 'desirable for the attainment of the common objectives, and to submit to it any appropriate proposals'.

The bare bones of articles 145–154 revealed the potential power of the Council as the preserve of the member states. It remains, in simple terms, the most obviously intergovernmental body of the Community. In the early years, it appeared that the Council did pretty much everything, initiating, executing, and vetoing legislation. As Weiler suggests, during the 'foundational period', the Council, and through it the member states, 'took control' over 'every phase of decisionmaking' very 'often at the expense of the Commission'. The member states, accordingly, 'assumed a dominant say' in all the Community's activities. (Weiler, 1991a, p 2423). This particular impression was further enforced by the Luxembourg Accords, a convention instituted at the behest of the French in 1965, and which permitted any member state to veto any policy initiative which it perceived to be against national interest. On a number of occasions, the Luxembourg Accords very nearly brought the Community to its knees (Nicoll, 1984a).

The role and responsibilities of the Commission were, in turn, described in articles 155–163. Whereas the security of the 'common objectives' of the Treaty was vested in the Council, article 155 handed the Commission a particular responsibility to 'ensure the proper functioning and development of the common market'. It also provided the Commission with a policy-forming role, one that equips it to 'participate in the shaping of measures taken by the Council and by the European Parliament'. Its membership of 20 Commissioners, at least one from each member state, was established in article 157. The number of Commissioners nominated from each nation state, together with the parcelling out of portfolios, has remained as another of the most political, and thus most sensitive, matters in Community politics (Lodge, 1993a, pp 7–8). Moreover, the quality of Commissioners has remained equally controversial, with rather too many rather too obviously being failed domestic politicians.

The relation between the Council and the Commission was always going to be critical to the future functioning of the Community, as article 152 had suggested. Article 162 further urged that the two institutions must 'consult each other' and 'settle by common accord their methods of co-operation'. According to its first President, Walter Hallstein, the Commission had 'three main tasks':

> First it draws up proposals to be decided by the Council of Ministers. Secondly, it watches over the execution of the Treaty and may call firms and governments to account. Thirdly, it mediates between the governments and seeks to reconcile national interests with the Community interests.

There was, he added, a further emergent task, 'whose importance is growing', that 'of executing those decisions of detail which for the sake of rapid and impartial treatment it is empowered to take itself' (Weigall and Stirk, 1992, p 125). It was the continued growth of this fourth 'task' that would allow the Commission to expand the borders of its own particular empire during the first decades of the Community. By the mid-1980s, the Commission had emerged as the dominant driving force behind further economic and indeed political integration.

The third institution was the Parliament, the role and responsibilities of which were described in articles 137–144. The composition of the Parliament was outlined in articles 137 and 138, the latter of which provided for a proportionate system of representation, with the number of Members or MEPs loosely reflecting the respective populations of each member state. It also provided for the method of selection to be decided by each member state. The remission of election procedures to the member states was a critical concession. Indeed, far too much remained in the gift of the member states. For whilst article 138 paid lip-service to the idea that there should be 'political parties at a national level', European elections are still blighted by the fact that they remain irreducibly national events, with national politicians representing national parties invariably promising to protect national interests.

But the real problem with the Parliament as it was established in the Rome Treaty lay in its legislative emasculation. As article 138 went on to affirm, the powers of the Parliament would be strictly limited, to 'giving its assent' to legislation presented to it, or to 'delivering advisory opinions' upon it. There was no power of legislative initiative and no power of veto. The nation states simply refused to countenance any possible rejection by the Parliament of policies pursued by the Council. The Parliament was always intended to be supine, a vague concession to the principle of democracy, present but certainly not empowered in any practical sense.

Whilst the principle of democracy was not one that overly troubled Monnet, the phrase 'democratic deficit' has come to haunt his creation. The more apparent has the economic and political power of the Community become, the more concerned critics have become regarding the blatant lack of democratic process and accountability. A parliament without the power to initiate legislation, or indeed to veto it, is an absurdity. Whilst the situation, as we shall see, might have improved marginally, the essential absurdity remains. The new Europe is fundamentally undemocratic, and the reason for this lies in the institutional structure established in the Rome Treaty. Hallstein spoke hopefully of an institution in possession of a 'degree of democratic control greater than ever imposed upon traditional international relations' (Weigall and Stirk, 1992, p 126). The critical word here, of course, is international. International parliaments may be emasculated. But the Community aspired to be something more, to describe a new kind of supra, rather than international, form of governance. It rapidly became apparent that an ocean of difference lay between the aspiration and the hard reality.

The difficulty in making sense of the institutional structure of the Community is compounded by the fact that there is no easy comparative analysis available. The institutional structure established in the Rome Treaty does not fit neatly into the kind of categories defined most famously, in the early modern period, by Locke and Montesquieu, and which tend to be most familiar in modern western liberal democracies. Most importantly, perhaps, the result of this ambiguity is a failure to respect the essential principle which lies at the heart of this constitutional tradition: the separation, and the balance, of powers. It would be convenient to suggest that the Council represents the executive, whilst the Commission and the Parliament represent the legislative. But this is clearly not the case.

The institutional structure of the new Europe is, quite simply, unique. This should not itself serve to condemn the Community. But the problems which result from the failure to observe the core principles of the separation and balance of powers are further compounded by a similar failure to respect the other essential components of liberal democratic constitutional thought. We will investigate these particular failings in greater depth elsewhere. But suffice to say that the Court of Justice has fallen critically short of the ideal of an independent judiciary, whilst the failure to respect the barest notions of democracy and citizenship has emerged as a crippling weakness.

Reviving the dream

The stagnation of the 1960s drifted unobtrusively into the stagnation of the 1970s. The heady days of Rome seemed to belong to a very distant past. Commentators coined the phrase Eurosclerosis. It seemed as if the various weaknesses and ambiguities written into the Rome Treaty were insuperable. Monnet had indeed 'built it badly'. In simple terms, the 1970s can be seen as a series of failed attempts to revitalise the Community. But if the effect was failure, the desire was notable. Indicative of both, the aspiration and the failure, was the Paris Intergovernmental Conference (IGC) of 1972, which concluded with a burst of rhetorical optimism, projecting an 'ambitious programme of substantive expansion of Community jurisdiction' and with it the 'revival of the dream of Europe'.

The responsibility for reviving this dream fell to two of the Community's institutions, the Council and the Court of Justice. The Council's capacity to rejuvenate political integration was defined in article 235, which stated that:

> If action by the Community should prove necessary to attain, in the course of the operation of the common market, one of the objectives of the Community and this Treaty has not provided the necessary powers, the Council shall, acting unanimously on a proposal from the Commission and after consulting the European Parliament, take the appropriate measures.

In time, a whole range of policy areas, from consumer protection to energy to the environment, were to be developed under the auspices of article 235.

The Court, in turn, used a different Treaty article, article 5, as a mechanism for further enforcing certain fundamental principles of Community jurisprudence, thus ensuring the progression of legal, as well as political, integration. Article 5 required all member states to 'take all appropriate measures' to 'ensure fulfilment' of Treaty 'obligations'. It further required that they should 'facilitate the achievement of the Community's task'. The Court was invited to make sure that they did. As we shall see in chapter 3, it agreed with alacrity.

The Paris initiative of 1972 is too often ignored. Whilst the immediate achievement might appear to have been slight, as Weiler rightly observes, with hindsight it can be seen as the first step in a 'brick-by-brick demolition of the wall circumscribing Community competences' (Weiler, 1991a, pp 2448–2449). The Paris summit is also significant for two other reasons. First, it saw the accession of two new members, Denmark and the United Kingdom; the first since the Community's inception.[5] Second, the IGC was set within the immediate political context of President de Gaulle's fall from power. Indeed, de Gaulle had repeatedly refused the accession of the United Kingdom, in 1963 and 1965, and in doing so had been condemned by many of those who strove most energetically to revive the 'dream'.[6] Only with the arrival of successively pro-European French Presidents, Pompidou and Mitterand, did the possibility of renewed economic and political integration seem possible. The irony is obvious. Denmark and the United Kingdom have proved to be the most consistently truculent members of the Community. If anyone has kept the spirit of de Gaulle marching on, it is they.

Throughout the 1970s various commissions were established with the increasingly desperate brief of trying to think of something to do. Their only common characteristic was that they all failed to various degrees. The Tindemans Report waxed lyrical on the subject of European integration as a 'self-evident good', and advocated all sorts of wholly unpalatable ideas, such as enhanced democratic accountability, and even more unacceptable measures, such as majority voting in Council. The Three Wise Men Commission was established in 1979 in order to examine the failures of the Community, and found plenty. The sense of crisis was tangible. The Secretary General of the Commission, Emile Noel, rued the 'institutional drift away from the spirit, and indeed the letter of the Treaties of Rome' (Weigall and Stirk, 1992, pp 173–174).[7] William Nicoll, the Director General of

[5] The peculiar, self-inflicted, agonies that accompanied the UK's accession will be considered in chapter 4.

[6] According to Spaak, de Gaulle's continued determination to champion the French national interest over and above all else had revealed his 'utter contempt' for the idea of European integration (Weigall and Stirk, 1992, p 132).

[7] Stein has suggested that the ineffectiveness of Community institutions left a vacuum that could only be filled by the Council, the intergovernmental institutions par excellence. The result is much rhetoric, little action. He concludes: 'The problem with the summit council has been that at times its ringing declarations end up in a way reminiscent of the Emperor's orders in Gilbert and Sullivan's *Mikado*. When the Emperor orders something to be done, it is as good as done and therefore, it need not be done' (Stein 1983, pp 648–649).

the Secretariat General of the Council, similarly suggested that there was an urgent need to reopen 'paths to European unity', if need be, through a multi-speed Europe (Nicoll, 1984b). This latter idea, which has become more familiarly known as 'flexibility', would come to the fore during the 1990s.

In 1982, the President of the Parliament, Peter Dankert, observed that the 'anniversary of the European Community does not seem to be an occasion for much celebration', adding that the 'infant which held so much promise 25 years ago has changed into a feeble cardiac patient'. Perceptively, he noted that now that there was no obvious financial inducement for further integration, no one appeared to want to take the Community any further. Aside from securing direct elections to the Parliament in 1979, and establishing the Community's 'own resources', or budget, the previous two decades had achieved precisely nothing. With equal perception, Dankert identified a critical failure to engage the 'peoples' of Europe, a fact which made the peoples' reciprocal apathy wholly understandable. The picture was bleak indeed:

> The Europe of today is suffering from a very complicated illness. The symptoms are unemployment, social unrest, growing insecurity and a sense of alienation on the part of our young people. The disorientation is so far-reaching that confidence in democracy as an institution has been shaken throughout Europe. (Dankert, 1982, pp 8–9.)

The comments are as prescient today as they were 20 years ago. The same is true of his concluding comment, that the new Europe lacks an 'identity'.

So what precisely was wrong? The essential problems remained the same: the financial drain of the CAP, and the question of governance. Whilst the former might be causing immediate economic stress, it was the latter which described a more deep-rooted problem. The Council remained the most powerful institution, trapped between the contradiction described by its responsibilities under article 235 and the countervailing desire to protect national interests through the invocation of the Luxembourg Accords. Whilst the Three Wise Men Report had noted that the accords were a fact of political life, both the Tindemans and then the later 1981 Genscher-Colombo Reports had hazarded the idea of majority voting in Council. As ever there was much wringing of hands and venting of spleens. In the end, the convention of the Luxembourg Accords was broken by the most unlikely champion of integration, the British Prime Minister Margaret Thatcher. Thatcher's use of the veto at every instance during the early 1980s, as a strategy to force through a revision of the United Kingdom's budgetry contribution, led to its effective abrogation at the 1984 Fontainebleau IGC. Once the decision was taken to ignore any mooted UK veto, then the 'convention' was itself finished. Few mourned its loss. It was as if a great weight had been lifted from the Community's shoulders (Nicoll, 1984a, pp 40–41; A Williams, 1991, pp 77–78).

The collateral problem of governance remained that of democracy, or the 'democratic deficit'. Writing in 1991, Shirley Williams commented that the problem of democracy was the most pressing issue of the 1980s, whilst the failure to resolve it described the most urgent task of the 1990s (S Williams, 1991). It remains the most urgent task. Paradoxically, one of the few achievements of the 1970s, the first elections to the Parliament in 1979, only served to underline the extent of the problem. The fear that the lack of democracy was both the product, and the primary catalyst, of popular disaffection was borne out by the low election turnouts of 1979, 1984 and 1989. Popular indifference complemented an impression that the Community was the plaything of political elites. Monnet had gaily assumed that democracy was a potential hindrance to integration, that popular support would follow success. It did not (Slater, 1982).

Slowly it dawned. The solution to the malaise of Eurosclerosis must be another Treaty. If Rome had been built 'badly', then it would need to be rebuilt, or at least prettied up a bit. And, most importantly, if this was to happen then someone would have to take the initiative. The question of leadership was one of the many which had been shirked in 1958. There is no head of state in the European Community or Union. It is sometimes thought that if there were it might be the President of the Commission. Perhaps so. But if the acid test for such a position is the exercise of power and influence within the Community, then there are various other candidates. The President of the Council is one. Sadly few would suggest that it is the President of the Parliament. At the same time, moreover, the Franco-German axis remains the bedrock of the new Europe, and the respective heads of state remain far and away the most important domestic politicians. The veracity of this claim was never clearer than during the second part of the 1980s. The impetus for renewed integration was provided by the arrival of a new French President, Francois Mitterand, in 1984, together with a new German Chancellor, Helmut Kohl, and also a new President of the Commission, Jacques Delors. Three new 'saints' were added to the host, three putative healers of a very sick patient.

Whilst Mitterand responded to the unbelievers, most obviously Margaret Thatcher, by threatening the prospect of a 'two-speed' Europe, Delors set about establishing the Commission as the spiritual temple of a Community that would be more responsive to the 'needs of capital', and better governed by an all-powerful, all-knowing executive (Ross, 1995, pp 28–37).[8] Council summits began to take on a greater urgency. The Fontainebleau summit, hosted by Mitterand, and the first at which Delors attended as President of the Commission, saw an end to the Luxembourg Accords, as well as the establishment of two new Committees, the Adonnino and the Dooge. The purpose of the former was to pursue the necessary administrative and symbolic reforms necessary to realise a prospective 'Europe of the citizens'. Its brief included such apparently vital tasks as the need to establish an EC radio station, an EC flag and an EC hymn, and also to investigate the viability of an EC space station. Such, it was assumed, would soon pull the crushingly indifferent citizenry into line. Rather more important perhaps was the Dooge Committee. Its brief was to investigate the vexed question of governance, and most particularly the possibility of institutional reform.

The Dooge Committee had another task as well; to deal with a draft Treaty which had emerged uninvited from the Parliament.[9] In this context, dealing meant minimising. The Committee, however, proved to be rather taken by the draft Treaty, and reported back approvingly

---

[8]   Ross's account of the Delors Commission is fascinating; the excessive, almost sclerotic, bureaucracy, the obsessive secrecy, the desperation to cultivate an image of infallibility. Little wonder that the Commission has developed the reputation for being something of an epitome for such bloated governance. The irony is, of course, that the Commission is actually smaller than the executives of most medium-sized member states. It just appears to be overblown, ridiculous and threatening.

[9]   The Parliament, of course, had no rights of legislative initiative. Still less was it expected to draft new treaties (Lodge, 1984, p 377).

to the Dublin IGC at the end of 1984. It was thanked, and then dismissed, the Council expressing a number of 'reservations and disagreements' regarding the proposed new Treaty. The origins of the draft Treaty can be traced back to 1979, with the arrival of the first tranche of elected MEPs. Bolstered by a sense of its own importance and ambition, the new Parliament decide to make its presence felt, and this, necessarily, in turn implied a challenge to the authority of the Council.

The leading figure in this new Parliamentary initiative was Altiero Spinelli. He, more than any, was convinced that Europe needed to be built again, and built better. And this meant that it had to be built on democratic foundations. Spinelli, as we have already noted, was hugely influenced by the early federalist movements, infused as they were by certain core tenets of liberal political thought, such as an effective separation of powers, a rule of law and a democratically elected legislative. Whilst he appreciated that the Council would never formally approve a full-blown federal union, Spinelli was convinced that a kind of 'federalism without federation' was Europe's best, indeed only, hope. In a lecture given in 1983, Spinelli declared that his initiative was aimed at transforming the Community into 'a genuine political and economic Union . . . with the authority and institutions which would enable it to respond effectively through democratic procedures to serious and growing problems' (Burgess, 1986).

In June 1980, Spinelli had sent a letter to his fellow MEPs inviting support for an initiative aimed at overcoming 'institutional deadlock'. A growing number of devotees became known as the 'Crocodile Club', named after a Strasbourg restaurant at which they ruminated earnestly about fine wine and institutional reform (Cardozo and Corbett, 1986). The Community looked to dine its way out of crisis. Rather than merely amending the Rome Treaty, Spinelli and his fellow *gastronomiques* were convinced that a whole new constitutional order must be created, in a whole new Treaty. There was also much careless talk on the desirability of democracy, and how it might be enhanced if the Parliament actually enjoyed any real legislative power. The Draft Treaty which finally emerged was unsurprisingly strong on the desirability of legislative power-sharing. Parliament, the drafters argued, should do rather more than merely advise.

Parliament itself was entirely convinced, and adopted the Draft Treaty in February 1984, by 225 votes to 32. Its 87 articles described a convergence of the existing ECSC, EEC and Euratom treaties, to which it also added the European Monetary System (EMS). Amongst its more radical measures, article 8 significantly incorporated the European Council as the effective head of state of the proposed all-encompassing new Union. The Council was thus defined, and limited. Article 12 entrenched the legislative supremacy of the Union, thus extending its competence still further, whilst article 23 formally ended the Luxembourg Accords. Articles 63–69 established a more comprehensive foreign policy.

The Treaty was radical and innovative, earning the conspicuous support of President Mitterand, who used the opportunity to reiterate his views regarding a formalised two-tier Community. It was also wholly unattractive to the overwhelming number of member states. The Council was certainly not emamoured with the prospective article 8. It did not wish to be defined or limited, and certainly not in such a way that it might become accountable before the Court of Justice (Feld and Mahant, 1986, pp 41–43; Freestone and Davison, 1986, p 126). The Commission was similarly unenthusiastic at the idea of sharing legislative initiative. And finally, when the results from the Parliamentary elections of 1984 came through, it was clear that the peoples of Europe remained crushingly indifferent.

It was the intent of Parliament, rather than its achievement, that was instructive. Aside from the proposed institutional reforms, there were two detectable political trends; a growing sympathy for pluralist democratic politics, and a renewed, if covert, interest in federalism, most obvious in the proposed article 12 (Lodge, 1984, pp 381–387; Lodge, 1986a). What article 12 announced, of course, was the desirability of a principle of subsidiarity, a mechanism for the formal demarcation of competences between Community institutions and the nation states. The idea would prove to be irresistible.

It is, then, the ideological, as much as the institutional, impetus that made the Draft Treaty significant. The Crocodile Club had dared to reintroduce the rhetoric of federalism to European debate. Along with subsidiarity, it was seen to be the natural complement to enhanced Parliamentary power, and thus democratic legitimacy. The political ideology was further complemented, elsewhere in the Treaty, by a renewed social ideology, most obviously in the mooted 'Policy for Society' which encompassed a number of new policy heads which had gained recent currency, including health, the environment and consumer protection. Again, the idea of a constitutionally enacted social policy would, in time, prove to be irresistible.

A Single Act

The snowball had begun to roll. The ensuing IGC, at Luxembourg in early 1985, revisited the subject of treaty reform. Appealing to their vanity, Delors attempted to lure the nation states into thinking that they could remain in charge of this process, the architects of their own Community, and perhaps Union. The nation states, however, felt themselves to be rather more impelled by economic need than any concern for democratic inadequacies. The successive global crises of the 1970s and early 1980s had hurt everyone. Europe did not appear to be working, literally.

The Commission duly produced the Cockfield White Paper describing all the vast economic gains that might be realised if only there could be renewed economic and political integration. It listed 279 proposals for the establishment of a comprehensive internal market through the removal of the various remaining physical, fiscal and technical barriers to trade. As impressed by Cockfield as it was irritated by the Parliament, the Council decided that if there was going to be new Treaty, it was best that they should draft it themselves. At the Luxembourg IGC, it was agreed that the Treaty structure should indeed be amended, that the market should be streamlined in accordance with the recommendations of the Cockfield Report, that there should be single currency in due course, and that there might even be room for a token enhancement of Parliament's ability to delay or amend legislation. There was, of course, no question of the Council surrendering its veto. There was no mention of the need for flags, hymns or space stations. Parliament, miffed by the rejection of its Draft Treaty, retaliated by rejecting the Council proposals by 243 votes to 47. The Council ignored them, and carried on anyway.

The result of all this endeavour and heartache was the Single European Act (SEA), the first substantive reform of the Rome Treaty. Its purpose, as stated in article 1, was to further the 'concrete progress towards European unity'. At its heart were two aspirations, to address the problem of governance, and to implement the recommendations of the Cockfield Report.

At first glance there did indeed seem to be some progress towards democratising Community institutions. Article 3.1 at least expressly acknowledged the existence of the Parliament, whilst articles 6 and 7 advanced a new process of legislative 'co-operation'. However, this latter innovation amounted to little more than an intensified process of consultation. The grail of legislative initiative remained elusive. Moreover, the 'co-operation' procedure was further limited by its restriction to legislation relating to the completion of the internal market in pursuance of article 8A. At first sight article 149 seemed to be similarly impressive, empowering Parliament to propose amendments or to reject the 'common position' communicated to it by Council. However, the labyrinthine technicalities of this procedure, together with the fact that the Council could in any case override any amendment or rejection, provided it did so unanimously, again militated against its real effectiveness.

All in all, the new powers amounted to nothing more than a marginally revised process of consultation, with only slightly greater powers of delay. Article 237 vested in Parliament a new power to veto new accessions to the Community. But these were hardly daily occurrences, and anyway Parliament was always the most enthusiastic supporter of such accessions. There was, in simple terms, no agreement in Council regarding the extent of necessary institutional reform. Those who were keenest to see the process of integration revitalised, in other words the poorest, such as Italy, were happy to countenance whatever reforms of governance were necessary. The rather wealthier Germans were altogether less convinced that institutional reform was necessary for the completion of the market and, even if it was, were not at all convinced that this should warrant a diminution of Council authority. The German government tabled counter-measures intended to limit severely any prospective enhancement of Parliament's legislative powers (Lodge, 1986b, pp 213–216).

When the smoke had cleared, it was obvious that the Council was the real, and predetermined, winner. The IGC had even adopted a Dutch proposal for the increase of the Council's supervisory power over the Commission. The vexed question of the Luxembourg Accords, and their proposed abrogation, had also been carefully ignored. The sentiment of the SEA was very different from that articulated by Spinelli and his fellow diners. In all, as one critic observed, by the time the SEA had finally come into being, it was clear that the institutional 'landscape' was all too 'familiar' (Bermann, 1989; also Bieber et al, 1986, p 767).

The real heart of the SEA lay in the second of the original aspirations, in the completion of the internal market, as enshrined in article 8A. All institutional reforms were subsumed under this overarching ambition, to implement the recommendations of the Cockfield Paper, and to do so, moreover, by the end of 1992. The enactment of a deadline was to prove totemic. It was article 8A that mattered to the member states, not esoteric debates about democratic legitimacy (Lodge, 1986b, p 213). It was for this reason that article 100A specified that there would be qualified majority voting in Council for the adoption of all:

> measures for the approximation of such provisions laid down by law, regulation or administrative action in Member States as have as their object the establishment and operation of the internal market.

Article 100A did not, however, extend to fiscal matters, to the free movement of persons, or to the rights and interests of the unemployed. The omissions are striking. There would be integration where there was money to be made, not where there were merely principles to be argued. Of equal significance is the fact that the SEA also acknowledged the fundamental instrumental importance of the legal system, and of legal integration, providing for the establishment of an additional court in article 168A. What emerged was a Court of First Instance.

For those concerned with the state of European integration, the SEA proved to be a bitter disappointment. The questions of democracy and governance had barely been addressed. The new co-operation procedure was more tantalising than empowering. The most that the Council could expect, and the most that it got, was a momentary cessation of hostilities. The war was certainly not over (Bieber et al, 1986, pp 775, 791–792). Parliament quickly realised that the Act, far from being a 'step towards Euro-dynamism', was in reality a 'retrograde move' (Lodge, 1986b, p 221). Neither did the Act move the Community any nearer to a genuine supranational identity. The whole exercise was commonly condemned as a 'cosmetic' version of the original, and rather more radical, Draft Treaty (Lasok and Bridge, 1994, p 26). Although the Act introduced new Community competences in the areas of the environment, regional development and technology, widespread dissent at the preceding IGC prevented any substantive proposals in the more politically contentious area of social policy.

In a particularly strident, and bitter, commentary, Pierre Pescatore condemned the perpetrators of the Act for abandoning the 'moral' idea of Europe, and enacting a 'fundamentally deceptive' statute, designed to convey the appearance of reform, whilst entrenching the power of member states:

> Putting into force the Single Act would therefore mark a severe setback for the European Community. I am among those who think that forgetting about the Single Act would be a lesser evil for our common future than ratification of this diplomatic document . . . The Single Act does not contain any tangible commitment by the Member States, no obligation which could be defined in precise terms. It opens or seems to open some new avenues, though most of them had already existed under the original EEC Treaty, but each new possibility is outweighed by corresponding loopholes, reservations and new unanimity requirements . . . As a whole, the Act is the worst piece of drafting I have come across in my practice in European affairs . . . Thus, the lip-service paid in paragraph 4 of the Preamble to the 'European idea' is no substitute for real progress towards democracy and political co-operation. (Pescatore, 1987, pp 9–18.)

Perhaps too much had been expected. The fate of the Draft Treaty should have alerted everyone to the fact that the Single Act was never likely to herald a substantive renewal of integrationist energy. The Council was simply not prepared to countenance genuine reform.

But at least there was talk of reform. Moreover, of perhaps greater importance, talk of institutional reform was being increasingly heard alongside that of market reform. As Emile Noel suggested, this particular 'synergy', between institutional and market reform, was the most important consequence of the all the debates surrounding the

Act (Noel, 1989, pp 3–4, 8–10). It is worth noting that the most substantive reforms, most obviously those articulated in article 100A, were an expression of precisely this synergy. At the end of the day, the Single Act was a political deal, not a moment of historic constitutional importance. Any impetus towards further integration was largely consequential (Edward, 1987).

The balance between the Community and the nation states remained tentative. In the words of one commentator:

> If proof were needed that the European Economic Community is still the product of a careful tempering of integrationalist impulses with preoccupations of national sovereignty, the recently ratified Single European Act . . . amply supplies it . . . Rather than place European integration on a new set of political foundations, as many influential voices had urged, the Single European Act brings a combination of programmatic change and limited structural reform. (Bermann, 1989, p 529.)

The 'new' Europe, it seemed, was far from built. Indeed, it was questionable 30 years on whether the foundations were even secure. Much, it seemed, was still to be done.

Chapter 2

An ever closer union

Another Treaty, it seemed, another disappointment. It was all too obvious that the Single European Act had not repaired the building that Monnet had constructed so 'badly'. In fact, it had barely papered over the cracks. The forebodings of the 1970s and early 1980s hung heavy. Commentators still mused on the possibility of fragmentation and disintegration, on the prospective demise of the European idea. And yet, there was something in the Act which turned out to be of enormous importance, something which was able to get everyone hoping once again. For the Single Act had projected still another Treaty, one that would finally effect the completion of the market, one that might even gesture towards some kind of governmental reform, perhaps even some kind of political union. Emerging from the depths of despair, Europe was about to venture out on its biggest adventure yet. Less than a decade after the Single Act, there would be a full-blown political union, complete with competences over justice and home affairs, and over foreign policy. And by the end of the century, there would have been three more Treaties.

Maastricht: an ever closer union

After the Single Act, as before, it was economic expediency which geared political progress. Just as the Rome Treaty had set itself a timetable, of twelve years, by which time the market would be complete, so too did the Act set itself a similar target, this time of just seven years. The enduring legacy of the Single Act was the '1992 Project'. The market, the Act confidently proclaimed, would be completed by the end of 1992. There would at least be jam tomorrow.

A sense of urgency was enhanced by the Cecchini Report which announced in 1988 that the completion of the market would realise savings of 200bn ECU. The figure seemed fantastic. Indeed, as later research revealed, it was more fantastical than merely fantastic, the product of some decidedly creative accounting. But it did the trick. Suddenly, everyone was taking the '1992 Project' very seriously indeed (Tartwijk-Novey, 1995, p 27). Moreover, given the reforms enacted in article 100A, most importantly the move to qualified majority voting in Council on matters relating to the completion of the market, completion of the Project did seem to be feasible. The member states were, to use Dehousse's metaphor, 'seduced' into making sacrifices of political sovereignty by the lure of considerable financial satisfaction (Dehousse, 1988, p 117). As Weiler commented, with similar acerbity, the Community finally set about trying to accomplish something in seven years which it 'should have accomplished in the preceding thirty' (Weiler, 1991a, p 2544).

The energy which the Project seemed to inspire attracted almost hysterical excitement amongst integrationists. Commissioner Ehlermann suggested that the Project, building on the foundations laid down by the Cockfield Report, was the 'most ambitious and successful legislative programme ever adopted by the Community'. For the first time, he added, the Community was actually taking the initiative, rather than leaving everything to whim of the Court of Justice. It was, he concluded, an 'outstanding success' (Ehlermann, 1990).

The immediate impetus for the '1992 Project' was supplied by the Delors Commission, which tabled proposals for its execution in early 1987. There were three main planks: first, a reform of the Common Agricultural Policy (CAP) which would prevent surpluses; second, an enhancement of the Community's income, or 'own resources'; third, a reform of the Community's structural funds. The proposals were radical. Indeed, certain aspects, most obviously the reform of the CAP, were even heretical. It certainly seemed that the Commission was taking the idea of economic reform seriously. The ultimate adoption of the Delors Plan sealed this impression (Ehlermann, 1990, pp 1109–1110).

Perhaps the most controversial substantive proposal in the Report related to the institution of monetary union; an idea which had bounced around for nearly two decades. The Report envisaged a three-stage process. First there would be a single financial area, with a free market in financial services, free circulation of financial instruments, the inclusion of all member state currencies in the exchange rate mechanism, and a substantially greater role for the Committee of Governors of Central Banks. The second stage would establish a European system of central banks, the 'Eurofed'. The final stage would be the irrevocable fixing of exchange rates and the assumption by the 'Eurofed' of full responsibility for monetary policy across the Community.

The seriousness with which economic reform was being taken in the context of the 1992 'Project' was evidenced by the establishment of complementary Intergovernmental Conferences on Political, and Economic and Monetary Union. The latter was an obvious complement to the 'Project', and particularly to the Delors Commission. Everyone except the United Kingdom proved willing to countenance the idea of monetary union. The establishment of the Intergovernmental Conference (IGC) on Political Union revealed a similar awareness, not merely that the next stage in European integration had to be political, but that such a development would require a renewed effort to deal with the seemingly intractable problem of governance. In a very real sense, it was also an admission that the Single European Act had failed lamentably in this particular matter. As ever, political union was always more likely to succeed if it could piggyback economic expediency (Heath, 1988).

Unsurprisingly, the most enthusiastic support for institutional reform came once again from the Parliament, whose Martin Report had recently repeated the case for an increase in rights of co-decision, along with parliamentary involvement in the appointment of the Commission. Noticeably, for once the Council did not reject these proposals out of hand. Indeed, a few heads of state, most notably President Mitterand of France, waxed lyrically about the projected virtues of social and political reform in the Community (Corbett, 1992; Pinder, 1991). A mood, it appears, had been set.[1] By 1990, all

---

[1]   The only consistent opposition, needless to say, came from the Thatcher administration in the UK. We shall revisit its particular fears in chapter 4.

eyes were focused, not only on the Community's past, but on the future of a projected Union.

In late 1992 the pilgrims finally arrived at Maastricht, weary but expectant. However, it rapidly became apparent that the celebrants would have to be patient. Things were not going to be simple. The Maastricht Treaty on European Union (TEU), was designed both to amend the existing Rome Treaty, as well as to establish a whole new constitutional structure for the impending Union. This structure was to be founded on three 'pillars': the first pillar being the Community Treaty, whilst the remaining two related to Common Foreign and Security Policy, and Justice and Home Affairs. The former was established in article J of the Union Treaty, and was intended to cover 'all questions related to the security of the Union'. The latter 'pillar', the various 'fields of Justice and Home Affairs', was then established in article K.

The Union thus supplements the Community, though it does so rather awkwardly under the one constitutional structure. In simple terms, it is intended that the Community should remain the supranational element in the Union, and also the fully justiciable one, whilst the two new pillars should be intergovernmental. This remains controversial, for the kinds of powers granted the Union in the two intergovernmental 'pillars' materially affect the real lives of real people, and in a modern liberal society, of the kind which the 'new' Europe purports to be, this lack of democratic and judicial accountability is plainly wrong. As we shall see shortly, subsequent Treaties, in 1997 and 2000, have largely failed to address this disquiet.

The Maastricht Treaty opened with a Preamble, replete with all the customary platitudes. There then followed a set of 'Common Principles', of which article A set a suitably grandiloquent tone, declaring that the newly established Union represents: 'a new stage in the process of creating an ever closer union among the peoples of Europe in which decisions are taken as closely as possible to the people'.

The phrase 'ever closer union' replaced an earlier explicit reference to a 'federal union' which had appeared in the Dutch draft of the Treaty. Needless to say, it was the United Kingdom that rallied opposition to the 'F-word'. It was this same opposition that pressed for the inclusion of article F, which declared that the Union would 'respect the national identities of its Member States, whose systems of government are founded on the principles of democracy'. The relationship between the Union and its constituent nation states remains acutely sensitive.

The homage to national identities was only one part of article F. Article F2 declared that the Union determined to 'respect fundamental rights, as guaranteed by the European Convention for the Protection of Human Rights and Fundamental Freedom'. It also expressed the Union's support for the principles of liberty, democracy and the rule of law. All very nice. But there is a critical ambivalence here. For the Union is not justiciable, and so the promise to respect the principle of the rule of law is vacuous, if not perverse. As Michael Zuern has drily observed, if the Union actually applied to join itself, its application would fail precisely because it failed to fulfil its own criteria as established by article F (Zuern, 2000, pp 191, 195–200). The Union would like all its members to be democratic and to observe the rule of law; but it does not seem particularly keen to do so itself.

So much for the new political Union. Of course, the heart of the Union remains the economic Community, the common market. Due deference to this reality was paid in article B of the Union Treaty, which declared that the overarching purpose of the Union was to:

> promote economic and social progress which is balanced and sustainable through the creation of an area without internal frontiers, through the strengthening of economic and social cohesion and through the establishment of economic and monetary union, ultimately including a single currency.

Of course, aside from the establishment of a political union, the Maastricht IGC was intended to celebrate completion of the single market. Unsurprisingly, therefore, there were a number of amendments to the Community Treaty or 'pillar', most of which were intended to realise the aspirations of article B. Of greatest significance, perhaps, was the enactment of the Delors Plan in articles 3A, 4A and 102–109, complete with timetable, an exchange rate mechanism, a common currency (the ECU) and a Central European Bank. In the years following the Delors Report, two alternative theses for transition to a single currency had been advanced, either a gradual evolution or a more rapid 'Big Bang'. The Delors solution was a 'two-tier' process, which bore a strong resonance with the idea of a 'two-speed' Europe, with each member state free to choose the speed with which they felt most comfortable. This approach gained implicit support at Maastricht, by virtue of the very strict criteria for convergence in article 109F, including narrow exchange rate bands, low long-term interest rates, limited deficit and a 'sustainable' price performance. It was not expected that everyone would fulfil these criteria, certainly not with the same degree of comfort. There was, therefore, one speed for the more stable economies, so that they could get richer more quickly, and another for the less stable, so that they would get rather less rich, and do so more slowly. This was another meaning of the word 'balanced'. The extremely rich Germans were very keen, the rather poorer Italians rather less so (Artis, 1992; Dunnett, 1994).

The extent to which there should be symmetry between the aspirations of the Union and the Community was reflected in the recasting of article 2 of the Community Treaty, much of which now echoed article B. The new article 2 made explicit reference to the idyll of 'economic and monetary union', alongside that of a 'harmonious and balanced development of economic activities'. Previously, the Community had merely sought harmony. The nature of this 'balance' was then fleshed out in the remainder of the redrafted article, which now sought to achieve:

> sustainable and non-inflationary growth respecting the environment, a high degree of convergence of economic performance, a high level of employment and of social protection, the raising of the standard of living and quality of life, and economic and social cohesion and solidarity among Member States.

The marrying of economic and social cohesion was a welcome admission that markets are more than merely economic entities; a theme we shall return to in chapter 5. The admission that unemployment required concerted attention was also significant. It has come to dominate European policy over the following decade.

Of course, what could not be found in article 2, or indeed in any of the aspirational statements in the Union Treaty, was anything that was terribly inspiring. Neither the Union nor the Community has ever sought to reach out to the 'peoples' of Europe, to excite their support. People do not lay down their lives in the cause of 'non-inflationary growth'. The failure to inspire lays behind the critical absence of a European identity, and of a concomitant popular affinity. It is a considerable failing, and one to which we shall return in greater depth in the final chapter of this book. The failure to properly address it at Maastricht was critical.

Bits and pieces

The failings of the Maastricht IGC, and its Treaties, rapidly became apparent. The lack of inspiration was hardly unexpected, the rather ambiguous notion of citizenship similarly disappointing. But these were certainly not the only failings. One of the burning issues, as ever, was that of governance. Maastricht had, once again, provided an opportunity to get to grips with the seemingly intractable problem, and given that the IGC had finally established a political union the moment had never been more apposite. Sadly, of course, the opportunity went begging. Three failures were immediate and obvious, and rightly attracted particular critical comment: the failure to address the problem of governance and the 'democratic deficit'; the failure to institute a meaningful conception of Union citizenship; and the failure to clearly define competences between the Union and Community, and the constituent member states.

With regard to the question of governance, the same institutional imbalances remained. The Parliament's role in the co-decision procedure was marginally enhanced, by a power to reject a Council proposal at the second reading. However, the Council could still override the rejection if it did so unanimously. A third reading stage was also introduced, in which conflicts between Council and Parliament were to be resolved through a conciliation process. Finally, Parliament also gained the power to veto Commissioners, together with some largely vacuous supervisory powers over both the Council and the Commission (Raworth, 1994, pp 18–21). Amongst the more glaring omissions in the Treaty was the refusal to allow Parliament full rights of access to the Court of Justice in order to take actions against other institutions. Overall, as one commentator observed, when push had come to shove, when the opportunity to grasp the nettle of legitimacy had been offered, the participants at Maastricht had plainly lacked the 'courage' to do so (Bradley, 1994, pp 199–204, 211). At the end of the day, the only institution in the new political union that could not itself adopt the various forms of secondary legislation, regulations, directives or decisions was the Parliament (Hartley, 1993, p 222).

The Commission's failure to gain enhanced executive power was equally significant. The power of the Council, however, was virtually untouched. Moreover, given the intergovernmental nature of the other two 'pillars' of the Union, it was clear that the Council was far and away the real winner at Maastricht. The question of legitimacy had never been more starkly presented. Operating beyond the effective purview of the Court of Justice, in breach of any principle of the rule of law, the new Union was even less legitimate as a constitutional entity than the Community. As a gesture towards democratic accountability, the reforms instituted at Maastricht were, as Philip Raworth commented, 'timid'. The 'persistence of national particularism', he continued, 'reflects a Community consciousness that is lacking or at least in its infancy'. Most importantly, Parliament remained a disempowered and 'idiosyncratic body', one that incorporated a 'European identity' that was still very obviously 'artificial' (Raworth, 1994, pp 22–23).

The second failure relates to the idea of Union citizenship, as introduced in TEU, article 8. Delors had advocated the idea of citizenship as a vital feature in the putative 'social face' that was supposed to be described at Maastricht. Its complement in this aspiration was to be the much-vaunted Social Charter, replete with its various rights for workers. Sadly, however, the very fact that the rights were limited solely to workers, immediately excluded over half of Europe's new citizenry. The disparity between the legal definition of a worker and the constitutional definition of a citizen has emerged as one of the more regrettable anomalies of the Union. There are millions of citizens who do not work, and millions of workers who are denied citizenship. The reason for this latter peculiarity lies in the regrettable assertion, stated in the second clause of article 8, that only those who are citizens of a member state can be citizens of the Union. Different member states have different criteria for citizenship, and so, accordingly, the criteria for Union citizenship is various in the extreme. We shall revisit the concept of Union citizenship in the final chapter, for it speaks to the far deeper, and seemingly intractable, problems of European 'identity' and affinity.

The third failure of the Maastricht Treaty, perhaps the greatest, related to the principle of subsidiarity. The history of the European Community can be written in terms of competence, of the often tense relationship between the Community itself and its constituent nation states. This relationship defines the European experience. It was clear to those who drafted the TEU that these problems would be just as great, if not greater, in a political union. The suggested solution was subsidiarity. However, there was a fatal confusion. As we have already noted, article A of the TEU referred to the idea that 'decisions' should be 'taken as closely as possible to the people'. Taken to an extreme this could mean that, where possible, decisions should be taken at the lowest viable political level; in parish councils, in workplaces, in housing co-operatives. Article A suggests a radical decentralisation.

However, article A must be compared to the explicit definition of subsidiarity in article 3B, which suggested that the Community may only take action,

> if and in so far as the objectives of the proposed action cannot be sufficiently achieved by the Member States and can therefore, by reason of its scale or effects of the proposed action, be better achieved by the Community.

Article 3B then suggests that there are really only two alternatives, the member state or the Community. There is no room here for the parish council or the housing co-operative. For some, such as British Prime Minister John Major, article 3B represented a great victory for decentralisation, but only if decentralisation meant power exercised at nation state level. Article 3B established a rebuttable presumption that policy should be developed by nation states, and only rarely by the Community. Others were not so sure. Certainly, the Germans, who were already very familiar with a principle of subsidiarity in their own political system, defined the principle in federal terms. Dutch Prime Minister Ruud Lubbers made precisely the same observation (Constantinesco, 1991, pp 38–41). But who decides who decides? If the federalists were right, the question of which body can 'better' achieve the objects of the Community would be decided by the Community. If Major was right, then the question of who decides was vested in the nation states.

The reason for this confusion was political. The ambiguities were not accidental. Indeed, they were a conscious attempt to obfuscate. The drafters wanted a definition that 'satisfied nobody completely', but which upset no one that much (Teasdale, 1993, pp 189–191). The principle was supposed to be infinitely interpretable; each member state, and each member state government, can define subsidiarity pretty much as they please. For Major, subsidiarity could indeed be represented as a triumph for the nation state. For the more federally inclined, it could equally well be presented as a further step towards a Europe that was more obviously federal in nature. So variable is the meaning of subsidiarity that one commentator calculated at least 30 different possible interpretations.

In a very real sense this conscious confusion written into the definition of subsidiarity was synonymous with the overall ambivalence of the TEU itself. At the end of the day, as Lord Mackenzie Stuart observed, the principle of subsidiarity was a 'prophylactic', a preventative treatment aimed at ameliorating the realities of legal and political integration in Europe (Mackenzie Stuart, 1992, pp 19–24). Pretty much the same could be said of the TEU, so proud of its political union, so shy of upsetting its constituent nation states, so reluctant to admit that the whole purpose of a European political union can only be to further dismantle the constitutional, political and economic integrity of the nation state.

It was all a bit of a mess; continuing institutional imbalance, the ambiguity surrounding the meaning of subsidiarity, to which could be added the oddly diluted form of citizenship, the various Protocols, enshrined in article 239, which allowed various member states to opt-out of various things, the statements in article F referring to a rule of law that was respected by the Union, but not actually effective in it, and of course the overarching oddity of the three 'pillar' structure, with one supranational pillar and two intergovernmental ones. The inauguration of the Union was, as Joseph Weiler observed, a critical 'constitutional moment', and it appeared to have gone rather awry (Weiler, 1999a, p 3).

The sharks circled. In perhaps the most stinging critique, Deirdre Curtin assailed a Treaty that had promised so much, and delivered so little, a Treaty that revealed 'more of a bricoleur's amateurism than a master-bricklayer's strive for perfection and detail'. Ultimately, she suggested, it was a Treaty of 'bits and pieces'. There were, she suggested, two primary reasons for the Treaty's failings. First, there was 'no overriding and consistent constitutional philosophy'. Second, the member states had 'behaved like almighty *Herren der Vertraege*', ignoring, almost whimsically at times, the unique nature of the Community legal system. The effect, ultimately, was to threaten the very coherence and integrity of the Community itself. Her conclusion was brutal:

The result of the Maastricht Summit is an umbrella Union threatening to lead to constitutional chaos; the potential victims are the cohesiveness and the unity and the concomitant power of a legal system painstakingly constructed over the course of some 30 odd years. And yet the European Parliament and the national parliaments (and the people in three member states) are presented with this *fait accompli* and bullied into believing that only 'bad Europeans' would reject it. And, of course, it does contain elements of real progress . . . but a process of integration, if it has any meaning at all implies that you can't take one step forward and two steps backward at the same time . . . It must be said, at the heart of all this chaos and fragmentation, the unique *sui generic* nature of the European Community, its true world–historical significance, is being destroyed. (Curtin, 1993, p 67.)

Others, whilst similarly disappointed, tried to put on a brave face. Whilst deploring the rather 'rudimentary' union established at Maastricht, Ulrich Everling sought to suggest that some kind of progress had been made (Everling, 1992). It was suggested by some that the Maastricht TEU had at least ventured the possibility of political, as opposed to merely economic, supranationalism, even if it had then scuttled back into a more familiar intergovernmental pose. It was a spiritual, if not a material, victory for supranationalism (Holland, 1994, pp 91–99, 108–114, 203–205). Paul Demaret suggested that honours were about even, marginally enhanced legislative competence for the Parliament balanced by the reinforcement of the power of the Council (Demaret, 1994).

In a perceptive commentary, Helen Wallace suggested that the ambiguities that riddled the Maastricht Treaty reflect a wider political malaise which beset late twentieth century government across Europe. Political debate in general has been stifled, suffocated by the rhetoric and the mythology of economics and free markets. The political fate of the new European citizen, she observed, is tossed around at the whim of economists and technocrats, who use a language of rights as a mere charade for exacting an economics of conscious inequality. Clearly, she concluded,

technocracy and an elite-driven process seem no longer an adequate basis for EC governance. The gap between governed and governors within and between countries is serious and created havoc in the debate about Maastricht to which technical and legalistic devices seemed an inappropriate response. (Wallace, 1984, p 96.)

The accusation is a considerable one. But it is also an accurate one. The 'new' Europe is, indeed, paradigmatic of questions of governance and public philosophy, questions that reach far beyond its competences and boundaries.[2]

Looking back with the benefit of hindsight, Weiler suggests that the critical 'moment' of the Maastricht Treaty is important, not because it founded a Union, or at least not only, but because it brought into question the limits of European integration. After 1992, the idea of Europe became 'contestible' (Weiler, 1999a, p 3). Suddenly, it was not just a handful of sceptics who doubted the energy of the enterprise. The Union, it seemed, might just have been a step too far, and its prospective history might be written in terms of decelerated integration, or perhaps even disintegration.

A crisis of governance

Such a lot of hope, and such a lot of heartache, for a Treaty that was so widely condemned. The immediate future stretched the agony a little further, for the Treaty had to be ratified by the member states. The British government very nearly fell in the struggle to pilot an amended version of the European Communities Act through Parliament.[3] The more democratic, and the more reckless, actually approached their citizenry directly in order to seek their approval. Only in Ireland did such an approach appear to be vindicated. Referenda in Denmark and France proved to altogether more tortuous. In Denmark, the people rejected ratification by 50.7 per cent to 49.3 per cent. Politely asked to have another go, the Danes were more obliging, and voted by 56.7 per cent to 43.3 per cent in favour of ratification. The French referendum produced a similar result to the first Danish vote, approving ratification by less than 2 per cent. They were not given a chance to reconsider and a second vote. This time, 2 per cent was just fine. Significantly, the French Conseil

---

2   We shall return to these questions in the final chapter.
3   We shall revisit this particular agony in chapter 4.

Constitutionnel had already declared that large parts of the Treaty, including articles 8A, 100C and 104J, were incompatible with the tenets of the French constitution. The constitution was simply altered. The sense of fudge and frustration was not so easily assuaged (Oliver, 1994).

In an even more damning ruling in the famous *Brunner* case, the German Federal Constitutional Court had reached a similar conclusion to its French counterpart. Although it had adjudged that ratification was constitutional, the Federal Constitutional Court did see fit to make a number of collateral observations, commenting that the Union, as a 'special compound of States', fell somewhat short of statehood, and that the sovereignty of the German state remained, accordingly, intact. It seemed that Europe was little more integrated in 1992 than it had been in 1957 or, for that matter, during the age of Charlemagne or Augustus Caesar (*Brunner*, 1994; Herdegen, 1994). It did seem to be something of a snub.

Most obviously, perhaps, there was a strong case for sober reflection. Something, quite clearly, had gone very wrong indeed.[4] Commentators mused. Some suggested that the final completion of the market was what really mattered, most obviously the effecting of a single currency (Cockfield, 1994). Others preferred a more political strategy, pressing ahead for a fully federal Europe (Wistrich, 1994, pp 153–166; Howe, 1995). Still others were inclined to be considerably more cautious. At an extreme, the more cataclysmic foretold the coming end of the 'new' Europe. Alan Milward prophesied a 'natural' dissolution, complemented by the reassertion of 'national diversity' (Milward and Soerensen, 1993, pp 16–21; Milward, 1993, pp 196–201; cf Therborn, 1995, p 74).

There was also a new shadow lurking over the Union's shoulder, that of enlargement. Along with it came the gnawing fear that the politics of diversity might indeed overcome the politics of integration. More sceptical politicians such as Prime Minister Major loudly championed the idea of a Europe that would be 'wider' rather than 'deeper'. The intergovernmental nature of the Union could certainly be interpreted

---

[4] In the words of Derek Urwin: 'The Treaty probably satisfied no one. It fell far short of the previous claims made for it, while nevertheless advancing Europe further along the integrationalist road than many sceptics would have wished' (Urwin, 1995, p 256).

in this way, and it was clear that the creation of the Union had, in large part, been effected in order to prepare the way for the possibility of future enlargement. The possibility of further accessions had been discussed for much of the previous decade and had received formal approval at the Copenhagen Council in 1992 which had established a raft of accession criteria, the more important of which related to economic viability, whilst the more notional mused on the desirability of democratic credibility.

Then, in 1995, the Union duly welcomed three new members, Austria, Sweden and Finland. The accession of these three countries was not particularly troublesome, for the simple reason that each was rich, richer indeed than the vast majority of existing member states. The problem lay in the next prospective tranche of accessions. The integration of East and West Germany cost the latter $1 trillion. Europe has still not recovered from the shock. The prospect of enlarging the Union to include perhaps 24 member states, maybe even more in the longer term, troubles many. For some, the more xenophobic, it is the age old fear of the barbarians at the gate. For others it is the more prosaic fear that the sheer expense of enlargement might cripple the Union.

It is suggested that Europe might need to double its regional aid budget in order to equip any new members financially (Tartwijk-Novey, 1995, pp 37–54, 118–123). Alternatively, it might just make drastic cuts to existing budgets. Neither prospect is popular. Current net contributors reject the former idea. Current net receivers reject the latter. For much of the decade following the Maastricht TEU, the Union has continued to flirt with its neighbours, teasing and tantalising, but stolidly refusing to let them join the party. We will take a close look at the prospect of enlargement in chapter 7. In the meanwhile, we should note that its very prospect presently sends shivers down the collective spine of Europe. Recent Councils, like the most recent Treaty, at Nice in 2000, have been obsessed with the prospect.

Enlargement, then, added a considerable frisson of anxiety. Just as important was the very obvious sense of disinterest amongst the newly enacted citizenry of the Union. The problem of affinity, of the search for some kind of binding and inspiring public philosophy, is of enormous importance, and we shall return to it in the final chapter.

Juergen Habermas suggested that the essential problem with the 'new' Europe, that of an overwheening concern for free market capitalism at the expense of democratic legitimacy, was just as great, perhaps even greater, after 1992 than it was before (Habermas, 1992, pp 8–13). The step from disinterest to dislike is not a large one. The need to address the legitimacy question, the seemingly intractable issue of governance and public philosophy, was more pressing than ever. Moreover, as Antony Smith noted, questions of affinity and legitimacy cannot be distinguished from those of diversity:

> It is one thing for elites in Brussels, Strasbourg and some European capitals to identify with and work for a united Europe, quite another to attribute such sentiments and beliefs to the great mass of middle and working classes, let alone the surviving peasantries of Southern and Eastern Europe. (Smith, 1992, p 72.)

In this context, Juliet Lodge suggested that the more immediate need post-1992 was somehow to 'personalise' the Union. There must, she observed, 'be an increase in the efficiency, effectiveness, accountability, democratic responsiveness and openness of the institutions' (Lodge, 1993b, pp 377–381). Now the economic Community had become a political Union, it would have to learn to behave like one. Emphasising the overarching 'crisis of governance' across the continent, she continued:

> The problem inherent in analysing European integration today rests with the implicit expectation that the EC/Union should 'act' whether internally or externally in an increasingly politically homogenous and cohesive manner across a growing number and range of issue-areas. The institutions do not have the capacity to deliver and meet these expectations.

Ultimately, the problem remained that of competence, the problem which the principle of subsidiarity had so singularly failed to resolve:

> The locus of political authority has not been agreed by the EC's member governments. Not only is the concept of a single or a central locus of political activity contested, but the location of the main institutions remains disputed . . . That the absence of agreement over the parameters of supranational authority is problematic is attested to by the continuing wrangling over the

political issue of the EC's democratic legitimacy. Member governments, by and large, still see supranational agencies as their rivals engaged in a zero-sum game for power, authority and the loyalty of their subjects.

Her conclusion was succinct, and apposite. The 1990s would need to be 'a time when the political face to integration' would have to be 'recognized and accommodated' (Lodge, 1993b, pp 383–385).

Amsterdam: reflections

Whilst academic commentators let rip, Europe's political elites desperately searched for some way of cobbling things together. After all, the finger of blame could only point one way. The crisis of governance and legitimacy was rooted in a failure of leadership (Rose, 1995, p 89). The solution of course was to project another Treaty. It is always the solution. It was clear that the Union, and indeed the Community, would need substantial revision. Commission policy during the years immediately following the Maastricht TEU had focused on three things: securing the common currency; revising the constitutional structure of the Union; and promoting enlargement. The resolution of all these goals, the Commission loudly announced, required a new Treaty. A date was set, 1997, and a place, Amsterdam.

However it was to be a very different Treaty. A so-called Reflection Group, set up to provide some kind of prospective focus, urged the IGC to concentrate on 'necessary changes' rather than embark on 'a complete revision'. Such changes were, of course, those demanded by the prospect of enlargement (Langrish, 1998, p 4; Maganza and Piris, 1999, p 35). A mood was set. Where the Maastricht IGC and resultant Treaty had been gaudy and overblown, Amsterdam was reserved and undersold, in the words of one commentator, little more than a 'routine service' (Langrish, 1998, p 19). In academic parlance, it is said to be a 'consolidating' Treaty. In other words it tinkers around a bit with the Maastricht Treaty, altering a few sentences here and there, changing all the article numbers, and hopefully addressing some of the more obvious and glaring ambiguities along the way.

Amongst the latter were various amendments to the Union Treaty. Article A, now recast as TEU, article 1, introduced the much-vaunted principle of 'transparency'. Henceforth, decisions would not only be taken as 'closely' as possible to the citizens, but also 'as openly as possible'. The need to address the issue of administrative obfuscation had emerged as a particular concern in the years immediately preceding the Amsterdam IGC. It was felt, quite sensibly, that the 'peoples' of Europe might feel a little more enamoured of their Union if they had the slightest idea about what it did and what it was supposed to do.

Article F, recast as article 6, was also reworked, so that it now stated that:

> The Union is founded on the principles of liberty, democracy, respect for human rights and fundamental freedoms, and the rule of law, principles which are common to the Member States.

But not, of course, principles that are common to the Union itself. The problem of the Union's legitimacy remained, for what did not change at Amsterdam was the overarching Treaty structure. The three 'pillars' still remain, even if their contents have been juggled around. The Community 'pillar' remains the only supranational one, and so, accordingly, the only one in which the principle of the rule of law is at all meaningful. The insertion of the phrase 'respect for human rights and fundamental freedoms', replacing the explicit reference to the European Convention in article F of the Maastricht TEU, was a tacit admission that the Union, not being a nation state, could not itself ratify the Convention. If it wanted to define a human rights profile, the Union would have to do so itself. Much of the post-Amsterdam agenda would be fashioned around this possibility.

Article 7 TEU added further provision for punishing any member state that is adjudged by the Council to be in 'serious and persistent breach' of the general principles listed in article 6. Such punishment, it was surmised in the second paragraph, might take the form of suspension from Council meetings. It was never seriously intended that any existing member state might be so punished (Verhoeven, 1998, pp 223–224). But it was thought to be a useful stick with which to beat a number of putatively new members of the Community. It would, for example, sound so much better if Turkey could be denied accession because the Union appeared to take articles 6 and 7 so very seriously, rather than merely because Greece was still peeved by the occupation of northern Cyprus and would refuse to give its assent.

The most important remaining amendments to the Union Treaty lay in the third pillar, in the former article K, newly recast as articles 29–42. The field of 'justice and home affairs' was transmogrified into an 'area of freedom, security and justice'. Most importantly of all, a whole raft of provisions relating to visas, asylum and various other policies relating to the free movement of persons was transferred to the Community 'pillar', taking residence in a new Title IIIA. In essence, these measures constituted what had become known as the Schengen *acquis*. Twelve member states accepted the *acquis*, three did not; the usual suspects, Denmark, Eire and the United Kingdom.

The transference was in part a response to widespread criticism that a large chunk of the Union Treaty provisions were clearly in breach of any number of international conventions, but most obviously the Geneva Convention which required matters relating to refugees and asylum to be subject to a rule of law. What remained in the third 'pillar' were various provisions for closer 'police and judicial co-operation in criminal matters'. These so-called 'flanking measures', including policies to combat terrorism, organised crime and drug trafficking, are designed to tighten external borders as a complement to the relaxation of internal borders. They are intended to make 'Fortress Europe' a reality, but to do so in a way in which the breaches of international refugee law are rather less obvious.

The incorporation of the Schengen *acquis* was not the only substantial amendment to the Community Treaty. The presence of new articles on employment policy, in Title VIII, and those on the environment, in Title XIX, were clearly intended to pander to wider popular concerns. And the same might be said of a new article 13, which stated that the Council could, 'acting unanimously on a proposal from the Commission and after consulting the European Parliament' elect to 'take appropriate action to combat discrimination based on sex, racial or ethnic origin, religion or belief, disability, age, or sexual orientation'. The value of this putatively liberal and progressive article will, of course, depend on the nature of derivative secondary legislation. Its greater significance, perhaps, rests in the tacit admission that the 'new' European Union must address the obvious questions of political morality that face any modern liberal democracy. Article 13 EC was cast in the same spirit as article 6 TEU. It represented an acknowledgment that something must be done, even if it did not say precisely what.[5]

Other than this, however, it was clear that the focus of the Amsterdam Treaty lay in the 'consolidation' of the Union. If the years between 1958 and 1992 had been consumed by the desire to complete the market, finally to establish an economic Community, it had become ever more apparent that the years after 1992 were to be devoted to the establishment of a political Union. In this vein, the more supportive such as Armin von Bogdandy argue that the Treaty, whilst appearing so modest, was in fact a significant, if rather covert, step towards 'supranational' political 'federation' (von Bogdandy, 2000a, pp 32–41). All the great, still unresolved questions, of governance and legitimacy, of enlargement, of the relation between the Community and Union, and the nation states, would be recast within this particular ambit, of divining and securing political Union.

The age of flexibility

Overall reactions to the Amsterdam Treaty were, once again, somewhat less than exuberant. A 'series of modest achievements' according to Joseph Weiler (Weiler, 1999b, p 1). Deirdre Curtin noted a 'sense of *déjà vue* about it all'; another Treaty, another opportunity lost (Curtin, 1999, p 71). To a certain extent, of course, the Amsterdam Treaty was never intended to be exciting. But even so, there was still much to disappoint. The overarching structure remained a mess. Governance remained an affront to precisely those principles of liberal democracy so vacuously declared in article 6. Rhetorical gestures to transparency and to combating discrimination were precisely that, rhetorical gestures.

In addition there was something else that gave rise to anxiety. Just as Maastricht had been haunted by the word federal, Amsterdam was haunted by another F-word, flexibility. And just as the very word 'federal' was exorcised from the Maastricht Treaty, so too the word 'flexibility' was cast beyond the bounds of polite debate. In its place, the peoples of Europe were invited to think in terms of 'closer co-operation', a phrase which, it was fondly hoped, might seem to be rather less obvious a snub to the very idea of an *acquis communautaire*

---

[5]   We shall return to article 13 in chapter 6.

(Gaja, 1998, pp 855–856). The immediate months leading up to the Amsterdam IGC were dominated by the idea of 'closer co-operation'. All the other planned amendments, to articles 1 and 6 and to articles 29–42, the anticipated movement of the Schengen provisions to the Community pillar, the invention of article 13; all paled in comparison. The time had come for a new dawning, for what has, anyway, come to be known as the age of flexibility.

Articles 43–45 enacted the principle in the Union Treaty. Article 43 establishes that those member states who 'intend to establish close co-operation between themselves' may do so within the purview of the Union, and may use the institutions of the Community in order to assist them. The article goes on to affirm that this principle of 'closer co-operation' is 'aimed at furthering the objectives of the Union and at protecting its interests'. It also adds that the principle should only be 'used as a last resort', that it does not affect the existing 'rights' of non-participating member states, and most importantly, that it does not in any way 'affect the *acquis communautaire*'. The specific reference to the Union is interesting, complemented as it was by the further proviso that 'co-operation' should not infringe upon areas of 'exclusive' Community 'competence'. Once again, there is a clear sense that if there are to be further innovations in the process of integration they will take place in the Union, not in the Community.

In simple terms, 'flexibility' is intended to allow different sets of member states to integrate in different areas at different speeds. Another phrase, 'variable geometry', is commonly used to describe pretty much the same thing (Phillipart and Edwards, 1999, pp 103–104). The principle is intended to furnish a constitutional sheen to the much criticised presence of Protocols, or opt-outs, in the Maastricht TEU. Accordingly, the fact that twelve of the member states subscribe to a single currency, whilst three do not, is no longer to be seen as a messy political fudge, but as an exemplar of 'closer co-operation' in action.[6] The same is true of perhaps the most important example of flexibility written into the Treaty framework, the article 14 EC opt-outs for the United Kingdom, Eire and Denmark, from various aspects of the 'area of freedom, justice and security'.

[6]   Of course, there are still problems, the most obvious of which is the status of those countries not participating in the single currency. All member states are bound to be affected by it, but which member states should have a say in how the currency operates? (Usher, 2000, pp 488–493.)

In the final analysis 'closer co-operation' is a clear admission that enlargement will necessitate a Europe of different 'communities' of member states, some richer, some poorer, some more closely integrated, some less so, some with open borders, some without. The fear, of course, is that with flexibility will come fragmentation. In a paradoxical sense, flexibility both guards against and promotes precisely this threat (Phillipart and Edwards, 1999, pp 104–105). The potential for fragmentation comes both from within the Union, in the form of residual political and cultural differentiation, and from without, in the form of pending enlargement which can only exacerbate the reality of political and cultural differentiation. Flexibility is intended to pre-empt this threat. But it could just as well be said to have invited fragmentation into the heart of the Treaty, and asked it to sit by the fire and warm its toes.

It is certainly a common impression. According to Weiler, the idea of 'closer co-operation' represented a 'failure masquerading as an achievement' (Weiler, 1999b, p 3). Suddenly the European citizen, for decades taught to worship the idol of the *acquis communautaire*, was supposed to welcome the idea that each member state should, from now on, feel free to pick and choose which bits of European integration they would like to support, at what speed they might like to integrate, and to what extent. Intangible though it might be, it was this sense of *acquis* that had been lost, a sense of harmony and common purpose, of everyone treading the same route together, even if they did have no clear idea of where it was leading.

Other commentators have noted the symbiosis between flexibility, and what Jo Shaw terms 'that other rather plastic concept, subsidiarity' (Shaw, 1998, p 66). The comparison is valid. Both seek a balance between the power of the nation states and that of the Union; both, ultimately, seek to cloak hard-nosed political reality with a fragment of constitutional nicety; and both describe concepts that seem to be almost infinitely definable. The Amsterdam Protocol on Subsidiarity affirmed the Edinburgh Declaration, that subsidiarity should be seen as a device for reinvesting primary competences in the nation states. It remains to be seen whether the same will in the end be true of flexibility. In the meanwhile, the age of flexibility does, as Grainne de Burca suggests, appear to reinforce an emergent 'teleology of subsidiarity', something that appears to be opposed to the original Community 'teleology of integration' (de Burca, 1998, p 218).

Flexibility, if not fragmentation, has clearly taken a strong hold of contemporary political discourse across Europe. In the run-up to the Amsterdam IGC, the Austrian Chancellor, Victor Klima, observed that the 'restitution' of 'certain powers in the area of national or regional responsibilities should not be a taboo subject'. Both President Chirac of France and Chancellor Kohl of Germany made similar, if rather more obtuse, intimations (Devuyst, 1999, pp 109, 112–113). The essential political question after Amsterdam was simple; has the age of flexibility superseded the age of integration? For some, the answer is clearly in the affirmative. According to Alan Dashwood, flexibility confirms the 'new orthodoxy', that the 'new' Europe will remain one of 'bits and pieces' (Dashwood, 1998, p 213). Moravcsik and Nicolaidis furnish the same conclusion with a slightly more positive spin, referring to flexibility as evidence of a 'new evolutionary pragmatism' (Moravcsik and Nicolaidis, 1999, p 79). Either way, and despite all the over-anxious protestations, it seemed that the price of the Union would be the end of the *acquis communitaire*.

Nice: leftovers

Shortly before his entire Commission were booted out for corruption, its President, Jacques Santer, was moved to admit that he could not 'hide the inadequacies, the weaknesses and the great gaps' that remained after Amsterdam. In more prosaic terms, there were 'leftovers' that would have to be resolved by the next IGC and then corrected in yet another consolidating Treaty, at Nice in December 2000. The need for such a strategy was strongly urged by successive Cologne, Tampere and Helsinki Councils during 1999. All emphasised the need to revisit the still unresolved problem of governance. Moreover, each further noted the ever looming prospect of enlargement. The previous year had seen the opening of official negotiations with six of the aspirants, Hungary, Poland, Estonia, the Czech Republic, Slovenia and Cyprus.

In the end, the Nice IGC produced three documents: the redrafted Treaties; a Charter of Fundamental Rights; and a Declaration on the Future of the Union. The latter two documents will be discussed in the next two sections of this chapter. With regard to the redrafted Treaties, once again, there were various miscellaneous amendments. Amongst the more complex were a series of amendments to article 133 EC relating to external trade policy. The general thrust of these amendments is to return control of Community trade policy to the Council, and thus, in effect, to the nation states. Most strikingly, revised article 133 curtails the power of the Commission to negotiate international agreements on the Community's behalf (Pescatore, 2001, p 266).[7]

Perhaps the most striking amendment to the constitutional principles established by the TEU is the addition to article 7 of a clause that allows the Council to issue recommendations whenever there is a 'clear risk of a serious breach' of the enumerated principles in article 6 'by a Member State'. Interestingly, article 46 TEU grants the Court of Justice a power of review over the procedures stipulated in article 7. The immediate political impetus here was a desire to avoid any future occurrence of the so-called 'Haider affair'. No one had seriously expected an existing member state to fall foul of articles 6 and 7, but the inclusion of Jörg Haider and two of his fascist cronies from the far-right Freedom Party in the Austrian government in early 2000 shattered that cosy complacency. There was, it seemed, a very rotten heart to Europe. A commission of 'Wise Men' was convened to investigate the affair. Fortunately, the wise men also proved to be malleable men, sufficiently malleable indeed that their Report largely excused the Austrian government of its temporary sojourn with its fascist friends. They were not really 'fascist', the Wise Men advised, just very 'extremist'. Hopefully, article 7 will preclude any future need for such supine obfuscation.

The amendment to article 7 was not really a 'leftover'; more an unforeseen lacuna. The precarious state of the 'closer co-operation' was, however, far more obvious, and very much in need of attention. Nice introduced a reinvigorated principle of 'enhanced co-operation', the practical difference being that article 44 TEU now requires that there should be a minimum of only eight member states wishing to pursue 'closer co-operation' in a given field of policy. A more ephemeral adjustment requires that co-operation should now 'respect' the *acquis communautaire*. The tenor is one of encouragement. Rather than being an exception, it is clearly intended that flexibility should become something of a norm (Shaw, 2001 pp 201–202; Bradley, 2001, pp 1114–1115).

The Nice Council was conducted in what one commentator termed an 'atmosphere of conflict' (Yataganas, 2001, p 269). Undoubtedly the

---

[7]   We shall revisit article 133 in chapter 7.

most fierce of many fierce debates surrounded the vexed issue of extending qualified majority voting in EC legislative matters. Whilst everyone could agree to extending the domain of qualified majority voting to a whole tranche of areas in the Community Treaty previously subject to unanimity, no one could agree to the mooted revisions to the voting ratios (Piris, 2000, pp 17–22, 24–28). The bickering between heads of state was endless, and not terribly edifying. The German Chancellor claimed a greater weight of votes for Germany for the simple reason that there were more Germans. The French President responded with the rather gnomic argument that France had a nuclear capacity. The squabble over voting ratios brought into the open a simmering dispute between Germany and France with regard to their relative political influence. Germany's ultimate victory in this particular matter, and in the complementary matter of Parliamentary representation, has been interpreted as signalling a final upsetting of the increasingly precarious Franco-German balance of power.

After hours of debate, a gruesomely complex formula for voting ratios was worked out.[8] The mantle of integration had passed, it seemed, from the visionaries to the statisticians. No one was entirely happy, but everyone was very tired. The Council was the longest in history, lasting four days, and ending at 2.30 a m on the Monday morning. Prior to Nice, heads of state had only ever spent weekends at their Councils, enjoying the food, drinking the fine wines, and strolling through the gardens of various castles, chateaux and Schlossen. But Nice was not fun at all. It had lasted 370 hours, involving ten meetings of foreign ministers and three meetings of the heads of state in Council. Prime Minister Blair emerged muttering that such a Council and such an IGC, must never be allowed to happen again (Yataganas, 2001, p 270; Wessels, 2001, p 198).

Tempted by rights

In the lead up to the Nice Council, there had been much discussion of a proposed Charter of Fundamental Rights. The recommendation had been strongly stated at the Cologne Council in summer

---

[8]   The compromise was based on a 'triple majority'. Decisions would be adopted in Council if they had the agreement of a majority of member states, between 71% and 74% of weighted votes, and if requested by any member state, at least 62% of the notional total population of the Union.

1999, where it concluded that there 'appears to be a need, at the present stage of the Union's development, to establish a Charter of fundamental rights in order to make their overriding importance and relevance more visible to the Union's citizens'. Despite the clear implication that appearance mattered as much as substance, the prospect of such a Charter, particularly if it could be said to describe a proper European 'constitution', caused great excitement. Academies buzzed, a Convention was established, to which all kinds of pressure groups, many of them religious, pleaded the case for their favourite rights (Eicke, 2000, pp 280–281; Liisberg, 2001, pp 1172–1182). Above all the braying, Europe's political elite pontificated on the need to symbolise what the German Foreign Minister, Joschka Fischer, rather obscurely termed a 'European Finality'. Such a Charter would seal the Union, giving it an unassailable moral and political legitimacy. The French President, Jacques Chirac, appealed to the memory of the 'genius of a few visionaries', to the cause of an 'empire forged for intellectual reasons', one which seeks the 'collective promotion of shared values'.

The root cause of the Charter can be traced to recital 27 of *Opinion 2/94* of the Court of Justice, which held that 'No Treaty provision confers on the Community institutions any general power to enact rules on human rights or to conclude international conventions in this field' (*Opinion 2/94*; Lenaerts, 2000, p 575). As we have already noted, the clear implication of article F of the Maastricht TEU was that the Union might wish to join the European Convention. *Opinion 2/94* brought that canard rapidly to earth. If the Union wanted some kind of charter of rights by which it might seek to enhance its own rather spartan political legitimacy, then it would have to write its own.

And so it did. Appended to the Nice Treaty was a Charter, the Preamble of which proudly proclaims that the 'peoples of Europe, in creating an ever closer union among them, are resolved to share a peaceful future based on common values'. Moreover, it confirmed, 'conscious of its spiritual and moral heritage, the Union is founded on the indivisible, universal values of human dignity, freedom, equality, and solidarity'. The Union is also, it added, 'based on the principles of democracy and the rule of law'. The echoes of article 6, and the European Convention, and similar statements in a series of domestic charters in member states were resonant. Less familiar perhaps was the even grander observation that all 'future generations' were also to be bound by the 'responsibilities and duties' enumerated. The 'new' Europe, it seems, intends to stick around.

There are, in all, 54 articles in the new Charter, listing all manner of rights, most of which are again taken from the Convention or from member state constitutions. The usual suspects are present, all the rights that commonly appear in such charters. Article 1 thus proclaims that 'Human dignity is inviolable. It must be respected and protected'. Article 2 secures the 'right to life', whilst article 6 suggests that 'Everyone has the right to liberty and security of person'. Article 7 adds a 'right to respect for his or her private and family life', whilst article 20 affirms that 'Everyone is equal before the law', and article 21 applies the principle to counter 'discrimination based on any ground such as sex, race, colour, ethnic or social origin'. Elsewhere can be found a series of more prosaic civil rights, to access ombudsmen, to petition, to fair judicial proceedings, and so on. A number of these latter rights, whilst again being common to many member state constitutions, also speak to the perceived need to enumerate Union citizenship rights (Goldsmith, 2001, p 1209).

There is nothing particularly unusual about Europe's Charter. And there is nothing particularly unique about the problems of interpretation that it, like any such Charter, must necessarily encounter. What, for example, does 'human dignity' mean? And what does the 'right to life' mean? In what jurists term 'hard cases', where there is no clear moral certitude, it is quite possible for such rights to be in direct contradiction. Does the 'right to life' forbid abortions? Does the right to 'human dignity' require that women have a right to abort? Charters of rights rarely provide answers, just lots of different interpretations and opinions.

There is anyway a much deeper criticism of the Charter, one which renders the classical problem of conceptual interpretation largely irrelevant. For, at the end of the day, despite all the fine words, the appeals to past visionaries and the expressed need to seal Europe's 'Finality', the politicians lost their nerve, and perhaps their interest. The Nice Council lost itself in the impenetrable world of voting ratios. The Charter of Rights slipped out, almost apologetically. There was to be no proud document describing the fundamental justiciable rights of all European citizens, merely a rather ephemeral Declaration. Accordingly, Europe's new Charter describes a series of rights, none of which can be enforced by any court.

And yet, it is clear that the Charter may still have a role to play in the development of a Union, and indeed a Community, human rights jurisprudence. As we shall see in the next chapter, the Court of Justice has already carved out a rather restricted human rights jurisprudence, and it may well take up the responsibility of translating the principles articulated in the Charter into Community, if not Union, law. In the recent *Broadcasting* case, Advocate General Tizzano advised that 'relevant statements of the Charter' could not be 'ignored' by the Court. The Charter, he added, could 'provide reliable and definitive confirmation' of what rights truly existed in Community law' (*BECTU*, 2001; Shaw, 2001, pp 199–200).

There is also precedent, for, as we shall see in chapter 6, the Community Charter for the Social Rights of Workers originally started life as a Declaration in 1989, only to be elevated to justiciable status in the Maastricht Treaty. It is quite possible that the Nice Charter will follow the same path. There is certainly a tangible sense of expectation. The final 'chapter' of the Charter contains a series of 'General Provisions', articles 51, 52 and 53, the tenor of which is to define justiciable limits. These articles were clearly drafted when it was intended that the Charter would be part of Community and Union law. The fact that they have been left in is striking.

Article 51.1 states that the 'provisions of this Charter are addressed to institutions and bodies of the Union with due regard for the principle of subsidiarity and to the Member States only when they are implementing Union law'. The immediate purpose here is to preclude 'horizontality', the possibility that Charter rights might be deployed against private bodies or against member states in areas outside Community law. Article 52 states that any 'limitations' on the 'exercise' of rights must be 'provided for by law', and must be 'subject to the principle of proportionality'. This particular concession pays homage to the existing jurisprudence of the Court of Justice. Charter rights, like Community human rights, will always be adjudged within the context of the wider 'general interests' of the Union. Article 53, in turn, states that 'nothing in this Charter' should be 'interpreted' to be in conflict with existing human rights provisions in member state constitutions or in the European Convention. The burning question, of course, not just for article 53, but for every other article in the Charter is simple; interpreted by whom? (Goldsmith, 2001, pp 1204–1207, 1210–1211; Ward, 2001, pp 118–120.)

Unsurprisingly, the Charter has enjoyed a somewhat mixed reception. Those who drafted it tend, not surprisingly, to be most supportive. Having said that, there is a certain paradox in Lord Goldsmith's confession that it is right that the Charter should have no greater force than that of Declaration simply because it 'lacks the precision of language necessary to allow it legal force'. Such an attitude would condemn just about any such Charter, including the European Convention, the comparable Canadian Charter of Rights, and even the US Constitution. More persuasive, perhaps, is Goldsmith's passing observation that the Charter may well emerge as a primary 'guiding resource' for the Court of Justice and for courts of member states (Goldsmith, 2001, p 1215).

Others are less forgiving, arguing that the failure to adopt a binding Charter can only send the 'message' that the Union's 'commitment to the protection of fundamental rights is less serious' than appeared in the run up to Nice (Herringa, 2000, p 112). The more optimistic assume that the Charter will anyway become a 'justifiable element' of Community and Union law in due course (Engel, 2001, p 153). For some, such as Armin von Bogdandy, much depends on the future development of Union human rights in general and the Charter in particular. With the common market 'exhausted as a vision for further integration', and with no clear vision of 'where European integration should go from here', human rights offers itself as perhaps the only 'intriguing prospect' (von Bogdandy, 2000b, p 1337). The observation is acute, as Europe's leaders appear to acknowledge. The Declaration on the 'Future of the Union', which was also appended to the Nice Treaty, conceded that the Charter's status would be a subject for review for the next IGC. If so, then articles 51, 52 and 53, and indeed the 50 that come before, may actually come to mean something. Until then they, like the Charter itself, hover like Banquo's ghost, the anticipated guest of honour who was rudely dispatched along the way.

A decade of Europe?

Three years on, the dust has still to settle on the Nice Treaty. But, once again, initial responses are rather downbeat. The Charter is only one disappointment. In a stinging commentary, Pierre Pescatore dismisses the Treaty package, including the Charter and Declaration, as 'amateurish', lacking in both 'imagination' and 'courage'. The entire venture into political Union has only served to enhance nation state recidivism, diverting attention and energy into 'false projections at its periphery', and detracting from the original core business of European integration, the completion of an efficient common market (Pescatore, 2001). Jo Shaw reaches a similar, if less visceral, conclusion, noting that the 'resurgence' of 'large state supremacy' reveals a 'continuing ambivalence among the Member States over the nature and purpose of the integration process, and of the Treaties which sustain that process' (Shaw, 2001, p 215). It is clear that the integrationist dynamic that drove the '1992 Project' and the completion of the market has long passed. The Union has never recovered from its bodged birth. A Union of 'bits and pieces' seems to have become a Union of 'fits and starts'.

Contemporary Europe, it is clear, is beset with problems. Some of these problems relate to the market. The value of the single currency, for example, whilst stabilising through 2001–02, has still fallen by nearly a fifth since the beginning of 1999. As we shall see in later chapters, various areas of the common market, of free movement, competition and social policy, remain to be 'completed'. The market, however, is no longer the primary focus of attention, and so, accordingly, neither is the Community. It is the fate of the Union that distracts everyone's attention, and it is here that the deeper problems can be found. One is the seemingly intractable problem of governance. Another is the impending anticipation, or perhaps more accurately fear, of enlargement. These two issues dominate the current political agenda.

This much is admitted by the presence of a 'Declaration on the Future of the Union' that was tagged onto the end of the Final Act of the Nice Council. The Declaration states that 'having opened the way to enlargement, the Conference calls for a deeper and wider debate about the future development of the Union'. It then went on to list four priorities, each of which would be addressed in the projected 2004 IGC. The first priority is a delimitation of competences between the Union and the member states and, more particularly, in a way that reflects 'the principle of subsidiarity'. In other words, another look at flexibility. The second admits the need to re-examine the 'status' of the Charter. The third priority suggests a need to simplify the Treaties. And the fourth priority relates to the possible role of national Parliaments in the European architecture. This is couched in terms of a 'need to improve and to monitor the democratic legitimacy and transparency of the Union and its institutions' in order to 'bring them closer to the citizens'. All very heart-warming, perhaps, but such sentiments have been expressed before, on numerous occasions.

However, what is perhaps distinctive about these more recent sentiments is the immediate context of pending enlargement. As we have already seen, this context dominated both the Amsterdam and Nice IGCs, giving birth, indeed, to the age of flexibility. The same is true of subsequent Councils. The Copenhagen Council at the end of 2002 reaffirmed that enlargement in 2004 would go ahead. Ten countries, the six with which negotiations had been opened in 1998, along with Slovakia, Lithuania, Latvia and Malta, remain officially 'on course'. Commentators speak in suitably cataclysmic terms of the pending 'Big Bang', of all aspiring members arriving in one, potentially shattering, go. Overnight the Union will be 25 per cent bigger, with an added population of around 75 million. Problems abound, many of them unresolved. Perhaps most obvious is the problem of structural support. All applicant countries will be 'beggar-nations', and the squabbling as to who will fund them, and to what tune, remains one of the least edifying aspect of successive Council meetings. It is clear that the CAP will need substantial reform, and it is equally clear that many existing members of the Community, whose economies are centred on traditional farming practices, such as France and Ireland, remain resistant to the very idea.

In this context, it is clear that institutional reform and reform of governance will be every bit as necessary as structural reform. Nice was overwhelmed by the resultant bickering that surrounded the question of voting weights in Council. The Commission will be equally in need of reform following enlargement. At present it is agreed that, from January 2005, there will be just one Commissioner for each member state, and that once it reaches 27 members, the Union will adopt a rotation system with Commissioners being nominated in turn by member states. The Parliament will also be reformed. Here the need to limit members, initially to 700 seats, was abandoned. There will, for a Europe of 27 member states, be 732 MEPs. It was decided that the efficiency of the Commission would be impeded if there were too many Commissioners. No one is so fussy about the Parliament. Indeed, the continued weakness of the Parliament, despite the enhanced process of 'co-decision' conceded at the

Amsterdam and Nice IGCs, does little to allay the basic charge of a 'democratic deficit.

The problem of governance has changed little in half a century. In simple terms, the 'new' Europe is governed in blatant disregard of the basic principles of democracy and accountability. And the problem is pervasive, as Joseph Weiler observes, located 'at all levels of European governance'. Small wonder that so few bother to vote in European elections, as few as 15 per cent in certain parts of the Union. There is no government to be elected, no government to be cast out. The age of flexibility is complemented by the age of *Comitology*, of government through an intricate web of unaccountable committees. This network, established by the Council in its Decision 87/373, strengthens its own power whilst further distancing governance from the principles of democracy, accountability and transparency. The failure to address this executive despotism was, as Weiler rightly concludes, the 'real black hole' of the Amsterdam Treaty (Weiler, 1999a, pp 98, 275–276; Weiler, 1999b, pp 6, 19). It is no less the case after Nice. As feared, fragmentation has accompanied flexibility. There are too many committees, too few opportunities for citizens to engage in their own government. Rhetorical gestures towards accountability and transparency in the Treaty merely underline their absence. As a House of Lords Select Committee commented, 'Leaving it in the hands of the Council alone to decide what principles and limits should apply is akin to leaving children unsupervised in a sweet shop and expecting them to exercise restraint' (Curtin, 1999, p 76, 87–89).

The dismissal of the corrupt and discredited Santer Commission in 1999 found the Union plummeting to new depths of popular disregard. A pervasive apathy, a mutual distrust of leaders and citizens, the fear of enlargement, everything seems to coalesce around the question of governance; the same problems, the same inability to resolve them. In an address to the European Parliament in early 2000, the new President of the Commission, Romano Prodi, announced a far-reaching review of governance. Two years on, this review produced a Commission White Paper on Governance. Sadly, but perhaps predictably, the Paper is rather stronger on rhetoric than substance. Five principles of good governance are identified; openness, participation, accountability, effectiveness and coherence. But the Paper makes no effort to present practical proposals to actually enhance any of these principles, save to recommend a strengthening of the 'Community method', and more particularly the Commission's role in driving forward further incremental integration. Clearly the White Paper was drafted as a Commission response to flexibility, and more particularly to the Council, and the member states that it sees as having promoted it. But what is perhaps most disappointing is the implication that the future lies with more governance, rather than greater democracy (Joerges, 2002; Wincott, 2001, pp 901–906, 909–910).

It might be that the current 'Convention' investigating the possibility of a new European 'Constitution' may address this disappointment. According to the likes of Juergen Schwarze such a radical overhaul of the constitutional structure of the Union is the 'only realistic choice for the future development' of the new Europe (Schwarze, 2002, p 252). It certainly chimes with the sentiment of the Declaration on the Future, which stated the need for a fresh look at the Treaties, as well as the 'status' of the Charter. But whether the Union, or more importantly the member states, actually have the courage to enact any radical recommendations must remain doubtful. The reform of the constitution, like the reform of governance, will require a reinvigoration of a now rather arcane ideology, that of European integration. It is not an ideology that has an obvious future in the age of flexibility.

Yet the rhetoric can still be heard. In the same address to the Parliament, in early 2000, Prodi, prophesied a 'decade of Europe'. It would be a decade of 'outstanding achievement and success'. 'If we act boldly and decisively together', he declared, 'we can shape the new Europe our citizens want and that we owe to future generations.' This will be a 'just, humane, inclusive Europe', an 'exciting, energetic, enterprising Europe'. It will, indeed, be 'everyone's Europe' (Ward, 2003, p 97). It is an inspiring thought. But it is the kind of statement that the 'new' Europe has heard many times before. If the Union cannot summon up the collective will really to tackle the 'democratic deficit' and reform its structures of governance, if it cannot summon up the courage to enact a meaningful, binding charter of rights, then it is unlikely to be any more just and humane, or indeed exciting and energetic, than it is at present. Very soon we will be half way through the 'decade of Europe'. It is clear that there is much still to be done.

Chapter 3

The foundations of Community law

It is often suggested that the law of the European Union can be found in its Treaties. This is only partly true. The Treaty articles certainly provide the 'primary' law of the Community and Union. But there is rather more to European law than this. There are various forms of 'secondary' law, law that is derived, or at least is supposed to be derived, from the 'primary' law. This comes, most obviously, in the form of regulations and directives. But again, there is rather more, for there is also the law that the European Court of Justice has made up. It is, of course, true that all law is to some degree made up by courts and their judges. Legal realists, for example, argue that the law is simply what a court says it is, no more and no less. Even so, the degree of overt political activism exercised by the Court of Justice is striking. It can be, and frequently is, argued that the Court has emerged as the most dynamic and purposeful of all Community and Union institutions in the furtherance of the idea of European integration. It has recently been suggested that the Court has taken on a role that 'closely resembles the equivalent institution of a fully-fledged federation' (Hartley, 1999, p 12). The purpose of this chapter is to investigate the veracity of this claim. In order to do so, we will take a look at the jurisdiction of the Court, at its powers of judicial review, at the founding doctrines of European public law, supremacy and direct effect, and at the Court's role in forging coherent bodies of administrative and human rights law.

A supreme court

As we have already noted, it was always intended that a supranational Community should have a supreme court. And so, accordingly, article 220 (ex 164) of the Rome Treaty established a Court of Justice. It stated, quite simply, that: 'The Court of Justice shall ensure that in the interpretation and application of this Treaty the law is observed.' Ensuing articles stipulated the constitution of the Court, listing the number of judges, presently fifteen, and the number of Advocates General, currently nine.[1] Rather whimsically article 223 (ex 167) then added that the judges and Advocates General 'shall be chosen from persons whose independence is beyond doubt'. It is not clear what they should be independent from, but the very merest experience of law reveals that no judge is ever truly independent of personal and social bias. It is ridiculous to suppose that they might be. It should also be noted that, from 1992, article 225 (ex 168a) institutes a Court of First Instance, with a more limited jurisdiction, to provide some kind of effective relief for the Court of Justice. For what very rapidly became apparent was the fact that the Court of Justice was going to be far more active than was originally conceived. Europeans, or more pertinently European member states, have proved to be peculiarly litigious.

Thereafter follow an array of articles prescribing the 'jurisdiction' of the Court of Justice. But that is it. There is no mention of any general principles of law, no doctrines, no suggestion of the kind of legal system, or principles, that the Court may wish to adopt, or indeed any direction as to its methodology, whether it should exercise a comparative approach, developing Community law from member state traditions, or even member state case law, or whether it should strike out for an altogether more original jurisprudence. That was left to the Court itself to determine.

Having established a Court of Justice, the next matter was to make it supreme. The pressing need to do so was not lost on the Court itself. As early as 1962, in the leading case of *Van Gend en Loos*, the Court declared that, rather than being subject to the ordinary norms of international law, the Community was instead constitutive of a 'new legal order'. Just two years later, in *Costa v ENEL*, the Court reaffirmed that:

---

[1]   By convention there is one judge from each member state. The role of the Advocate General is to provide an expert opinion to the Court.

By contrast with ordinary international treaties, the EEC Treaty has created its own legal system which on entry into force of the Treaty became an integral part of the legal systems of the Member States and which their courts are bound to apply. By creating a Community of unlimited duration, having . . . powers stemming from a limitation of sovereignty, or a transfer of powers from the States to the Community, the Member States have limited their sovereign rights, albeit within limited fields, and have thus created a body of law which binds both their nationals and themselves. (*Costa*, 1964, 593.)

The arrogation of judicial sovereignty was uncompromising, and has been reinforced on countless occasions, perhaps most famously and forcefully in *Internationale Handelsgesellschaft* in 1970 and in *Simmenthal* in 1978. In the former case, the Court emphasised that the very idea of Community law depended upon the entrenchment of a principle of supremacy:

In fact, the law stemming from the Treaty, an independent source of law, cannot because of its very nature be overridden by rules of national law, however framed, without being deprived of its character as Community law and without the legal basis of the Community itself being called into question. Therefore the validity of a Community measure or its effect within a Member State cannot be affected by allegations that it runs counter to either fundamental rights as formulated by the constitution of the State or the principles of a national constitutional structure. (*Internationale Handelsgesellschaft*, 1970, 1134.)

This latter idea, that there might be a conflict between Community law and certain fundamental public laws of member states was revisited again in *Simmenthal*, where the Court made a particular effort to reaffirm that national courts must always give precedence to Community law over any conflicting domestic law. It held:

Furthermore, in accordance with the principle of the precedence of Community law, the relationship between the provisions of the Treaty and directly applicable measures of the institutions on the one hand and the national law of the Member States on the other is such that those provisions and measures not only by their entry into force render automatically inapplicable any conflicting provision of current national law but – insofar as they are an integral part of, and take precedence in, the legal order applicable in the territory of each of the Member States – also preclude the valid adoption of new national legislative measures to the extent to which they would be incompatible with Community provisions . . . It follows from the foregoing that every national court must, in a case within its jurisdiction, apply Community law in its entirety and protect rights which the latter confers on individuals and must accordingly set aside any provision of national law which may conflict with it, whether prior or subsequent to the Community rule. (*Simmenthal*, 1978, 643–644.)

This jurisprudence, originating in *Van Gend* and *Costa*, and then reasserted in *Internationale Handelsgeselschaft* and *Simmenthal*, entrenches the principle of supremacy in Community law.

What it means, in effect, is that the validity of Community law cannot be questioned by national courts. Community law is the highest source of law. It, or, more accurately, the Treaty from which it is notionally derived, provides what jurists sometimes term a *Grundnorm*. All subsequent Community law, together with all implementing legislation drafted in the member states, flows from this one critical principle (Eleftheriadis, 1996, pp 34–35). With regard to this latter matter, the drafting of implementing legislation, as the Court made clear in the above statement in *Simmenthal*, the principle also means that member states are pre-empted from legislating in such a way that might contradict existing Community legislation. This doctrine of 'pre-emption' is collateral to that of supremacy. Anything else, the Court confirmed, would 'imperil the very foundations of the Community' (*Simmenthal*, 1978, 629; Caranta, 1993, p 280).

The doctrine of supremacy is, then, of enormous importance, and it is easy to see why commentators such as Pavlos Eleftheriadis have declared it to be 'the most important constitutional issue of the Community legal order' (Eleftheriadis, 1998, p 257). The question as to whether the Court had any authority to create it is, of course, a different matter. As we shall see in the final part of this chapter, it is also a controversial one.

Vertical direct effect: the first step

The establishment of a doctrine of supremacy was in fact the first of two stages by which the effective supremacy of Community law was ensured. The second stage was the development of a doctrine of direct effect. In order to understand this doctrine it is first necessary to revisit the principle forms of secondary legislation prescribed in article 249 (ex 189) of the Rome Treaty. Aside from decisions, which are relatively rare, and which apply only to specific situations, there are two primary forms of legislation: regulations and directives. Regulations are 'directly applicable', binding member states as to both the manner and the form of their implementation in national law. Directives are 'directly effective', prescribing policy ends, but not prescribing the particular manner of their enforcement in national law. The intention that lies behind directives is to provide the nation states with a certain latitude when it comes to the implementation of Community law. A collateral effect is that member states can also be held responsible for the success, or failure, of their implementing legislation (Curtin, 1992a, pp 33–49).

The doctrine of direct effect has evolved in this particular area in the implementation of directives. The reason for this is simple. For it is here that member states might, in the drafting of implementing legislation, be tempted to mitigate, or even nullify, the impact of Community law. From its earliest days, the Court of Justice assumed the responsibility for countering any such temptation. As a number of commentators have noted, the development of the Court's jurisprudence in the field of direct, and also indirect, effect, is probably the most 'remarkable' example of its judicial activism. The development of the doctrine of direct effect has revealed a tripartite judicial function, with the Court appearing to be the legislator, the enforcer and the monitor of Community law; a legislative, a judiciary and an executive all in one (Caranta, 1993, p 279; Martin, 1994, pp 26–27; Craig, 1992).

The seminal case for the establishment of direct effect is, once again, *Van Gend en Loos*. Although the case involved the effecting of Treaty articles, rather than directives, it was most significant that the Court chose to emphasise that direct effect extended rights of action, not only for member states and Community institutions, but also for individuals against member states. Anyone, it was suggested, could take a member state to court for its failure to render Community law 'fully effective'. What the Court in *Van Gend* established was a second of the fundamental principles of western jurisprudence. Alongside the doctrine of supremacy, there must be a complementary doctrine of the rule of law. It is this latter doctrine that direct effect is supposed to ensure.

The Court in *Van Gend* supported the Advocate General in suggesting that the two principles were inextricable:

> The conclusion to be drawn from this is that the Community constitutes a new legal order of international law for the benefit of which Member States have limited their sovereign rights, albeit within limited fields, and the subjects of which comprise not only Member States but also their nationals. Independently of the legislation of Member States, Community law therefore not only imposes obligations on individuals but is also intended to confer upon them rights which become part of their legal heritage. These rights arise not only where they are expressly granted by the Treaty, but also by reason of the obligation which the Treaty imposes in a clearly defined way upon individuals as well as upon the Member States and the institutions of the Community. (*Van Gend*, 1963, 12.)

The ruling was seminal indeed. It has been suggested that *Van Gend* 'represented the first step in the judicial contribution towards the building of a more federal Europe' (Craig, 1992, p 458). Judge Mancini even went so far as to suggest that legal historians will look back at the decision as 'the unique contribution' made by the Court to the 'making of Europe' (Mancini, 1999, p 40). It was certainly an uncompromising ruling. And yet the member states of the Community have showed considerable ingenuity in trying to make it rather less so, an ingenuity that has led to a long-running battle with the Court, and to the development of a considerable and complex case law.

A major step was affirmed in *Van Duyn* where the Court extended the principle introduced in *Van Gend* to directives (*Van Duyn*, 1974). The decision represented a clear extension of the Court's determination to assume an executive function as the monitor of Community law (Lewis and Moore, 1993, p 153). Critical reactions to this step have varied, some hailing it as a necessary advance, others going so far as to denounce it as 'breathtaking radicalism' amounting to 'judicial legislation', 'contrary to the Treaty', and even a prime example of 'revolting judicial behaviour' (Mancini, 1989; Hartley, 1999, p 29; Rasmussen, 1986, p 12; Wincott, 1995, p 591). The Court turned the screw a little further in *Ratti* in 1979, extending rights of action against member states which failed to implement Community law within prescribed time limits (*Ratti*, 1979). This principle, of providing individuals with rights of action against member states that fail to implement Community law 'effectively' and within a certain time, has become known as 'vertical' direct effect.

It might have been thought that there should be a complementary principle of 'horizontal' direct effect, meaning the provision of rights of action for individuals or private parties against other individuals or parties whose actions infringe their rights under Community law. The Court of Justice has, however, consistently rejected the idea, doing so most famously in 1986 in the *Marshall* case (*Marshall*, 1986). There are various reasons for this stance, some explicit, some implicit. The explicit reason was simple. Article 249 (ex 189) clearly stated that directives are only 'binding' upon member states. Amongst the implicit reasons, it has been suggested that such is the complexity of Community law, that it might be unreasonable to expect individuals to abide by it. This argument is compromised by the fact that precious little domestic law is any more readily comprehensible. It has also been suggested that the approach emphasises the Court's determination that national courts should be seen to be holding their governments to account (Curtin, 1990a). It is certainly the case that the Court appears to be determined that member states should remain fully responsible for any loss suffered by an individual, if that loss has been caused by a failure of implementing legislation. In simple terms, a principle of 'horizontal' effect would allow member states to shirk these responsibilities, and the Court is simply not prepared to countenance this possibility.

Horizontal direct effect: a second step?

At least, it has not done so overtly. The Court's stance regarding the notion of 'horizontal' effect has attracted criticism, much of it suggesting that it restricts unduly the ethos as well as the practice of direct effect, and in doing so prejudices the uniform and coherent applications of Community law. Individuals should be as responsible in Community law for their actions, as they are in domestic law (Martin, 1994, p 28). This position was even argued before the Court by the Advocate General in *Vaneetveld* in 1994 (*Vaneetveld*, 1994).

Whilst the Court has remained unmoved by such arguments, it is clear that there has been a 'retreat' from the rigours of the *Marshall* principle. An immediate gesture in this direction can be seen in the ever-widening definition of which institutions might be said to be an 'emanation' of the state, and thus constitute a 'public body'. In *Foster* this definition was extended to include a utility corporation, with the Court asserting that such a body could be defined as one that was 'subject to the authority or control of the state or has special powers beyond those which result from normal relations between individuals' (*Foster*, 1990, 3339). The nature of supposed public bodies has continued to develop through the case law of domestic judiciaries. Thus in the United Kingdom, the High Court in *Griffin* decided that a 'public body' could include a privatised utility. In *St Mary's School* the Court of Appeal extended the definition to include the board of governors of a state school (*Foster*, 1990; *St Mary's School*, 1997). Judicial activism is not the sole preserve of the Court of Justice. Indeed, part of its strategy is to make sure that everyone is implicated.

Perhaps the most striking example of the Court's supposed 'retreat' has been the development of a doctrine of 'indirect' effect, the purpose of which is to hold member states responsible if private individuals act in such a way that in their relation with other individuals they breach Community law. In such a circumstance the Court will again hold the member state liable for implementing legislation that must, by definition, have been at fault. Thus in *Von Colson*, the Court held that a member state must interpret domestic legislation to be consistent with the demands of a directive, and if it fails to do so it will be liable for any resulting infraction by an individual. Citing article 10 (ex 5) EC, the Court made much of the need for 'effective' implementation, even in the context of legislative action by the member state that was otherwise perfectly lawful (*Von Colson*, 1984). Such obligations are incumbent on the member state, demanded indeed by the very spirit of article 10, by the very need to 'facilitate the achievement of the Community's tasks'.

In *Marleasing* the Court went a step further, holding, not only that implementing legislation must be consistent, but also that any prior existing legislation must likewise be interpreted so that it is consistent with subsequent Community law. The Court made it clear once again that the doctrine of direct effect exists to reinforce that of supremacy. The difficulty with *Marleasing*, however, is that the Court's rationale, that interpretation is merely fulfilling legislative intent, is rather less convincing when applied to the interpretation of legislation which was never intended to effect or indeed affect Community law, or its spirit. Moreover, as it clearly requires that legislation should be retrospectively reinterpreted, it also compromises the principle of legitimate expectations, one of the most hallowed principles of modern public law (de Burca, 1992, pp 224, 227–229; Curtin, 1990b, pp 723–726). Such uncertainty is often the hallmark of a creative, perhaps overcreative, judiciary.

Some of the most controversial recent developments in direct, and indirect, effect jurisprudence have been in the area of remedies for state liability. In the *Factortame* litigation, to which we shall return in greater depth in the next chapter, the Court of Justice insisted that remedies must be fully effective, even if this meant that national courts must deploy remedies that had not been hitherto available in domestic public law (*Factortame*, 1990). This approach was developed still further in *Francovich*, where the Court again cited article 10 as a general authority in supporting the Advocate General's advice that member states should be held liable in damages for any 'failure' to implement directives effectively. Such a remedy, it was agreed, was 'particularly essential' if Community law was to be fully effective (*Francovich*, 1991; Hartley, 1999, pp 59–61). It is notable that, as is so often the case, the politicians have followed the judges' lead. Article 228 (ex 171) now includes a provision whereby the Court is authorised to 'impose a lump sum or penalty payment' on member states that fail to implement legislation effectively 'within the time-limit' specified.

Similarly controversial has been a further development in the direct effect jurisprudence, to include principles of 'triangular' and 'incidental' horizontal effect. Both principles have admitted the possibility of private parties using directives in such a way that they directly or indirectly effect the legal rights of other private parties. In doing so, they clearly breach the otherwise rigorous refusal of the Court to extend a formal principle of horizontal direct effect. The first of these principles, 'triangular' effect, relates to situations where private parties invoke directives that impose specific obligations on member states, but which will also have a necessary effect on the legal position of third parties (Timmermans, 1997, pp 17–19). The most common examples here relate to environmental provisions. The right of a private party to invoke such provisions in order to force public bodies to act, often to the detriment of third parties, was accepted by the Court in the *Grosskrotzenburg* case in 1995 (*Grosskrotzenburg*, 1995; Lackhoff and Nyssens, 1998, pp 397–398, 401–404).

The second, and rather broader, of these principles, 'incidental' horizontal effect, is again derived from case law, and suggests that private parties can rely upon Community directives in order to defend themselves against actions brought by other parties. The Court of Justice first accepted this kind of 'incidental' effect in three 1996 cases, first in *CIA Security International*, and then subsequently in *Ruiz Bernaldez* and *Parfitis* (*CIA*, 1996; *Ruiz Bernaldez*, 1996; *Pafitis*, 1996). It has been said that the Court has permitted 'incidental' horizontal effect to be used in these cases as a 'shield', but not as a 'sword' (Lenz et al, 2000, pp 516–517). The situation has, however, been confused in subsequent cases. The refusal to allow a 'shield' defence in *Lemmens* suggests that the Court prefers a case-by-case approach to the establishment of any firm principle (*Lemmens*, 1998). The situation regarding 'incidental' horizontal effect has become murkier still following the recent *Unilever Italia* case in which the Court was happy to allow a private party to use a directive as a 'sword', in other words, as a cause of action against another party (*Unilever Italia*, 2000).

The development of 'incidental' horizontal effect, or more precisely the confusion which surrounds its development, has been much criticised. According to Michael Dougan, the 'incidental' effect case law 'merely joins the unfortunate parade of bizarre nuances which already characterises' the wider doctrine of direct effect (Dougan, 2000, p 610). Far simpler, many commentators have suggested, would be to permit a simple and straightforward principle of horizontal direct effect. It is, indeed, the 'logic of a Europe of Citizens rather than a Europe of States' (Szyszczak, 1996, pp 352–353; Douglas-Scott, 2002, p 309). This was also the strong recommendation of Advocate General Lenz in *Dori*. The Court, however, has remained adamant, affirming in *Dori* that its primary concern is to 'prevent' any member state 'from taking advantage of its own failure to fully comply with Community law' (*Dori*, 1994).

Yet it cannot be denied that the various related doctrines of 'indirect' and 'incidental' effect do mitigate the rigour of the *Marshall* decision. At the same time, moreover, these collateral doctrines provide still further examples of the Court's determination to assume the responsibility for creating general principles of Community public law, even if the process can seem, at times, to be wholly inconsistent and unpredictable. All in all, the direct effect jurisprudence is vast. According to some commentators it is too vast, its sheer complexity underlining the fact that legal integration has reached such a stage that there is no longer any need for a doctrine of direct effect. According to Sacha Prechal, Community law is now so well established in the member states that there is no need for national courts to worry about whether European legislation is directly effective or not (Prechal, 2000, pp 1067–1069). Such a situation can be taken two ways. The size and complexity of direct effect jurisprudence could be seen as a tribute to the juridical ingenuity of the Court of Justice. It could also be seen as a vivid illustration of what can happen when legal regimes are carved out by an over-active judiciary. Perhaps both views are correct. We shall return to this debate in the final part of this chapter.

Making references

The principles of supremacy and direct effect are the foundations of Community public law. Whilst there has, as we shall shortly see, been some criticism of the Court's jurisprudence in the creation of these principles, it can be argued that they enjoy an implicit legitimacy through article 220. At the same time, it must be appreciated that neither principle would enjoy any practical credibility if it was not for another critical Treaty article. According to some commentators, the 'keystone' of Community public law is found in article 234 (ex 177) (Mancini and Keeling, 1991, pp 2–3). For without this article there could be no meaningful principle of supremacy. Indeed, there would be very little Community law at all.

In simple terms, article 234 lays down conditions under which matters of Community law should be 'referred' to the Court of Justice by national courts. It vests 'jurisdiction' in the Court so that it can 'give preliminary rulings' in a series of matters, including the 'interpretation' of the Treaty, and the 'validity and interpretation of acts of the institutions'. It goes on to state that:

> Where such a question is raised before any court or tribunal of a Member State, that court or tribunal may, if it considers that a decision on the question is necessary to enable it to give judgment, request the Court of Justice to give a ruling thereon.

The critical word here is 'may'. It bears a sharp contrast with the use of the word 'shall' in the following paragraph of the article. It affirms that:

> Where any such question is raised in a case pending before a court or tribunal or a Member State against whose decisions there is no judicial remedy under national law, that court or tribunal shall bring the matter before the Court of Justice.

The word 'shall' makes things easy. The word 'may' has the capacity to make things very much more difficult. For, very obviously, in the instance where there is no capacity for 'judicial remedy' in national law a reference must be made. But in the rather more common instance where there is such a remedy, references may or may not be made, and the decision whether to do so, most importantly, rests with the relevant national court.

The philosophy behind article 234 is that the national courts of the member states might be best able to make Community law effective. It also adds a veneer of enhanced legitimacy to Community law, making it appear that such law, being administered by national courts, must somehow be part of national law. It adds to the feint that the member states might have retained some measure of legal sovereignty, whilst also foisting on national courts the responsibility for actually implementing laws that might be controversial or unpopular.

At the same time, whilst the spin should not be underestimated, the Court has made it clear that the use of article 234 is not a matter of jurisprudential whimsy. The reference procedure may place the Court one step away from the immediate action, but its clear intent is to play an instrumental role in the fashioning of Community law (Arnull, 1985, pp 169–170). The proper observation of article 234 is, therefore, vital. In the early case of *Foglia*, the Court made it clear that the reference procedure is the artery which keeps the heart of the

Community pumping (*Foglia*, 1981, 3045). It is, perhaps, for this reason that the Court has, on occasion, been happy to widen its own jurisdiction. In *Dzodzi*, for example, the Court even declared itself willing to receive references in matters of purely domestic law, if that law is based on Community law (*Dzodzi*, 1990). This latter development has proved to be controversial, not least because in more recent cases, such as *Meilicke* and *Banchero 1* and *2*, the Court has tended to be more robust in declining to hear cases in which references on 'irrelevant' matters have been made (*Meilicke*, 1992; *Banchero*, 1993, 1995; Barnard and Sharpston, 1997, pp 1127–1141).

Much, then, depends both on the Court of Justice knowing when to accept and when to decline references, and on national courts knowing how to refer and when to refer. On the latter score, it might more prosaically be said that everything depends on the goodwill and blind ignorance of the national judiciaries (Arnull, 1989, pp 639–640; Mancini and Keeling, 1991, pp 1–5). Of course, goodwill is the more desirable quality. In *Meilicke*, the Court waxed nostalgically about the development of a 'spirit of cooperation' (*Meilicke*, 1992, 25). Whilst the story that champagne corks popped when the first preliminary reference was made in Luxembourg may be apocryphal, there was a clear anxiety that national courts might have sought to circumvent the reference procedure by simply declining to use it (Douglas-Scott, 2002, pp 234–235). And there are occasional instances of this, perhaps most famously when the French *Conseil d'Etat* refused to make a necessary reference in the politically sensitive *Cohn-Bendit* case (Bebr, 1983).

It is, however, blind ignorance that has really made the system tick. The sheer weight of referrals to the overwhelmed Court has been a testament to the utter incomprehensibility of so much Community law. The number of references increased by 87 per cent during the 1990s (Douglas-Scott, 2002, pp 252–254). National courts have proved to be only too happy to refer, not merely in difficult hard-case scenarios, but also where the ruling of the Court of Justice was always predictable.[2] In a bid to reduce the number of referrals, the Court has occasionally sought to provide guidelines. It made a concerted effort to do so in 1982 in the *CILFIT* case. Here it impressed that a national

---

[2]　According to one Court of Justice judge, Federico Mancini, in many instances the reference procedure is an exercise in 'child's play' (Mancini, 1991, p 185).

court was under no obligation to make references if it felt that it was any way capable of interpreting Community law either because it was straightforward or, reinforcing the earlier decision in *Da Costa*, because the Court of Justice had already given a ruling on the same kind of matter in a previous case (*CILFIT*, 1982; *Da Costa*, 1963). What a national court could not do, however, as the Court of Justice confirmed in *Foto-Frost*, is rule that an aspect of Community law was invalid. If it thought that it might be, it must first seek a reference under article 234 (Foto-Frost, 1987).[3]

Whilst intended to reduce the number of references, the *CILFIT* ruling did represent, in a paradoxical way, a more intrusive approach. Previously, as it had emphasised in the early *Rheinmuhlen* case, national courts had enjoyed the 'widest discretion in referring matters to the Court of Justice' (*Rheinmuhlen*, 1974, 3). After *CILFIT* there were guidelines which, if not exactly clear, were at least clearer. A more supple statement as to what these guidelines actually meant was given by Lord Bingham in *ex parte Else*, a decade after *CILFIT*. According to Bingham 'the appropriate course is ordinarily to refer the issue to the Court of Justice unless the national court can with complete confidence resolve the issue itself' (*Else* 1993, 534). Bingham's comments reinforce the feeling that the Court of Justice has actually enhanced its overarching control of Community law whilst at the same time trying to reduce its own hands-on involvement.

It is generally recognised that *CILFIT* established a principle of *acte claire* and, along with *Da Costa*, perhaps even one of precedent. Taken together with *Foto-Frost* it also reinforces the authority, or supremacy, of Community law. This latter point frames one of the hoariest of debates surrounding article 234. On the one hand, the article might be read as arrogating interpretive authority to the Court of Justice. On the other hand, particularly in the light of *CILFIT*, it might equally appear that the article actually delegates interpretive power back to national courts. This latter view might be reinforced by the Court's own attitude in *Meilicke* and *Banchero*, though, once again, it is an attitude that is immediately contradicted by the line of cases following *Dzodzi*. There is little consistency here, and the situation has been rightly described as 'puzzling' (Douglas-Scott, 2002, p 240).

[3] As Gerhard Bebr has noted, in this case the Court deliberately went further than the remit of the matter referred to it, in order to impress the hierarchical reality of article 234 (Bebr, 1988).

According to some commentators, such complexities are born of the inherently contradictory nature of article 234, an article that was, at once, intended both to empower and to constrain national courts (Rasmussen, 1984, p 256).

Fundamental principles: a common administrative law

The development of the twin doctrines of supremacy and direct effect, together with the evolution of the article 234 jurisprudence, can be seen as the first phase in the Court's strategy of legal integration. Whilst this phase is still ongoing, during the last three decades, the Court has embarked upon a second phase, focusing upon the development of common rights and principles of administrative law, as well as the foundations of a human rights jurisprudence. We will examine the latter jurisprudence in the next part of this chapter. Taken in the whole, the presence of certain fundamental principles of constitutional law, such as supremacy and direct effect, together with common principles of administrative law, and recognised principles of human rights law, represent a discrete Community public law. Or at least that is the idea.

In his seminal study of Community administrative law, Juergen Schwarze noted that throughout the 1970s and 1980s, the Court of Justice had engaged in a 'prolific interaction' with national courts in order to 'harmonise' common rights and principles. The strategy was twofold, with the Court either emphasising certain common rights in the administrative law of the member states, or selecting certain particularly desirable rights and then enforcing their uniform acceptance across the Community (Schwarze, 1991, pp 17–19). Back in 1992, the conclusion of Schwarze's *European Administrative Law* emphasised the role of the Court, not just in the past, but in the future too:

> As regards the future perspectives for the completion of EC administrative law, at present and for the foreseeable future, all hopes, with the exception of partial and sectoral legislative codifications, rest upon a gradual, cautious and pragmatic further development of case law in the Community. (Schwarze, 1992, p 1440.)

With regard to the past, Schwarze noted a series of important cases, many of which straddled the borderline between fundamental principles of human rights and administrative law. These cases included

Transocean Marine Paint Association, which enforced the right to be heard in all administrative actions involving Community law, *National Panasonic, AM & S* and *Heylens* (*Transocean Marine Paint Association*, 1974; *National Panasonic*, 1980; *AM & S*, 1982; *Heylens*, 1987).[4] The decision of the Court in *AM & S*, to seek guidance on the appropriate operative principles of administrative law in the member states, was a striking example of what Koopmans has termed the 'comparative dialectic' approach to developing common principles of administrative law (Koopmans, 1991).

In the *Heylens* case, which upheld the argument that administrative bodies are under a duty to provide the reasons for their decisions, the Court made one of its most strident assertions with regard to the fundamental nature of administrative law rights. It held that:

> Effective judicial review, which must be able to cover the legality of the reasons for the contested decision, presupposes in general that the court to which the matter is referred may require the competent authority to notify its reason. But where, as in this case, it is more particularly a question of securing the effective protection of a fundamental right conferred by the Treaty on Community workers, the latter must also be able to defend that right under the best possible conditions and have the possibility of deciding, with a full knowledge of the relevant facts, whether there is any point in their applying to courts. (*Heylens*, 1987, 4097.)

There is an implied duality here; a fundamental right is one thing, but a fundamental right enshrined in the Treaty is quite another. Such a right is a particularly fundamental right, and worthy of suitably particular and fundamental support. Some rights, it seems, are more fundamental than others.

Schwarze made particular use of *Heylens* as illustrative of his wider thesis regarding the 'convergence' or harmonisation of Community administrative law:

> This decision demonstrates first of all the potential overlapping of the general principles of constitutional and administrative law. In order to guarantee a fair administrative procedure and

---

4   Basing her conclusions on the *Transocean Marine Paint Association* case, Deirdre Curtin also suggested that Court's primary focus lay in the prospective harmonisation of administrative law (Curtin, 1992b).

adequate judicial review, the Court refers to the constitutional traditions common to Member States and also to the relevant articles of the European Convention for the Protection of Human Rights and Fundamental Freedoms. The judgment also shows that the Court aims at the optimum of procedural guarantees for citizens in the Community, orienting its standards for the protection of individual rights and judicial review in the Community on the most developed national administrative systems. (Schwarze, 1991, p 14.)

Nothing has happened during the last decade to rebut Schwarze's overarching thesis. The harmonisation of common principles of administrative law has gone on apace.

At the same time, it is equally clear that the nature of this 'convergence' has been further refined. First, it has become ever more obvious that the impact of Community principles of administrative law have had a considerable impact on the domestic administrative law of the member states (Millett, 2002, pp 321–322; Jacobs, 1999).[5] Second, it is also clear that the focus has moved from the establishment of certain administrative law rights to the reinforcement of general principles of administrative law (Schwarze, 2000, pp 163–165, 180–181). The two most important of these principles are proportionality and legitimate expectations.

In one of the leading early cases, *Internationale Handelsgesellschaft*, the Court had suggested that proportionality, as deployed in the administrative law of a number of member states, most notably Germany, should be a 'fundamental' principle of Community administrative law. In its interpretation of the principle, the Court affirmed that 'the individual should not have his freedom of action limited beyond the degree necessary for the public interest' (*Internationale Handelsgesellschaft*, 1970, 1127). In practice, the principle is intended to act as a bulwark against public law bodies, requiring them to justify actions which might unnecessarily infringe the rights of ordinary citizens. In the *Germany* case in 1997, the Court of Justice defined the principle in the following terms:

> In order to establish whether a provision of Community law complies with the principle of proportionality, it must be ascertained whether the means which it employs are suitable for the

---

[5]   We will examine this further in the next chapter.

purpose of achieving the desired objective and whether they do not go beyond what is necessary to achieve it. (*Germany*, 1997.)

Despite difficulties experienced in jurisdictions in which proportionality was not already a recognised principle of administrative law, such as the United Kingdom, by the end of the 1990s, the principle has indeed come to be widely recognised as fundamental in Community law.

The same is true of legitimate expectations, a principle which operates to protect individuals who have acted in reliance of measures taken by the Community and, of course, effected by the member states. In essence, legitimate expectations is a principle that exists to enforce a necessary degree of legal certainty. It is common to the legal systems of all the member states of the Community though, as we shall see in the next chapter, it has only secured a place in UK public law during the last couple of decades, and very much as a result of the influence of Community law. The Court of Justice has repeatedly deployed legitimate expectations as a fundamental principle of Community administrative law, providing a succinct interpretation in the *Efisol* case, where it held that the principle should extend to 'any individual who is in a situation in which it is apparent that the Community administration, by giving him precise assurances, has led him to entertain justifiable expectations' (*Efisol*, 1996).

The development of certain common rights and principles in Community law is, yet again, a striking instance of the Court of Justice's creative impulses. Supporters of the process, such as Schwarze, deem it simply necessary, and argue strongly for the movement now to 'horizontal codification'. Such codification could only enhance legal certainty and transparency in administrative law procedures, and it should, he argues, now be possible for the member states to 'reach an agreement about the basic rules' necessary for the administration of Community law (Schwarze, 2000, pp 176–178, 181).

Without making the express case for codification, Adam Tomkins has similarly argued that the Court should continue to focus its attention on the entrenchment of 'transparency' as a fundamental principle of administrative law (Tomkins, 1999). This certainly chimes with the rhetoric of the Amsterdam and Nice Treaties, wherein the general idea of transparency in all aspects of Community governance was much trumpeted. A number of the decisions with which the Court

,trative law 'rights', most obviously *Heylens*,
.ms of transparency, and in more recent cases,
national and *Hautala*, which involved more pre-
.1e release of documentation and information, the
.1rmed the fundamental nature of the principle
national, 1999; *Hautala*, 1999).

Fur. .nental principles: human rights

Along with the development of certain common rights and principles
of administrative law, the Court of Justice has also endeavoured to add
a distinctive human rights dimension to Community law, or at least it
has from time to time. As we noted in the last section, in cases such as
Heylens and *Internationale Handelsgesellschaft*, the Court clearly understood administrative law rights to be 'fundamental' rights. And during
the past three decades the Court has, on occasion, sought to venture
further still. The clear limitation, however, has been the demarcation
of Community competence. Whilst it might be desirable for
Community public law to inhere a human rights dimension, the
innate dualism of the Community legal order has militated against
such rights ever being truly universal. Member states have remained
protective of their 'margin of appreciation' in human rights issues,
and domestic courts have, as a result, occasionally come into conflict
with the Court of Justice over the issue.[6]

A second related problem is that of definition. All kinds of things can
be described as being 'fundamental' rights, just as all kinds of things
can be presented as 'human' rights. The definitional problem afflicts
any human rights jurisprudence. Community law is no exception. If
anything, indeed, the situation is worse in Community law than in
most jurisdictions, for the simple reason that its primary focus is upon
regulating a market, rather than a discrete political community.
Accordingly, many of the mooted 'fundamental' rights in the
Community have been cast in terms of social and economic 'rights',
including presumed rights to strike, to move across national borders,
even to fish (Churchill and Foster, 1987). The idea of administrative
rights being 'fundamental' rights is, of course, another example of this
tendency (Schwarze, 1986).

---

[6]   We shall examine this particular problem in the next chapter.

In this situation, there is always a danger of losing sight of what a 'human' right is really supposed to be. It might reasonably be suggested that most people would recognise the need for some sort of conceptual distinction between the right to fish and the right not to be subjected to torture. Although, it should be noted, the new Union Charter does not, having lumped together all manner of supposed rights, from the most revered fundamental rights, to human dignity, to life and to liberty, to the altogether more prosaic rights to access ombudsmen, to 'conduct' a business and to a 'high level' of consumer protection.

In a famous essay, Koen Lenaerts endeavoured to make a series of definitional distinctions, presenting a 'concentric circles' model for a 'catalogue' of fundamental rights. At the heart of the model could be found those rights protected in the European Convention. Each successive circle of rights then catalogued, in turn, the general principles of Community law, citizenship rights, and then finally 'aspirational' rights, into which were bundled a motley set of economic and social rights (Lenaerts, 1991, pp 376–389). The distinction between 'fundamental' and 'aspirational' rights has proved to be popular. But categorising the catalogue can still be problematic. As we shall see in chapter 6, for example, there remains a fierce debate as to whether gender-related rights, such as rights to equal pay, are really fundamental human rights or merely aspirational social rights.

As ever, whilst it intimated that certain free movement rights might be especially important, the Rome Treaty provided no definitive statement on the subject of fundamental or human rights. Such rights were, as Weiler has suggested, never part of the original 'conception' of the Community, and for the first couple of decades the Court seemed unwilling to vary this sentiment (Weiler, 1986, 1110–1114). Advocates General occasionally mooted the possibility of a Community human rights jurisprudence (*Nold 1*, 1959; *Geitling*, 1960). But it was only with the landmark *Stauder* decision in 1969, that the Court acknowledged its responsibility to protect 'the fundamental human rights enshrined in the general principles of Community law' (*Stauder*, 1969).

In the following year, the Court reinforced this commitment in *Internationale Handelsgesellschaft*, accepting the Advocate General's argument that the human rights provisions of member state constitutions:

contribute to forming that philosophical, political and legal substratum common to the Member States from which emerges through the case law an unwritten Community law, one of the essential aims of which is precisely to ensure the respect for the fundamental rights of the individual. (*Internationale Handelsgesellschaft*, 1970.)

Critics suggested that this essentially comparative approach was minimalistic, somehow lacking in genuine commitment to the idea of human rights (Rasmussen, 1986, p 399). In cases such as *Nold 2* and *Hauer*, however, the Court retained this particular methodology, whilst also advancing the idea that the rights articulated in the European Convention might also be adopted as part of the 'general principles' of Community law. Such largesse was, however, immediately mitigated by the observation, in *Nold*, that a balance must always be made between 'the substance' of fundamental rights and 'certain limits justified by the overall objectives pursued by the Community' (*Nold 2*, 1974; *Hauer*, 1979; Dallen, 1990, p 781; Bibas, 1992, pp 264–267). Such objectives being, of course, the kind of essentially economic aspirations articulated in articles 2, 3 and 4 of the Community Treaty.

For much of the next two decades, the Court maintained this twofold strategy, adopting certain provisions from member state human rights charters, together with those found in the Convention.[7] Unfortunately, the status of the Convention in Community law was never entirely clear. The situation changed in 1992, with the inclusion of a rhetorical commitment to the principles articulated in the Convention in article 6 (ex F) of the Union Treaty. But, aside from it being purely rhetorical, the value of this statement was diluted by the uncertain constitutional relation between the Union and the Community. It was far from clear whether article 6 was binding on the Community. It was certainly not binding as such on the Union. Moreover, the ruling of the Court of Justice in its *Opinion 1/94*, which

---

[7]   This approach was specifically approved by Lenaerts, who suggested that there was a division of responsibilities between the two supranational legal orders, with the Community providing a human rights jurisprudence at Community level, and the Convention providing such a jurisprudence at nation state level (Lenaerts, 1991, pp 371–372). Of course, this only worked for those member states that fully recognised their responsibilities under the Convention, and so omitted the likes of the UK which singularly did not.

led to the omission of the explicit reference in the revised article 6 at the Amsterdam Treaty, added still further uncertainty.

The Court's approach met with a mixed reception for much of the 1980s. Some praised its activism, arguing that the Court was teasing out a collective political morality in the new Europe (Bibas, 1992, pp 294–295). Others were rather less convinced. Weiler expressed his doubts regarding a human rights jurisprudence that was the product of a 'judicial leap' of the imagination, and which had resulted in the regressive desire to 'exercise' a 'balancing test' between rights and so-called Community 'objectives'. Weiler rightly sensed that the problem was less that of 'excessive zeal' on the part of the Court, and more one of its 'reluctance' to 'exercise a sufficiently robust individual protection policy' (Weiler, 1986, pp 1109, 1118; Weiler, 1999a, pp 103–129). This fear was borne out in a series of cases during the late 1980s and early 1990s in which the Court appeared to be retreating ever further from a firm commitment to the idea of human rights across the Community. In *Klensch*, *Demirel* and *Bostock*, the Court expressly recognised the strict limitation of its competence in the area of supposed fundamental or human rights, to Community matters only (*Klensch*, 1986; *Demirel*, 1987; *Bostock*, 1994).[8] In *Wachauf*, moreover, it reinforced the reality that so-called Community rights were never 'absolute', but always balanced, even overreached, by the wider interests of the Community itself (*Wachauf*, 1989).

The overall sense of muddle and prevarication was reinforced by a series of controversial Irish cases involving one of the hoariest of law and morality issues, abortion. Article 40.3.3 of the Irish Constitution forbids abortion. In the first of these cases, *Open Door Counselling*, in 1988, the Irish Supreme Court duly prohibited the distribution of leaflets giving advice on abortion. The matter became one of immediate political controversy, and rumbled on into a second case, *Grogan*, in 1991. Here, however, the Irish Court referred the matter under article 234 (ex 177) to the Court of Justice, on the grounds that suppression of such material might be a breach of article 50 (ex 60) of the Community Treaty which provides for the free movement of services. The suspicion was justified. The Court of Justice refused to

---

8   In doing so, as Henry Schemers and others have noted, the Court further threatened the sanctity of its own core constitutional principle of supremacy (Schermers, 1990).

countenance the thought that any supposedly fundamental 'moral' right enshrined in a domestic constitution could detract from the overarching authority of a Community 'market' right. The decision attracted much criticism, appearing to be the starkest example of an economic 'objective' undermining a deeply held ethical right. In the words of one commentator, *Grogan* 'was the product of a contingent mode of legal thought which, if unchecked, will shape both the normative structure and the substance of fundamental rights in the European Union' (Phelan, 1992, p 689).

The treatment of human rights issues before the Court of Justice during the later part of the 1990s remained largely piecemeal. At times, the Court seemed willing to affirm certain alleged fundamental rights, particularly when they were reinforced by the European Convention. Two famous cases involving the Commission are illustrative, one seemingly progressive, the other oddly regressive. In the first, *X v Commission*, the Court held that, in requiring an employee to take an AIDS test, the Commission had breached a fundamental right to privacy (*X v Commission*, 1994). In the second case, *Connolly*, the Court of First Instance decided that a fundamental right to freedom of expression, as recognised by article 10 of the Convention, was limited by the duty that a Commission employee had towards the 'dignity' of his position (*Connolly*, 2001). So a Union employee can be sacked for exercising a right to free expression, but not if his right to privacy is breached. The discrepancy underlines the irreducible truth that afflicts any human rights jurisprudence; the fundamentality of any fundamental right is dependent upon the contingency of the particular case.

Even so, it is clear that the Court of Justice has, at times, acted in a peculiarly inconsistent and unconvincing manner. The examples provided by the Irish cases and the Commission cases are not exceptional. We shall encounter others in chapter 6 when we take a look at Community 'social' rights. Unsurprisingly perhaps, in the light of these difficulties, criticism of the Court's human rights jurisprudence has continued to grow. In a seminal article in 1992 Coppel and O'Neill argued that 'it must be questioned whether' the Court of Justice 'has ever been motivated by a concern for the supposed lack of adequate protection of fundamental rights within the European Community'. The Court, they continued, 'has employed fundamental rights instrumentally, so as to accelerate the process of legal integration in the Community'. Accordingly, it 'has not protected these fundamental rights for their own sake', and so it can only be concluded that it 'has not taken these rights seriously', but has rather used the 'rhetoric of human rights' as a 'vehicle' with which to 'extend the scope and impact of European law' (Coppel and O'Neill, 1992, pp 227–228, 245).

The opaque statements included in the Union Treaty only added to the sense of disquiet. Patrick Twomey suggested that the Treaty's 'failure to deal adequately with human rights issues' represented a 'lost opportunity and a fundamental defect' in the creation of a new Europe (Twomey, 1994, p 121). As we noted in the last chapter, following the impetus provided by the Cologne summit in 1999, the Union has responded with the presentation of 'declaratory' Charter of Fundamental Rights at the Nice Treaty. However, as we also noted, the extent to which this either clarifies the situation or indeed enhances human rights protection in the new Europe remains dubious. The collective rights articulated in the case law of the Community, in the articles of the Union Treaty, and now in the declaratory Charter, still add up to depressingly little.

An honest broker?

Thus far, the principles of European public law that we have investigated in this chapter – supremacy, direct effect, common administrative law and human rights – have been primarily developed as a means by which the Court of Justice can train member state judiciaries; not merely train in the sense of educate, but also train in the sense of constrain. They all seek to harmonise, to provide a foundation of common principles of European public law. There is, however, a further aspect of Community public law that must be examined. This is the Court's capacity to review the actions of the Community institutions, including actions brought by institutions against member states. Once again, whilst there is a broad statutory authority for this power of review, much has depended upon the evolving case law of the Court. Moreover, given the obvious political sensitivity that always attaches to judicial review, whether domestic or supranational, it has proved to be a controversial area.

The Court's jurisdiction is laid down in article 230 (ex 173) which states that it 'shall review the legality of acts' adopted by the institutions of the Community. It also grants the various institutions rights of action, as well as any 'natural or legal person', who may 'institute proceedings', though only against decisions that are either 'directed to that person' or of 'direct and individual concern'. We must immediately note that the Court has adopted the most rigorous interpretation of this clause, in the *Plaumann* case requiring evidence of a high degree of 'individual' and 'peculiar' suffering (*Plaumann*, 1963). Subsequent case law has occasionally, as in the anti-dumping case *Extramet* and then again in *Codorniu*, suggested that the Court has softened its stance (*Extramet*, 1991; *Codorniu*, 1993). But it is difficult to uncover a consistent line here, with other cases such as *Zunis Holding* and *Greenpeace* remaining faithful to the more restrictive interpretation of what constitutes 'individual' and 'peculiar' suffering (*Zunis Holding*, 1996; *Greenpeace*, 1995). Once again the overarching impression is a clear one. The ordinary citizen is distanced from the process of Community law.

We should also note that article 231 (ex 174) gives the Court the power to declare certain actions 'void'. The interpretive width of both articles 230 and 231 was reinforced most famously in the *ERTA* case in 1971, in which the Court held that any measure of a Community institution could be annulled if it was 'intended to have legal force', whether or not it was enacted in accordance with article 249 (ex 189). Accordingly, in this particular case the Court supported the Commission's argument that the Council's attempt to introduce measures outside article 249 must be struck down (*ERTA*, 1971). The Court's willingness to take the broadest view of what can be considered a reviewable act was reinforced more recently in *France* (*France*, 1997). Given the inevitable lack of clear guidelines regarding institutional competence in the Rome Treaty, much has, once again, been left to the Court, and the *ERTA* and *France* cases have affirmed the Court's willingness to take this creative responsibility (Bradley, 1987, p 41).

However, much the greatest evidence of this willingness can be found in a series of cases regarding the status of the Parliament. Since the Nice Treaty, article 230 now states that the Court shall 'have jurisdiction in actions' brought not merely by the member states as well as the Council and the Commission, but also by the Parliament. It might seem only reasonable that it should. But this particular statement is the product of a long, and sometimes bitter, litigation. The first instance was the *Les Verts* case in 1986, in which a French political party sought annulment of certain measures adopted by the Parliament (*Les Verts*, 1986). At the time, article 230 was conspicuous in failing to make reference to the Parliament. The Court waxed lyrically on the need for the Community to accept a principle of the rule of law. It held that:

> It must first be emphasised in this regard that the European Economic Community is a Community based on the rule of law, in as much as neither its Member States nor its institutions can avoid a review of the question whether the measures adopted by them are in conformity with the basic constitutional charter, the Treaty. (*Les Verts*, 1986, 1339.)

The references to the rule of law and to the Treaty as the 'constitutional charter' of the Community are justly famous. At the same time, the actual judgment cannot be understood as anything other than an act of extreme judicial activism. The Court reasoned that the Parliament by the mid-1980s represented something very different from that originally conceived in the Rome Treaty, and so, being able to effect legal rights, must then also be subject to judicial review. This was, of course, precisely what the Parliament wanted to hear. Accordingly, it declined to contest the action, in the hope that if it was subject to article 230 it must also be able to initiate actions under the same article.

Such hopes were, however, quickly dashed by the Court in the *Comitology* case two years later (*Comitology*, 1988). Parliament had not become that important. Or, perhaps, it was too important. Either way, the notion of the rule of law suddenly seemed to be rather less compelling. The interests of the Parliament, the Court decided, could be adequately looked after by the Commission, and so Parliament needed no powers to initiate actions. The decision was clearly inconsistent with the spirit of *Les Verts*. The Court, however, seemed to be quite unperturbed (Weiler, 1989; Bradley, 1988). Shortly afterwards battle was rejoined in the *Chernobyl* case, and once more the Court changed its mind, allowing an action of annulment brought by the Parliament, but only in defence of its own prerogatives. In doing so, it placed the Parliament in a position analogous to that of a private individual 'directly and individually concerned' (*Chernobyl*, 1990).

The reason for the abrupt change of heart is nothing more sinister than judicial whimsy, and the changing face of the Court. Different judges have different opinions, and the newly constituted Court was simply more sensitive to the ongoing debate surrounding the legal position of the Parliament (Bradley, 1991). Subsequent amendments to article 230, culminating with that adopted at the Nice Treaty, renders the *Les Verts–Chernobyl* jurisprudence to be of largely historical interest. But it remains another striking example of the extent to which judicial activism has triggered subsequent political reforms, in this case a series of important amendments to a Treaty article.

Thus, whilst its relationship with both the Parliament and the Council has often been rather fraught, the Court has always enjoyed a far better relationship with the Commission (Mancini, 1989). *ERTA* is, of course, a prime example of this. Article 226 (ex 169) always envisaged that the Commission should act as the 'watchdog' of the Community, and so should enjoy special access to the Court, particularly in matters relating to the implementation of Community law by member states. Whilst article 226 stipulates that the Commission must provide member states with the 'opportunity to submit its observations' in any putative dispute, the Court has always been quick to support the Commission once its patience has run out. In *Ireland*, the Court flatly rejected any 'practical difficulties' which were alleged to have delayed implementation (*Ireland*, 1990). In *Italy*, the Court even agreed that where national courts interpret conflicting national legislation in such a way as to be compatible with Community law, there is still a failure to implement effectively (*Italy*, 1973). Since 1992, article 228 (ex 171) has further vested in the Court the power to 'impose a lump sum or penalty payment' against any persistent failure to implement. It is striking that the provision lays down no limit to state liability in actions brought by the Commission under article 226.

The close relationship between the Court and the Commission is further evidenced by the operation of article 232 (ex 175), which addresses actions against institutions for failure to act. Whereas the Court has been singularly unsympathetic with regard to actions brought by individuals under article 232, it has been much more supportive of the Commission. In the *Transport* case in 1985, for example, it was quick to support the Commission in an enforcement action against the Council (*Transport*, 1985).

The Court has shown itself to be marginally more supportive of individual actions under article 235 (ex 178), which gives it 'jurisdiction' in 'disputes relating to compensation for damage' caused by Community institutions, more particularly for non-contractual liability actions brought under article 288 (ex 215). Once again, however, appearances can be deceptive. In cases such as *Schoeppenstedt* and *Zuckerfabrik*, the Court applied the most rigorous tests requiring evidence of a 'flagrant violation' of Community rights (*Schoeppenstedt*, 1971; *Zuckerfabrik*, 1971). In *Amylum* it went further still, and suggested that the action of the Community institution must have been 'verging on the arbitrary' (*Amylum*, 1979). Although, in the subsequent *Sofrimport* case, the Court appears to have retreated from this latter requirement, once again the same broad conclusion recurs (*Sofrimport*, 1990). Successful legal actions taken by individuals against Community institutions are as rare under article 235 as they are under article 230. In this area of public law, the Community does not appear to welcome the involvement of the European citizen.

Running wild?

Although there are certain key Treaty articles, such as articles 220, 234 or 249, the substance of European public law has been created by the Court of Justice. The principles of supremacy and direct effect are the most notorious examples of this, to which can now be added the more recent developments of a common administrative law and certain principles of human rights. At the same time, it is just as clear that the operation of the reference procedure, as well as the reach of interinstitutional review, owes much to judicial creativity. As one of their number admits, from the very earliest days, it was clear that the judges in the Court had '*une certaine idée de l'Europe* of their own' (Pescatore, 1983, p 157). The question is whether they should have allowed this political prejudice to influence their judicial responsibilities.

Those who seek to defend the Court's activism tend to follow Federico Mancini's famous claim that the responsibility to create fundamental principles of Community public law was inherent to the Rome Treaty. Mancini readily admitted that: 'If one were asked to synthesise the direction in which the case law produced in Luxembourg has moved since 1957, one would have to say that it coincides with the making of a constitution of Europe' (Mancini, 1989, p 595). He also admitted that we should be 'in no doubt as to the degree of activism the Court displayed in fostering the integration of Europe and forging a European identity' (Mancini and Keeling, 1994, pp 183–184, 189). However, this particular responsibility, for the Court to create a European 'constitution' was implied in the Treaty, most immediately in articles 220 (ex 164) and 234 (ex 177). It is this implication that legitimates the creation of certain fundamental principles of Community public law. Deploying a famous metaphor, Mancini argued that:

> The preference for Europe is determined by the genetic code transmitted to the Court by the founding fathers, who entrusted to it the task of ensuring that the law is observed in the application of a Treaty whose primary objective is an 'ever closer union among the peoples of Europe'. (Mancini and Keeling, 1994, p 186.)

Using a different metaphor, but in pretty much the same vein, Martin Shapiro refers to 'path-dependent' consequences (Shapiro, 1999, p 331). The same sense can also be gleaned from the observation of a former President of the Court, Hans Kutscher, who wondered how else the Court was intended to operate, except in a way that was 'dynamic and teleological' (Douglas-Scott, 2002, p 209). Such an approach, to use original Treaty articles in a 'creative' way, has been clearly favoured by the Court. The most obvious example of this is the constant citation of article 10 (ex 5) EC, which requires member states to 'take all appropriate measures' to 'facilitate the achievement of the Community's tasks'. It is for the Court, the Court assumed, to ensure that they do (Jacobs and Klarst, 1985, p 191).

Some, however, are not so easily convinced. For them the so-called genetic coding of European legal integration has mutated alarmingly. Foremost amongst its early critics was Hjalte Rasmussen. In his *On Law and Policy in the European Court of Justice*, Rasmussen accused the Court of acting quite beyond its constitutional jurisdiction as defined by the Community Treaty. In actively pursuing the integration of the Community, the Court had strayed into political, as opposed to legal, terrain. The Court, he asserted, 'has successfully acted as an unequivocal and indefatigable promoter of centralism, uniformity and unification' (Rasmussen, 1986, p 377). Worse still, the Court had refused to admit that this was so, preferring instead to spin the 'pernicious myth' that its role was 'essentially passive', extending no further than ordinary processes of judicial interpretation (Rasmussen, 1986, p 36).

Such activity, and such deceit, contravenes one of the basic jurisprudential principles of liberal democracy, that of judicial neutrality and
independence. It is for democratically accountable politicians to
create the law, not for judges. Judges should merely interpret the law
as it stands. In a famous passage, Rasmussen repeated the advice of his
compatriot, the jurist Alf Ross, that a judge should not be 'like the
Homeric king who received his *themistes* direct from Zeus, or like the
Oriental Cadi who makes his decision out of esoteric wisdom'
(Rasmussen, 1986, p 29). This, however, is precisely what the Court
of Justice had appeared to do, using the windy rhetoric of the
Preamble and articles 10 (ex 5) and 308 (ex 235) in particular to justify quite enormous judicial leaps of the imagination. The Court, he
concluded, was 'running wild' (Rasmussen, 1986, pp 31–32, 508–512).

Reactions to Rasmussen's accusations were fierce, not surprisingly
fiercest of all amongst the judges of the Court. Mauro Cappelletti
responded that Rasmussen's entire study was based on 'factual exag-
gerations' (Cappelletti, 1987). However, Rasmussen's criticisms have
been echoed elsewhere. Andre Bzdera emphasises the 'centralist' and
supranational 'inclination' of the Court, whilst Martin Holland similarly notes that the Court has been an 'implacable adversary of
intergovernmentalism' (Bzdera, 1992, p 124; Holland, 1994, p 108).
Mary Volcansek voices a common complaint against the seeming
arrogance and complacency of a Court that makes little effort to
justify its activism. And she is little more impressed by those who have
watched from the wings. What is 'truly remarkable' about the Court's
activism, she observes, has been 'the almost total lack of criticism
and virtual sycophantic praise' that it has attracted (Volcansek, 1992).
Few seem to care that the supreme Court of the new Europe is
pursuing a virulently political agenda.

One who does is Trevor Hartley who, alongside Rasmussen, has
emerged as one of the most compelling critics of the Court.
According to Hartley, on a number of occasions the Court has ventured to 'give judgments outside, or contrary to, the text of the
Treaties' (Hartley, 1996, pp 101–102). In his *Constitutional Problems of
the European Union*, Hartley has chronicled in some depth the Court's
deliberate strategy in creating certain essential principles of
Community public law, including most obviously direct effect. This
process, he confirms, has been quite outside the remit granted the
Court by the Community Treaty. It might, in time, be 'regarded as

justified' (Hartley, 1999, p 58). But that does not make it right, at least not legally.

The debate that has engulfed the activity of the Court of Justice is common to public law in many jurisdictions, particularly those with 'written' constitutions. There are always 'literalists', who hold that constitutional documents must be interpreted strictly, just as there are also 'interpretivists', who hold that such interpretation is evolutionary, and thus can, and should, change over time. In a sense the critics of the Court, such as Hartley and Rasmussen, take a more literal view of what is ultra vires the original constitution, the Rome Treaty. For Hartley, what matters is 'words on paper', not clever metaphors such as Mancini's genetic code (Hartley, 1999, pp 49–50). The defenders of the Court, however, adopt the interpretivist position, seeing the practice of judicial reasoning in any court as being necessarily creative and metaphorical (Tridimas, 1996, pp 203–206; Arnull, 1996). Such a position chimes further with the realist argument, that all courts create law. The European Court of Justice has, perhaps, been just a little more brazen in its interpretive creativity.

The legal philosopher Ronald Dworkin suggests a possible solution to this common problem of constitutional interpretation. According to Dworkin's renowned 'integrity' thesis, whilst judges might appear to create law, their powers of creation are limited by political and ethical context, by the constructed 'rationality' and the 'political morality' of the community within which they operate. This argument has been applied to the European Community and its Court of Justice by Joxerramon Bengoetxea in his influential study *The Legal Reasoning of the European Court of Justice*. According to Bengoetxea, the Court pursued an integrationist strategy in order to complete the market. It did so in accordance not merely with the stated ambitions of the Community itself, but also with due regard to the wider 'political morality' of its citizenry. Though necessarily 'activist', the Court, he observes, has consistently displayed a 'self-conscious effort to achieve rationality' (Bengoetxea, 1993, pp iv, 9, 99–101, 135, 193–196, 260–270).

A number of commentators have emphasised the historicity of the Court, with alternating periods of activity and passivity. Karen Alter has argued that the defining feature of the Court has been its determination to set an agenda that is quite distinct from that adopted by the politicians. As such, the Court has often provided an integrationist impetus that has been otherwise lacking (Alter, 1998). Such an analysis can go some way to explaining the more obvious inconsistencies that afflicted the development of general principles. The continuing agonies that surround the idea of horizontal effect, the treatment of the Parliament in matters of institutional review, the somewhat uncertain and unconvincing attempts to carve out a human rights jurisprudence; all are very obviously products of historical, as well as political, contingency.

This historical approach to analysing the Court's activity has also been pursued by Joseph Weiler, who has charted periods of consolidation and 'mutation' in the Court's history. Within this context, whilst acknowledging that the Court has striven to become ever more prudent, meaning less confrontational, he has rightly prophesied that the advent of a political Union suggests an ongoing period of 'volatility' (Weiler, 1999a, pp 188–218). The sense that the Court is presently in 'retreat' has been advanced by other commentators. Such an ambition, to concentrate more upon the responsibilities of Treaty guardianship, rather than those of political activity, was even declared by the President of the Court in 1996 (Douglas-Scott, 2002, pp 219–220).

In a very real sense, then, the basic arguments are commonly accepted. The Court has been activist. For some this activism was necessary and desirable. For others it was unwarranted and inexcusable. But it may be that the question as to whether the Court should have been activist, or has exceeded its remit, is the wrong one. A better question might be the classic 'virtual history' question, 'what if?'. What if the Court had not been active in promoting legal integration through the creation of certain fundamental principles of public law? The question carries a particular potency when placed in the context of a political elite that has appeared to be singularly unable to pursue a common vision with any kind of consistency. The fate of the Union since 1992 reinforces the sense that the future of Europe cannot sensibly be left to its politicians (Curtin, 1993, pp 62, 64–65). Of course, the observation raises huge democratic questions. The clash of law and politics is ever-present in any community. It is no less so in the European Community, and, particularly in the context of the present Constitutional 'Convention', it promises to be no less so in the future (Schwarze, 2002, pp 251–254).

Chapter 4

The law of integration

It is often said that the European 'project' is unique; the idea of a number of sovereign nation states banding together within an overarching legal and political community. The assertion is controversial. As we have already noted, various such communities have existed in the past, and various exist today, from the mediaeval *respublica Christiana* to latter-day international and transnational commercial bodies such as the North Atlantic Free Trade Area (NAFTA) and the Association of South-East Asian Nations (ASEAN). Yet it must be admitted that the 'new' Europe is, clearly, more than a mere trading arrangement. The reason for this is the depth of European 'integration'. This idea of 'integration' is of enormous importance, and it has become a familiar term in modern European studies. The expressions of integration are various: legal, political, social, economic, even cultural. The purpose of this chapter is to investigate the idea of 'integration', and more particularly the idea of legal and political integration. The primary focus will be upon the experience of legal and political integration in the United Kingdom. Necessarily, this experience is in some ways quite distinct. In other ways, it describes an experience that has been common to many member states of the 'new' Europe.

The question of competence

The very idea of integration suggests a coming together. It is, in other words, a process, a means to an end. The same is, of course, true of law and politics; both are processes, means to ends. These ends might be 'liberty, equality and fraternity', as was famously declared in the French Revolution or perhaps 'life, liberty and the pursuit of happiness' as stated in the US Constitution. It is not easy to discern such a clear statement in the 'new' Europe, where there is a residual confusion of means and end in the statement that the purpose of the Union appears to be to promote the 'ever closer union of the peoples of Europe'. Closer and closer and closer, but never, apparently, actually united. And so we are left with the clear impression that, at least in today's Europe, process is everything. It is a conclusion that makes the idea of integration absolutely fundamental.

The unifying principle that aligns questions of legal and political integration is that of national sovereignty. And the common point of tension in the process of European 'integration' is that which exists between residual notions of national sovereignty and the overarching challenge of European legal and political supremacy. The legal doctrine of supremacy was described in the previous chapter and, as was noted at the time, its most striking feature is its uncompromising statement. The Court of Justice has tolerated no derogation from the doctrine of supremacy, and has, indeed, reinforced it through the often tortuous creation of a collateral doctrine of direct effect. The creation of a human rights profile in the Community, along with certain common principles of administrative law, has added a further dimension to this jurisprudential challenge.

Moreover, there is much discussion at present about the prospects for a common private law, perhaps even a codified law of contract or obligations. To a considerable extent this discussion is premised upon the assumption of a common legal tradition across much of the continent, a tradition founded on civil law. This assumption can often seem anomalous in the United Kingdom, with its very different common law system. Proponents of a harmonised private law, and most particularly a common contract law, follow those public lawyers who argue that a common administrative law can be secured on a pre-existing *ius commune*, or common European jurisprudence. At the same time, aside from the conceptual convenience, they also argue from the position of efficiency. A common private law, it is suggested, would aid the working of the market. This latter argument has attracted the repeated support of the European Parliament. Once again, it is widely recognised that the Treaty provides no express provision for the harmonisation of private law, and so much would, as ever, rest with the creative energy of the Court of Justice, possibly acting under the broad authority of articles 94 and 95 (ex 100 and 100A) (Basedow, 1996, 1998; Van Gerven, 2002). For the present, however, we must wait and see.

The process of legal integration is, thus, not just of historic importance, but of prospective importance too. The jurisprudential integrity of the member states has been challenged, and will continue to be challenged, by the experience of integration. Whilst this chapter will concentrate primarily on reactions in the United Kingdom to this challenge, it should be remembered that a number of other member states have, from time to time, articulated certain anxieties in the difficult process of trying to mediate this basic tension between sovereignty and supremacy. Aside from the difficulties experienced in the United Kingdom, perhaps the most notorious have been those expressed by the Federal Constitutional Court in Germany.

The root of the Federal Constitutional Court's particular anxieties lay in the area of human rights. In its ruling in *Solange 1*, the Court asserted that it would continue to review the constitutionality of Community law in Germany,

> as long as the integration process has not progressed so far that Community law also receives a catalogue of fundamental rights decided on by a parliament and of settled validity, which is adequate in comparison with the catalogue of fundamental rights contained in the Constitution. (*Solange 1*, 1974, 452.)

In what amounted to a clear rejection of the principle of absolute supremacy, the Court retained the authority to decide on the legitimacy of Community law in Germany. As we shall see shortly, UK courts have adopted a similar sleight of hand in order to rationalise the relation of supremacy and sovereignty in British public law. But no UK court has ever made such a bald statement as that which emanated from the Constitutional Court in *Solange 1*.

The same Court then appeared to take a step back from such an assertive stance in *Solange 2* in 1987. Here it held that:

> so long as the European Communities, and in particular the case law of the European Court, generally ensure an effective protection of fundamental rights as against the sovereign powers of the Communities which is to be regarded as substantially similar to the protection of fundamental rights required unconditionally by the Constitution, the Federal Constitutional Court will no longer exercise its jurisdiction to decide on the applicability . . . of Community legislation. (*Solange 2*, 1987, 494.)

This might seem to be a critical concession. But it should be noted that whilst the Constitutional Court declares that it will 'no longer exercise its jurisdiction' of review, it does so 'so long as' the Community appears to 'ensure' effective protection of human rights. It is not, then, an unconditional surrender of competence, and so, by implication, the Constitutional Court retains the authority to adjudge whether Community law is automatically applicable in Germany.

The matter recurred for a third time in the famous *Brunner* decision in 1993. This case followed the proposed ratification in Germany of the Maastricht Treaty, and the complementary amendment of the German Constitution to include a new article 23. This new article stated that, for 'the realisation of a unified Europe', the German Federation 'may by legislation with the consent of the *Bundesrat* transfer sovereign powers'.[1] Whilst it approved both ratification and the amendment to the Constitution, the most significant aspect of the Constitutional Court's ruling was its willingness to assume jurisdiction. Once again, there was a clear implication that the Court would adjudge all important matters relating to either the legal or political sovereignty of Germany, and it would do so in the light of the German Constitution. As far as it was concerned, the *Grundnorm* in German law is the German Constitution, not the Union Treaty and not Community law (*Brunner*, 1994; Eleftheriadis, 1998, pp 262–265; Weiler, 1998, pp 288–289; Hartley, 1999, pp 154–157).

In essence what the German Constitutional Court is clearly determined to reserve is the 'competence' to rule on any potential tensions that exist between domestic and Community law. And it is not alone

---

[1]   The *Bundesrat* is a chamber of the German parliament.

in doing so. The Italian Constitutional Court followed its German counterpart by asserting, in the *Fragd* case, that it would retain competence to consider the compatibility of Community law with the human rights provisions of the Italian Constitution. In France, meanwhile, various courts have revealed an inconsistent response to the challenge of Community law, and more particularly the doctrine of supremacy. Whereas the *Cour de Cassation* has consistently accepted the doctrine, the *Conseil d'Etat* has not, and in refusing to do so has compromised the ultimate constitutional authority of the *Conseil Constitutionnel*,[2] Most famously in the *Cohn-Bendit* case the *Conseil d'Etat* refused to accept the immediate direct effect of directives, and continued to do so for a number of years. This assumption of constitutional authority to review Community legislation was only softened in the *Nicolo* case in 1989 (Douglas-Scott, 2002, pp 264–266).

An awkward partner?

Whilst the doctrine of supremacy might be firmly established in Community law, it is just as clear that the very idea of legal integration continues to create anxiety, both legal and political. The attitudes of the German, Italian and French courts excited considerable popular interest, if not disquiet. The legal and political aspects of integration cannot be readily distinguished, and this is certainly no less the case in the United Kingdom. For much of the rest of this chapter, we will concentrate on the legal and constitutional aspects of EU–UK relations. But first, it is important to establish a broader historical and political frame.

In political terms, the United Kingdom has been commonly termed an 'awkward partner' (George, 1990). There is clearly much truth in this assessment. The history of UK–Community relations during the second part of the last century is littered with all too many examples of bitterness, obfuscation and sheer silliness. As we have already noted, the attitude of various UK governments to the inception of the Community was far more contemptuous than constructive. Britain, Nye Bevan announced, had 'the moral leadership of the world'. The British, he

---

[2]   The *Cour de Cassation* is the highest court in the ordinary judicial courts of France. The *Conseil d'Etat* is the supreme administrative court. The *Conseil Constitutionnel* is the supreme constitutional court.

added, were 'simply more cultivated than they are'. As mentioned in chapter 1, following his attendance at a miners' rally, Herbert Morrison voiced the similarly inane opinion that the United Kingdom could never join the Community because the 'Durham miners won't wear it' (Young, 1993, pp 33–34; Hattersley, 1997, pp 41–42).

The same tone, unfortunately, has characterised much of the period since the United Kingdom's accession to the Community in 1972. Of course, the very act of accession was a tacit admission of error, an admission that the United Kingdom should, after all, have joined the Community back in 1958. By the time it joined a decade and a half later, the terms under which it did so, particularly the financial terms regarding contributions to the Community budget, were dramatically more onerous. Eden's bluster and Macmillan's anti-Semitic suspicions had their price. According to Roy Hattersley, the refusal to take a constructive part in the formation of the Community was the defining 'historical error of post-war Britain' (Hattersley, 1997, p 54).

That a mistake had been made had quickly become apparent. As Prime Minister, Macmillan swallowed his contempt and made repeated applications for association during the first months of the Community's existence. Trading deficits with the Community grew throughout the 1960s, and UK applications for some kind of association continued. The sterling crisis of 1966 served to underline the increasingly precarious condition of the UK economy outside the Community. President de Gaulle of France, however, remained studiously opposed to the prospect of UK accession. Never one to seek recourse to persuasion where an insult would do, Macmillan accused de Gaulle of 'bidding high for the hegemony of Europe', and wanting to be the 'new Napoleon' (Greenwood, 1992, p 86–89; Young, 1993, pp 63–64, 83). De Gaulle remained resolute, dismissing applications from the succeeding Wilson administration with equal alacrity, revelling in the opportunity to dismiss the United Kingdom as an economically untenable candidate for accession. It was only with the fall of de Gaulle in the wake of popular rioting in 1969, that the possibility of UK accession became viable.

A fresh application for membership, submitted by the new Heath administration, was finally accepted at the Paris Council in 1972, along with similar applications from Ireland and Denmark. Even then, Heath's work was far from over. An unconvinced House of

Commons barely approved the statutory instrument of accession, the European Communities Act, by a mere eight votes. 'Joining the Community', Heath sought to reassure his Parliamentary colleagues, 'does not entail a loss of national identity or an erosion of essential national sovereignty' (Hattersley, 1997, p 224).[3] The essential word here was, of course, essential. For the last 30 years, successive British governments, and their citizenry, have struggled to make sense of what this one particular linguistic caveat means. In 1975, the Wilson government held a referendum on continued membership of the Community. The nation voted by 2 to 1 to remain. Wilson himself had refused to campaign for either a 'yes' or a 'no'. Such ambivalence spoke volumes, both of Wilson and of Britain.

The real tensions came to the fore during the 1980s, as a fundamentally Eurosceptic Prime Minister, Margaret Thatcher, led successive administrations. As is so often the case, there is a certain irony in Thatcher's virulent scepticism. Thatcher had campaigned for a 'yes' vote in 1975, and whilst still in opposition during the final crisis-ridden months of the Callaghan government in 1978–79, had fiercely argued the case for some kind of common European currency as a means to bolstering the pound sterling. It was, of course, Thatcher who finally signed the Single European Act and who, in so doing, paved the way for both the completion of the market and the inception of a political Union. By her own admission, this one signature was the most serious 'mistake' of her career'. Such mistakes, and such inconsistencies, are, however, the privilege of the professional politician. It should be noted that the present vice-President of the Commission, Neil Kinnock, campaigned fiercely for a 'no' vote in the 1975 UK referendum.

For much of the rest of the time, Thatcher was an implacable opponent of further European integration.[4] The Conservative Party election manifesto in 1979 had made much of the need to force a

---

[3]   The statement repeated the assertion given in a 1971 White Paper, that 'There is no question of any erosion of essential national sovereignty. What is proposed is a sharing and an enlargement of individual national sovereignties in the general interest' (Duff, 1998, p 36).

[4]   Personal relationships were also, perhaps not surprisingly, somewhat fraught. By the time of the famous 1984 Council at Fontainebleau, Chancellor Kohl of Germany refused to speak to Thatcher. The nature of French President Mitterand's admiration can be discerned in his evocative suggestion that his British counterpart, and invariable opponent, had 'the eyes of Caligula and the mouth of Marilyn Monroe'.

readjustment in the United Kingdom's contributions to the Community budget, and Thatcher duly arrived at her first Council meeting announcing that she was no longer prepared to 'play Sister Bountiful to the Community', and that she was only attending in order to 'get our own money back' (Greenwood, 1992, p 108; Young, 1993, p 141; Thatcher, 1993, pp 79–82). Europe was not so easily bullied, and the arguments trundled on for four years. At the Fontainebleau Council in 1984, a frustrated Thatcher finally announced that she would deploy the Luxembourg 'accords' in order to bring the effective government of the Council to an indefinite halt. This, as we have already seen, only succeeded in achieving the effective abolition of the 'accords' themselves. Yet again, Thatcher had made a striking contribution to the future integration of Europe. In the end, after all the fuss, the United Kingdom was merely granted a rolling rebate of 66 per cent.[5]

As the 1980s progressed, Thatcher's opposition to further integration became increasingly explicit. In a notorious speech given at Bruges in 1990, Britain's Prime Minister waxed poetically, if a little incredibly, about the threat which the Community posed to the Magna Carta, whilst creating the equally implausible Orwellian spectre of an 'identikit European personality' (Thatcher, 1993, pp 744–745). Such overt Euroscepticism could only lead to division within the party and the government. Some Ministers, such as Nicholas Ridley, revelled in the opportunity to indulge in a little visceral xenophobia, dismissing the French as a nation of 'poodles' and the whole idea of European integration as a German 'racket'. Others, however, were horrified, and matters came to a head with the resignation speech of former Chancellor Geoffrey Howe, which ridiculed his Prime Minister's suspicions of a 'continent that is positively teeming with ill-intentioned people, scheming in her words, to extinguish democracy'.

The Thatcher government never recovered from Howe's speech, and fell months later. Her successor, John Major, inherited a poisoned chalice. Almost immediately, the European question was reopened by the 1992 Exchange Rate Mechanism (ERM) crisis, when the pound sterling was unable to maintain its position within the loose currency

---

[5]   By which was meant a guaranteed import–export ratio, with required at least 66 per cent of exports to be balanced by imports, and with any differences made up through adjustments to budgetary contributions.

bands provided by the European Exchange Rate Mechanism. Whilst the United Kingdom had studiously remained outside the single currency, it was committed to the ERM. The attempt to bolster the pound sterling failed, but not before 40 per cent of UK gold reserves had been squandered in the process.

The passage of the 'Maastricht Bill' through Parliament in 1992 proved to be equally fraught. Having inherited a slim majority of just 19, and carrying an intransigent complement of around 30 to 40 Eurosceptic MPs, piloting the legislation was always going to be difficult. Major desperately triumphed the United Kingdom's various protocols, from the single currency and the Social Chapter. Eventually, after much heartache, and various labyrinthine legislative procedures, the Bill staggered through. But not before the government had been humiliated by the loss of one Commons division, and had squeaked through another only by the casting vote of the Speaker. In the end it had sought recourse to the constitutionally dubious tactic of attaching the final reading of the Bill to a confidence motion (Rawlings, 1994a; Major, 1999, pp 278–288, 346–389).[6]

The rest of the Major administration remained mired in the European question. The *Sunday Times* ridiculed a Prime Minister with an unleadable party, one reminiscent of a 'panto horse – the front had no relation to the back' (Baker et al, 1993, p 163). In 1994, in an action which bore some resemblance to the *Brunner* case in Germany, Lord Rees-Mogg challenged Parliament's ability to approve the Maastricht Bill (*Rees-Mogg*, 1994). The action failed, for reasons that we will examine in the next section. But the mood of recriminations continued. In 1996, Major even resigned as leader of his party in order to try re-establish his authority. He won the subsequent election, but established little, other than reaffirming the reality that his party was ungovernable. By the time of the 1997 election, Tory candidates were writing their own manifesto commitments on Europe, some supportive, most sceptical in various degrees. The subsequent crushing defeat

---

6   The atmosphere in the Commons surrounding the events of the various votes on the amendments was described by one national newspaper to be one of 'mass hysteria'. At one point, the Deputy Speaker's refusal to table opposition amendments had led to the call for a vote of no confidence in his position. Whilst not unknown, such a demand is rare in the extreme. On another occasion, the tellers counted wrongly, and declared a tied vote, when in fact the government had won by one.

was, in no small degree, the consequence of these festering internal divisions on the subject of European integration.

The manifesto of the succeeding Blair government promised to place the United Kingdom back at the 'heart of Europe'. But then Major had made precisely the same promise on his assumption of power. We shall see if 'new' Labour has been any more successful in the final part of this chapter.

The question of sovereignty

The real tension, as we have already noted, continues to oscillate around one essential myth within which the British 'constitution' is shrouded. This is the myth of parliamentary sovereignty. All the United Kingdom's many and various legal and political anxieties can be traced back to this one all-consuming constitutional mythology, the 'keystone', as the renowned Victorian jurist, Albert Dicey, termed it, of the British constitution. Dicey's *The Law of the Constitution*, within which the concept of sovereignty took such a central position, represented the epitome of a jurisprudence that was based on the power of individual nation states. The concept of parliamentary sovereignty provided a sheen of constitutional legitimacy to the exercise of this power. It was, moreover, thoroughly ingrained in the psyche of the English public lawyer, the product of two centuries of faith in the 'great and glorious' revolutions of the seventeenth century (Dickinson, 1976; MacCormick, 1999, pp 123–126). To a considerable extent it remains so, even though, as we shall see in the final chapters of this book, it is difficult, it not impossible, to give the classical idea of sovereignty any sensible meaning in the contemporary 'new world order'.

The putative threat to the concept of parliamentary sovereignty could be found in the European Communities Act 1972, section 2.1, which stated that:

> All such rights, powers, liabilities, obligations and restrictions from time to time created or arising under the Treaties, and all such remedies and procedures from time to time provided for under the Treaties, as in accordance with the Treaties are without further enactment to be given legal effect or used in the United Kingdom shall be recognised and available in law, and

be enforced, allowed and followed accordingly; and the expression 'enforceable Community right' and similar expressions shall be read as referring to one to which this subsection applies.

In the jargon of constitutional theory, the 1972 Act is an 'enabling' Act. It is intended to proscribe the future manner of legislative enactment. The burning question, of course, is whether section 2.1 represents an infringement of 'essential' sovereignty.

The initial response, most famously articulated by Lord Denning in *Macarthy's*, was that it did not, but that it did not in a rather unusual way. Faced with subsequent legislation that appeared to be inconsistent with the 1972 Act, Denning was insistent that there could be no implied repeal of the former. Short of an express reservation, he opined, British courts must interpret subsequent legislation to be in accord with Community legislation, no matter how creative they might have to be. The Diceyan idea of 'continuing' sovereignty might have suggested that the opposite was true, that in the instance of inconsistency, subsequent legislation repealed former legislation. Denning, however, adhered to the alternative idea of 'self-embracing' sovereignty. According to this latter idea of sovereignty, the 1972 Act had bound the 'manner and form' with which it might be later repealed. In this instance it meant that the provisions of the 1972 Act could only be repealed expressly.[7]

The 'priority' of European law, Denning suggested, 'is given by our law'. He continued:

> It is given by the European Communities Act 1972 itself. Community law is part of our law: and, whenever there is any inconsistency, Community law has priority. It is not supplanting English law. It is part of our law which overrides any other part which is inconsistent with it. (*Macarthy's*, 1981, 200.)

In making this statement, and in excavating this alternative idea of sovereignty, Denning hoped to be able to accommodate classical ideas of parliamentary sovereignty with the all-encompassing principle of the 'supremacy' of Community law; the principle which, as we have already seen, has been so rigorously enforced by the European Court of Justice. Trevor Allan termed it 'Lord Denning's dexterous revolution',

---

7   It should be noted that this particular, self-embracing, theory of sovereignty has precedent, most famously perhaps, parts of the Act of Union.

adding that his statement could 'be interpreted as lying on the borderline between interpretation and (non)-application' (Allan, 1983).

Aside from certain residual doubts regarding the constitutional pro-
priety of Denning's 'revolution', there are certain other problems.
First, the idea that the 1972 Act is a different kind of statute, founded
on a particular species of sovereignty, and that Community law, in
turn, exists as a kind of adjunct part of British law, runs quite against
the Community view of a holistic legal order (Anav, 1989, pp
648–650). A second problem relates to the working of Denning's 'revolution' in practice. In simple terms it invites a 'dualistic' conception
of British constitutional law. On the one hand, for matters relating to
Community law there is one set of rules of judicial interpretation
and reasoning derived from one tradition of constitutional sovereignty, whilst, on the other hand, for the rest of British public law
there is another set of laws and rules derived from another tradition
of constitutional sovereignty. As Allan observed, Denning's interpretation of the 1972 Act as a 'self-embracing' statute effectively
established a super-law, and with it a super-system of law, which must
now 'operate alongside national law' (Allan, 1983, p 25).

It follows, therefore, that British citizens are subject to two rather different sovereignties; a limited UK sovereignty and a superior
European sovereignty. At the same time they are, unavoidably, subject
to two sets of rights; a problem which, as we shall see shortly, has
increasingly unsettled senior members of the judiciary. For much of
the intervening two decades, however, this dualist system of public
law has been adopted widely in dealing with matters of Community
law. It was accepted by the Court of Appeal in the leading case of
Garland in 1983, and then again by the House of Lords in *Pickstone*
and *Lister* in 1989 and 1990 respectively (*Garland*, 1983; *Pickstone*,
1989; *Lister*, 1990). Whilst it seemed rather less comfortable with the
idea in the cases of *Duke* and *Finnegan*, the House of Lords expressed
its most fervent support for the principle of constitutional duality in
the seminal *Factortame* case which was also decided in 1990. We shall
also take a closer look at the *Factortame* cases shortly.

A third problem is consistency, a problem that can be readily exacerbated by the politically dissident. The repercussions of this problem
were revealed in Lord Rees-Mogg's legal action initiated in the wake of
the Maastricht legislation. According to Rees-Mogg, legislative

enactments such as the statute incorporating the Maastricht Treaty breached earlier commitments, most immediately those provided in the 1978 Parliamentary Elections Act. The potential breach of the 1978 Act was a technical matter. The real challenge was directed against the idea that Parliament could bind itself in terms of the 'manner and form' of legislative repeal. For, if Parliament was not bound by the 1978 Act, then the idea that it was bound by the conditions of the 1972 Act was equally uncertain. The question was, of course, just as much political as legal. In anticipating the Divisional Court's decision, the Speaker of the Commons made a florid appeal to article 9 of the Bill of Rights, a document which itself enjoys a dubious constitutional provenance, and the stated inalienability of Parliament before the judiciary. The Court duly took the hint and declined to support Rees-Mogg's action, in doing so avoiding any suggestion that it might have been acting as a court of constitutional review (*Rees-Mogg*, 1994; Rawlings, 1994a, pp 256–261; Rawlings, 1994b; Chalmers, 2000, pp 84–85).

The European way

In a famous passage from his judgment in *Bulmer v Bollinger*, given in 1974, Lord Denning observed that the Community Treaty was 'quite unlike any of the enactments to which we have become accustomed'. He continued:

> It lays down general principles. It expresses aims and purposes. All in sentences of moderate length and commendable style. But it lacks precision. It uses words and phrases without defining what they mean. An English lawyer would look for an interpretation clause, but he would look in vain. There is none. All the way through the treaty, there are gaps and lacunae. These have to be filled in by judges, or by regulations or directives. It is the European way . . . Seeing these differences, what are the English courts to do when faced with a problem of interpretation? The must follow the European pattern. No longer must they argue about the precise grammatical sense. They must look for purpose and intent . . . They must divine the spirit of the treaty and gain inspiration from it. If they find a gap, they must fill it as best they can . . . These are the principles, as I understand it, on which the European Court acts. (*Bulmer*, 1974, 1237–1238.)

It was not, then, merely the question of sovereignty that troubled Denning. It was the very notion of the 'European way', the idea that judges and lawyers must 'divine' the 'spirit' of the Treaty, that they must root out its 'purpose'. Obviously things have become a little clearer since 1974. But it is equally true that the British judiciary has continued to be bothered by the European 'way'. We shall encounter specific examples shortly.

The present continuing state of confusion can be stripped down to three primary elements. First, there is uncertainty as to what the role of the domestic judiciary now is. More particularly, there is a concern that domestic courts should be required to act as courts of constitutional review. Such a responsibility runs directly against the classical conception of parliamentary sovereignty. The nature of this challenge was vividly described by Lord Mustill in *Peterborough*, as late as 1991:

> According to the doctrine of the separation of powers, as understood in the United Kingdom, the legislative acts of the Queen in Parliament are impregnable. The United Kingdom has no constitutional courts in the same sense as in other countries . . . it is axiomatic that the courts have no supervisory or revising powers in relation to primary legislation. If Parliament speaks, the courts must obey. This is the fundamental principle of our constitutional law, but it has more recently been overlaid with qualifications of increasing importance to daily life stemming from the accession of the United Kingdom to the European Communities. Since then the courts have been obliged to read statutes of the United Kingdom in the light of general principles laid down in the EEC Treaty, as developed in instruments of the Council and the Commission, and as expounded by the Court of Justice of the European Communities. (*Peterborough*, 1991, 196–197.)

The House of Lords was just as troubled in the *Factortame* case, when the granting of an interim injunction against a parliamentary statute was perceived to be a potential usurpation of the legislative function, and thus tantamount to constitutional review. In *Stoke* in 1991, Hoffmann J, whilst admitting the reality that the 1972 Act demanded a 'partial surrender of sovereignty', steadfastly refused to concede that judges were now endowed 'with quasi-legislative powers' (*Stoke*, 1991). There is, it seems, still a distance between acknowledging the potential demise of sovereignty and embracing the complementary responsibilities of constitutional review.

A second confusion surrounds the nature, and appropriateness, of various principles of Community law. The idea that such principles might somehow be restricted in use to cases concerning matters of Community law only has proved to be illusory. The emergence of various principles of Community administrative law, a number of which we examined in the last chapter, has caused especial concern. Two in particular have given rise to considerable debate. The first of these is legitimate expectations, a principle that has been increasingly used as an additional head of action in domestic public law since it famously received Lord Diplock's approval in the *CCSU* case (*CCSU*, 1985). It was notably deployed more recently by Lord Donaldson in *Cunningham*, paradoxically as a means of evading the suggestion that Community law had introduced another new 'principle' into public law, a general right to know the reasons for decisions made by public bodies (*Cunningham*, 1991).

The *CCSU* case also touched upon the second of these controversial principles, for Lord Diplock also suggested that proportionality might be a principle that could be used by British courts in order to determine the appropriateness of administrative actions or decisions. However, domestic courts have been chary of accepting this suggestion. In *Brind*, a case more directly concerning the status of the European Convention in domestic law, Lord Lowry voiced the collective concern of his colleagues in the House of Lords:

> In my opinion proportionality and the other phrases are simply intended to move the focus away from the hitherto accepted criteria for deciding whether the decision-maker has abused his power, and into an area in which the court will feel more at liberty to interfere. The first observation I would like to make is that there is no authority for saying proportionality, in the sense in which the appellants have used it, is part of the English common law and a great deal of authority the other way. This, so far as I am concerned, is not a cause for regret. (*Brind*, 1991, 766–767.)

As we shall shortly see, domestic courts revealed a similar antagonism, and no little confusion, when faced with the suggested deployment of proportionality in the Sunday Trading cases. And the confusion has continued in more recent cases still, such as *International Trader's Ferry*, in which the Court of Appeal and the House of Lords came to directly opposing views as to what constituted disproportionate action on the particular facts of the case in question (*International Trader's Ferry*, 1997).

It has been suggested, rightly, that principles such as legitimate expectations or proportionality, cannot be introduced in a piecemeal fashion, but can only work effectively as part of a far wider recasting of domestic administrative law. As Sophie Boyron writes, such 'concepts cannot be viewed in isolation, but are integrally related to the whole theoretical framework which exists within a particular legal system' (Boyron, 1992, p 238). Anxieties regarding the appropriateness of such juridical concepts attaches to wider concerns regarding the activity of the Court of Justice, and its imagined imperialism (Coppel and O'Neil, 1992, pp 244–245). At root, of course, the fundamental problem with British public law has been its singular failure to embrace the idea of rights, and much of the confusion regarding the application of apparently alien principles of Community law can be traced to this particular failing (Loughlin, 1992, pp 184–210).[8] However, as we shall see in the final part of this chapter, in this particular respect it might be that the times are finally changing.

The third and final concern relates to the nature of judicial reasoning. As Lord Denning had opined in *Bulmer*, British judges have never been comfortable with the idea of purposive, or teleological, interpretation; in other words, of interpreting legislation, not in line with its strict linguistic meaning, but in the wider context of its apparent purpose. This discomfort found expression Schiemann J's observations in *Peterborough*:

> Reaching a decision as to what is the aim in view, when one is considering primary legislation is, given English styles of statutory drafting, a difficult task since the aim is frequently not stated and indeed different components of the legislature may have had differing aims in view. (*Peterborough*, 1991, 219.)

Hoffmann J expressed a similar feeling of discomfort when faced with seeking the purpose of Treaty provisions 'expressed in language capable of being given a wider or narrower interpretation' (*Stoke*, 1991).

---

8   Loughlin has also argued that this failure, to embrace the idea of rights in UK public law, has similarly led to a refusal to understand or develop coherent theories of judicial reasoning and interpretation (Loughlin, 1992, pp 15–39, 139–183).

Yet, of course, judicial reasoning in any legal jurisdiction is purposive to some degree. Interpreting the meaning of statutes is always a contextual activity, dependent upon each judge's understanding of the meaning of certain words and certain concepts at a particular time. Meaning does not stand still, even for judges. The challenge of Community law is that it requires British judges to confront head on an activity which they have never felt inclined to embrace, at least not with any enthusiasm. The fact that British judges must now do so was explicitly emphasised by the Advocate General in *Factortame*. Not only must British courts recognise their responsibility to act as courts of constitutional review, but so too, he opined, must they adopt a more 'substantive' and less 'formal' approach to matters of statutory interpretation and judicial reasoning (*Factortame*, 1991).

The shopkeepers' tale

A series of cases involving the status of legislation concerning Sunday trading offers itself as the first of two particularly enlightening examples of judicial confusion regarding the status and the nature of Community law. Both were set during the late 1980s and the first part of the 1990s, and thus took place within a particular political context of comparable antagonism and uncertainty. In a sense they represent the high-point, or perhaps more appropriately low-point, of British judicial attitudes to the challenge of European legal integration.

It is rare for any litigation, let alone EC litigation, to become a matter of wider public interest. The issue of Sunday trading, however, emerged during the early 1990s as a semiotic for general attitudes towards Europe. To a considerable extent, related questions, such as the ability to display weights and measures in 'imperial' pounds and ounces, rather than kilos and grams, remain a matter of loud protest, and futile legal challenges. Everybody shops, and so everybody feels involved in these kind of questions, even if the legal niceties are far removed from ready comprehension.

The main issue revolved around the Shops Act 1950, section 47 of which states that 'Every shop shall, save as otherwise provided by this Part of this Act, be closed for the serving of customers on Sunday.' The origins of the Shops Act lay in theological, as well as industrial, arguments relating to the beneficial prohibition, not so much of shopping but of working on Sundays. Shopping on Sunday, it was feared, courted eternal damnation. The exceptions 'provided' rendered much of the Act itself ridiculous, and have passed into legal folklore. The fifth schedule, for example, permits the sale of intoxicating liquors, and cooked meals, except for fish and chips if cooked in a fish and chip shop, as well as partly cooked tripe partly cooked anywhere. Pornographic magazines can be sold on Sunday mornings, but Holy Bibles cannot be sold at any time on any Sunday. In simple terms, section 47 was a mess.

Moreover, more and more companies were treating the statute with contempt, whilst more and more local authorities, though empowered under section 222 of the Local Government Act 1972 to seek a civil injunction to prevent them trading, were turning a blind eye. In what was very much part of a wider campaign to secure the final repeal of section 47, a number of larger DIY stores raised article 28 (ex 30) of the Community Treaty as a defence against any possible injunction. Article 28, as we shall see in the next chapter, is one of the central pillars of the common market, preventing any member state from imposing 'quantative restrictions on imports and all measures having equivalent effect'. In the leading case of *Dassonville*, the Court of Justice had reinforced the scope of article 28 by declaring that 'measures having equivalent effect' included 'all trading rules enacting by Member States, which are capable of hindering, directly or indirectly, actually or potentially, intra-Community trade' (*Dassonville*, 1974). Whilst the equally important *Cassis de Dijon* case had suggested that what it termed 'indistinctly applicable' measures might be defended in terms of national 'characteristics', the DIY stores suggested that section 47 was prima facie inconsistent with article 28, and that the later, as an instrument of Community law, enjoyed legislative 'supremacy'. Sunday closure, they alleged as a matter of fact, created a potential reduction in the volume of imports from other member states.

The first reference on the matter to the Court of Justice was made by Cwmbran magistrates in *Torfaen* in 1989. In what Trevor Hartley rightly termed a 'famously opaque' decision, the Court held that section 47 was indeed in breach of article 28, unless it could be otherwise justified. Such a justification, it added, could only be 'legitimate' if it could be shown to be 'part' of 'economic and social policy, consistent with the objectives of public interest pursued in the Treaty' (Hartley, 1999, pp 78–79). Such matters, it further added, were for national courts to decide. The real comedy in the Court's decision came in the suggestion that their Worships might like to employ the principle of proportionality in order to ease their confusion. Article 3 of Directive 70/50 was supposed to provide some guidance on this matter, stating that 'the prohibition laid down in article 30 [now 28] covers national measures governing the marketing of products where the restrictive effect of such measures on the free movement of goods exceeds the effects intrinsic to trade rules'.

Unfortunately, few, in Cwmbran or anywhere else, had much idea what this really meant (Barnard, 1994, p 453; Rawlings, 1993, pp 315–317; Arnull, 1991). It appeared that some restriction on trade might be acceptable, provided it was not disproportionate in terms of the potential benefit to trade. Chaos ensued, with various courts up and down the country reaching various conclusions. Some injunctions under section 222 were granted by some courts. Some were not. In some areas Sunday trading seemed to be permissible. In others it was not. In was decided that trading was ungodly in Wellingborough and Stoke-on-Trent, and was thus forbidden (*Wellingborough*, 1990; *Stoke*, 1991). It was also thought to be ungodly in Shrewsbury, but the burghers of that town were free to risk their own damnation if they felt compelled to spend their Sundays touring out of town DIY stores (*Shrewsbury*, 1990). As Rawlings concluded, the Court of Justice had left British courts to juggle issues that they were 'not remotely equipped to handle' (Rawlings, 1993, p 17).

Judicial confusion appeared to be widespread. In *Stoke*, Hoffmann J expressed his particular admiration for the 'traditional English Sunday'. It was not something, he opined, that could be hazarded against the alternative interests of a common market, and it was certainly not an exercise in which judges should be engaged:

> It my judgment it is not my function to carry out the balancing exercise or to form my own view on whether the legislative objective could be achieved by other means. These questions involve compromises between competing interests, which in a democratic society must be resolved by the legislative. The duty of the court is to inquire whether the compromise adopted by the United Kingdom Parliament, so far as it affects Community trade, is one which a reasonable legislature could have reached. The function of the court is to review the acts of the legislature

but not to substitute its own policies or values. This is not an abdication of judicial responsibility. The primacy of the democratic process is far more important than the question of whether our Sunday trading laws could or could not be improved. (*Stoke*, 1991, 235.)

Like Hoffmann, Lord Mustill's judgment in *Peterborough* provided further evidence of judicial confusion, and banality. According to Mustill, it was impossible to decide which was the more important, keeping 'the Sabbath Holy' or promoting the interests of the common market. And he too had something to say about proportionality. Such 'balancing' processes, he declared, 'would be difficult to the point of impossibility in any but the simplest case, where the balance is to be struck, not between two conflicting trade interests, but between the community free trade interest on the one hand, and an intelligible and elusive national moral, social or cultural norm on the other' (*Peterborough*, 1991, 210).

It was clear that there would need to be further recourse to the Court of Justice, which had, in the meantime, given rulings on very similar cases referred from France and Belgium, *Conforama* and *Marchandise*. In these cases, it had ruled that 'the restrictive effects on trade which may stem from such rules do not seem disproportionate to the aim pursued', and therefore article 28 (ex 30) did 'not apply to national legislation prohibiting the employment of staff on Sundays' (*Conforama*, 1991; *Marchandise*, 1991; Barnard, 1994, p 455). Although the law seemed to be clear, British courts persisted in making references, and so the Court of Justice finally decided that it must rule on the particular matter itself. In doing so, it appeared to rescind the notion that such matters were best decided, on their particular facts, by national courts. The Court held that 'it had all the information necessary for it to rule on the question of proportionality of such rules', and, unsurprisingly, decided that the Shops Act was not disproportionate in its effect on the market (*Stoke*, 1992).

A final, and interesting, point was raised by the issue of temporary relief. As the Court of Justice typically takes up to two years to make a judgment following a referral under article 234, the companies against which injunctions might have been issued, argued that they stood to lose considerable revenue in the meantime. This would, they added, be a particular injustice if the final decision was given in their favour. In answer to this, certain domestic courts required local authorities to given 'cross-undertakings' to recompense any companies, in damages, for any losses, if the case was indeed decided in their favour (*Rochdale*, 1988). Unsurprisingly, local authorities shied away from making such undertakings, and so, to all intents and purposes, both section 47 of the Shops Act and section 222 of the Local Government Act were effectively disapplied (Diamond, 1991). Equally unsurprisingly, the various companies realised that there was benefit in threatening litigation, even as it became ever more apparent that the final decision of the Court of Justice would go against them. Local authorities simply could not take the chance of losing. The companies most certainly could. This particular discrepancy came to an end in the *Kirklees* case, decided in the wake of the *Francovich* ruling. There was, it was decided, no longer a need to require cross-undertakings, when damages could anyway be secured against public bodies such as local authorities (*Kirklees*, 1991; Rawlings, 1993, pp 324–330; Robertson, 1993, pp 27–30).

It has been suggested that the Sunday shopping litigation was something of a 'classic saga', an epic replete with so many different plots and sub-plots, of paramount importance and yet at times verging on the farcical. It certainly provided a vivid example of the difficulties which British courts have experienced in trying to make sense of European legal integration. More than this, as Richard Rawlings observed, it provides a similarly unedifying picture of the darker side of the common market, where 'powerful corporate interests' can use and abuse the law in order to pursue narrow economic interests (Rawlings, 1993).

The fishermen's tale

Once again, the distinguishing feature of the fishing cases, which also took place against the particular political backdrop of the early 1990s, was their ability to generate public interest. During a period of particular volatility in domestic politics, any number of minor backbenchers could be found trundling around remote Cornish fishing ports bemoaning the perfidious French and Spanish trawlermen who floated across the Channel and stole 'our' fish. The perfidy seemed to be all the more galling in that Community law appeared to condone such acts of larceny, and in so doing prevented the British government from taking measures to protect the livelihood of British fishermen.

The origin of the dispute which kept hundreds of lawyers in gainful employment for the best part of a decade could be found in the Common Fisheries Policy. This Policy, like the more famous Common Agricultural Policy, is an anomaly, a regime that is exempt from the ordinary rules of the common market. It is designed to preserve fishing stocks, whilst also balancing the relative interests of different fishing communities throughout the Community. In rather more prosaic terms, it was hoped that the Policy would encourage British, Spanish and French fisherman to desist from attacking one another on the open seas (Shackleton, 1985). It is a vast, unwieldy beast, and has long been in need of substantial reform.

EC Regulation 170/83, article 4 establishes certain fishing 'quotas'; in other words it sets limits to the amount of fish landed by vessels registered in each country. During the later part of the 1980s, the British government became increasingly suspicious that Spanish fishing vessels were being registered in the United Kingdom, and were thus fishing from the UK quota. The government's initial reaction was to impose restrictive conditions on the issue of licences for registration. This approach was duly declared unlawful by the Court of Justice in *Agegate* (*Agegate*, 1990). In response, the government then decided to revamp its entire legislation, so that the redrafted Merchant Shipping Act 1988 and the complementary Merchant Shipping (Registration of Fishing Vessels) Regulations 1988, SI 1988/1226 required that all previously registered vessels must be re-registered. Ninety-five vessels, all of which were Spanish, were unable to re-register for a licence due to the new nationality requirements written into the Regulations.

A number of Spanish companies applied, in the UK courts, for judicial review of the Secretary of State for Transport's refusal to re-register their vessels. The Divisional Court duly requested a preliminary ruling from the Court of Justice (*Factortame 2*). In the meantime, it granted interim relief and set aside the 1988 Act and Regulations. This latter decision went expressly against the orthodoxy recently restated in *Bourgoin*, that courts could not grant interim relief against public bodies or in order to provide a temporary disapplication of legislation (*Bourgoin*, 1986). Unsurprisingly, perhaps, the Court of Appeal promptly reversed the interim relief decision, at which time the Commission then intervened in order to apply for interim relief under article 234 (ex 186). The matter then passed to the House of Lords which upheld the Court of Appeal's decision to reverse the interim relief, but which also decided that it should seek a preliminary ruling on the matter from the Court of Justice (*Factortame 1*, 1990). There were, thus, two legal actions running alongside one another; one on the substantive issue in question, and one on the collateral issue of interim relief.

The Court of Justice decided the interim relief question first, albeit after 12 months, ruling that the House of Lords must grant effective relief, even though this would clearly require it to act as a court of constitutional review, at least in matters of Community law. Its judgment was based on article 10 (ex 5) EC, and the principle of supremacy established in *Costa* and *Simmenthal*. If the sole obstacle to the granting of effective relief was a national rule, then that rule must be set aside. The Court commented:

> It must be added that the full effectiveness of Community law would be just as much impaired if a rule of national law could prevent a court seised of a dispute governed by Community law from granting interim relief in order to ensure the full effectiveness of the judgment to be given on the existence of rights claimed under Community law. It follows that a court which in those circumstances would grant interim relief, if it were not for a rule of national law, is obliged to set aside that rule. (*Factortame 1*, 1991, 70.)

Amidst considerable contemporary political controversy, the House of Lords duly applied the Court of Justice's reasoning, and granted interim relief, thus disapplying the statute. In order to mask what appeared to be a naked exercise of constitutional review, Lord Bridge sought recourse to Denning's 'dualism'. He said:

> If the supremacy within the European Community of Community law over the national law of Member States was not always inherent in the EEC Treaty it was certainly well-established in the jurisprudence of the European Court of Justice long before the UK joined the Community. Thus, whatever limitations of its sovereignty Parliament accepted when it enacted the European Communities Act 1972 it was entirely voluntary. Under the terms of the Act of 1972 it has always been clear that it was the duty of a UK court, when delivering final judgment, to override any rule of national law found to be in conflict with any directly enforceable rule of Community

law. Similarly, when decisions of the Court of Justice have exposed areas of UK statute law which failed to implement Council directives, Parliament has always loyally accepted the obligation to make appropriate and prompt amendments. Thus there is nothing in any way novel in according supremacy to rules of Community law in those areas to which they apply and to insist that, in the protection of rights under Community law, national courts must not be inhibited by rules of national law from granting interim relief in appropriate cases. It is no more than a logical recognition of that supremacy. (*Factortame 1*, 1991, 107–108.)

It seemed to be so obvious, which makes it something of a shame for the Spanish companies, many of which had been reduced to the verge of bankruptcy and which now sought in a third *Factortame* action to seek damages under the *Francovich* principle for their losses during the intervening period. Unsurprisingly, their frustration was all the greater when the Court of Justice finally ruled on the original reference, on the substantive matter, and duly held that the 1988 Act was in breach of Community law, and must accordingly be disapplied (*Factortame 2*). The Court of Justice's ruling in *Factortame 3*, on the matter of damages, arrived in 1996, and provided a strong reinforcement of the *Francovich* principle. The 'right to reparation', the Court held, 'is the necessary corollary of the direct effect of the Community provision whose breach caused the damage sustained' (*Factortame 3*, 1996; Emiliou, 1996; Downes, 1997). The British taxpayer was left to foot the substantial bill.

In effect, *Factortame 3* instructed UK courts to provide damages against public bodies where appropriate, just as *Factortame 1* and 2 had required the same courts to provide both interim and permanent relief respectively. By the end of the *Factortame* saga, UK courts were clearly under an obligation to provide a full range of remedies in actions against public bodies, at least when it was shown that a Community right had been breached.[9] And it was just as clear that, in such circumstances, domestic courts do now act as courts of constitutional review. After 20 years or more, the full jurisprudential implications of

---

[9] It should be noted that the resolution of *Factortame 3* did not actually bring the entire saga to an end. There was to be both a *Factortame 4* and a *Factortame 5*, involving various collateral aspects of state liability and statutory duty, and mooting the possibility that the nature of such liability might be best described in terms of a breach of tortious duty (Downes, 1997).

accession to the European Community had finally come home to roost. Whilst some, such as Lord Bridge, revealed a residual discomfort, for others this constitutional revolution was a matter for celebration, offering the possibility of a full-scale reform of the founding principles of UK public law (Craig, 1991, pp 254–255; Wade 1991a).

Anomalous and wrong

The final step was always going to be the biggest. The time had come to do away with Lord Denning's concept of constitutional 'dualism'. The pressing nature of this step was underlined, shortly after the first two *Factortame* cases, in a famous immigration case, *Re M (Re M)*. The case, which again caught the transient attention of the wider public, involved the forced deportation of a Zairean asylum-seeker, in direct contravention of a court order. Although it was of little use to M, who had been returned to Zaire, and who had immediately disappeared to meet an unenviable fate, his legal representatives decided to mount an action against the Home Secretary alleging contempt of court, whilst also requesting interim relief and an interlocutory order for the return of M. Whilst the substantive immigration issues are not immediately relevant to us, a series of collateral comments relating to the influence of Community law, made in both the Court of Appeal and the House of Lords, most certainly are.

In the Court of Appeal, Lord Donaldson said the following:

> It is anomalous, and in my judgment wrong in principle, that whereas the law gives the courts comprehensive power to preserve rights and to 'hold the ring' pending a final decision in a dispute between citizens (including companies) or between citizens and local authorities, its powers where central government is involved are more circumscribed. It is even more anomalous that, as a result of *Factortame Ltd v Secretary of State for Transport (No 2)* . . . and the operation of European Community law, they now have comprehensive power even where central government is involved, but only in relation to rights under Community law. (*Re M*, 1992, 139.)

It is striking that Lord Donaldson should have felt moved to make this statement whilst acknowledging that it was incidental to the immediate facts of the case in question. It was, he clearly thought, a matter of 'principle' that the patent injustices brought about by the continuing faith in Denning's 'dualism' should be made starkly apparent. The two sentences in the above extract deserve closer attention. In the first sentence, Lord Donaldson finds that the inability to 'preserve' individual 'rights' against government is just plain 'wrong'. In the second sentence, he adds that the ability of courts now to do so, but only in matters of Community law, merely compounds one 'anomaly' with another. The criticism of Denning's 'dualism' may not be overt, but it is as clear as it could otherwise be (Wade, 1991b; Ward, 1994).

On appeal to the House of Lords, Donaldson's comments received the particular endorsement of Lord Woolf, who, commenting on the considerable effects of the *Factortame* case, observed that:

> The unhappy situation now exists that while a citizen is entitled to obtain injunctive relief (including interim relief) against the Crown or an officer of the Crown to protect his interests under Community law he cannot do so in respect of his other interests which may be just as important. (*Re M*, 1993, 448.)

The fact that such senior members of the British judiciary should feel compelled to criticise what is a central principle of British public law as being anomalous, wrong and unhappy warrants attention.

The immediate root of this dissatisfaction, as another senior member of the judiciary, Lord Slynn, has observed, lies in the essential incoherence of British administrative law. Community law has simply made this incoherence all the more apparent (Slynn, 1987). It has, more particularly, underlined the especial injustices that attach to the law of remedies. The core of both the Sunday trading and the *Factortame* litigation concerned the absence of effective remedies in domestic public law, an absence that had been relatively recently reaffirmed in the leading case of *O'Reilly v Mackman* (*O'Reilly*, 1982).[10] Yet, as the years have progressed, it has become ever more obvious that the anomalies must be addressed. As Francis Jacobs has recently asserted, the experience of European legal integration has reinforced the sense that a 'right to an effective remedy is a fundamental principle' of any 'developed legal system', a right that is, moreover, 'inherent in the very notion of a rule of law' (Jacobs, 1999, p 244).

---

[10] In which the House of Lords had reinforced the fact that availability of what is anyway a severely restricted range of remedies remains purely discretionary.

So we return to the essential issue, that of sovereignty. The absence of effective remedies in domestic public law is solely due to the particular reverence which British public lawyers have reserved for this particular mythology. The evolution of constitutional 'dualism' has simply sought to bolster one fiction with another. It is against this series of fictions, and the psyche which nurtures them, that Lords Donaldson and Woolf expressed their dissatisfaction. In simple terms, the incoherence of domestic administrative law is a direct cause of the absence of an established power of constitutional, as opposed to merely judicial, review.

As we noted earlier, the very idea of classical sovereignty is now barely tenable. As Neil MacCormick has concluded, the apparent ability of courts to disapply legislation 'seems to drive a wooden stake through the heart of the old constitution' and 'the doctrine of parliamentary sovereignty' (MacCormick, 1999, p vi). In similar vein, Trevor Allan has argued that the arrival of Community law undermines the credibility of any unitary conception of political or legal sovereignty (Allan, 1985, pp 619–623). Two centuries ago, the radical iconoclast Tom Paine wrote that all constitutional mythologies must, in time, be brought before the 'altar of reason' and raised up as 'burnt-offerings' to 'common sense' (Paine, 1985, pp 51–66, 81, 142–143). Never has the metaphor seemed more appropriate.

Yet, despite all the evidence to the contrary, the psyche of parliamentary sovereignty clings tenaciously to its foothold in our constitutional mindset. As Francis Jacobs and Peter Goodrich both predicted a decade ago, Britain's legal elite still seem to be somewhat bemused, if not suspicious, of Community law (Jacobs, 1992; Goodrich, 1992, pp 207, 228). As MacCormick has repeatedly urged, the future direction of British public law lies 'beyond' the classical idea of Diceyan sovereignty, just as it lies 'beyond' the nation state (MacCormick, 1993; MacCormick, 1999, pp 73–75, 95, 131–133).[11] And so, in the meantime, we are left to ponder the possibilities of a fundamental reform of UK public law, one that recognises the need to reach beyond classical ideas of sovereignty, and which will, at the same time, finally cast aside the related ambiguities brought about by Denning's 'dexterous' revolution and the various collateral injustices that have emerged under the auspices of constitutional 'dualism'.

---

[11]   We shall return to this latter thought, that the age of the nation state has reached its natural end, in the final chapters.

Back in 1987, Lord Mackenzie Stuart hazarded the thought that the *CCSU* judgment, in its ready acceptance of the principles of legitimate expectations and proportionality, laid the foundations for the emergence of a coherent administrative law, one that properly embraced the demands of European legal integration (Mackenzie Stuart, 1987, pp 416–419). A decade or more later, and we are still listening to the same kind of prophecies, and we are still waiting (Jacobs, 1999, pp 238–245; Amos, 2001; Millett, 2002). Recent case law has continued to reveal the kind of anomalies that so troubled Lord Donaldson, with courts granting one set of remedies in cases involving a breach of Community law, such as *Hedley Lomas*, and then denying the same remedies in cases which involve similar breaches in domestic law (*Hedley Lomas*, 1996). In 1998 in *Factortame 5*, Lord Woolf took the opportunity to revisit the ground he had covered five years earlier in *M*, suggesting that 'it might be right on some future occasion to re-examine' the continuing anomaly regarding the dissonance between remedies in Community and domestic law (*Factortame 5*, 1998, 469). Meanwhile the years drift past, and the anomalies remain, and so do the injustices.

A culture of rights

As we have already noted, the United Kingdom has gained the dubious reputation of being a politically 'awkward partner' in the new Europe. Moreover, the accusation has proved to be just as true of the 1990s as was of the decades before. As Andrew Duff has recently suggested, the United Kingdom has proved to be 'the single greatest obstacle to reform in the European Union' (Duff, 1998, p 38). The agonies of the Major administrations in earlier part of the decade have already been examined. The presentation of a Memorandum on the Court of Justice, intended to curtail its allegedly 'political' propensities, to the Intergovernmental Conference (IGC) in 1996, represented yet another attempt by a British government to retard the process of deeper integration (Chalmers, 2000, pp 91–94).

The most extreme Eurosceptics in the Conservative Party continued to voice a visceral distaste for such integration. The present leader of the Party, Iain Duncan Smith, went so far as to present a Bill to Parliament in 1996 which was intended to furnish domestic courts with the power to disapply the 'judgments, rules and doctrines' of the

Court of Justice. The Court, he added, was a 'political' one, and one that 'sees its role as the architect of European integration' (Chalmers, 2000, p 90). There might be something in the suggestion, as we have already seen, but the passage of such a statute would have caused jurisprudential chaos. The present Conservative Party appears to be still entranced by the prospect of such grand, if not anarchic, gestures.

The succeeding Blair government, however, which came to power in 1997, appeared to be rather different. It certainly appeared to be unique in that it represented the election of the first UK government since 1972 which claimed to be pro-European in sentiment. And to a certain extent it can, indeed, be argued that the United Kingdom's relations with the rest of Europe have been rather less fraught (Duff, 1998, pp 45–46). However, in considerable part this is due to the fact that, having witnessed the seemingly endless agonies experienced by the Conservative Party, 'New' Labour has been determined to marginalise the subject of Europe. As Hugo Young observed, 'Within a week of the election, Europe was rendered into a quotidian banality' (Young 1998), p 490). Moreover, the reason for the apparent marginalisation of European issues during the years of the Blair government may lie in a deeper, and more genuine, ambiguity, even mistrust, of Europe. Rawnsley has charted the extent of Blair's own ambivalence, noting that the man who can so merrily declare his personal ambition to be a 'leader in Europe' on one day, can, on the next, present himself to readers of *The Sun* as a latter-day St George determined to slay the 'dragon' of European integration (Rawnsley, 2000, pp 73–75).

Perhaps the most obvious example of this apparent ambiguity regarding Britain's future in Europe has been the debate, or more accurately lack of debate, surrounding the possibility of joining the single currency. As Rawnsley observes, the subject hardly dares breathe its name (Rawnsley, 2000, pp 235–236). Whilst both the 1997 and 2001 Labour Party manifestos included commitments to conduct a referendum on the subject, there has been no firmer commitment to the timing of such an event, or, more importantly perhaps, what form any question might take. Meanwhile, the government sticks religiously to the dubious argument that its own recommendation to join will be dependent upon the fulfilling of certain 'key' economic criteria. The implication, that the question of whether the United Kingdom should adopt the single currency is a purely economic one, is untenable. It is certainly economic. But it is just as much a political and constitutional question too, as Blair has himself occasionally admitted (Rawnsley, 2000, pp 73, 76–81), and as such it warrants a genuine, open and, indeed, vociferous, public debate. The latest Eurobarometer surveys, it should be noted, reveal that only 31 per cent of UK citizens express any enthusiasm for a single currency, whilst 41 per cent admit that they know little or nothing about the European Union at all.

Doctrinally, it is often suggested that there is an immediate affinity between the European experience and the notion of a political 'Third Way', something that has periodically been touted as the ideology of New Labour. In an address to the 1997 European Socialist Congress, Blair advised that the 'people's Europe' describes a 'third way', not one that is 'old left or new right, but a new centre and centre-left agenda' (Young, 1998), pp 490–491). To the extent that a 'Third Way' ideology can properly be discerned, it appears to chime with communitarian and social democratic ideas of 'rights and responsibilities', of active citizenship, perhaps even forms of deregulated and participatory politics. For 'Third Way' prophets such as Antony Giddens, the European 'model' offers an enticing example of such forms of government and politics in action, a 'prototype' for a 'life-politics' that is defined in terms of 'consensus' and effected through multi-layered, differentiated political 'spaces'. The obvious consonance here is with the related ideas of proportionality and subsidiarity (Giddens, 1998, pp 130–134, 141–142; Mullender, 2000; Ward, 2001, pp 112–140). For the moment, however, subsidiarity remains an essentially notional concept, whilst the ridicule which has more recently attached to the politics of the 'Third Way' has rather quieted its prophets.

In a broader sense, the most striking example of the apparent impact of European politics on recent domestic UK politics can be seen in the institution of a Human Rights Act in 1998. The arrival of the Act was greeted with acclaim in many quarters. 'Something is happening', Helena Kennedy opined, 'a different *Zeitgeist*, a shift in the legal tectonic.' Francesca Klug referred to a 'new spirit of the age' (Klug, 2000, pp xi, 6–7). Conor Gearty suggests that the Act represents the emergence of a new 'culture' of rights, whilst Murray Hunt, in broad agreement, refined this 'culture' to be one that is essentially communitarian rather than libertarian, a culture, in other words, that chimes with the vagueries of 'Third Way' rhetoric (Gearty, 1999, pp 169–170; Hunt, 1999, pp 89–90). The invocation of a new 'culture' of rights echoes the words of the then Home Secretary, Jack Straw, who advised the House of Commons that the Act would 'bring about the creation of a human rights culture in Britain'. In a subsequent speech, Straw sought to develop this vision in terms of a new political 'culture' founded on 'considerations of common humanity' (Klug, 2000, pp 7, 49, 66).

This might be true. Certainly, the campaign to incorporate some form of the European Convention has been a long one, and there can be little doubt that the wider project of European legal and political integration has been instrumental in securing its ultimate success (Bingham, 1993, pp 398–400; Woolf, 1995, pp 69–70; Beyleveld, 1995). Of course, the juridical distinction between the Convention and the European Union remains valid. But, as we saw in the previous chapter, it also remains fine. Indeed, it can be said that the incorporation of the Convention in UK law, in the Human Rights Act 1998, mirrors the incorporation of much of the Convention, and perhaps most importantly its spirit, in the new Union Charter of rights. If there is a new 'culture' of rights it might reasonably claim to be pan-European.

At the same time, just as we noted the critical weaknesses of the Union Charter, so too must we acknowledge similar weaknesses in the Human Rights Act. Most importantly, its potential impact is dulled by the absence of article 13 of the Convention, which provides for 'effective' remedies. The alternative notion, that judges can make 'declarations of incompatibility' and invite government to amend apparently offending legislation, is no substitute for immediately enforceable rights (Ewing, 1999, pp 84–86). Once again, the hallowed fictions of parliamentary sovereignty appear to have hamstrung the possibility of providing British citizens with a genuinely effective charter of rights. The Act is certainly not all that it might have been, and there is perhaps some truth in the suggestion that it 'excites lawyers' rather more than it is likely to empower citizens (Young, 1999, p 37).

In a sense, only time will tell as to the extent of its practical effectiveness. The Joint Select Committee Report on the possible incompatibilities that might exist between it and the Anti-Terrorism, Crime and Security Bill, drafted in the wake of the September 11 atrocities in 2001, reveals both the power and the potential weakness of the Human Rights Act. The potential can be found in the existence of the Committee Report, and its ability to state incompatibilities. The weakness lies in its ability to do nothing more (Bonner and Graham, 2002, pp 179, 181–183). So far the reaction of British courts in those cases in which breaches of the Act are alleged, reveals an inconsistency that is not dissimilar from that which afflicted initial judicial attempts to make sense of European legal integration. In *R v A*, for example, various judges in the House of Lords came to quite different opinions regarding the responsibilities demanded by section 3, which requires primary legislation to be given effect in a way that is compatible with Convention rights (*R v A*, 2001).

But even if the final statute disappoints, it would be wrong to dismiss the Act in its entirety. If nothing else, the Act does represent a considerable gesture towards a more 'European' idea of citizen rights and responsibilities. As Sir Stephen Sedley noted, in anticipation, the passage of such a statute would represent a fundamental break with Britain's particular jurisprudential tradition (Sedley, 1995, pp 386, 391). Another member of the current Bench, Sir John Laws, went further still, welcoming prospectively a statute that would redefine British public law, recognising that effective 'democracy' must be underpinned by certain 'fundamental principles'. According to Laws, the resultant 'culture' of human rights will be evolutionary, forged in the 'crucible of a life shared with others', the reflection, above all, of a 'shared morality' which defines the 'good' community (Laws, 1996, pp 624–627, 635). More recently, David Feldman has enjoined that 'if properly internalised by administrators and legislators', the Act should 'contribute to a sound ethical base for political and constitutional decision-making' (Feldman, 1999, p 171). It is, of course, a critical 'if'. But if Britain has gained little else, and is to gain little more, from the experience of European political integration, the possibility of this advance in our public philosophy at least is surely to be welcomed.

Chapter 5

The law of the market

The primary reason that the European Community exists is to make money. Denis MacShane puts it succinctly:

> Europeans can prattle on about humanist traditions as much as they like, but this will cut little ice unless there is a successful material base to European construction. (MacShane, 1995, p 26.)

Prosperous Europeans, the rationale assumes, will make peaceful and contented Europeans. Much therefore depends, not merely on the Community making money, but on it appearing to make money. Great store has been placed on the virtues of a single market, upon its establishment, and then its ultimate completion. As we shall see, the idea of a free market is one of the centrepieces of modern liberal political thought, and in a very real sense post-war Europe has been offered up to this particular ideological idol. At the same time, there is a very obvious paradox here; for the one thing that a free market seems to need is lots of legal regulation, and lots and lots of laws. Moreover, as we shall also see, at the root of this free market philosophy, is the assumption that markets are discrete entities, enjoying their own immanent rationality. But they are not; markets are political, social, even cultural phenomena, affecting our everyday lives in a multitude of ways. For this reason, this chapter must be read alongside the next, which takes a look at the other side of the coin, at those who live and work in the market.

The idea of a free market

The idea of a free market in Europe is not new. The Roman Empire operated a kind of free market. The same is true of the Hanseatic League which, though more obviously mercantilist, still operated through a series of customs agreements designed to reduce the external expenses that could hinder cross-border trade. It was, however, during the eighteenth century that the idea of a free market really took off. It seemed to represent all the highest ideals of Enlightenment political thought, of liberty and progress, the spread of ideas and the making of money. Kant's vision of a 'cosmopolitan' Europe was based on precisely this, a continent united by a common interest in free trade.

Undoubtedly, the greatest advocate of such a market was Adam Smith, whose famous *Inquiry into the Nature and Causes of the Wealth of Nations*, published in 1776, is still regarded as the founding text in classical neo-liberal economics. According to Smith, the most efficient economies are those that run themselves, with the least intervention from central government authorities, either in the form of laws and regulations, or customs and tariffs. The purpose of laws, to the extent that there should be any, must be to liberate individuals to pursue their own particular material interests. The politics of liberty coincides with the politics of efficiency.

This assertion, that people do things in order to improve their lot in the world, was at the root of Smith's utilitarian vision of human nature. Individuals, he held, invariably put their interest before that of the society within which they live. In a famous passage from the *Wealth of Nations*, he held that it 'is not from the benevolence of the butcher, the brewer, or the baker, that we expect our dinner, but from their regard to their own interest'. Accordingly, 'We address ourselves, not to their humanity but to their self-love'. A free market runs itself because it expresses everyone's desire to be free to promote their self-interest. Every 'man', he observed, 'lives by exchanging, or becomes in some measure a merchant' (Smith, 1976, 1.4.1). To this extent, a free market preserves, not just liberty, but the democratic equality of all its actors.

Smith termed this self-interest the 'invisible hand' of the market. At an extreme, of course, the *Wealth of Nations* recommended a free market utopia where every man:

as long as he does not violate the laws of justice, is left perfectly free to pursue his own interest in his own way, and to bring both his industry and capital into competition with those of any other man, or order of men. (Smith, 1976, 4.9.51.)

Elsewhere, Smith argued that 'all duties, customs, and excise should be abolished', and that 'free commerce and liberty of exchange should be allowed with all nations and for all things' (Ross, 1995, pp 318–322).[1] The reason for this concentration on removing all forms of customs and excise was the need to minimise what liberal economists term 'transaction costs'. The lower the overall costs of trade, the higher the profit, and the greater the incentive to continue production. And, so the logic continues, if production is improved, society must necessarily progress.

The neo-liberal thesis has been supported by various leading economists over the intervening two centuries. One of the most famous was John Stuart Mill, whose *Principles of Political Economy* again placed the ability to engage in a market at the centre of his broader argument in support of the principle of liberty. At the same time, however, as his later *Chapters on Socialism* also revealed, Mill was acutely aware of the social implications of a free market, and in particular of the danger that certain individuals may simply fail to compete and be left to starve to death. For their benefit, therefore, there must be a 'necessary' social 'provision'. Such provision, he added, must also be 'authoritative'. It is a responsibility of liberal government. It is for this reason that the Community, like each of its member states, legislates for precisely such provision, even if it appears to be rather begrudging in the process. Free markets, Mill conceded, are never entirely free, and nor should they be (Mill, 1994, pp 59–65, 311–316, 363–365).

This latter reality was, of course, well understood by Karl Marx, whose *Capital* remains perhaps the ultimate critique of liberal economics. According to Marx, the idea of the free market actually alienates individuals, setting them against each other in an orgy of self-interested destruction. We shall return to Marx in the next chapter, when we explore the rationale that lies behind the provision of social laws. It was, however, the particular fear of Marxism that nourished neo-liberal economics for much of the rest of the twentieth

---

[1]   An observation that carries a certain irony, given that Smith ended his working life drawing a salary as a government customs officer.

century, and more particularly, perhaps, during those immediate post-war decades in which the European 'common market' came into being.

Friedrich von Hayek, one of the most influential of these neo-liberal economists, specifically wrote against the incipient 'slavery' of Marxism. Following the intellectual path beaten out by Smith and Mill, for Hayek the free market was essential, not merely because it might promote wealth, but because it preserved liberty. In his famous *Road to Serfdom*, Hayek opined that the reality of free market 'dispenses with the need for social control' (Hayek, 1962, pp 27–29). The 'fight' against the 'myth' of socialism, as he confirmed elsewhere, is the fight against the 'closed society', and is the 'last battle against arbitrary power' (Hayek, 1992, 2.62–96, 3.1–18, 43–60). In a very real sense the case for a European 'common market' was made within this particular, and particularly zealous, intellectual context.

At the end of the day, however, despite the undoubted intellectual ascendancy of the neo-liberal free marketers for much of the twentieth century, Mill's prophesy remains valid. A free market can never be completely free. Contemporary 'law and economics' scholars, such as Richard Posner, readily concede that a free market needs an array of laws in order to preserve the freedom it cherishes. Whilst laws might create 'transaction costs' of their own, the presence of such legal regulation is necessary in order to counter the various tendencies that markets inhere to hinder trade and create monopoly positions that actually close off 'open' markets (Posner, 1986). The experience of the European 'common market', as we shall shortly see, provides compelling evidence in support of this argument. Rarely has a market that has so championed its freedom, appeared to be so dependent upon such an array of laws.

Free markets, then, need legal regulation in order to survive. And they need it for another reason too, as we shall see in the next chapter. For every liberal community must also take the responsibility for securing, not merely the liberty of all, but also the equality of all, and with it the happiness of all and, more prosaically, the necessary capacity to survive. Although Hayekian economics would experience a revival during the 1980s, translated into 'Reaganomics' across the Atlantic, and lionised by Margaret Thatcher in the United Kingdom, the more extreme variants of the neo-liberal political vision are no

longer taken so seriously. By the end of the century, as the prominent
Nobel economist, John Kenneth Galbraith, commented, the idea of
an unregulated free market was 'leading an increasingly esoteric existence, if indeed, any existence at all' (Galbraith, 1991, p 260).
Galbraith's conclusion provides an intriguing context for any examination of the European single market.

The single market project

The economic reconstruction of Europe was a priority in 1946, and
the idea of some kind of 'common' market, whether it be a customs
union or something altogether grander, rapidly gained its adherents.
Moreover, whilst the desire to provide some kind of social framework
should not be ignored, it is striking that the first President of the
Commission, Walter Hallstein, should assert that the market would
'walk in the spirit of Adam Smith'. At the same time, it must also be
recognised that whilst the rhetoric might be one of open borders, the
reality was rather more prosaic. As Alan Milward has emphasised,
the common market was created in order to service its member nation
states (Milward, 1992, pp 21–43). Ideology has repeatedly given way
to political expedience, and it is for this reason that the history of the
market gives the appearance of 'fits and starts' (Tsoukalis, 1991, pp
2–4). It was Hallstein, once again, who observed, 'we are not in business at all – we are in politics (Holland, 1980, p 3).

The free market lay at the centre of the Treaty of Rome. The sentiments which lay behind it can still be found in article 2, which waxes
lyrically about the need for the Community to 'promote' a 'harmonious, balanced and sustainable development of economic activities',
as well as 'a high degree of competitiveness and convergence of economic performance', and article 14 (ex 7a) which affirms that the

> internal market shall comprise an area without internal frontiers
> in which the free movement of goods, persons, services and cap-
> ital is ensured in accordance with the provisions of this Treaty.

These four 'freedoms' are the heartbeat of the common market, and
have been the subject of considerable legal reinforcement. Much of the
rest of the Treaty was devoted to fleshing out further the nature of the
market, and its 'freedoms'. Articles 23–31, or Title I of the Community
Treaty, describe the free movement of goods, including the remnants of

the original Customs Union enacted in the Rome Treaty, whilst articles 39–60, presently comprising Title III, establish the primary legislation for the free movement of persons, services and capital.

Although there was, and still is, a considerable legal framework, in reality much was left, in 1958, to 'market mechanisms'. It was thought that the market would largely complete itself (Swann, 1992, pp 9–10). Neo-liberal economics certainly suggested that it should. The twelve-year 'transitional' period stated in the Treaty, however, proved disappointing. By 1970, the market was barely any nearer to completion that it had been in 1958. To a considerable extent this was due to the fact that the nation states continued to operate in largely autonomous units (Lavigne, 1995, pp 98–99). A stark example of this attitude was evidenced by President de Gaulle's liberal use of the Luxembourg 'accords' in order to veto any collective measure that might threaten to damage the French national interest. The stagnation that continued to beset the Community through much of the 1970s can be laid at precisely the same door.

Throughout this period, extending to the late 1970s, it can fairly be said that Community policy was somewhat schizophrenic. Whilst the Community talked the language of free markets, and vigorously engaged in the emerging global markets, the order of the day within remained firmly regulatory, and determined by national interests. In the words of one commentator, it was very much a case of 'Keynes at home, and Smith abroad' (Gilpin, 1987, p 355). The problem with this approach became ever more apparent. Not only was the common market failing to create extra wealth, but so too was it polarising existing wealth. The richer nations were getting richer, the poor, poorer. In the face of this 'wealth diversion', the need to genuinely open up the market became increasingly urgent (Tovias, 1994).

The Hague summit in 1969 called for precisely this, introducing at the same time, not merely a refined budget or 'own resources' programme, but also the idea that the market might be most effectively 'completed' with the aid of 'economic monetary union'. Any exuberance which flowed from this initiative was, however, quickly crushed by the oil crisis of 1973, and the resultant global recession. Europe was trapped in a cycle of 'stagflation', of alternating periods of inflation and stagnation (Aldcroft, 1993, pp 195–204). It was not to emerge for nearly a decade. By the middle of the 1970s, average unemployment in certain areas of the Community exceeded 20 per cent (Tsoukalis, 1991, pp 34–56). Some still advised the need to press on with liberating the market. Others were suddenly rather less enthusiastic. Monetary union was off the agenda, at least for a while. In its place emerged a limited system of currency exchange parameters, something we will revisit later in this chapter.

The nation states, as ever in periods of economic crisis, went their own way, with Germany and the Benelux countries adopting strong anti-inflationary tactics, whilst France and the United Kingdom preferred the monetarist solution of curtailing the flow of money. What was clearly missing was any Community-wide macroeconomic initiative.[2] In the meantime much of the Community's energies, and particularly those of the Court of Justice, were engaged in trying to counter the many and various forms of 'non-tariff' barriers which the nation states were deploying as a means of protecting their individual economies against one another. Such barriers, as we shall shortly see, commonly took the form of technical standards or forms of indirect taxation. In 1981, the Commissioner for Industry, Etienne Davignon, asserted that the 'industrial activism' of the member states had 'become a veritable challenge to the Community' (Tsoukalis, 1991, p 39).

As the recession bit ever deeper, the Community's economists peered ever closer at their slide rules. Much attention was paid to 'trade diversion'. Even more was paid to the potential benefits of forcing the completion of the market (Kemp and Wan, 1976, pp 95–70). Some began to wonder whether free markets actually create wealth at all. Everyone bemoaned the apparently irreversible rise and rise of monopolies (Tovias, 1994, pp 65–67). Others argued the case for macroeconomic management. In perhaps the most strident critique of the common market, Stuart Holland argued that the very idea of a free market and its 'invisible hand' was a fallacy. Markets need both political impetus and economic regulation, otherwise they will never benefit from the necessary harmony of capital and labour interests. The real failure of the common market, Holland concluded, lay in the

---

2   As Tsoukalis observes, the 'nation states behaved as autonomous political units, and the dialectic of economic, political, and social forces differed considerably from one to another. Under such circumstances, monetary union became a totally unfeasible objective. In complete contrast to their verbal commitments, individual member countries showed hardly any interest in using the EC as a framework for an effective co-ordination of macroeconomic policies' (Tsoukalis, 1991, pp 35–36).

Treaty itself, in its faith in market 'mechanisms', and its concomitant failure to give explicit political objectives, and, above all, in its failure to protect itself against voracious multi-nationals that seek to establish monopoly positions (Holland, 1980, pp 49–82). There was more than a scent of Marxism, and truth, in his conclusion that:

> The failure of economic union and positive integration, in this sense, is not merely an accident of botched institutions or a failure of will in leadership elites. It reflects the basic dominance of economics over politics in a capitalist system, and the key interest of a capitalist class in maintaining its prerogatives over the rest of us. (Holland, 1980, p 113.)

But then everything appeared to change. Suddenly everyone began to hope again. This reversal of mood, during the second half of the 1980s, has been described as 'absolutely remarkable' (Tsoukalis, 1991, p 43). In one sense the reason for this reversal lay in the sheer depth of despair itself. The economic condition of the Community had reached a critical point. Between 1973 and 1985, its global market share of manufacturing goods had fallen from 45 to 30 per cent, whilst between 1979 and 1985, its industries had experienced a mere 3 per cent growth in demand, in comparison with Japan where the figure was closer to 17 per cent. Productivity was chronically low, and import penetration in certain areas, such as information technology, had increased by over a third (Wise and Gibb, 1993, pp 50–56).[3] Something had to be done, even if it meant overriding the interests of individual nation states. Even the nation states realised as much.

A pivotal moment came at the 1984 Fontainebleau Council, when it was agreed that the Commission should draw up a fresh programme for the radical reform of the market. The result, as we have already noted, was the Cockfield Report, entitled *Completing the Internal Market*. The ambition of the Report can be gleaned from its concluding observations:

> Europe now stands at the crossroads. We either go ahead – with resolution and determination – or we drop back into mediocrity. We can now either resolve to complete the integration of

---

[3]   The Commission was particularly fearful of falling behind in the area of information technology, and responded by creating a flurry of projects, such as EUREKA and ESPRIT.

the economies of Europe; or through a lack of political will to face the immense problems involved, we can simply allow Europe to develop into no more than a free trade area. (Cockfield, 1990, pp 4–5.)

The final observation attested to an ambition that had progressed considerably further than that articulated in 1958.

The primary recommendations of the Report concerned the abolition of remaining barriers to trade.[4] Three types of 'non-tariff' barrier were noted: physical barriers, such as import quotas for non-EC goods, licensing, inspections and notional 'safety' checks at national borders, in all costing around 8m ECU a year; technical barriers, of which around 100,000 were still in operation; and fiscal barriers, providing for all kinds of disparate tax regimes, and more importantly tax disincentives operating against imports (Tsoukalis, 1991, pp 68–74; Wise and Gibb, 1993, pp 70–89). The specific recommendations advised the removal of all frontier controls, the purging of remaining controls on the passage of capital, the reassessment of public procurement provisions, and the extension of a principle of 'mutual recognition' in technical and other specifications.[5] The striking absence was the lack of proposals regarding tax harmonisation, the most obvious way of addressing fiscal barriers. Tax harmonisation remains the hottest of political potatoes.

The Cockfield Report was accepted with great enthusiasm by the Delors Commission. As we have already noted, the Single European Act of 1986 incorporated the vast majority of its 279 recommendations, and by 1992, 90 per cent of the Report had been enacted in secondary legislation (Pinder, 1993, p 59). But, it was the provision of the 'magic number', of 1992, which was the stroke of real genius (Whynes, 1995, p 69). As perhaps the 'most successful marketing campaign of the decade' it served to concentrate everyone's attention (Kay, 1989, p 28).[6] And, most importantly, the Single European Act appeared to work. An upsurge in investment, together with a massive

---

[4]   A testament, as Tsoukalis observes, 'to the omnipotence of the State' in European economics (Tsoukalis, 1991, p 68).

[5]   As opposed to harmonisation of specifications.

[6]   As Wise and Gibb observed, the 1992 Project created a 'vision' which was designed to inspire the necessarily 'vast political commitment' of Europe and its citizenry (Wise and Gibb, 1993, p 97).

restructuring of manufacturing and goods, resulted in a compound growth rate of an average 4 per cent per annum. Unemployment fell. The Commission redoubled its efforts to deal with the vexed problem of monopolies, whilst the Court of Justice embarked upon an even more rigorous enforcement of the free movement provisions. The paradox was evident. The market became more and more regulated, as its various barriers appeared to fall (Campbell et al, 1990, pp 138–139).

The Cockfield Report and the apparent 'completion' of the market in 1992, was not universally applauded. Suspicions were exacerbated when, as we noted earlier, it was discovered that the financial gains projected by the Cecchini Report, commissioned in 1988 to provide a complementary account, and which airily hazarded the figure of around 200bn Euro, were at best amateurish, and at worst down right fictitious (Pinder, 1993, pp 60–65; McDonald, 1995, pp 150–152; Wise and Gibb, 1993, pp 119–124). Some feared that the entire 1992 'Project' was rather more delusion than vision. Stephen George suspected that it was merely another mask for 'national interests', and he was not alone (George, 1991, p 162; Kastendiek, 1990, pp 82–84; Milward and Soerensen, 1993, pp 27–28; Story, 1990, pp 50–60). Socialist critics continued to flay a Community that was so ready to regulate the market in order to promote competition, but so reluctant to do so in order to protect social interests (Jacobi, 1990, pp 24–25).

For now, however, regardless of its social, and indeed moral, short-comings, we are told that the single market has been completed. And in its place comes a new aspiration, stated in article 2 TEU, to secure and 'promote economic and social progress . . .' through 'the estab-lishment of economic and monetary union, ultimately through a single currency'. It is this ambition that has emerged as the new totem for further European integration, and it is this ambition that is still with us. We shall return to it in the final part of this chapter.

The free movement of goods

In many ways, the free movement of goods is the heartbeat of Community law. Far more of the original Rome Treaty was devoted to it than to the free movement of anything else, and although we shall consider each of the other free movement 'rights' in due course, it is entirely appropriate that we should embark upon our examination of the substantive law of the market with this fundamental Community 'right'. The founding provision is article 23 (ex 9) which states that:

> The Community shall be based upon a customs union which shall cover all trade in goods and which shall involve the prohibition between Member States of customs duties on imports and exports and of all charges having equivalent effect, and the adoption of a common customs tariff in their relation with third countries.

The sentiment of article 23 is then fleshed out in two further sets of articles; one set relating to the establishment of a 'customs union', and the other set devoted to the 'prohibition of quantitative restrictions between member states'. We shall consider each in turn.

The establishment of a 'customs union', in articles 25–27, speaks the language of post-war Europe. In a very real sense, it describes the original purpose of the Community. The importance of this 'fundamental principle', of free trade without barriers, was clearly stated in cases such as *Ramel*, and has been repeatedly reaffirmed since (*Ramel*, 1978). There is little that is controversial here. However, in its prohibition of all 'duties on imports and exports and charges having equivalent effect', article 25 then opens up a particularly contentious area.

The early case law, most particularly two cases involving Italian government bodies, emphasised that the Court of Justice would take a rigorous approach to dealing with such 'effects'. In the first case, despite recognising that the tax in question might be commendable in terms of its purpose, the Court of Justice struck down a duty intended to deter the export of cultural artefacts (*Italy*, 1968). In the second case, a tax intended to fund the study of trade patterns met a similar fate. Once again, the Court affirmed that it was the 'effect' of the tax that mattered, not the purpose (*Italy*, 1969). It was clear from these two cases that the Court of Justice intended to take the most uncompromising approach when faced with any apparent attempt to hinder internal trade, no matter what the purported reason.

Case law relating to other types of charge having 'equivalent effect' is equally rigorous. In yet another Italian case, *Bresciani*, the Court of

Justice struck down charges intended to fund veterinary inspections of imported animal carcases (*Bresciani*, 1976). This particular issue has become ever more controversial throughout the 1980s and 1990s, particularly in the wake of the BSE crisis. The need to monitor the condition of animals transported across the Community has also become a common subject of animal welfare group campaigns. But whilst charges might be made for inspections required by Community law, the Court has steadfastly refused to permit any charges sought by individual nation states (*Germany*, 1988). As ever, the interests of the market override all else.

The article 25 jurisprudence should be read alongside the case law relating to article 90 (ex 95) which reinforces, in section 1, the prohibition of 'internal taxation of any kind in excess of that imposed directly or indirectly on similar domestic products', and in section 2, a similar prohibition against taxation intended to 'afford indirect protection to other', meaning dissimilar, 'products'. And, once again, the Court of Justice has done its utmost to take the widest interpretive approach to article 90. Thus, with regard to taxes on 'similar' goods, it has struck down examples of direct discrimination in cases such as *Hansen*, which involved the provision of tax relief to home producers of spirits, and also indirect discrimination in cases such as *Humblot*, where the French government had devised a scheme of vehicle excise which could only benefit French car manufacturers (*Hansen*, 1978; *Humblot*, 1985).

With regard to 'other' products it has been just as uncompromising, striking down, in the 1980 *France* case, a differential French tax on spirits which had the 'effect' of benefiting those, generally French, spirits manufactured from fruit rather than grain. Although it might be thought that fruit and grain based spirits were materially different in composition, the Court had little difficulty in holding that their intended market was 'common' (*France*, 1980). The same approach was taken in the *UK* case, where the Court was just as happy establishing a 'competitive relation' between wines and beers, and so struck down a tax regime that disadvantaged the former. It was not the kind of alcohol that mattered, the Court opined, but its 'strength' (*UK*, 1983). The 'common' market that the Court established is, it seems, defined rather less by the connoisseur than by the alcoholic.

It might be thought that such was the vigour of the Court's approach in these article 25 and article 90 cases that the nation states would be cowed. But the reality proved to be rather different. All kinds of non-tariff barriers have been employed in the attempt to benefit national producers and present some kind of deterrent against imports. As we noted before, the Cockfield Report noted that nearly 300 of these kinds of barriers were still in operation 30 years after the 'customs union' was originally established. Most have now been exorcised, laid to rest by the 'completion' of the single market. But the case law remains significant, not least because it includes two of the seminal examples of judicial activism in Community jurisprudence: *Dassonville* and *Cassis de Dijon* (*Dassonville*, 1974; *Cassis de Dijon*, 1979).

Both these cases sought to flesh out the second set of articles relating to the free movement of the goods, those prohibiting 'quantitative restrictions between member states'. The ambit of this injunction was fleshed out in article 28 (ex 30) which prohibited both 'quantitative restrictions on imports' and 'all measures having equivalent effect'. The former prohibition is fairly straightforward, defined in cases such as *Geddo*, as measures which 'amount to a total or partial restraint' of 'imports, exports, or goods in transit' (*Geddo*, 1974). The difficulties arose from the second clause, and the attempt to work out what such 'measures' might be and what 'equivalent effect' meant in practice.

The defining case, here, was *Dassonville*, in which the Court of Justice held that:

> All trading rules enacted by Member States which are capable of hindering directly or indirectly, actually or potentially, intra-Community trade are to be considered as measures having equivalent effect to quantitative restrictions. (*Dassonville*, 1974.)

It was, self-evidently, an expansive ruling, and wholly in line with the Court's generally strident approach to defending the principles of free movement in the market. This extent of this vigour was evidenced in a number of ensuing cases, including the *Ireland* case, in which the Court held that a government sponsored 'buy Irish' campaign could be deemed to be a 'measure' capable of 'hindering' trade, and the *UK* case, in which a similar fate befell the government's attempt to require goods to register national or regional origin (*Ireland*, 1982; *UK*, 1985).

The matter, however, was far from settled. Whilst the Court had no difficulty in applying the *Dassonville* 'principle' in a series of cases relating to such clear examples of 'direct' discrimination, alleged examples of 'indirect' discrimination, where 'measures' might be 'indistinctly applicable', were altogether more awkward. Here the Court was faced with rules that appeared to apply equally to domestic and imported goods, but which nevertheless created a considerable barrier to trade. The classic example was provided in the *Cassis de Dijon* case, where the German authorities had refused to permit the importation of a particular French liquor on the grounds, rather oddly perhaps, that its alcoholic strength was insufficient (*Cassis de Dijon*, 1979). Under German law such liquors, whether or not imported, were required to have an alcohol content of 25 per cent or more. The strength of Cassis de Dijon is considerably less. It was claimed that such laws were actually intended to prevent a proliferation of alcoholic drinks, and could be defended on the grounds of public health and policy.

Of course, article 30 (ex 36) had always provided member states with a measure of control insofar as they could prohibit the transit of goods on the 'grounds of public morality, public policy and public security', as well as protect 'national treasures' and so forth. But this has proved to be a relatively uncontroversial area of law, with the Court duly refraining, wherever possible, from interfering with the resolution of national courts in their particular interpretation of these 'grounds' (*Henn and Darby*, 1979; *Sandoz*, 1983). The Court was not, however, impressed by the invocation of these 'grounds' in the *Cassis* case. It held that such laws were acceptable only if they satisfied certain 'mandatory requirements' relating to the protection of health, the fairness of commercial transactions and consumer interest, and were anyway sufficiently 'significant'. Otherwise, the Court would enforce a principle of 'equivalence', or mutual recognition, of standards. What counts as alcoholic in one member state should, prima facie, count as alcoholic in another. It further added that any such 'requirements' must be proportionate, and that it would operate a 'rule of reason' in order to form its judgments.

It all added up to a formidable hurdle, and the *Cassis* ruling is often taken to represent something of a high-water mark in the Court's creative capacity to interpret Treaty articles in order to secure the underlying ideology of the free market. Its introduction of a principle of 'equivalence', together with its application of proportionality, in order to defeat spurious attempts to use countervailing Treaty articles in order to promote national economic interests, has been termed 'heroic'. It coincided, of course, with a period in the Community's history where the Court clearly felt impelled to promote market integration despite, or perhaps because of, the inability of politicians to take on that responsibility (Alter and Meunier-Aitsahalia, 1994, pp 535–570; Weatherill, 1999, pp 82–84).

However, with the apparent success of the 1992 'Project' and the 'completion' of the market, it has been suggested that the Court has since preferred to take a more reserved approach. The case which is invariably cited as the seminal example of this judicial reticence is *Keck* (*Keck*, 1993). In this case, decided in 1993, it appeared that the Court was determined to redefine the extent of its *Cassis* judgment, and to recast the ambit of article 28. At the same time, it was becoming ever more apparent that member states were unhappy at the impact of such an expansive ruling, one that seemed to extend article 28 to all kinds of rules that were never intended to 'hinder' trade. Of course, in forging its jurisprudence relating to the free market of goods, the Court had always looked to 'effect' rather than intention. Its apparent willingness to resile, if not from the principle itself, from the primary responsibility of monitoring it from case to case, was significant.

An early case which, in hindsight, seemed to prepare the ground was *Cinetheque*, in which the Court accepted a ban on the sale of videos in France during the first year of the film's release. Although this was a hindrance to trade, and might distinguish against certain other member states' video industries, the measures was not 'intended' to fall within article 28 and were anyway 'proportionate' (*Cinetheque*, 1985). This invocation of proportionality was also invoked, as we recall, in the Sunday trading cases in the United Kingdom. It is, perhaps, the great virtue of principles as fluid as proportionality that, applied on a case by case basis, they can admit a degree of interpretive subtlety consonant with the immediate political and economic context.

In *Keck*, however, the Court seemed to be altogether more brazen in its determination to be reticent (*Keck*, 1993). In this case, it was suggested that a provision in French law prohibiting traders from selling stock at a loss was in breach of article 28, as it might restrict the quantity of goods traded. The Court held that such a 'selling arrangement', whilst it might indeed restrict trade, was never intended to fall under article 28. It could have simply decided the case on the application of proportionality. But it chose not to, instead admitting the need for a fundamental review of article 28 jurisprudence. Henceforth, the Court held, such rules that affect all traders and inflict an 'equal burden' should be taken as falling outside article 28.

And most importantly, it determined that the burden of proof must be shifted. Where, in cases such as *Cassis* and even *Cinetheque*, the onus had lain with member states to justify the presence of indistinctly applicable 'measures having equivalent effect', now, following *Keck*, that responsibility lies with the complainant, both to prove that the measures do indeed have an 'equivalent effect', and also that they have that effect in practice. In doing so, it reduced the possible application of the *Dassonville* principle to article 28 cases, removing the 'potential' from the test of 'actual or potential' interference with trade. The complainant must be able to provide evidence of hindrance 'in fact'. To a certain extent such a resolution still chimed with the principle of adjudging 'effect', not 'purpose'. But the mood of the Court implied rather more.

The so-called *Keck* 'revolution' has led to a vigorous debate regarding the role of the Court in the creation of the free movement of goods law, and its possible limits (Chalmers, 1994; Weatherill, 1996; Oliver, 1999, pp 793–799). As we noted before, the Court has long laboured under accusations of unwarranted judicial activism in the area of forging general principles of public law. And whilst the relatively esoteric nature of the article 28 jurisprudence has shielded the Court from a comparable degree of public scrutiny, similar arguments regarding the Court's role in the wider area of free movement law has attracted critical commentary. The idea that the Court has, post-*Keck*, focused more on consolidation than on integration certainly chimes with the broader mood in the Union in the lead up to the Amsterdam and Nice Treaties (Chalmers, 1994, pp 401–403). Stephen Weatherill has recently affirmed that the history of free movement of goods case law during the 1990s was essentially one of deregulation. It is certainly true that cases such as *Clinique* and *Mars* reinforce the sense that post-*Keck* the Court is increasingly willing to allow national judiciaries to wrestle with the countervailing demands of public and Community interest (*Clinique*, 1994; *Mars*, 1995; Weatherill, 1996, pp

896–897, 904–906; Weatherill, 1999). It seems that the responsibility for judging how free the free market should be, and more particularly how free the free movement of goods should be, is passing.

The albatross of agriculture

Articles 32–38 provide for a Common Agricultural Policy (CAP), stating, rather prosaically, that it extends to all the various 'products of the soil, of stockfarming and of fisheries'. Its 'objectives' are stated in article 33, and include the increase of 'agricultural productivity', the security of 'supplies' of food, the control of prices and the need to 'ensure the standard of living for the agricultural community'. These provisions describe the three pillars of the CAP, market unity, Community preference and financial solidarity. Very obviously, the sentiments expressed in article 33 made rather more sense in 1958 than they do now. Today there is plenty of reasonably cheap food. The reason that the CAP remains is found in the latter of these objectives: the need, in short, for certain member states to pander to one particular political constituency.

The rest of the provisions in the CAP Title relate to the establishment of 'agricultural markets', including provisions for the proper regulation of prices, state aids and control of trade flows. Two of the more contentious articles, 44 and 45, have now been repealed. Article 44 sought to define pricing policy, permitting national governments to fix prices, thereby subsidising farmers against the market, and necessarily against the consumer. Article 45 permitted individual 'contracts' between member states to limit trade in certain products, thereby creating a shortage or at least a limitation on the availability of a certain product, which would, in time, lead to the raising of prices.

The very existence of a special regime relating to agriculture has been a bone of enormous contention since the very inception of the Community. It was, of course, based on the myth of the 'blooming peasant' so beloved of President de Gaulle. As a result, the farmer became a protected species, kept in a permanently rarefied economic atmosphere. The myth of the 'blooming peasant' aligned with another, particularly beloved of Monnet, that the essence of the European idea could be found in its agriculture. Ultimately, however, it was vested interests that really counted. The CAP was created in deference to the particular national interests of France, and to a lesser degree, the Netherlands, and its presence as Alan Milward has noted, remains a testimony to the original conception of a common market as a mechanism for defending the European nation state in the midst of dire economic straits post-1945. The CAP has continued, Milward concludes:

> like some clumsy prehistoric mastodon, incapable of evolution into the present world where the political influence of agriculture on parliamentary systems is small indeed, an awesome reminder of the strength which integration could add to the rescue of the nation state. (Milward, 1992, 317.)

It became ever more obvious, as one decade passed to another, that the CAP was a huge economic drain, as well as the cause of considerable resentment on the part of certain member states who felt disadvantaged by the particular financial support given, in effect, to certain other member states. The CAP has done little, either, for the wider reputation of the Community. The butter mountains and wine lakes of popular imagination have been superseded by squabbles over fishing quotas, of the kind we encountered in the last chapter when we examined the *Factortame* saga.

As Tsoukalis observes, it was clear as early as the late 1960s that the CAP had been 'transformed into an albatross hanging from the neck of an embattled Community' (Tsoukalis, 1991, p 40). For much of the last half century, the CAP has swallowed up between 70 and 80 per cent of the Community's budget. The first attempt at serious reform of the CAP was the Mansholt Plan in 1968. According to Mansholt, the CAP had reached the 'end of the road':

> Dairies churn out subsidised butter regardless of market needs; no one worries about packing the stuff, because no matter whether it is bought, stored, sold cheaply or destroyed, the producer gets the guaranteed price. At the same time, the Member States spend their money to nobody's advantage on farms so small as to condemn their occupants to constant want. (Weigall and Stirk, 1992, pp 136–137.)

Financing 'farms with five cows', Mansholt concluded, 'is tantamount to financing chronic destitution'. The Plan thus proposed a new system of co-operative farming, and retraining programmes. Eighty-thousand farmers blocked Brussels for a week, and the Plan was dropped. Nothing, as Fiona Butler observed, better revealed the enduring power of 'strong economic and political constituencies of interest' than the demise of the Mansholt Plan (Butler, 1993, pp 114–115).

The problems did not, however, go away. The United Kingdom made reform of the CAP a primary reason for its obstructionism during the1980s, whilst the EU's steadfast refusal to donate its surpluses as 'gift aid' to Africa at the same time, for fear of disrupting world 'trade flows' in cereals, left a sour taste in the mouth. Writing in 1987, Brian Gardner voiced a general frustration, referring to a continuing and 'unwritten, but none the less effective conspiracy of the agricultural constituency against the consumer and taxpayer'. It was a conspiracy, moreover, that seemed to be 'dedicated to neutralising any initiative aimed at improvement or even reform of policy' (Gardner, 1987, p 169). Aside from the matter of economic expense and efficiencies, the overriding problem with the CAP is one of principle. There is no reason, outside political expediency, why one area of the market should be protected. Moreover, there is no reason why the expense of protecting one area should, of necessity, be passed on to other areas. The specially protected regime of the CAP is funded by all the other unprotected regimes in the common market.

The combined weight of the arguments from efficiency and from principle led to renewed calls for reform during the 1990s. The Commission was particularly concerned that the anomaly of the CAP would appear to be even starker in a 'completed' market. Confirming that the 'status quo cannot even be defended or maintained', the 1992 MacSharry proposals once again recommended the need for 'root and branch' reform, not least because the United States had refused to sign off the Uruguay 'round' of the General Agreement on Tariffs and Trade (GATT) until there was reform of the European CAP (Butler, 1993, p 17; Daugbjerg, 1999, pp 408–409, 418–119).[7]

At the centre of the MacSharry proposals were three mooted reforms; an intensification of price-stabilisers, a reduction of milk quotas and,

---

[7]   The intention of the the General Agreement on Tariffs and Trade (GATT) was to collect a series of agreements regarding tariffs which could operate at a global level. It has now been superseded by the World Trade Organisation (WTO). We will revisit GATT and the WTO in chapter 7.

most importantly, a series of 'accompanying measures', which included 'set-asides' and retirement schemes. As Carsten Daugbjerg observes, these reforms were, in truth, hardly radical. Yet, once again, vested interests consigned much of the MacSharry proposals to the shredder (Daugbjerg, 1999, pp 415–416). The Parliamentary Committee on Agriculture concluded that the Report had 'overestimated' the 'adaptability' of the farming industry. Sadly, the conclusion was probably justified. The Council demanded that the proposals be 'watered down'. In effect, the Council was presented with a severely modified series of proposals, with limited price reductions in the contentious areas of cereals and milk and a very much more expensive system of compensation (Butler, 1993, pp 119–122; Colman and Roberts, 1994, pp 116–117).

The events of the 1990s, however, continued to reinforce the sense that something must be done. Throughout the late 1980s, the CAP budget had increased by over 18 per cent. Cereal intervention stock continued to rise, reaching 29m tonnes by the middle of the 1990s (Ackrill, 1995, pp 213–214). The particular protected currency of the CAP, the 'green' ECU, originally designed to facilitate the provision of 'monetary compensation amounts', or grants to farmers for setting aside land or reducing production, struggled to survive (Colman and Roberts, 1994, pp 96–98). The consumer, meanwhile, picked up an ever more exacting bill. The BSE scare, which provided a number of member states with the excuse to ban British livestock products, and thereby bolster their own industries, further revealed the capacity for self-interest that lay at the heart of the CAP. Finally, in 1997 at the Amsterdam Council, the first significant steps were taken with the repeal of articles 44 and 45, and with them the statutory conditions for pricing policy. The Union was left to ponder precisely what really remained of a Policy that had been stripped of its most important, and most controversial, facet.

The repeal of articles 44 and 45 also removed much of the most important case law regarding the CAP, the critical weight of which had been developed in response to pricing policies developed by certain member states that were alleged to be in breach of Policy provisions. One of the most striking features of the CAP, however, is the relative paucity of legal actions in comparison with other areas of the market. Aside from those that flowed from pricing policy, the more remarkable cases, of which *Bela-Muehle* is the most famous example, are those that reinforce the sense of inter-institutional conflict, and the need somehow to maintain a balance between vested interests. In *Bela-Muehle*, the Court was asked to adjudicate between a Commission that wanted to limit milk surpluses, and a Council, fired by nation state interests, that was reluctant to support any such reforms. It is significant that the Court, which in other areas of the market has been so keen to support the Commission, on this instance came down on the side of the Council (*Bela-Muehle*, 1977; Snyder, 1985, p 56). It is equally significant that the Court has felt no particular compunction to support the interests of the consumer against the vast agricultural cartel that is the CAP. In cases such as *Germany* and *Balkan*, it has consistently defended higher prices if they are 'reasonable' within the context of the Policy as a whole (*Germany*, 1963; *Balkan*, 1973).

The Commission's *Agenda 2000* paper readily admitted that the diluted McSharry reforms were wholly inadequate, and recommended their 'deepening and extending'. It further noted two particular reasons which make the need for further reform compelling. First, there is the Union's position in the wider global market, and secondly there is impending enlargement. Accordingly it suggested further price decreases, together with greater reliance on direct payments to farmers in the current 15 member states. There is sense in the proposals, even if they follow the now established, and decidedly hoary, tradition of paying farmers to produce less and less (Daugbjerg, 1999, pp 424–425; McMahon, 2002, pp 16–17). Needless to say the Commission's proposals were again watered down by the Council at the end of 1999. But the Report remains, as Joseph McMahon concludes, an 'important milestone' in the reform of the CAP (McMahon, 2002, p 19). Or so everyone hopes.

Regulating competition

In some ways, the idea of competition is the purest element of the free market ideology. The neoclassical ideal of 'perfect competition' described a position of equilibrium which confirmed the optimal allocation of resources in any active market. For this reason, of course, the existence of competition law is something of a perversity. However, the need for some degree of regulation has been understood since the very inception of the European common market. Half a century ago, Walter Hallstein spoke of the need for 'regulated competition' (Tsoukalis, 1991, p 16). Economists today readily concede that the practicalities of 'workable' competition, as opposed to the idylls of 'perfect' competition, make law, not merely necessary, but desirable (Young and Metcalfe, 1994).[8]

There are generally recognised to be three forms of uncompetitive behaviour: monopolies; positions of 'dominance', which usually relate to forms of price control; and mergers. All threaten to 'close' open markets. Critics of capitalism have seized on these forms of market 'distortion' as evidence of an innate disequilibrium in free market ideology. They are the legitimate, if undesired, offspring of a 'free' market; determined, moreover, to devour the very same parent that nourished them. In the context of a critique of monopolies, Marx famously commented that 'One capitalist always kills many' (Marx, 1975, 1.763). Historically, there have been two ways of dealing with uncompetitive behaviour. There is the 'Anglo-American' approach, which deals with such behaviour on a case by case basis, and there is the 'continental' approach, which takes a broader policy-based attitude. It is often suggested that the European Community adopts aspects of both.

In truth, the area of competition law is one of those most encumbered by statute, and one of the most stridently litigated in the common market. The centrepiece of Community competition law can be found in article 81 (ex 85), which addresses 'undertakings' which seek to distort the market, and article 82 (ex 86), which is directed against the abuse of 'dominant positions'. Once again, however, much has depended upon the Court of Justice, together with the Commission, which has been granted a particular responsibility to monitor and enforce competition policy under Regulation 17/62.[9] The task has not been simple, as we shall see, for whilst both the Court and the Commission have wanted to enforce articles 81 and 82, they have also sought to respect all the contradictions of interest that are hidden within the ideology of a 'free' market (Young and Metcalfe, 1994, pp 131–135).

Article 81.1 states that the 'following' are 'incompatible with the common market':

---

[8]   Workable competition is sometimes termed 'ongoing' competition.

[9]   This power was enhanced in the *Camera Care* case, when the Court agreed that the Commission also carried interim powers, allowing it to suspend market activity as necessary (*Camera Care*, 1980).

all agreements between undertakings, decisions by associations of undertakings and concerted practices which may affect trade between Member States and which have as their object or effect the prevention, restriction or distortion of competition within the market.

It then provides a series of specific examples, including price fixing and agreements to limit production. Article 81.2 renders any such 'agreements' to be 'automatically void', whilst article 81.3 provides for certain exemptions which can be deemed by the Commission to contribute 'to improving the production or distribution of goods' or 'to promoting technical or economic progress'. In practice, the Commission has tended to issue 'block exemptions' in order to stimulate certain markets. The idea is that exemptions are acceptable if the consumer benefits. In reality, of course, the consumer only benefits if the producer can see a profit.

Article 81 left a series of interpretive matters to the Court of Justice. The first was the definition of 'undertakings'. Typically the Court has deployed a liberal interpretation, in the *Chemiefarma* case, easily including a so-called 'gentlemen's agreement' within the definition of an 'undertaking' (*Chemiefarma*, 1970). In the 1972 *ICI* case, it also included oligopolies, and, moreover, held that 'apparent' evidence of a 'concerted practice' was sufficient, unless it could be disproved in fact (*ICI*, 1972). This position was softened slightly in the famous *Woodpulp* case, where it was held that the Commission needed to provide some evidence of a 'concerted practice'. Interestingly, the Court further admitted in *Woodpulp* that a degree of price fixing might be acceptable if it was a 'rational response to the need to limit commercial risk in a long-term market' (*Woodpulp*, 1988). Competition, in other words, must be reasonably gentle competition; not too brutal and not too destructive. The concession was a vivid testimony to the need to balance the ideal of competition with the sometimes alternative needs of a supposedly 'free' market (Lange and Sandage, 1989).

The second matter that required further definition related to the 'object or effect' of distorting the market. And, once again, there is a fundamental contradiction at play, for all contracts are intended to 'distort' a market by limiting market activity. In this area, the Court has, of necessity, followed a case by case approach, and again the inevitable result has been a degree of inconsistency required by the need to balance the countervailing demands of competition and the market interest. Thus in *Consten*, the Court deemed an agreement to grant sole distributions rights in return for a guaranteed rate of purchasing to be uncompetitive, whilst in *Nungesser*, the Court similarly voided an exclusive license which bound a research institute to disseminating its discoveries to one sponsoring company (*Consten*, 1966; *Nungesser*, 1982). In *Pronuptia*, however, the Court accepted a franchising agreement which granted a trademark license in return for a 'royalty' payment and agreement to purchase original materials. This agreement was held to be in the wider interests of the market insofar as it guaranteed quality, and disadvantaged no one franchisee (*Pronuptia*, 1986). Although the Court has more recently denied that it operates a 'rule of reason' approach to article 81 cases, it remains true that the search for balance continues to militate against consistency (*Metropole Television*, 2001).

Article 82 further addresses the particular problem of monopolies by prohibiting 'Any abuse by one or more undertakings of a dominant position'. Again the Court of Justice has adopted a case by case approach to deciding what a 'dominant position' might be. As the famous *United Brands* case revealed, much here depends upon defining a market. In this case, the Court had to decide whether there was a definable 'market' in bananas, or merely a 'market' in fruit. Deciding that bananas were distinct in their 'appearance, taste, softness, seedlessness' and 'easy handling', it was decided that there was, therefore, a particular market in bananas, one that might be easily distorted (*United Brands*, 1978).

The 'abuse' of such a position can come in three different forms. The first is a refusal to supply products to potential competitors (*ICI*, 1974). The second is price discrimination, which can include various forms of 'predatory' pricing, as well as other 'selling arrangements' geared to favour certain companies. In the *Hoffman-La Roche* case, the Court voided such an arrangement, in which Hoffman granted rebates to certain distributors of their products who agreed not to offer discounts (*Hoffman-La Roche*, 1979). The third form of 'abuse' is merger activity. During the era of merger 'mania', during the 1980s and 1990s, this 'abuse' caused considerable anxiety in the Commission, as it became apparent that more and more transnational corporations (TNCs), generally centred outside the Community, were gobbling up former 'national champions.' The 1980s witnessed a 400 per cent increase in such activities.

Initially, the Court of Justice tried to control mergers through article 82. The limitations of this approach were apparent in the *Continental Can* case, where the Court tried to rationalise which kind of merger might or might not be acceptable in terms of the relative interests of business and consumer (*Continental Can*, 1973). In time the Commission determined to take a more active policy role, producing a Regulation, 4064/89, which empowered it to act if a merger lead to a 'concentration' in the market, whilst also fulfilling three additional criteria; that the aggregate global turnover of the new corporation would exceed 5bn ECU, that the aggregate turnover in the Community of at least two of the 'undertakings' would exceed 250m ECU, and that each of the 'undertakings' had less that two-thirds of its turnover in any one member state.[10] As further evidence of the Commission's seriousness, the Regulation also included a complex system of 'notification' to a designated Mergers Task Force, together with powers to either bar mergers or require 'modification', or indeed to levy fines of up to 10 per cent of aggregate turnover.

Yet, despite all this apparent vigour, it remains true that only the most 'mega' of mergers will be caught by Regulation 4046/89 (Hoezler, 1990, pp 14–19). This has impacted in two ways. First, the rate of merger activity has, unsurprisingly, continued apace during the last decade. In 1997 alone, there were $384bn worth of mergers in the Union; a 50 per cent increase on the previous year. The following year saw $256bn worth of mergers involving EU–US companies alone. By the end of the decade, the rate of mergers was 400 per cent higher than it was in 1990 (Balanya et al, 2000, p 9). And yet subsequent proposals to lower the relevant thresholds have met with concerted resistance in Council, most particularly from the United Kingdom and Germany (Downes and MacDougall, 1994; Young and Metcalfe, 1994, pp 134–136).

Secondly, for all potential mergers which fall outside the Regulation, the only recourse is to the Court of Justice operating under article 82. And, once again, partly in its need to adopt a case by case approach, and partly also because of the need to balance the various interests at play in the market, the Court has had to reconcile itself to a degree of inconsistency. One of the most famous article 82 merger cases, *Re*

---

[10]   If the figure was higher than two-thirds, then the merger would anyway be matter for national competition regulation in the appropriate member state.

Nestle and Perrier, provides a vivid example of this, with the Court accepting that the merger of the two companies did represent a 'dominant' position, but also accepting that it might go ahead provided it was 'modified' by an agreement to supply its product, bottled water, to a third minor competitor (*Re Nestle and Perrier*, 1994).

The law of 'workable' competition is a jurisprudence of such compromises and inconsistencies, no more 'perfect' than the free market is 'free'. Whilst some commentators continue to urge the case for a renewed determination to achieve the idyll of 'perfect' competition, for the majority it is clear that in the area of competition law, as in any other aspect of the market, reality militates against any ideological zeal (Montagnon, 1990, pp 1–4; Snyder, 1990, pp 63–99). The present determination of the Commission to decentralise the enforcement of competition policy, brought about largely because of the administrative burden of dealing with thousands of notifications brought under Regulation 17/62, further reinforces the sense that the pursuit of the idylls of competition is no longer such a compelling passion (Ehlermann, 2000, pp 537–544, 588–590).

Consumers

Whilst the law of the common market might appear to be concerned chiefly with those who seek to trade in it, it is not exclusively so. As we shall see in the next chapter, it is also concerned with those who work in it. And it is also concerned, very much so indeed, with those who shop in it. Markets need lots of enthusiastic shoppers, at least as much as they need willing traders and workers. Since 1997, the Community has recognised, in article 153 EC, the particular interests of consumers, stating that it will 'promote the interests of consumers' and 'ensure a high level of consumer protection', and will do so by 'protecting the health, safety and economic interests of consumers'. The idea of 'economic interests' is not further defined, though the article subsequently lists specific rights to information, education and organisation.[11]

The Rome Treaty had provided the basis for a series of directives, generally founded on article 94 (ex 100) EC, which sought to curtail various forms of misleading advertising (84/450), as well as define

---

[11] This recast the earlier recognition of consumers in Chapter XI of the Maastricht Treaty.

product liability (85/374), the labelling of foodstuffs (79/112) and consumer credit (87/102). The single market project saw an intensification of directives intended to promote consumer confidence, including specific measures on package holidays (90/314), unfair contract terms (92/13), general product safety (92/59), and, rather more recently, certain aspects of sale of goods and guarantees (99/44).

The consumer represents the flip side of the market in at least two ways. First, it is often argued that the consumer is the beneficiary of competition policy (Stuyck, 2000, pp 368–377). This is only partly true. As we have seen, despite the intermittent energy of the Commission, there are still a variety of weaknesses in the Community's competition regime, most particularly those relating to monopolies and mergers. At the same time, it must also be noted that the balance between the European consumer and big business is not an equal one. This inequality was graphically revealed during the popular furore surrounding the EU's supine protestations to the US government regarding genetically modified foods (Balanya et al, 2000, pp 98–101, 125–126). The second way in which the consumer represents a flip side of the market is the fact that he or she represents the alter ego of the worker. The only derogation here, of course, is that those who are denied the opportunity to work are still subject to the laws relating to consuming goods. They merely act from a position of obvious disempowerment.

Liberal political economy highlights the consumer as the ideal rational economic actor, the person who will invariably act in his or her own immediate self-interest. There are two critical assumptions, and misconceptions, here. First, the expectation assumes that no one will spend more money than they need to in order to purchase an item. But of course, this is nonsense. Every day, millions of us buy certain items at inflated prices because of a multitude of intervening factors, perhaps environmental, perhaps moral, perhaps attached to various health and safety concerns. Consumers are less predictable than the economic analyst likes to concede. Secondly, the expectation also assumes that everyone has equal access to the market. This again is nonsense. There is no equality of access between a millionaire and an itinerant migrant worker, still less between the millionaire and the itinerant migrant worker's unemployed partner.

However the myth of the rational economic actor remains a centrepiece of free market ideology. As Michelle Everson observes,

Community law, and more particularly its much-vaunted rights of free movement, were intended to fashion the ideal 'market actor', someone who can be 'expected' to act in a certain way, primarily as an 'aggressive' competitor in the marketplace (Everson, 1995, pp 85–87). This attitude has been taken on further by the Court of Justice in its various attempts to balance the relative interests of business and consumers in the law of the common market. In a series of cases, such as *Tommaso Morellato*, *Clinique* and *Mars*, the Court has invoked the rational economic actor model in order to define the consumer as someone who enjoys formal access to the market and who will act rationally within it (*Tommaso Morellato*, 1997; *Clinique*, 1994; *Mars*, 1995).[12] Once invoked, the model permits the Court to refrain from intervening in the market in order to preserve fairness in transactions.

There are occasional exceptions. The Court has, for instance, intervened in order to 'protect the provision of information' (*GB Inno*, 1990).[13] But, in general, rational consumers are adjudged to be 'reasonably circumspect', and to be able to look after themselves. Neither the Court nor the Commission has paid heed to any argument that all economic transactions are based on some measure of inequality between parties. Yet, even Adam Smith admitted that there is no such thing as equality of exchange; the 'invisible hand' of the market is dependent upon the motivation of 'profit', of the market price being higher than the original value of the product purchased. Capitalism presumes such imbalances in all transactions.

Formal equality of access to a market is, then, no guarantor of fairness. Indeed, the very opposite is true. The market operates on the assumption that the consumer is in a position of weakness. Recent arguments have dwelt on the idea that Community consumer law and policy would be better focussed on the idea of 'market access' (Weatherill, 1996, pp 896–897, 904–906; Barnard, 2001, p 52). The Advocate General hazarded the thought in *Leclerc-Siplec*, and the Court has tentatively followed in *De Agostini* and *Graf* (*Leclerc-Siplec*, 1995; *De Agostini*, 1997; *Graf*, 2000) However, the argument

---

[12]   It should be noted that in the *Clinique* case, the Court went against the strong recommendation of the Advocate General; a recommendation based on the fact that consumers in one country might be disadvantaged more than in another.

[13]   A right which has, since 1997, been subsequently enacted in the amended form of article 153 EC.

concentrates on the relatively narrow point of breaking down measures that represent a 'direct and substantial' impediment to access in article 30 cases post-*Keck*. Whilst the development is suggestive, there is a far wider, and far more radical, argument here that the Community could take on; one that relates to fundamental ideas of fairness and market 'rights'.

The idea that consumer rights should be based on something other than equality carries with it a particular intellectual baggage. Critical legal scholars such as Roberto Unger have long argued the case for 'market rights', in terms of rights of real, rather than merely formal, access. Moreover, according to Unger, the right to access a market in practice is not merely economic. It is a matter of democracy. Indeed in a polity in which forms of representative democracy are so clearly limited, the ability to act within the market is probably the most important form of democracy that any citizen can enjoy. The ability to buy food is dramatically more important than the ability to vote for parliamentary representatives. Unger places the 'market right' of access at the heart of what he terms 'superliberalism' (Unger, 1983, pp 32–41).

A similar argument has been advanced from within the tradition of 'political liberalism' by Martha Nussbaum. Explicitly developing the critique of the Nobel Laureate, Amartya Sen, Nussbaum has argued that access to the market should again be judged, not in terms of formal equality, but in terms of 'human capabilities'; meaning in terms of 'what people are actually able to do and to be – in a way informed by an intuitive idea of life that is worthy of the dignity of the human being'. Nussbaum's 'capabilities approach' to political economy also echoes the appeal of another Nobel Laureate, John Kenneth Galbraith, in his championing of a reinvigorated sense of the 'good society'. We shall revisit Galbraith's idea of a 'good society' in the next chapter. In simple terms, the 'capabilities approach' asks the question: is the market regulated in such a way as to take account of everyone's capability to access it? (Nussbaum, 2000, pp 5–6, 11–15, 298–303). Rarely can the answer be given in the affirmative. It certainly cannot in the 'new' Europe.

A further argument that is often attached to the notional consumer 'interest' is that of a rationalised private law of contracts across the Community. As we have already noted, it is often presented as the next inevitable step in the process of European legal integration. Such arguments are invariably presented in terms of efficiency (Basedow, 1996; Van Gerven, 2002). And efficiency is important. But the reformation of Community contract law could be something more than mere harmonisation and the minimising of transactions costs. The idea of contract law based on 'relations of interdependence', rather than 'antagonism' lies at the heart of Unger's idea of 'market rights' (Unger, 1983, pp 59–90). If the 'new' Europe really wanted to embrace a radically different vision of social 'solidarity', then it could forge such a law of contracts, not in terms of autonomous and notionally rational economic actors, but in terms of real people, some economically empowered, some less so, but all bound together by a common economic interdependency. A consumer law, and a contract law, that dealt in terms of capabilities and real market access would be a first step in this direction.

Capital and currency

Despite all the efforts, all the rhetoric, and all the laws, the market is still not yet completed, at least not properly. The 'completion' of the single market in 1992 refused to admit that the absence of a single currency was a failing. Instead, the Maastricht Treaty merely redefined 'monetary union' as its next goal. As Kenneth Armstrong suggests, the evolution from single market to single currency carried its own particular 'logic'. The pursuit of the single currency offered itself as a new 'regulatory strategy, not simply in terms of the functional and efficient pursuit of goals, but also in terms of the creation of powerful symbols which are institutionalised and shape actor-integration' (Armstrong, 1999, p 751). In more prosaic terms, having apparently 'completed' the market, the pursuit of a single currency gives the Commission something to do; so much was, indeed, tacitly admitted in the Commission's own 1996 paper *The Impact and Effectiveness of the Single Market*.

The drive to establish a single currency flows from one of the original 'rights' of 'free movement' in the common market: the removal of 'restrictions' on the 'movement of capital between member states' found in articles 56–60 (ex 73) EC. What such restrictions might be, and what indeed capital might be, was, inevitably, left to the Court of Justice to determine in due course. Significantly in the *Sanz de Lera* case, the Court affirmed that article 56, which prohibits such 'restrictions', is directly effective, and so in need of no implementing legislation (*Sanz de Lera*, 1995). Although article 58 provides certain exemptions regarding taxation policy, the Treaty 'Chapter' on capital movements is both rigorous and also relatively uncontroversial. The primary reason for liberating the movement of capital is to reduce 'transaction costs'. Capital could be subject to the same kinds of fiscal barriers that hinder the movement of goods. In turn, of course, the logical extreme that lies behind the removal of such costs is the establishment of one 'common' currency.

As we have already noted, the idea of a single currency has been around for a long time. Article 105 (ex 105) of the Rome Treaty had established a Monetary Committee to monitor 'monetary policy' in the Community, and, as early as 1964, Commission memoranda were venturing the idea of some kind of 'monetary union'. By the time of The Hague summit in 1969, the idea had earned the official sanction of the Council. During the 1970s, the Community attempted to employ a system of currency exchange parameters, which became known as the 'snake in the tunnel'. In practice, the 'snake' provided a means by which weaker currencies could measure themselves against the German Deutschmark (DM), making the DM the de facto common currency of the Community (Snyder, 1999, pp 421–429).[14]

Talk of a common currency was then resurrected in the lead-up to the pivotal Fontainebleau Council in 1984 and, four years later, the Third Capital Directive linked the need to abolish all remaining restrictions on the free movement of capital with the need to clear the ground for a single currency. The Hanover Council of that year duly announced the establishment of the Delors Commission on Monetary Union. The resultant Delors 'plan' recommended a system of binding rules for the financing of national budgets, and did so through three 'stages'. The first stage was the establishment of an Exchange Rate Mechanism (ERM) currency 'band', and the complementary 'convergence' of economic performance with regard to interest rates, inflation and fiscal management. The second stage concerned the necessary institutional reforms to be effected in the Maastricht Treaty, and complemented by a final co-ordination of economic policies

---

[14]   Noting that nothing then happened for the rest of the decade, Tsoukalis dismisses the 'snake', and the idea that it might provide the inspiration for monetary union, as the 'biggest non-event of the 1970s' (Tsoukalis, 1991, p 165).

between member states. The third and final stage was to be the establishment of the single currency in 1997, to be joined by all those countries that had fulfilled the 'convergence' criteria. The Report was accepted, timetable and all, by the Madrid Council in late 1989 (Snyder, 1999, pp 430–433).

Two years later article 4 (ex 3a) of the Community Treaty was drafted to include amongst the Community's 'activities', the

> irrevocable fixing of exchange rates leading to the introduction of a single currency, the ECU, and the definition and conduct of a single monetary policy and exchange rate policy the primary objective of both of which shall be to maintain price stability and, without prejudice to this objective, to support the general economic policies in the Community, in accordance with the principle of an open market economy with free competition.

The alignment of the single currency with the completion of the single market could not have been made clearer. Although the ERM effectively collapsed later that year, the case for a single currency was energetically pressed by both the Commission and the business sector throughout the 1990s, leading to its taking centre stage in the 1995 Council Resolution on the 'Stability and Growth Pact', which required all governments to gear their economies around limiting 'deficits' so as to refine existing 'convergence programmes'.

The very language of the Resolution betrays the audience to which it is addressed. In a very real sense, the idea of a single currency has always been an essentially elitist one, created by a handful of monetary experts, and then seized upon enthusiastically, both by politicians desperate to resuscitate a flagging political enterprise, and by business leaders desperate to maximise their profits (Snyder, 1999, p 420). Engagement with the wider public is, at best, marginal. The audience that the Council and the Commission have always been keenest to reach is that of business. And the interest has been reciprocated in full. Relishing the removal of governmental control of currency and interest rates, the critical mass of business interests have enthusiastically welcomed the idea of a single currency, establishing a dedicated Association for Monetary Union (AMUE), and issuing a stream of pamphlets arguing the case for a single currency. In asking the question, 'Japan has one currency. The United States has one currency. How can the Community live with twelve?' in its 1991 paper,

Reshaping Europe, the European Roundtable of Industrialists (ERT), revealed the extent to which the nature of the argument had been seized by those who seek to frame the argument solely in economic terms.

Yet, whilst the economic arguments are clearly relevant, expert opinion remains divided, with many leading economists arguing that the economic case for a single currency is neither compelling nor forbidding (Snyder, 1999, pp 436–437, 442–443). Moreover, regardless of its merits or demerits, such deregulation has very obvious political, social and cultural consequences. The introduction of the single currency has been rightly described as a 'Trojan Horse', a means by which to usher in further deregulation of industry (Balanya et al, 2000, pp 50–57). A single currency will play a massive role in shaping the future of all European citizens. Its economic impact will only be one facet of this. As much has been admitted by the French President Jacques Chirac, for whom the single currency epitomises not the market 'Project' so much as the 'entire political project' of European Union (Snyder, 1999, p 437). The admission warrants remembrance. As the United Kingdom contemplates a referendum on joining the currency, its government remains grimly determined to peddle the fiction that voters need only consider certain financial 'tests' which relate to the United Kingdom's ability fully to acquit itself of the necessary 'convergence criteria'. Given that this 'criteria' has been readily waved by a number of entrants to the currency, and that they are anyway infinitely interpretable, the fiction is compounded still further.

The importance of the single currency as a 'metaphor' for the 'new' Europe has been emphasised by Francis Snyder, who has observed that the 'debate' about the currency is thus, 'a debate about the future of the EU as a polity, the European social model, and the nature of European identity'. It was always intended to be 'milestone in the history of European integration'. In truth, however, it may well prove to be 'millstone around the neck of a fledgling, causing the young European Union to sink in the turbulent waters of deflation, enlargement, postmodern politics and globalisation'. Indeed, Snyder goes on to hazard the suggestion that if the single currency fails, then 'European integration as we know it may be in danger' (Snyder, 1999, pp 418, 473).

Completing the market?

It would be easy to think that the final establishment of a single currency, within which every member state is a participant will complete the market. Unfortunately, this is not so. As Susan Strange has commented, ten years after the Maastricht Treaty, it is clear that 'Europe is still not nearly as much of a common market as North America' (Strange, 1998, p 108). There is, for a start, a huge question regarding what the European market is supposed to do. Can a market in which so many millions are unable to find work, or are denied the capacity to engage effectively as consumers, be said to be complete?

Moreover, the question regarding the claimed 'completion' of the market aligns with the prospective fate of the much-vaunted 'decade of Europe'. As the new century beckons, the European 'community', as we have already seen, faces various challenges of governance, to which must also be added a number of residual problems facing the 'common' market. The extent of these problems was acknowledged in the Commission's 1997 *Action Plan*, which admitted the continuing need to improve the framework of judicial enforcement, to eliminate residual 'distortions' in the market, particularly those caused by the failure to harmonise taxation policy, to remove remaining 'sectoral obstacles', and to deliver a market that was truly for the 'benefit' of all Europe's citizens (Mortelmans, 1998, pp 108–115).

Though a striking admission that the completed market was still some way short of completion, the *Action Plan* focused more on refining the existing legal and political strategies. As Kamiel Mortelmans observed, it lacked 'vision', a longer-term 'view' of what the market should become (Mortelmans, 1998, pp 128–129). The deeper problems lie elsewhere. But before we take a look at these, it is important to set the pervasive judicial context. There can be no doubt that the forging of the market has, indeed, owed much to an aggressive judiciary. The *Dassonville* and *Cassis* jurisprudence, for example, was created, in the words of one commentator, 'at a time' of legislative 'paralysis' in the Community (Weatherill, 1999, p 82). The Court's rigorous support of the Commission's competition policy is equally striking. Back in 1990, Francis Snyder could rightly conclude that:

> The European Court is not simply an institution which adjudicates disputes between two parties or which decides questions of

interpretation or validity. On the contrary, it has a central role in the creation of the European Community and of the internal market, for the European Court is a major creative force in Community law-making, policy-making and politics. (Snyder, 1990, p 26.)

A decade later, however, and there is a distinct feeling today that the Court of Justice is rather keener to assume a quiet life. The *Keck* judgment is suggestive of a clear change of judicial mood, as is the determination of both the Court and the Commission to encourage national authorities and their courts to undertake greater responsibility in monitoring competition law and policy, reserving only those cases of immediate Community 'significance' for their own consideration. The Commission's 1993 'Notice' which intimated this determination followed the Court's firm ruling in *Automec*, that Community institutions should only be responsible for adjudging those competition cases in which there was a clear 'Community interest' (*Automec*, 1992; Shaw, 1995, pp 128–129; Hiljemark, 1997, pp 84, 89–96; Maher, 1996).

It is an attitude that clearly owes much to the idea of subsidiarity which bounded onto the stage of Union policy in 1992. And for this reason, given the confusion which surrounds subsidiarity, it is perhaps no surprise that national courts have so far proved to be rather bemused by their new found responsibilities (Wesseling, 1997). However, it is this mood of 'decentralisation' that is instructive, and it is a mood that has been reinforced in the Commission's 1999 White Paper on Competition. The Paper's tacit conclusion is both prosaic and ironic; given the sheer weight of referral 'notifications', the Community's monopoly on considering monopolies is no longer practicable (Ehlermann, 2000).

Above all, it is a mood that resonates with the broader sense that the onus in the 'completed' market should be one of consolidation rather than further integration. Indeed, it might be said that the limitations of law have been reached. Kenneth Armstrong identifies post-1992 Europe as one of intensified 'regulation' rather than intensified legal integration (Armstrong, 1999, pp 745, 784–788). Whilst those problems admitted in the Commission's *Action Plan* might benefit from further specifically legal integration, the deeper problems cannot. The institution of the single currency is perhaps the most notorious of these remaining problems. But it is not alone. A series of further problems are outstanding. One, alluded to by the Commission, is the fate of the European 'consumer'; another is unemployment.

A further problem relates to regional disparities. The statistics tell much of the story. German salaries average up to 500 per cent higher than those in poorer countries such as Portugal (Curwen, 1995, pp 192–193). These disparities were only exacerbated after 1992, and are likely to be even more so after the various stages of enlargement in 2004 and 2007. It requires a considerable stretch of the imagination to assume that the German middle class can engage in the market on an even footing with the impoverished peasantry of the Romanian steppes. Aside from the social and ethical issues at play here, such regional disparities are economically destabilising; subverting employment trends, inflationary policy and the sub-optimal use of national and transnational economic infrastructures. More dangerous still, from a political perspective, such disparities only serve to nurture xenophobic resentment (George, 1991, pp 190–198; Harvie, 1994, pp 22–35, 66–79).

As Joanne Scott emphasises, with regard to regional disparities, it is a case of too little law, rather than too much. Regional disequilibrium necessitates legal intervention, and, as yet, the Community's response has been unconvincing (Scott, 1995, pp 1–15). Community regional policy still prefers the indirect approach, seeking to lure investment, rather than directly funding projects for social and economic growth. Thus it promotes tourism in countries such as Greece and Portugal, in the hope that investment in a sunny disposition will suffice. Hundreds of thousands of ECU are spent on restoring ruined temples and dilapidated museums, rather than on hospitals or schools. Regional development is futile if it fails to improve the quality of life of the underprivileged and impoverished (Scott, 1995, pp 44–49, 65–70).

The need to address regional disparities is also one of the central arguments behind Stuart Holland's plea for greater macroeconomic management in the Community. It is placed at the root of the wider need to create the more 'balanced' Europe so lionised in Treaty rhetoric. As long as certain individuals, and certain groups of individuals, are so obviously wealthier than others, then it is futile to expect any genuine sense of European 'solidarity' to emerge (Holland, 1993, pp 9–30).

At the same time, however, speaking in the more immediate context of agricultural reform, Joseph McMahon has just as virulently argued that regional disequilibria can only be properly addressed by a more coherent regional policy. The two apparently converse solutions can, as McMahon comments, be reconciled by application of the principle of subsidiarity, with regions governing their own agricultural policy wherever possible, and the Community intervening only where its capacity to act is needed (McMahon, 2002, pp 26–27). As always, however, it is a matter of political will, and in the area of European agriculture that will has been conspicuous in its absence for the most of the last half century.

Aside from agriculture, the area of Community law that is perhaps most immediately engaged with the problem of regional disparity is that which relates to state aids. Articles 87–89 (ex 92–94) frame Community law relating to state aids. Apart from certain listed exceptions, such as 'aid having a social character' or aid granted to ameliorate 'natural disasters', article 87 condemns state aids as 'incompatible with the common market'. The question of state aids, understandably, remains a contentious one, with the nation states keen to maintain their control over matters that so obviously affect national interests. It is for this reason that article 89 preserves the ability of the Council to determine 'exempted aid'. But with that caveat in place, it can also be noted that the Commission, specifically empowered under article 88 to monitor state aids, together with the Court of Justice, has taken a rigorous approach to rooting out such forms of market distortion (*Intermills*, 1984; *Van der Kooy*, 1988). As ever, regulating the market is far more about balancing conflicting interests, than it is about reinforcing any ideal or ideology.

The challenges of regional disparity, like those of unemployment, the consumer and the single currency, should not be underestimated. But, perhaps, the deepest problem lies at the very heart of the notion of a 'free' market. For, whilst the 'common' market might be 'free' in the economic sense, it is certainly not free in the political or ethical sense. Joseph Weiler rightly observes that the 'culture of the Market' describes a 'highly politicised choice of ethos, of ideology and of political culture' (Weiler, 1991b, p 430). Francis Snyder reaches a similar conclusion, emphasising that the four 'freedoms' which underpin the law of the European 'market' carry a very particular ideological baggage, one that polarises economic power and marginalises alternative conceptions of redistribution. In other words, the common market, like any other, favours certain individuals and interests over others and, being unregulated, provides no instrument with which to restore balance. Economic freedom in the 'new' Europe has come at the price of political freedom (Snyder, 1990, pp 24–26, 35–42, 49–56).

The experience of the European 'common' market has, then, reinforced the reality that no market is really 'free', but rather the reflexive instrument of various interest groups, amongst which the consumer is usually the weakest and the larger corporation is invariably the strongest. Between these two mismatched competitors, the institutions of the European Union, including national institutions, are supposed to ensure fair play. In reality, however, the Commission has never made the slightest effort to hide its lust for business.

The statistics are telling. Brussels has become the Shangri-la of big business. Over two hundred of the largest TNCs have permanent offices in Brussels, from which over ten thousand lobbyists ply their trade, acting in the words of one recent commentary 'as a replacement for the citizen-based constituency that the Community lacks'. Over three thousand lobbyists flutter around the European Parliament alone (Balanya et al, 2000, pp 3–5). The Union is awash with business groupings, many of which are peopled not only by representatives of business, but also by members of the Commission. The largest, such as the European Roundtable of Industrialists (ERT), pride themselves on their capacity to pick up a phone and chat to a head of state or a Director General of the Commission. According to the former President of the Commission, Jacques Delors, organisations such as the ERT are the 'main driving forces behind the Single Market'. It is certainly true that the ERT played a major role in drafting Delors' 1993 White Paper on *Growth, Competitiveness and Employment*, and it continues to be true that the many of the working parties set up by the various directorates of the Commission are packed with members of the ERT and similar interest groups (Balanya et al, 2000, pp 22–25).

The assertion that the ERT might be one of the 'driving forces' of the market may well be true. But it is a shame. The main driving force behind the common market should be those who work in it and shop in it, whilst the main driving force behind the Union should be its citizens. The extent to which public concerns regarding various aspects of the market, such as the environment and advances in biotechnology, are swept aside is depressing. The 1998 Life Patents Directive, permitting what the Nobel Laureate, Dario Fo, terms 'genetic manipulation', was opposed by nearly two-thirds of the Union's citizens. It was, however, fervently supported by biotechnology corporations and business interests. The Directive might have been justified in terms of principle, and it is possible that public concern is ill-founded. But the fact that the Directive will enable a series of US TNCs to speculate on billion dollar profits is not a good enough reason for the institutions of the Community to abrogate their responsibility to engage public concerns (Balanya et al, pp 83–88). The case for democracy in the common market is every bit as pressing as it is for democracy in the Union itself.

Chapter 6

The law of persons

It would be easy to think that the law of the market is the law relating to the free movement of goods and capital, to agriculture and to competition. It is, however, rather more. The law of the market also relates to those who work in it, and to those who shop in it. The original Community Treaty identified workers as a category of Europeans worthy of particular legal recognition. There is, as we shall see, a series of specific worker's rights, including particular rights for women. These form the basis of what is sometimes termed European social law and policy. Two of the four famous 'freedoms' also relate to workers, the freedoms of movement and the freedom of establishment and to provide services. These laws are supposed to provide Europe with a social 'face'. At the same time, they further fashion a distinctive Community law of persons. But what is most striking is the extent to which, in endeavouring to fashion this 'law', the 'new' Europe appears to promote all kinds of differentiation, and with it all the inevitable sources of discrimination and disempowerment. In the final chapter we will take a closer look at the idea of European citizenship, inaugurated in 1992 as the foundation for a new European public philosophy. But, as we shall see in this chapter, such rhetorical and essentially ephemeral gestures pale in comparison with the reality of a Union that seems to find the idea of a 'good' and inclusive society so difficult to realise.

Europe's social face

Although article 2 of the Rome Treaty paid homage to the idyll of 'solidarity' between nations, it paid scant attention to the idea of social solidarity amongst its constituent peoples. The only immediate concessions were concerned with certain labour law provisions, namely article 118 (now 137–140), which addressed various aspects of working conditions, and article 119 (now 141) which related more specifically to equality of pay between the sexes. Limited as they were to certain categories of workers, these provisions ignored the condition of millions of European citizens. They also failed to provide any kind of grander social vision, a failure which, as Loukas Tsoukalis rightly observes, represents one of the most serious of the Treaty's many failings (Tsoukalis, 1991, p 19). The reason for the Community's lack of commitment to matters of social welfare has two roots. First, it is anxious not to impinge upon what it presumes to be the efficiency of the market and, second, it is just as concerned not to impinge on an area of policy jealously guarded by member states (Moxon-Browne, 1993; Barnard, 1999, pp 481–482).

Bounded by such constraints, during the early years of the Community the Commission struggled to make any serious impression in the area of social policy. The first sign of a more concerted effort came with the 1974 Social Action Programme, which dedicated itself to the ideal of full employment, to an improved standard of living and working and to social dialogue in the workplace. The harsh economic climate of the 1970s and early 1980s ensured that little more practical progress would be made. Europe, it seemed, was unable to address the polarised social conditions within which so many of its citizens lived and worked (Holland, 1980, pp 20–64, 89–116). The possibility of finally redressing this failing came with the forging of the single market initiative during the mid-1980s. Jacques Delors was rightly convinced that the completion of the market was as much dependent upon making social 'solidarity' a reality, and forced through a 'new Social Action Programme' at the pivotal Fontainebleau Summit in 1984.

Accordingly, social policy made an altogether more robust entry into the Single European Act, with article 118b (now 139), articulating the need for a genuine 'dialogue' between management and labour, whilst articles 130a–e (now 157–62) stressed the complementarity of economic and social progress. The presence of such a 'dialogue', as a necessary component of fair 'working conditions', had become increasingly popular following the political unrest of the late 1960s (Wise and Gibb, 1993, p 144). For some, however, its presence in the Treaty described the essential tension that could be said to exist between competitive Europe and social Europe, whilst for those who seek to elevate various workers' rights to the status of human rights, the ambiguities are greater still (Schermers, 1989; Wedderburn, 1991).

At the centre of the Commission's renewed vigour in the late 1980s was a particular concern with 'social dumping', of companies moving from country to country looking for the cheapest workforce, and in so doing merely perpetuating regional disparities. A common labour market, it seemed, was the only sensible way in which this problem might be resolved. The Marin Report of 1988 reinforced the sense of urgency. Writing at the time, Paul Teague noted that there were at least five key areas for prospective social reform: making the free movement of both workers and those seeking work genuine, increased co-operation between national labour markets, leading to a 'convergence' of training programmes, an enhanced Social Fund, statutory reinforcement of existing social policy initiatives, and refined processes of social 'dialogue'. All in all, it amounted to the institution of 'principles of social co-operation and consensus' (Teague, 1989, pp 7–92, 108–111).

The first step towards the institution of such principles was the drafting of a Charter for the Social Rights of Workers in 1989, designed, in the words of the Commission, to 'form a keystone of the social dimension in the construction of Europe in the spirit of the Treaty of Rome' (Wise and Gibb, 1993, p 126; Barnard, 1999, pp 483–484). Though rhetorical, and, as a 'solemn declaration', devoid of legal force, the Charter did establish both a mood and a process. Anything more would anyway have been vetoed by those member states that were keen to spin the line that workers' rights necessarily infringed market efficiency (Lodge, 1990, pp 137–141, 149–150; Wise and Gibb, 1993, pp 162–172). Whilst Delors celebrated the final emergence of a 'social dimension' and a 'social face', critics were altogether more sceptical, dismissing the Charter as a 'placebo' to placate workers (Lodge, 1990, p 135; Wise and Gibb, 1993, p 178). Not least because of its declaratory status, the tenor of the Charter gestured much more towards 'soft' than 'hard' law, encouraging and seeking to co-ordinate national activities, rather than actually forcing anyone to do anything (Watson, 1991, pp 36–38, 44–48; Riley, 1989, pp 80–86; Gould, 1989, pp 223–226).[1]

The value of the Charter ultimately rested in its capacity to set a tone. The reinvestment of the idea of a social 'dialogue' between management and labour, of 'consultation and worker participation', was hailed by one commentator as 'unique' and 'daring' (Bercusson, 1990). Moreover, the number of directives that were clearly founded on the Charter, including those relating to pregnancy and maternity leave, and to part-time and temporary labour, was striking.[2] Later directives, including a significant number relating to health and safety, have continued to reveal their original pedigree in article 118 and the 1989 Charter.[3] Moreover, the sceptics appeared to be ultimately vanquished by the inclusion of a Protocol to the Maastricht Treaty in 1992, in which 11 of the member states, the unsurprising exception being the United Kingdom, announced their desire 'to continue along the path laid down' in the 1989 Charter. The annexed Agreement on Social Policy, and the Protocol on Economic and Social Cohesion, duly noted that the completion of the market was dependent upon both 'economic and social cohesion' running together.

As ever, much of the Social Charter that was adopted at Maastricht was rather higher on rhetoric than concrete policy. Its Preamble made much of the social 'dialogue' as 'an essential condition for ensuring sustained economic growth', whilst articles 3 and 4 of the Agreement finally entrenched the principle in the Treaty framework. In turn, article 1 revisited its commitment to the 'promotion of employment, improved working conditions, proper protection, dialogue between management and labour, development of human resources with a

[1] To a certain extent such an approach was rendered inevitable by the refusal of one of the member states, the UK, to participate at all.
[2] As each of these directives was technically based on articles 100 and 118, rather than the declaratory Charter, they could be passed by qualified majority voting in Council, something that attracted the particular enmity of the UK, which had mistakenly assumed that by emasculating the Charter it had evaded its provisions.
[3] One commentator suggested that this tranche of directives represented one of the most 'significant' of all areas to effect a more integrated social Europe (Szyszczak, 1992, pp 3–14).

view to lasting employment and the combating of exclusion'. More importantly, article 2 laid down that secondary legislation could follow in the form of directives.

Whilst some applauded further recognition of the need for social 'dialogue' in the workplace, rather more were troubled by vague aspects of the Charter (Whiteford, 1993; Shaw, 1994; Bercusson, 1994). Particularly troubled by the exemption secured by the United Kingdom, Erika Szyszczak regretted a social policy 'so long the Cinderella of the common market' being 'transformed, not into a fairy princess', but into an 'ugly sister of the internal market' (Szyszczak, 1994, p 313). As Paul Teague observed, European social policy remained trapped in the 'crossfire', between the desire to carve out a social 'face' and the countervailing urge to deregulate the market. He further prophesied that that industrial relations in post-1992 Europe would be increasingly defined in terms of subsidiarity and flexibility (Teague, 1993). He was right.

Present Commission initiatives in the related areas of industrial relations and employment talk in an unadulterated language of 'flexibility'. The European Pact for Employment, inaugurated at the Cologne Summit in 1999, confirmed that the idea of social 'dialogue' had been subsumed within the greater desire to promote 'flexible' labour strategies. Collateral statutory evidence can be found in the two major directives relating to working conditions which emerged during the 1990s. The Works Council Directive (94/45), for example, which, together with an overarching European Works Council, seemed to suggest a radical new policy line, on closer inspection turned out to be a very 'soft' piece of law, giving employees the right to be consulted but nothing more (McGlynn, 1995b). Much the same is true of the Working Time Directive (93/104), which was seriously emasculated in order to gain the support of the United Kingdom, and has ended up, as Catherine Barnard suggests, as an odd piece of legislation, at once trying to enforce 'rigidity' in the limitation of working hours per week, whilst also promoting 'flexibility' in the calculation of working time and the array of permissible derogations (Barnard, 1999, pp 488–493).

Since 1992, the Commission has become more and more focused on the socially corrosive problem of unemployment. By 1994, unemployment in the Union had reached over 11 per cent, and it was clear, as the Council recognised in the issuing of its 'Essen Priorities' in 1993, that only a coherent pan-Union approach could hope properly to address the problem. The Commission agonised about unemployment for much of the 1990s, its 1993 White Paper on *Growth, Competitiveness and Employment* being followed by Communications on the subject in 1995 and 1997, and then, perhaps most significantly, by the introduction of an Employment 'Title' in the Amsterdam Treaty'. Article 2 EC was also recast to include a 'high level of employment' amongst the 'tasks' of the Community. Despite the rhetoric, at first glance the Title appears to offer little more than various 'soft' law strategies for encouraging cross-border initiatives, with the Commission acting in what article 127 EC declares to be a 'supporting' role (Sciarra, 1999, pp 164–165). There is, for example, no new initiative to address the effect of merger 'mania', one of the most immediate causes of instability in the employment market.

The Commission preference for 'soft' law approaches to employment and social policy chimes very obviously with the broader mood of 'flexibility' which currently pervades Union policy. The era of 'prescriptive' social legislation appears to have passed (Armstrong, 1999, pp 767–772; Barnard, 1999, pp 487–491). The language articulated in the various directives addressing employment and working conditions which have emerged since the 'Essen priorities', focuses explicitly upon the need to facilitate 'a more flexible organisation of work in a way which fulfils both the wishes of the employees and the requirements of competition'. As we shall see shortly, this is certainly true of the more recent, and putatively radical, Framework, Race, and Equal Treatment directives, all of which are centred more immediately upon the related problem of discrimination. The idyll of 'flexibility' also lies at the heart of the Commission's Social Policy Agenda for 2000–2005, as well as the Employment Strategy unveiled in 2001, which urges the various nation states, recast as 'social partners', to 'develop' employment strategies 'in accordance with their national traditions and practices', and in doing so to 'define their own contribution' to the wider European ambition of 'full' employment.

At the Lisbon Summit in 2000, the Commission termed this approach an 'open method of co-ordination', something which Erika Szyszczak hails as a 'new paradigm' in European social policy. It represents, she suggests, an example of a 'new form' of Union 'governance', one of 'self-organising networks' dedicated to the 'processes of consensus-building', and should be seen as replacing the traditional Community 'method' of attempting to enforce the harmonisation of social policy through legal mechanisms. The Commission hopes that its new paradigm will 'create a virtuous circle of economic and social progress' that 'should reflect the interdependence of these policies and aim to maximise their mutual positive reinforcement' (Szyszczak, 2001, pp 1125–1128, 1135–1153; Adnett, 2001, pp 353–356). The rhetoric, as ever, is fine. But the proof of the pudding will be in the eating.

Back in 1993, Stuart Holland prophesied that the process of social dislocation would only be exacerbated in the new Union. There was a real risk, he suggested, of 'two different societies developing', one 'active, well-paid, well-protected socially, and with an employment-conditioned structure', the other 'poor, deprived of rights and devalued by inactivity' (Holland, 1993, p 125). Nearly a decade on, and 20 million remain unemployed in the 'new' Europe, whilst 50 million subsist below the poverty line (Balanya et al, 2000, p 59). In its recent judgment in *Albany International*, the Court of Justice glowingly acknowledged the 'equivalence' of social and economic 'objectives' in the Community Treaty (*Albany International*, 1999). It should never have been in doubt. The fact that it has means that we shall have to wait a generation, perhaps more, before the reality comes to match the rhetoric.[4]

Treating women the same

The second of the substantive areas of social policy addressed in the Rome Treaty was established in article 141 (ex 119), which stated that 'Each Member State shall ensure that the principle of equal pay for male and female workers for equal work of equal value is applied'. In effect, article 141 provides the foundation of Community sex equality law, an area which has, to a considerable extent, now been subsumed within the broader notion of discrimination. Before we take a closer look at article 141 and the jurisprudence that has flowed from it, we must set the general issue of sex equality within three particular contexts.

[4]   As Catherine Barnard concludes, writing in 1999, Union social policy 'now stands at a crossroads' (Barnard, 1999, p 511).

First, gender distinction cuts to the very heart of the 'new' Europe, and, in doing so, it represents something of a semiotic for the entire problem of discrimination which pervades the Union's law of persons. In simple terms, as Jo Shaw has recently affirmed, the Union is a 'gendered constitutional order' (Shaw, 2000a, p 417). Second, the idea of a free market militates against the strategic support of anybody or any one group of persons. Capitalism thrives on inequality. It needs losers just as much as it needs winners. Women, it might be argued, are simply one category of persons who seem to be destined to lose rather more than they win. However, for those who do not believe in such a fatalistic sociology, the idylls of a free market cannot justify such discrimination and disadvantage. For them, the idea of sex equality is a fundamental right, not merely a matter of market efficiency (Docksey, 1991). Dealing with sex discrimination becomes an imperative of moral and social justice. For still others, it should be noted, the need to regulate the market in order to promote female participation might also be defended in terms of efficiency. For very obvious reasons, the Community and its particular free market is entrapped within this particular debate.

The third context, however, poses rather greater conceptual difficulties. At the heart of modern feminist debate is a critical intellectual schism, one that is often described in terms of a 'sameness–difference' debate. For some, feminist strategy should be directed at erasing all forms of 'difference', to creating, in effect, a situation where all women are treated in just the 'same' fashion as men. In jurisprudential terms, this translates into an acceptance of 'formal' equality between the sexes. For others, however, the better strategy is to recognise 'difference' and to transcend it, employing, wherever appropriate, social and legal instruments to ensure that this difference does not result in discrimination. For the latter, equality is about 'substance' as well as 'form'. The debate is virulent, and seemingly irreducible. As the leading feminist critic Deborah Rhode has admitted, this virulence both fuels the vigour of feminist debate, whilst also fracturing, even debilitating, it (Rhode 1990). It is for this reason that some feminists, as we shall see, are so supportive of positive discrimination, in the workplace or in the family, whilst others are so critical of strategies that appear to merely perpetuate existing gender stereotypes.

To a certain extent such theoretical arguments might seem to be rather esoteric, certainly in the context of article 141, the motivation for which was altogether more prosaic. The original purpose behind article 141, as the Court agreed in *Defrenne 2*, was clearly to remove potential 'distortion' in the market, with some member states suffering economic disadvantage by virtue of implementing more rigorous policies of equal pay.[5] The Court talked of a 'double aim', of levelling the market and protecting core social values that lay at its 'foundations' (*Defrenne 2*, 1976; Barnard, 1999, pp 497–501). Unsurprisingly, the attitude revealed in *Defrenne 2* has caused considerable concern amongst those critics who see sex equality as a fundamental right, and not as some kind of 'by-product' of market regulation (Scheiwe, 1994, p 245).

However, whilst the Court might have felt primarily motivated by the desire to promote the interests of the market, this does not mean that it could insulate itself from the broader social and cultural issues relating to sex equality and discrimination. At some point in each case, and in each area of alleged discrimination, the Court has been forced to take a stand on the 'sameness–difference' debate; even if that stance has often proved to be quite contradictory, even tortuous.

Certainly, its earlier jurisprudence regarding the scope of article 141 seemed to suggest that the Court was broadly supportive of the 'sameness' argument. In other words, whilst seeking a progressive interpretation of the article, the Court was able to adopt a largely formalist view of sex equality. Its interpretation of the meaning of 'pay' provides a good example. In *Sabbatini*, the Court held that 'pay' means anything defined by an employer–employee relationship (*Sabbatini*, 1972). And in a series of subsequent cases, the Court used this definition in order to permit 'notional' pay in *Worringham*, contractual pension schemes in *Bilka-Kaufhaus*, contracted-out pensions in *Barber*, and statutory social benefits in *Rinner-Kuhn* (*Worringham*, 1981; *Bilka-Kaufhaus*, 1986; *Barber*, 1990; *Rinner-Kuhn*, 1989). Within the context of a particular, formalist, view of what sex 'equality' means, it could be said to be an impressive jurisprudence. And the Court appeared to be similarly liberal in its interpretation of 'equal work', refusing to countenance either direct or indirect forms of discrimination per se (Banks, 1992, p 112).

5   The member state most immediately concerned in 1958 was France.

However, there were limitations. Most obviously, the Court continued to feel bound by the overriding need to promote the interests of the market. Thus, whilst it condemned the idea of indirect discrimination, in the form of channelling women into forms of employment that are intended to evade the full rigour of social and sex discrimination legislation, in cases such as *Jenkins* and *Bilka-Kaufhaus*, the Court admitted that such discrimination might be permissible within the context of 'objectively justified factors' (*Jenkins*, 1981; *Bilka-Kaufhaus*, 1986). The riposte is an obvious one. Such forms of discrimination are never justified in anything but the most utilitarian of terms. Writing in 1994, Evelyn Ellis rightly noted that the Court continued to take 'fright' when there was a danger that a progressive ruling would cause 'wide-scale financial disruption' (Ellis, 1994a, p 75).

This essentially formalist approach could also be seen in the Court's interpretation of the five major directives which were intended to flesh out article 141. These directives sought to implement its provisions (75/117), as well as extend its principle in such areas as equal treatment in employment (76/202), equal treatment in matters of social security (79/7), equal treatment in occupational pension schemes (86/378) and equal treatment in self-employment (86/613). A number of the cases in which the Court wrestled with the meaning of 'pay' engaged with these directives. In general these directives have been condemned as being 'weak', and there is relatively little interesting jurisprudence to be discovered. Directive 75/117 was rendered largely redundant by *Defrenne 2*. Directive 79/7 is perhaps most conspicuous insofar as it evidences the failure of the Community to achieve any sort of consensus for the harmonisation of social security schemes within member states. Unsurprisingly, it has had little impact on the various forms of indirect discrimination women face in social security access, defined as it is in relation to employment (Luckhaus, 1990, pp 655–658; Ellis, 1991a, pp 185–186; Sohrab, 1994). In its original requirement that the member states should establish contributory social security schemes, and nothing more, Directive 86/613 has been shown to be equally toothless. Only the wealthier self-employed women have benefited (Ellis, 1991b, pp 175–178). In requiring member states merely to undertake the revision of any discriminatory occupational pension schemes, Directive 86/378 has been similarly dismissed as largely ineffective.

This leaves one so-called 'strong' directive, 76/207. In its prohibition of any discrimination 'whatsoever' in the area of equal treatment in employment, Directive 76/207 appears to be the most far-reaching of all. The inclusion of sexual harassment in the workplace, in article 5 of the draft directive, was certainly progressive. In Council, however, it was relegated to the status of a mere resolution. Moreover, as the Rubinstein Report and subsequent Commission reports acknowledged, harassment remains embedded in workplace culture, and thus requires more than the flourish of the legislator's pen (Ellis, 1991a, pp 149–150). The recommendation of the Vogel-Polsky Report in support of positive discrimination in the workplace, was also consigned to the realm of good intentions, its prospect so bleak that the Commission did not even bother to campaign for its enactment. The idea would, as we shall see, be revisited in the Court of Justice.

The most notorious failing of the Directive, however, is the exceptions permitted by article 2. Article 2.2 provides exemption for 'activities' for which 'the sex of the worker constitutes a determining factor', whilst article 2.3 provides a similar exemption for 'provisions concerning the protection of women, particularly as regards pregnancy and maternity'. The Court's decision in *Johnston* (*Johnston*, 1987), which involved the activities of a woman employed by the police service, revealed the extent to which it was willing to leave the determination of article 2.2 exemptions to national courts. The case law surrounding article 2.3 is rather more ambivalent, leading to a famously contradictory sequence of decisions. First in *Dekker*, the Court decided that dismissal from employment for reasons of pregnancy was unlawful, in doing so rejecting the idea that there might be some constructed male–female comparator (*Dekker*, 1990). But then, in *Hertz*, the Court decided that dismissal resulting from a pregnancy-related illness was acceptable, because illnesses were capable of male–female comparison (*Hertz*, 1990). In *Webb*, however, the Court of Justice reaffirmed that any dismissal for reasons of incapacity relating to pregnancy is illegal, in the process rejecting the bizarre argument advanced in the House of Lords that pregnancy could itself be compared to forms of illness. The later suggestion was only marginally less ridiculous than the suggestion, voiced along the way, that leave for pregnancy could be compared with leave granted to enable an employee to compete in the Olympic Games (*Webb*, 1994). There are occasions when judicial stupidity, and tastelessness, almost beggars belief.

The *Hertz* anomaly has passed; the Pregnant Workers Directive (92/85) specifically precludes any such 'analogy between pregnancy and illness'. But its passage has not precluded severe censure from a number of feminist critics (More, 1992; McGlynn, 1995a).[6] Paradoxically, of course, the impact of the Court's final rejection of a male–female comparator can militate against the interests of women. In *Gillespie*, for example, it allowed the Court to dismiss the suggestion that lower payments during maternity constituted direct discrimination (*Gillespie*, 1996).[7] The absence of a male equivalent of maternity pay did little to help the pregnant women in these cases. Once again, it reinforced the sense that juristic niceties were not really capable of resolving deeper problems of cultural discrimination that lay at the heart of the labour market. At the root of this search for a comparator, which seemed constantly to tempt the Court, was the sense that if women are indeed the 'same' as men, then such a comparison must be possible.

Treating women differently

The attempt to make sense of pregnancy under article 2.3 of Directive 76/202 was not the only time that the Court found itself mired in the controversies that beset modern feminism. During the 1990s, the Court found itself called upon to deal with two further and particular gender-related strategies, positive discrimination and the 'reconciliation of paid work and family life'. In both instances, the Court was asked to lend its support to the provision of political and legal instruments designed to erase, not difference, but the effect of that difference. In doing so, it was also being called upon to recognise the distinction between formal and substantive equality.

The issue of positive discrimination was addressed in two conflicting and controversial cases during the middle of the 1990s. In the first of these, *Kalanke*, the Court held that a practice of positive discrimination, which presumed in favour of female appointees when choosing between equally qualified applicants to positions in public service,

---

[6]   An exception was Evelyn Ellis, who argued that the decision might be excused insofar as it reflected a labour market in which employers might otherwise be 'unwilling to employ potential mothers at all' (Ellis, 1991b, p 162).

[7]   A decision used by the Court of Appeal in a similar case, *Clark* (*Clark*, 1997).

was contrary to article 2.1 of the Equal Treatment Directive (*Kalanke*, 1995). In the second case, *Marschall*, decided only two years later, in 1997, the Court reversed its decision, acknowledging that 'the mere fact that a male candidate and a female candidate are equally qualified does not mean that they have the same chances' (*Marschall*, 1997).

To a certain extent, the debate surrounding positive discrimination has been settled by the inclusion of the following proviso, in a newly drafted section 4 of article 141:

> With a view to ensuring full equality in practice between men and women in working life, the principle of equal treatment shall not prevent any Member State from maintaining or adopting measures providing for specific advantages in order to make it easier for the under-represented sex to pursue a vocational activity or to prevent or compensate for disadvantages in professional careers.

It is certainly no coincidence that the redrafting of article 141 coincided pretty much with the decision in *Marschall*. The controversy following the *Kalanke* decision had impacted upon both the Court and the Commission. More recent jurisprudence has seen the Court readily accepting various forms of positive discrimination. In *Abdoulaye*, it even accepted that extra payments made to women on maternity leave did not represent a form of discrimination against men, whilst in *Lommers*, it was prepared to accept the provision of specific childcare places for working mothers (*Abdoulaye*, 1999; *Lommers*, 2002).

But whilst the matter of positive discrimination might be settled as regards Community law, the debate surrounding the merits and demerits of positive discrimination will continue, not least insofar as they impact upon the much-vaunted 'reconciliation of paid work and family life'. In *Abdoulaye*, for example, the Court was clearly driven by a preconception of family life. The need to facilitate this particular reconciliation, of 'paid work and family life', has its roots in the Commission's fear that Europe might one day run short of Europeans. Statistics suggest that Europeans are not breeding as efficiently as they might, and for this reason purposeful fornication should be better supported in Community law and policy. To this end, the Commission, and indeed the Council and Parliament, issued a stream of resolutions and recommendations on the subject throughout the 1990s. The 'family', the Commission opined in its 1998

Communication, *Family Values*, is a vital 'part of the economic sector, for it raises future producers and is a unit of consumption' (McGlynn, 2000a, pp 229–231; McGlynn, 2001a, pp 252–263). The age of romance, it seems, has passed; or at least it has passed by the Commission.

The Court of Justice has also articulated its support for the general idea, holding in *Hill and Stapleton* that:

> Community policy in this area is to encourage and, if possible, adapt working conditions to family responsibilities. Protection of women within family life and in the course of their professional activities is, in the same way as for men, a principle which is widely regarded as being the natural corollary of the equality between men and women, and which is recognised by Community law. (*Hill and Stapleton*, 1998, 42.)

To a certain extent it might be thought that such a statement was remarkably progressive. And in a sense it was. But, at the same time, as critics such as Clare McGlynn have consistently pointed out, it continued to subscribe to a rather traditional, if not arcane, view of the family (McGlynn, 2000a, pp 228–229; McGlynn, 2001a, pp 267–268; Moebius and Szyszczak, 1998, pp 148–150).

Of course, the Court had set about forging a constructive definition of the 'family' long before it was called upon to deal with the 'reconciliation of paid work and family life'. In the process of dealing with the rights of 'persons', it could not do other. As far back as 1984 it could be found in *Hofmann* waxing poetically on the 'special relationship between a woman and her child', and opining that it was the duty of the Community to preserve this beatific image (*Hofmann*, 1984; McGlynn, 2000b, pp 37–39). Various forms of discrimination founded on the presumed definition of the family can be found scattered across Community jurisprudence. In some instances the sin is one of omission, whilst in others it is rather more obviously one of commission. The Court has, for example, resisted the temptation to enforce the individuation of social security benefits, preferring instead to accept the common practice amongst member states, of directing them to the 'spouses' of workers. More often than not, of course, such spouses prove to be female (Scheiwe 1994, pp 248–251; Meehan, 1990, p 191). A rather more notorious example, which we shall encounter shortly, is the Court's determination of workers' families in the sphere of the free movement of persons, one which has been said to promote a 'male breadwinner family model' (Moebius and Szyszczak, 1998).

The attempt of the both the Commission and the Court to describe some sort of idealised European 'family' has, then, proved to be controversial. For some, the Community's attempt to reconcile paid 'work' with 'family' life has merely reinforced a whole array of undesirable gender stereotypes, of the kind that can be found lurking in the jurisprudence relating, not merely to various aspects of the family, including pregnancy and maternity, but also in the equally vexed area of positive discrimination. According to McGlynn, if the Community continues to promote such stereotypes, the 'model European family' will turn out to be both 'regressive' and 'repressive' (McGlynn, 2000a, p 241; McGlynn, 2000b). The inclusion of a 'right' to 'reconcile family and professional life' in article 33 of the new Charter of Fundamental Rights suggested that it intends to (McGlynn, 2001b).

The difficulties experienced by the Court in relation to positive discrimination and to the 'reconciliation of paid work and family life', compound those encountered in dealing with the vexed issue of pregnancy and maternity. It has become ever clearer that formal notions of equality are of little use in dealing with deep-seated forms of cultural and economic discrimination (Scheiwe, 1994; Fenwick and Hervey, 1995). Indeed, more often than not, they merely perpetuate gender stereotypes, establishing male norms, and encouraging women to emulate them (Ellis, 1991a, pp 206–207). Strategies of positive discrimination, in particular, merely reinforce the sense that disempowered groups of women are somehow exceptional, something of an 'economic underclass' deserving of pity and the occasional legislative handout (Ellis, 1991a, pp 36–37; Ellis, 1994b, pp 653–654; Ackers, 1994).

With this realisation comes a collateral truth, that the law cannot itself erase gender discrimination. And there is still another, not particularly palatable, truth, as Sonia Mazey pointed out. In its existing form, the Community labour market actually promotes gender discrimination, not least in its perpetuation of forms of labour activity and job segregation. A preponderance of women in the relatively underprotected realm of part-time employment is only the most obvious example (Mazey, 1988, pp 64–67). Another is the Court's dogged refusal to recognise various forms of unpaid and care work as 'work', most recently in *Martinez Sala*, and earlier in *Drake* and *Johnson* (*Martinez Sala*, 1998; *Drake*, 1986; *Johnson*, 1991; Moebius and Szyszczak, 1998, pp 128–141). As we shall see shortly, such rulings are consonant with the Court's restrictive view of what proper work really is. For whatever reason, however, Kirsten Scheiwe is right to conclude that the Community depends upon a foundation of 'unpaid servicing work and care done mainly by women in families' (Scheiwe, 1994, p 255; Cullen 1994, pp 413–417).[8]

Writing in the wake of the Maastricht Treaty, which appeared to fail women in much the same way as it had appeared to fail everyone else, Sandra Fredman voiced a common realisation. The law, she recognised, 'is necessarily limited in this context'. Legal strategies, she added, 'must be accompanied by a much more radical focus on structural disadvantage and the causes thereof' (Fredman, 1992, p 134). The challenge was laid. And it was taken up. The baton passed, from a battered and bewildered Court to a Commission that appeared to be genuinely possessed by a zeal to counter discrimination in all its forms. For much of the later part of the 1990s, a flow of reports and statements emerged, culminating ultimately in a dual strategy which focused, on the one hand, on the notion of 'gender mainstreaming', and on the other hand, on a wider approach to the problem of discrimination in all its forms.

We shall take a closer look at the latter of these strategies in the final part of this chapter. In the meantime, we must take note of the 'potentially revolutionary' idea of 'gender mainstreaming' (Pollack and Hafner-Burton, 2000, p 432). According to the Commission, 'gender mainstreaming' can be defined as:

> The systematic integration of respective situations, priorities and needs of women and men in all policies and with a view to promoting equality between women and men and mobilizing all general policies and measures specifically for the purpose of achieving equality by actively and openly taking into account, at the planning stage, their effects on the respective situation of women and men in implementation, monitoring and evaluation. (Pollack and Hafner-Burton, 2000, p 434.)

---

[8] The value of which, it has been suggested, in global terms amounts to $11 trillion of the $23 trillion world economy (Moebius and Szyszczak, 1998, p 153).

Advocates of 'gender mainstreaming' argue that it can affirm the 'equal valuation of different characteristics among and between women and men' (Bretherton, 2001, p 61). In order to give the concept some bite, the Commission set up a network of 'mainstreaming officials' within the institutions of the Union, with a responsibility for promoting mainstreaming across all Union policy. Unsurprisingly, various reports on gender mainstreaming strove mightily to emphasise the potential efficiency gains in terms of growth and competitiveness. As the Council noted, 'if mainstreaming is to become institutionalised through practice, practitioners will need initially to be persuaded of the effectiveness of mainstreaming in generating efficient policies'.

Above all, however, the practice of 'gender mainstreaming' reflects the age of flexibility and subsidiarity. It returns the buck to the member states. Although this may be desirable for a number of reasons, including perhaps effectiveness, it has the less desirable result of promoting further differentiation within the Union. Thus, whilst there have been some notable initiatives within some member states, in others the picture is altogether less convincing. It is interesting, for example, that such initiatives are prominent in certain devolved parts of the United Kingdom, but rather less so in England (Beveridge et al, 2000). For this reason, the more sceptical can, at least for now, conclude that 'gender mainstreaming' has generated little of substance (McGlynn, 2001a, p 255).

If 'mainstreaming' can be categorised as an essentially 'soft' law strategy, the Commission has not refrained from providing an altogether harder reinforcement in the form of new gender-related Directives. Of a slightly earlier vintage was the 1992 Pregnancy and Maternity Directive (92/85), which guaranteed minimum amounts of maternity leave. Rather more recent are the 1997 Part-Time Workers Directive, which we encountered earlier, and which was clearly intended to impact upon female working practices, and also the 1996 Parental Leave Directive (96/34), which provides a right of three months' parental leave on the birth or adoption of a child, and does so, significantly, to either father or mother.[9] There was a clear resonance here, with the desire somehow to promote the 'reconciliation of paid work

---

[9] Although the fact that it remains an entitlement to unpaid, rather than paid, leave has attracted criticism (McGlynn, 2000b, p 44).

and family life'. Most recent of all is the newly redrafted Equal Treatment Directive, which emerged as part of a series of new Directives cast in the mould provided by the new article 13 of the Community Treaty. We shall return to article 13 shortly.

It might be argued that there is a new mood of responsibility abroad, that the 'new' Europe is finally tackling the problem of gender discrimination. Regardless of their intrinsic merits, and regardless of which brand of feminism they appear to endorse, the judgments of the Court in cases such as *Hill and Stapleton* and *Abdoulaye* do seem to reveal a progressive urge. The same could be said of *Thibault*, in which the Court deployed the Equal Treatment Directive in order to support women who had suffered career disadvantage due to maternity leave, and also *Melgar*, in which the Court extended the broad principle of employment protection affirmed in *Webb* to workers with fixed-term contracts (*Thibault*, 1998; *Melgar*, 2001). It could certainly be said of its judgment in *Deutsche Telekom*, in which the Court declared that the 'economic aim' which underpins article 141, 'namely the elimination of distortions of competition between undertakings established in different Member States', must be 'secondary to the social aim' which 'constitutes the expression of a fundamental human right' (*Deutsche Telekom*, 2000). Such a statement represents a marked evolution when compared with that articulated two decades earlier in *Defrenne 2*.

The free movement of some persons

The Community's law of persons does not relate solely to matters of discrimination in the workplace or the family. It also impacts upon two of its four famous 'freedoms', the freedom of movement of workers and the freedom of establishment and to provide services. The former relates to the employed, the latter to the self-employed and to companies. These freedoms are supposed to complement the free movement of goods and capital which we considered in the previous chapter. On closer inspection the 'free movement of persons', as heralded by Title III of Treaty, actually turns out to mean a particular type of person, those in work or those seeking work, or those with plenty of money. No one else is given the right to move anywhere.

Article 39 (ex 48) secures the basic freedom of movement for 'workers', as well prohibiting 'discrimination based on nationality' as 'regards employment, remuneration and other conditions of work and employment'. The final part of the article then states that certain exceptions can be justified 'on grounds of public policy, public security or public health'. We will return to this clause shortly. Article 39 is then reinforced by a series of supplementary provisions in articles 40–42 (ex 49–51).

Article 40 gives the Council the authority to issue directives or regulations in order to ensure 'cooperation between national employment services', and to abolish assorted mechanisms that might hinder this cooperation. Article 41 states the Community's particular desire to 'encourage the exchange of young workers', whilst article 42 addresses the need to ensure adequate social security provision for workers, including specific reference to 'migrant workers and their dependants'. We will return to this latter clause too in due course, for, as we shall see, some kinds of migrant workers are rather better protected than others.

Article 43 (ex 52) provides a general right of establishment for 'self-employed persons', to 'set up and manage undertakings'. Article 44 (ex 54) then replicates for the 'self-employed' what article 40 did for the employed, whilst article 46 (ex 56) replicates the notorious article 39.3 exemptions, and article 47 (ex 57) provides for the 'mutual recognition' of various kinds of 'formal qualifications'.[10] The difficulties of effecting this kind of harmonisation in the context of various member state prejudices has been illustrated in cases such as *Vlassopoulou*, in which the German Bar refused to accept the qualifications of a Greek lawyers, and in which the Court of Justice then felt obliged to do more than clarify that the relevant body had actually bothered to check whether there was any notional 'equivalence' of qualifications (*Vlassopoulou*, 1991).

The freedom to 'provide' services is given in article 49 (ex 59), whilst the definition of services is given in article 50 (ex 60). Interestingly, the Court has famously expanded article 49 to include, not merely the provision of services, but also the receipt. In doing so, it has, of course, been motivated by the desire to facilitate the market actor, even if, as it has in a number of highly controversial cases, appeared to

---

[10] Though article 44 explicitly restricts the form of secondary legislation to directives.

challenge certain deeply held ethical positions. Economic determinants are always likely to force the most creative interpretation of Treaty provisions. Thus, in the *Grogan* case, as we have already seen, the Court notoriously suggested that 'ethical' provisions in the Irish constitution regarding the 'right to life' should not be allowed to detract from the overarching Community right to receive services (*Grogan*, 1991; Coppel and O'Neill, 1992, pp 239–242).

A similar case which contrasted economic with ethical consideration, and which reached the same result, was *Blood*, in which a UK court held that article 49 allowed a woman to take sperm abroad for artificial insemination, despite the fact that the absence of written assent from her deceased partner would prohibit such a medical intervention in the United Kingdom. One commentator has gone so far as to say that the ruling in *Blood* is 'amoral' (*Blood*, 1997; Chalmers, 2000, pp 114–115). The pervasive power of economic determinants can be tasted in the whimsical declaration given in article 53 (ex 64), which voices the member states' 'readiness to undertake the liberalisation of services', but only 'if their general economic situation and the situation of the economic sector concerned so permit'.

Perhaps most importantly, it rapidly becomes apparent that the supposedly 'free' movement of persons is no more free than any of the other so-called free movement rights. Only certain kinds of persons can move and only in certain conditions. The ambit of the free movement provisions, to include only 'workers' rather than 'persons', has attracted considerable criticism, and rightly so (O'Leary, 1995, pp 534–535). It might be understandable that the original Treaty should deal in terms of 'workers'. It is no longer justifiable in a political Union. Moreover, the definition of what a 'worker' is has thrown up a further array of inconsistencies. From the very outset, in the early *Hoekstra* case, the Court arrogated for itself the capacity to determine the characteristics of a 'worker' (*Hoekstra*, 1964). This assumed definitional competence has proved to be something of an interpretive minefield (O'Leary, 1999, pp 392–396).

Whilst the Court has, on occasion, tried to be expansive, it has refused to countenance any but a strictly economic determination of what work is (Mancini, 1992, pp 76–81; O'Leary, 1999, pp 397–399). In other words, it looks for 'economic activity' and remuneration (*Lawrie-Blum*, 1986). In doing so, it excludes any number of activities which might otherwise be thought to be work. Whilst the Court accepted notional payment in the *Steymann* case as evidence of 'work', it refused to accept purely voluntary work for a drug rehabilitation organisation in *Bettray* (*Steymann*, 1988; *Bettray*, 1989). The general sense of incoherence spreads into the area of work-seekers. In *Antonissen*, the Court decided that such 'persons' enjoy the 'semi-status' of workers, and so are in possession of certain rights to move; though not too many (*Antonissen*, 1991).[11] In *Levin*, meanwhile, the Court struggled to make sense of part-time work, deciding that whilst it should not be excluded in principle, such work had to be in 'pursuit of effective and genuine activities', and not be 'purely marginal and ancillary' (*Levin*, 1982). Much part-time work is, by its very nature, ancillary, and although the Court applied a liberal test of marginality in *Kempf*, the distinction remains specious, and unnecessary (*Kempf*, 1986). As we have already seen, it is also constructively discriminatory; against women, against the elderly, against all those sections of society for whom part-time work is a primary activity.

Incoherence is compounded by bigotry. Here the Court's discriminatory interpretation of Regulation 1612/68, which was intended to allow for workers to be accompanied by their 'spouses and their descendants', and certain 'dependent relatives', provides further testimony. In *Reed*, for example, the Court agreed that the definition of spouse could not be extended to unmarried cohabitees, whilst in *Sandhu* a UK court felt able to interpret Community law so as to exclude a spouse who was subsequently divorced (*Reed*, 1986; *Sandhu*, 1982). The idea that a separated couple were still in a spousal relationship, as accepted in *Diatta*, merely adds hypocrisy to bigotry (*Diatta*, 1985). Whilst the recent *Baumbast* case, in which the Court accepted that a stepchild is a 'member of the family', and that a divorced spouse retains residence rights during the period of their child's education, has been hailed as more progressive, the overall reliance on one particular form of formalised interpersonal association, what the Court gnomically describes as a 'wholly internal situation', reinforces the impression that the Community's model 'family' is of a decidedly traditional vintage (*Baumbast*, 2002).

11   They are, for example, denied unemployment insurance and most other forms of social security provision.

The most notorious restrictions on free movement are, of course, those 'justified' in article 39.3, 'on grounds of public policy, public security or public health', and also article 39.4 which provides a general exemption to 'employment in the public service', and the similar provision in article 45. The very existence of the latter exemption, based, as David O'Keeffe has suggested, on an increasingly dated conception of national autonomy, is anomalous (O'Keeffe, 1992a, p 105). The greater controversy, however, relates to the meaning of the various 'grounds' listed in article 39.3, a meaning that has been fleshed out by both the Court of Justice and national authorities. Significantly, the willingness of the Court to support the UK government's exclusion of a member of the Church of Scientology in *Van Duyn* typified its general reluctance to question resolutions made by member states authorities (*Van Duyn*, 1974). In *Rutili*, a case involving an alleged danger to public security, and then later in *Adoui and Cornuaille*, which involved suspected prostitutes whose activities were alleged to be 'suspect from the point of view of morals', the Court affirmed that, provided there is no undue discrimination between migrant and national workers, then national authorities would retain residual jurisdiction to exclude on the basis of article 39.3 (*Rutili*, 1975; *Adoui and Cornuaille*, 1982).

Unsurprisingly, the latitude with which article 39.3 has been interpreted has attracted considerable criticism. For some, the idea of free movement of 'persons' only makes sense if it is inclusive, and if, indeed, it is recognised to be a fundamental, even human, right (Dallen, 1990, pp 777–779; Hall, 1991). For this reason cases such as *Gallagher*, which involve a piece of domestic legislation of dubious status in international human rights law, cause particular concern. In *Gallagher*, it was argued that the Secretary of State had issued an exclusion order under the Prevention of Terrorism Act, despite having failed first to gain an opinion from a competent, and independent, authority, as required under Directive 64/221. Despite the obvious misgivings of the Court of Justice, and its tacit agreement that such proceedings were clearly prejudiced, it shied away from making a more controversial intervention which might have challenged the interpretation of 'public security' adopted by the UK government (*Gallagher*, 1995; O'Leary, 1999, pp 411–412).

The presence of the article 39.3 exceptions remains controversial. Their possible infringement of international human rights conventions, together with their clear infringement of the very idea of a 'common' market, is exacerbated by the rather more prosaic argument that they have the continuing potential to militate against optimal market efficiency. If the market is truly to be completed, then the article 39.3 exceptions will have to be amended, perhaps even abrogated (O'Keeffe, 1992a, pp 89–106).

The reasons for these various restrictions on the 'free' movement of persons, some statutory, some interpretative, is predictable (O'Leary, 1999). The first is the oft-stated 'overriding' objectives of the Community. Free movement is only free so long as it does not cost money (Shaw, 1993, pp 324–325). The mere fact that the Commission has, historically, been so much keener to promote the movement of professionals, tells its own story (Papandreou, 1990). So does the case law. In *Gebroeders Beentjes*, for example, the Court allowed a contractor to evade Community provisions designed to aid the long-term unemployed, in order to protect 'freedom of contract' in the public procurement field (*Gebroeders Beentjes*, 1988). The desire to protect an area of economic activity that is so hedged by supposedly national interests leads to the second reason. As is the case with the retention of the article 39.3 exceptions, the Community, and particularly the Court, is reluctant to trample on an area of 'policy' so obviously cherished by the member states. Thus, whilst it recognised, in cases such as *F v Belgium*, that the free movement of workers is a 'social' right, the Court has rarely felt sufficiently impelled to interfere in a domain which nation states are so inclined to cherish (*F v Belgium*, 1976; *Lawrie-Blum*, 1986). The Court has also been more than happy to entertain the absurd. In the notorious *Belgium* case in 1989, it attempted to balance national interests with the desire to open borders, accepting sporadic but not permanent national border-checks (*Belgium*, 1989). Belgium could thus be entered freely, but only some of the time.

The constitutionalisation of the Schengen Convention in 1992 was intended to set a mood. The Convention had been set up by a number of the member states in 1985 in order to promote free movement across the Community. In truth, whilst pretending to open up borders, the Convention was as much about streamlining visa procedures, establishing vast databases and monitoring movement, particularly that of third-country nationals. It remained outside the auspices of the Treaty framework, because certain countries, including the United Kingdom and Eire, could not countenance their agreement. But in 1992 it entered the Treaty as part of the 'third pillar', on Justice and Home Affairs, whilst in 1997 large parts of it were transferred into the Community 'pillar'. We shall revisit the implications of the Convention and its passage into the Treaty in the next chapter, for its particular impact upon both migrants and indeed immigrants is considerable, and far from commendable.

In the meantime, without touching upon the status of this latter category of 'persons', it is clear that the supposed 'free' movement of persons is something of a charade. Article 39 still refers to 'workers', and it still provides exemptions which the Court of Justice, by and large, is willing to leave to the interpretive whimsy of national authorities. The Schengen databank continues to whir, and migrants, as we shall see, continue to encounter various impediments to their movement around the Community. And, perhaps most strikingly, a number of countries, including inevitably the United Kingdom, as well as Eire, remain stubbornly resistant to the entire enterprise. Border controls seem to matter in one distant corner of the Union, even if they do not seem to matter quite so much everywhere else. The idea of an 'area' in which there is the genuine 'free' movement of all 'persons' remains a distant hope.

The others

It remains particularly distant for some. Millions who live within the Union also live outside some or all of its various legal and political domains. Perhaps the most notorious group of those who exist, at least partially, outside the domain of the 'new' Europe are those who reside in the Community as third-country nationals, and one of the most immediate forms of discrimination that such 'persons' suffer relates to their rights of movement. Recent figures suggest that around 12 million fall into this category (Hansen, 1998, p 753). Their ability to move within the Union represents the flip side of a migration and immigration policy that also seeks to exclude those who wish to pass through its external borders; something we will examine in the next chapter. At the same time, their fate is a direct product of the Union's continuing identity crises. In simple terms, the 'new' Europe does not really know what to do with 'others', with all those who, for whatever, reason are not already citizens of member states. The 'others' who are already working within the Community, meanwhile, are treated with the kind of suspicion normally reserved for unwelcome gatecrashers at a private party.

The Union's record in dealing with these gatecrashers is less then edifying. Writing in 1992, David O'Keeffe rightly observed that the impact of free movement provisions on third-country nationals continued to nourish an ethic of 'discrimination, racism, xenophobia, and incitement to hatred and racial violence (O'Keeffe, 1992b, p 19; O'Keeffe, 1994). It is a prophecy that has proved to be all too accurate. The same sentiment is echoed, at the end of the same decade by Jef Huysman, who concludes that the Union's treatment of migrant workers is so closely defined in terms of 'restrictions and control' that it can only serve to sustain 'public expressions of racism and xenophobia' (Huysmans, 2000, p 764). The briefest survey of the Union's half-hearted attempts to erase this marginalisation reveals how sadly apposite the conclusion is.

The root of the particular problems attached to the 'free' movement of third country nationals can be traced to the formalising of the Schengen Convention in 1990.[12] Purportedly opening all borders between the Benelux countries, France, Germany, Spain and Portugal, the Convention pretended to new commitment to the free movement of all persons in the Community, or at least parts of it. In truth, Schengen was a lot more about security, and a lot less about encouraging free movement. At the heart of the Convention, as we have just noted, could be found a range of security provisions, including a databank designed to monitor the movement of third-country nationals in particular. Understandably, the Convention was subject to a barrage of criticism, not just from those who assailed the obvious infringement of norms enshrined in the European Convention, the Geneva Convention, and elsewhere, but also by the Community's own Meijers Commission, which reported that the Schengen 'procedures' were indeed an infringement of civil liberties, as well as a retrograde step in the process of opening internal borders (Spencer, 1995, pp 5–67; O'Keeffe, 1992b, pp 12–19; Curtin and Meijers, 1995).

The incorporation of the Schengen Convention into the Union

---

12   The Convention was originally conceived in 1985, but was not formally instituted until 1990.

Treaty in 1992 was intended to be a step forward. However, the fact that the Convention was consigned to the non-justiciable Justice and Home Affairs 'pillar', merely meant that institutionalised xenophobia was introduced to the Treaty framework itself. As one commentator observed, the integration of the Schengen Convention into the Treaty merely served to reveal the Union's 'fear', not just of 'uncontrolled migration', but of its own citizens too (D'Oliveira, 1994). The essential tenor of the Schengen Convention, inside the Treaty framework or outside, has always been 'security' (Kostakopoulou, 1998, pp 652–653)

The arrival of Union citizenship in article 17 (ex 8), restricted as it is to existing citizens of member states, merely intensified the sense that the Union really did fear its own migrants. The particular fate of millions of 'guest-workers', most famously in Germany, but also across much of the rest of the Union, is notorious; studiously denied national citizenship and therefore Union citizenship too, subject to the same regimes of taxation, but denied the same level of social support, as well as the full range of legal and political rights. There can be no possible excuse for such naked economic exploitation (Pugliese, 1995, p 55; Hedemann-Robinson, 1996, pp 328–329; Peers, 1996; Hansen, 1998, pp 757–761). Writing in 1995, Michael Spencer condemned a Europe that consigned so many of its migrants to a life that was 'little short of slavery' (Spencer, 1995, pp 20–21, 108–112, 129–144). The obvious solution to this injustice is to align citizenship with residence. It is not a difficult resolution, merely one that the nation states are unsure that they can sell to their respective electorates (Kostakopoulou, 1998, pp 646–648; Hansen, 1998).

The transfer of the Schengen provisions to the Community 'pillar' in the Amsterdam Treaty represented something of a triumph, albeit a largely symbolic one.[13] The essential problems remained, the ethic of xenophobia is just as virulent, the discrimination just as real. Moreover, the particular anomalies surrounding the peculiarities of Union citizenship merely exacerbate, once again, the kinds of racism that feeds on pretended political and social distinctions (Geddes, 1995, pp 197–215). The treatment of third-country nationals remains trapped within Europe's present 'security' mindset. The creation of Title IV of Part III of the Community Treaty, to which most of the

---

[13]   The Schengen Protocol, it should be remembered, provides exemptions from its provisions for the UK, Eire and, in a slightly different form, Denmark.

Schengen provisions relating to third-country nationals, as well as visa and asylum procedures, was consigned in 1997, was intended to bolster the aspiration, enshrined in article 61 EC, to establish 'an area of freedom, justice and security'.

To a degree, the tenor of the new Title appeared to be rather more progressive. Although set within a transition period of five years, article 61 (ex 73i) went on to prescribe a series of prospective measures 'aimed at ensuring the free movement of persons', including, as article 62 (ex 73j) confirmed, 'nationals of third countries'. However, tucked away in article 68 (ex 73p) could be found a clause removing the potential justiciability of any apparent breach of this undertaking, if it was 'pursuant' to 'the maintenance of law and order and the safeguarding of internal security'. The situation for migrant families in particular has improved little, with member states clinging tenaciously to their capacity to 'reserve the right' to impose various collateral conditions on the entry and residence of family members regardless of what the Community 'pillar' might say about the supposed rights of migrant workers (Peers, 1998, pp 1239–1242, 1252–1262, 1271–1272).

Given the pervasive tenor of the statutory provisions, and residual member state suspicions, the resultant case law has been predictably unedifying. As a basic principle, in cases such as *Meade*, *Demirel* and *Eroglu*, the Court has repeatedly affirmed that the basic free movement 'rights' under article 39 (ex 48) only apply to nationals of member states (*Meade*, 1984; *Demirel*, 1987; *Eroglu*, 1994). Such an approach can only lead to serial injustice. The 1985 *Diatta* case, which we have already encountered, is notorious. Here, a Sengalese national separated from her French husband was granted leave to remain only insofar as she remained technically within a spousal relationship (*Diatta*, 1985). The implication that otherwise she would have been deported was clear. So was the collateral implication: that not only can husbands divorce their wives, but so too can they have them deported. As we have also noted, in the more recent *Baumbast* case, the Court has recognised that divorced spouses should be entitled to rights of residence during the period of their children's education (*Baumbast*, 2002). This might seem to be rather more progressive. But appearances deceive. Once the young Baumbasts have progressed through school, their mother can expect to be summarily thrown out of the Community.

Commenting on the *Diatta* case, Joseph Weiler observed:

> In no situation can she be stripped of her humaneness. And it is that humaneness which guarantees her fundamental rights. Under Community law she must be accepted not simply as a means to ensure free movement but as a person, a universe unto itself. Once an individual, for whatever reason or on whatever basis, comes within the field of application of Community law, his or her fundamental rights must be granted. For the Court to say that at the moment of her divorce she does not only lose her derivative rights under Community law (which is acceptable), but also the protection of fundamental rights, is to strip her of humaneness. It is to acknowledge that under Community law she is mere instrumentality. (Weiler, 1992, p 90.)

The alignment of the right of free movement with human rights is compelling. The extent to which the Union's current provisions are in breach of the European Convention is well-documented (Marin and O'Connell, 1999). Devoid of the basic recognition of migrant human rights, the possibility of such injustice is writ large, whilst the idea that Europe is moving towards a border-free community becomes a risible delusion.

Two relatively recent events might suggest that the 'new' Europe is taking steps to address its appalling record with regard to the treatment of its internal 'others'. The first, and most recent, is the adoption of the Race Discrimination Directive. We shall take a closer look at this directive shortly. Ultimately, though, we must wait to see if it will prove to be more than merely cosmetic. In the meantime, it must be noted that it makes no explicit reference to the condition of third-country nationals. The second is the attitude of the Court of Justice in the notable *Martinez Sala* case. Although, as we have already seen, the Court in this case reaffirmed a rather restrictive view of what work is, with regard to the vesting of rights in third-country nationals, its decision has been rightly welcomed. More particularly, the Court of Justice aligned articles 12 and 17.2 EC in order to hold that the principles of equal treatment and non-discrimination must be accorded to any migrant lawfully resident in a member state (*Martinez Sala*, 1998; More, 1999, p 548; Moebius and Szyszczak, 1998, pp 128–132). This approach, it should be noted, has been reaffirmed in *Baumbast* (*Baumbast*, 2002). These developments warrant applause.

But they cannot detract from the overwhelming sense that the situation of third-country nationals in the 'new' Europe describes a peculiar and unnecessary form of discrimination. It also confirms that the so-called 'area' of free movement remains a rhetorical delusion.

Dealing with discrimination

The fact that millions of Europe's citizens suffer from various forms of discrimination does not appear to be entirely lost on Europe's leaders. As a gesture of recognition, the Treaty of Amsterdam announced a new article 13 EC, which proudly stated that:

> within the limits of the powers conferred by it upon the Community, the Council, acting unanimously on a proposal from the Commission and after consulting the European Parliament, may take appropriate action to combat discrimination based on sex, racial or ethnic origin, religion or belief, disability, age or sexual orientation.[14]

Whilst the absence of any statement of deeper moral principle caused concern, the article was widely interpreted as evidence of a determination to provide the Community with a more secure human rights foundation (Flynn, 1999). It represented a further evolution in the Union's troubled history of dealing with gender discrimination, one that sought to use this experience in order better to address itself to all, or at least rather more, of those forms of discrimination that are prevalent in the today's Europe.

Of course, such rhetorical flourishes are not uncommon in the history of the 'new' Europe. But it is the presence of a series of resultant directives that is rather more impressive. The most recent of these directives is a recast Equal Treatment Directive, which has been updated to include various features common to this new tranche of directives, most importantly, perhaps, the inclusion of harassment as a form of discrimination. Conceptually, of course, this revised directive revisits familiar ground, established in original form back in 1958 in article 141. Rather more distinctive, perhaps, are two directives specifically directed against forms of discrimination hitherto unaddressed in Community law (Waddington and Bell, 2001).

---

[14]   Needless to say, the greatest opposition to article 13 came from the UK.

The first of these directives is the Racial Equality Directive. Racial discrimination is pervasive across Europe. Statistics produced during the last decade are damning: one in five Turkish job applicants discriminated against in Germany, one immigrant murdered every three days in Italy, over 47,000 reported racist incidents in the United Kingdom in 1999/2000, 55 per cent of Belgians admitting to be racist, 48 per cent of French men and women confessing the same, 20 per cent of Union 'citizens' agreeing that all immigrants, legal or otherwise, should be sent back to their country of origin (Bell, 2002, p 54). The need for the Community to address the reality of race discrimination had been recognised as long ago as 1985, in the Evrigenis Report. Various Council and Commission declarations had subsequently condemned such discrimination. But it was only with article 13 that it finally found expression in the Treaty. Until then, to the extent that Community law addressed the problem of racism, it did so as a matter of collateral impact. Moreover, as we have already noted, in relation to its treatment of third-country nationals under the supposedly 'free' movement provisions, it could be said that Community law actually nurtures racism.

The Racial Equality Directive (2000/43) was adopted in June 2000, and prohibited racial discrimination in a range of areas. The fact that the prohibition extended beyond the workplace is significant. The definition of 'harassment', which is distinguished from workplace discrimination, is broad enough to encompass a range of other relationships, indeed any in which there is 'unwanted conduct' that has the 'purpose or effect of violating the dignity of a person and of creating an intimidating, hostile, degrading, humiliating or offensive environment'. The kinds of relationships that can fall under the ambit of the Directive could include those of landlord and tenant, teacher and student, doctor and patient. The width is exceptional within Union discrimination legislation. The Directive emerged within the immediate context of the furore surrounding Jörg Haider's Freedom Party in Austria, and can be seen as a specific, if slightly oblique, Commission riposte, and the Council's willingness to adopt such a broad-ranging directive owes much to this context (Bell, 2002, pp 72–80).

The second directive was the Framework Employment Directive, which emerged in late 2000. It forbids discrimination in employment on the grounds of religion, belief, age, disability or sexual orientation. To a considerable extent, the Framework Directive replicates the

Race Directive. However, the fact that discrimination is only prohibited in employment is a significant reservation. It seems that
discrimination on the basis of religion, age, disability and sexual orientation is either not quite so important, nor perhaps so pervasive, or
perhaps it is just too ephemeral. Whilst the context within which the
Racial Equality Directive was adopted reinforced the sense that such
discrimination is a specific taboo, other forms of discrimination still
seem to occupy a rather lesser position in the hierarchy of differentiation (Bell, 2002, pp 113–118).

Whilst these three directives might provide some encouragement to
those who advocate the need for a more inclusive Union, there are
two important caveats. The first is that the presence of article 13 is
contradicted by much of current Union law. The rhetorical support
for the ending of discrimination on the base of 'racial or ethnic origin'
rings rather hollow so long as free movement provisions, together
indeed with the idea of Union citizenship, so clearly continues to
nurture various kinds of social, economic and political exclusion
which impacts most immediately upon those whose ethnic origins
are deemed to be 'other'. The symbolic presence of article 13 must
not be underestimated. As Patricia Williams has argued, speaking
within the context of the struggle for civil rights in the United States,
oppressed racial minorities need symbols. But they also need real
political reform (P Williams, 1991, pp 146–165). It is for this reason
that the reform of the free movement provisions for third-country
nationals, and indeed the reform of Union citizenship, would mean a
great deal more than the vague rhetorical niceties of article 13 and the
Racial Equality Directive. It is significant, if sadly predictable, perhaps, that article 3.2 of the Racial Equality Directive provided a
specific exemption for national practices which aimed to restrict the
market access of third-country nationals (Bell, 2002, pp 76–77;
Hervey, 1999).

The second caveat applies to those various groups of persons listed in
article 13 that are still waiting for similar legislative commitment.
Perhaps the most notorious example here is discrimination inflicted
on the grounds of sexual orientation. The nature of this discrimination, and the difficulties which the Court experienced in trying to deal
with it, have been evidenced in a series of three recent cases, *P v S*,
Grant and *D v Council*. In the first of these cases, *P v S*, the Court
accepted that adverse treatment of transgendered individuals falls

within the scope of the Equal Treatment directive, even where trans-gendered persons of both sexes are equally vulnerable to discrimination. As the Advocate General opined, such discrimination was based on an 'obsolete' political morality (*P v S*, 1996).

However, in *Grant*, the Court decided that same-sex couples could be discriminated against, in relation to different-sex couples, provided the discrimination was the same against same-sex couples of both gender. The Court explicitly held that Community law made no pro-vision to counter 'discrimination based on sexual orientation', even though it was specifically denounced in article 13 (*Grant*, 1998; Bamforth, 2000). Of course, given the fact that the Reflection Group has specifically rejected the notion that any projected article should be directly effective, the Court could clothe its reticence in jurispruden-tial nicety. And the Framework Directive did, in due course, provide for explicit prohibition of discrimination based on sexual orienta-tion.[15] But, it should also be noted that such reticence is selective and in this case was wilfully insensitive to the pervasive political mood (Bell, 1999; Bell, 2002, pp 107–112).

Moreover, the case of *D v Council* is even more troubling, not least in that it revealed, and endorsed, discrimination at the very heart of the Union itself. Here, the Court upheld the Advocate General's view that there is a fundamental difference in 'nature' between heterosex-ual and homosexual couples regardless of the law, such that a gay man could be legitimately denied employment benefits in respect of a 'registered' partner working for the Council. Such benefits were only granted to 'married officials'.[16] The Court declined to accept the obvious, that the discrimination was founded on perceptions of sexual orientation, instead preferring to accept that it was derived from the legal distinction between 'registered' and 'married' partners (*D v Council*, 2001). The best that can be concluded, as Mark Bell has suggested, is that the Court remains reluctant to 'take the lead on morally sensitive questions', preferring instead to defer to member states (Bell, 1999, pp 76–77; Bell, 2002, 101–103, 111–112, 207). The worst is that it remains trapped within a reactionary cultural mindset

---

[15] The Court could also hide behind the rather specious distinction that article 13 was not formally ratified; even if such ratification was pretty much inevitable.

[16] The 'registration' was in line with domestic Swedish legal provisions which recognise such personal associations alongside that of marriage.

which, despite occasional tentative forays, it seems unable properly to escape.

As has become clear in the area of gender discrimination and, indeed, the free movement of persons, the European Court of Justice is not the place to expect radical reform. And perhaps it should not be. As we noted in chapter 3, in recent years, the Court has anyway become ever less activist in many areas of Community law. And so, accordingly, in this context it becomes all the more important that the Commission, or perhaps as article 13 intimates, the Council, should take up this responsibility. The fate of the Nice Charter of Fundamental Rights, however, suggests that the Council is relatively unconcerned by the condition of its citizens, still less by that of its myriad categories of 'others'. The Charter, of course, reinforces the rhetoric of anti-discrimination; article 21 replicates much of article 13 EC, whilst more specific rights, such as 'freedom of thought, conscience and religion' in article 10, and the 'rights of the elderly' in article 25, can be found scattered about. But, in its present declaratory form, the Charter remains a wholly emasculated document.

The Union, it appears, is prepared to acknowledge the presence of various kinds of discrimination, and the need to do something about it. But it seems to be hesitant, selective and contradictory. Advocate General Tesauro sounded the warning in *P v S*, when he reminded the Court that:

> The law cannot cut itself off from society as it actually is, and must not fail to adjust to it as quickly as possible. Otherwise, it risks imposing outdated views and taking a static role. In so far as the law seeks to regulate relations in society, it must, on the contrary, keep up with social change. (*P v S*, 1996, 2149.)

Yet, in general, the Court appears to be both reticent and confused, whilst the Council is preoccupied with other issues, and the Commission, though full of good intentions, seemingly incapable of getting to grips with the deeper issues. Meanwhile millions of persons in the 'new' Europe continue to suffer discrimination, in terms of gender, sexual orientation, race, disability, age and so on. Much of Community law promotes this discrimination, whilst continuing to decry it. And above all, so wedded is the Union to the basic tenets of liberal political economy that it seems to be quite unable to appreciate the nature and extent of what is perhaps the most pervasive form

of discrimination of all: that which is suffered by those who are
excluded, either totally or in large part, from an effective capacity to
engage in the activities of the common market itself.

The idea of a good society

Discrimination matters, for no society can claim to be just so long as
certain groups of individuals suffer institutional or strategic discrimination. And, more particularly, no free society can claim to be free so
long as it presumes that the presence of a free market suffices for a
public philosophy. For, as we have already noted, there is, in reality,
no such thing as a completely free 'free' market, just lots of markets,
all of which seek to balance freedom with a necessary measure of
regulation. And, in turn, there is no sensible public philosophy, no
matter how wedded to the basic tenets of free-market liberalism, that
does not admit the need for some kind of social provision. In his
Autobiography, one of the great advocates of free market economics,
John Stuart Mill, prophesied that the 'social problem of the future we
consider to be, how to unite the greatest individual liberty of action,
with a common ownership in the raw materials of the globe, and an
equal participation of all in the benefits of combined labour' (Mill,
1989, p 175). For Mill, the liberty of the individual was always paramount. But, at the same time, he was just as sure that the happiness of
the individual depended upon the collective solidarity of the community within which they lived.

The same insight was noted in a very different, but no less influential,
text written again in the middle of the nineteenth century, Karl Marx's
Capital. According to Marx, the liberal idea of 'political economy'
only serves to:

> Mutilate the labourer into a fragment of a man, degrade him to
> the level of an appendage of a machine, destroy every remnant
> of charm in his work and turn it into a hated toil. (Marx, 1975,
> 1.645.)

At the heart of *Capital* lay the demand for specific workers' 'rights':

> For protection against the serpent of their agonies, the labour-
> ers must put their heads together, and, as a class, compel the
> passing of a law, an all powerful social barrier that shall prevent

the very workers from selling, by voluntary contract with capital, themselves and their families into slavery and death. In place of the pompous catalogue of the 'inalienable rights of man' comes the modest Magna Charta of a legally limited working-day, which shall make clear when the time which the worker sells is ended, and when his own begins. (Marx, 1975, 1.302.)

The case for workers' rights has remained a centrepiece of socialist, and more latterly social democratic, thinking. It has also been accepted by liberals such as John Stuart Mill. Most importantly, perhaps, as we have already seen, it was recognised by those who drafted the Treaty of Rome.

But, as we have also seen, the idea of a 'good society' demands rather more than the mere provision of workers' rights, important though these might be. For a good society is inclusive. It concerns itself with the well-being of all, not just those who are employed. And it is also democratic. Real democracy, as John Kenneth Galbraith has suggested, is the ability to engage, not merely at the margins of political institutions, but at the economic heart of the community in which a citizen lives (Galbraith, 1996). True democracy lies in the capacity to participate in the marketplace, not merely the voting booth. The very idea of a liberal society is premised upon the equal capacity of all to engage effectively within it, and to do so, not merely as economic agents, but as morally driven beings. In the last chapter we noted the likes of Roberto Unger and Martha Nussbaum adopting a similar approach in their respective arguments for market rights and for a strategy based on effective 'capability'.

Understood in these terms, the marketplace becomes an irreducibly ethical environment, wherein the work people do, and the choices they make, have a very real impact upon the well-being of those with whom they live. Amartya Sen reaches the same conclusion, emphasising that free markets are never free, either from legal regulation or from moral responsibility. In every economic decision made, either by government or by the ordinary shopper, there is, Sen asserts, a 'multiplicity of ethically valuable considerations involved'. Moreover economic activity can never be considered to be autonomous. Every economically active agent, no matter how disempowered and disadvantaged, operates in a state of 'mutual' interdependence. For this reason, those who engage in the market are never purely workers or consumers, but citizens too, with moral and political concerns and responsibilities (Sen, 1987, pp 62, 85–89).

According to Galbraith, the present neo-liberal vision of the free market is ethically perverted, governed by a majority of the uncaring 'affluent' that appears to be quite unwilling to accept a collective responsibility for the disempowered minority. Galbraith's collateral suggestion, that the most damning evidence of this perversion is the 'retreat' of the public sphere, and the abandonment of law as an instrument of progressive social reform, carries an obvious resonance for the lawyer and legal theorist (Galbraith, 1987). Devoid of this ethical component, and devoid of a progressive conception of social justice, markets simply become instruments of terror and tyranny. 'Nothing', Galbraith asserts in his essay *The Good Society*, 'so comprehensively denies the liberties of the individual as the total absence of money' (Galbraith, 1996, pp 4–5). The responsibility of good government in a 'good society' is to ensure that everyone who lives in it can both work in it and shop in it, whilst also enjoying a full array of collateral political, social and human rights. The 'decisive step toward a good society, is to make democracy, genuine, inclusive'. His conclusion is visionary, and made within the context of a European project that offers itself as an 'imperfect' example of the kind of society which must develop in the future:

> Let there be a coalition of the concerned and the compassionate and those now outside the political system, and for the good society there would be a bright and wholly practical prospect. The affluent would still be affluent, the comfortable would still be comfortable, but the poor would be part of the political system. Their needs would be heard, as would the other goals of the good society . . . With true democracy, the good society would succeed, would even have an aspect of inevitability. (Galbraith, 1996, p 143.)

In the final chapter, we will take a look at current debates surrounding the need for Europe to craft for itself some kind of inspiring public philosophy. Galbraith's vision will be worth recalling. The idea of a 'good society' is worth our consideration. But, as we have seen, there is, sadly, a long way to go before the 'new' Europe can claim to be one.

Chapter 7

Beyond Europe

There is a tendency to assume that the law and policy of the 'new' Europe concerns only internal matters, the completion of the market, the effecting of a social face, the forging of fundamental legal principles, perhaps even the making of a constitution. Yet this is wrong. The Union is part of a wider, and rapidly changing, world. On the one hand, ever since its inception in 1958, the Community has engaged in various, mostly commercial, relations across the globe. It has a distinctive position, with distinctive responsibilities, within the broader framework of international law. Moreover, as the much-vaunted 'new world order' has emerged during the final decades of the twentieth century, the Union has found itself at the centre of this rapid transformation. The establishment of the Union in 1992 was an explicit recognition of this fact. The drive to establish a political Union was far less the product of any principled desire to realise a 'united' Europe, than it was the altogether more prosaic, and defensive, response to what was going on at its borders. We cannot understand the 'new' Europe, its politics and its law, outside the broader global context.

The new world order

In his 1991 State of the Union speech, US President George Bush, announced a 'big idea', a 'new world order' which had as its ambition 'to achieve the universal aspirations of mankind', or at least American perception of mankind, and these were 'peace and security, freedom and the rule of law'. The sentiment seemed to fit. It resonated with the end of the Gulf War, the immediate trigger for Bush's musings on a 'new world order', and with the end of the Cold War too, with the tearing down of the Berlin Wall, and with the equally important, if rather less symbolic, tearing down of trade barriers. Bush's 'big idea' carried a very obvious resonance with Francis Fukuyama's provocative suggestion that history had come to an 'end'. At the heart of Fukuyama's thesis was the assertion that there was a 'remarkable consensus' that the 'ideal' of liberal democracy could not be 'improved on' (Fukuyama, 1992, pp xi–ii, 13–18, 31).

Many shared this sense of triumph. Others were not so sure. According to George Soros, globalisation announces a new kind of 'totalitarianism', representing a greater threat to the 'open society' than anything that Marxism or Nazism could throw up (Barber, 2000, p 299). On these terms, the much-vaunted 'end of history' is simply an attempt to provide an intellectual sheen to an otherwise brutal experience, to prescribe for the collective imagination what has been termed a 'global dream', or rather more prosaically, a 'global consciousness' (Rosow, 2000, p 40; Lipschutz, 1992, p 399). In the final analysis, history defies the suggestion that we have reached the 'end of history'. The 'spectres' of modernity, as Jacques Derrida terms them, defy such a simple and such a complacent conclusion. The mythology of the 'new world order', Derrida asserts, is merely the most recent and the most mischievous of poltergeists, the harbinger of 'violence, inequality, exclusion, famine' (Derrida, 1994, pp 56–75, 85).

Of course, the idea of a 'new world order' cannot be divorced from the experience of globalisation. But what is globalisation? Precise definitions are elusive; but most operate within a broadly economic framework. Whilst its impact can be cultural, political, jurisprudential indeed, globalisation is generally seen to be most immediately an economic experience. The global 'village', it is suggested, has been constructed 'from the economic ground up' (Rosow, 2000, p 29). According to the founding Director General of the World Trade Organisation, the 'new world order' finally came into being with the completion of the Uruguay Round of the GATT (Dunkley, 2000, p 7). Before then, it was just so much hot air. Money does, it seems, make the world go round.

The question of what globalisation is cannot be detached from our particular experiences of it. It is often said that the destabilising effect of globalisation is rooted in its capacity to disrupt received senses of time and space. Boaventure Santos has spoken of an overlapping relation of the global and the local, of 'globalised localism', meaning the globalisation of local phenomena, and 'localised globalism', meaning changes in local conditions in response to global pressures (Santos, 1995, p 263). International relations scholars have coined the phrase 'glocalism' in order to give this rather bewildering experience a shorthand expression. It is intended to account for the fact that only a tiny fraction of those who wear replica Manchester United football shirts have ever visited the United Kingdom, and to explain why the people of Baghdad can sip their Cokes whilst listening to their leaders denounce the US President as the 'son of Satan'. The world is suddenly a lot smaller place, and a lot more ambiguous.

In a controversial article published in 1992, Benjamin Barber prophesied that this tension would lead to an inevitable fragmentation. Globalisation, he suggested, was haunted by two 'specters':

> The first is a retribalization of large swaths of humankind by war and bloodshed: a threatened Lebanonization of nation states in which culture is pitted against culture, people against people, tribe against tribe – a Jihad in the name of a hundred narrowly conceived faiths against every kind of interdependence, every kind of artificial social cooperation and civic mutuality. The second is being borne in on us by the onrush of economic and ecological forces that demand integration and uniformity and that mesmerize the world with fast music, fast computers, and fast food – with MTV, Macintosh, and McDonald's, pressing nations into one commercially homogenous global network: one McWorld tied together by technology, ecology, communications, and commerce. The planet is falling precipitantly apart and coming reluctantly together at the very same moment. (Barber, 1992, p 53.)

There is certainly much support for the notion that the most serious challenge of globalisation is directed against traditional national identities. In pronouncing the collateral 'end of the nation state', Keniche Ohmae advised that 'in terms of the global economy, nation states have become little more than bit actors', their power now dispersed amongst consumers and transnational corporations, global institutions and regional 'states'. The 'old world', he concluded, has quite simply 'fallen apart' (Ohmae, 1996, pp 7, 12, 15–16, 80–85). The idea of a countervailing process of global integration and disintegration is further reinforced by cold statistics. In 1975, for example, total foreign investments worldwide amounted to just $23bn. By 1997, that figure was $644bn. By the end of the 1990s, daily currency exchanges amounted to around $1.5 trillion; a vast 'virtual economy' that exists only in the minds of its currency trading junkies. There is no doubt that we are all rather more economically dependent upon one another than we immediately realise.

In the final analysis, as Will Hutton suggests, globalisation is just another form of politics, an 'exercise of raw power' (Giddens and Hutton, 2000, p 41). Importantly, however, it is not optional. According to Thomas Friedman, 'All politics is now global. Not every country may feel itself part of the globalisation system, but every country is directly or indirectly being shaped and affected by this system' (Friedman, 2000, p 76). In similar vein, Stephen Gill refers to a pervasive, malignant spirit of 'commodification' (Gill, 1995, pp 402–410). Philip Allott puts it eloquently:

> With the globalization of mass culture, the many of humanity are adrift in a sea of collective fantasy, sleepwalking in a waking dream, formed and manipulated by the few who manage the great systems of mental production, the mass reality industry. (Allott, 1992, p 233.)

More and more, we find our lives propelled by external dynamics, by the myriad forces of globalisation; forces over which we appear to have limited democratic control.

The Community and the global market

The 'new' Europe has been thrust into the 'new world order'. It is often said to symbolise it. Indeed it is often said to symbolise its ambiguities. As Francis Snyder has suggested 'Europeanisation and globalisation are complementary, partly overlapping, mutually reinforcing, but also competing processes'. As he has also affirmed, it is impossible to understand the truly innovative nature of European legal and political 'integration' without appreciating that this process has both internal and external aspects, and that the two are inextrica-ble (Snyder, 2000, pp 293–294). This is self-evidently true, for whilst the law of the common market might seem to be intrinsically European, it exists primarily so as to equip the Community to com-pete all the more successfully in global markets. What happens outside the Community dictates what happens inside.[1] As we shall see in due course, precisely the same is true of an emergent Union for-eign and security policy.

Whilst the 'new world order' is generally traced back no further than 1989, 'globalisation', of course, has a rather older lineage, as do, therefore, the jurisprudential adjustments that it has required within the realm of classical international law. The so-called Westphalian system, in which international law and order could be described simply in terms of relations between nation states has been increas-ingly disrupted for much of the twentieth century by a succession of inter- or trans-national organisations. The Community is, of course, a vivid testimony to the truth of this fact. Moreover, the presence of article 281 (ex 210) EC, which states that the Community shall have 'legal personality', most obviously in international law, adds further confirmation that the Community was fully aware of the changing nature of international law and order. This awareness has increased with each passing year. As Dominic McGoldrick has rightly sug-gested, as the 'new' Europe has flexed its muscles as an 'international actor', so has the 'interface' between Community and Union law and international law become ever more 'evident' (McGoldrick, 1999, p 263). Indeed, according to another commentator, so close is their symbiosis that Community and international law are 'natural part-ners' (Timmermans, 1999, pp 181–184).

Whilst some of the Union's relations with international organisations have political or humanitarian roots, the vast majority are economic and relate to the organisation of the world economy: the World Bank, the International Monetary Fund (IMF), the International Trade Organisation (ITO), in time the General Agreement on Tariffs and Trade (GATT) and its successor, the World Trade Organisation (WTO). The European Community has engaged with these economic organisations since the early days. Once again, the

---

[1]   Marjoleine Hennis has provided a compelling account of how this inter-relation plays out in the specific field of agriculture (Hennis, 2001).

Community Treaty acknowledged that this would be the case, with article 310 (ex 236) providing express authority for the Community to 'conclude' agreements with 'international organisations'. Title IX of the Community Treaty, furthermore, is devoted to a 'Common Commercial Policy' (CCP), the object of which, according to article 131 (ex 110) EC, is to promote the 'harmonious development of world trade, the progressive abolition of restrictions on international trade and the lowering of customs barriers'. Article 133 (ex 113) further states that the CCP 'shall be based on uniform principles' regarding 'tariff and trade agreements', principles which, in other words, would bind all member states.

Whilst the relevant Treaty articles provide the residual statutory authority, as ever, the juridical shaping of Community external commercial policy has been fashioned by the Court of Justice. There is an internal aspect to this competence. It has, for example, fallen to the Court of Justice to adjudge the legality of certain agreements concluded by the Community (*Opinion 1/91*; *Opinion 2/94*; Lenaerts and de Smijter, 1999, pp 98–104). It has also fallen to the Court to marshal the inevitably contentious area of 'two-headed' representation, where the Community and the member states have both been parties to international agreements, but have found themselves at variance with regard to the nature of their respective commitments. In *Opinion 1/94*, the Court was required to rule on the respective competences of the Community and its member states to conclude agreements relating to trade in services and intellectual property. A number of member states specifically challenged the Community's capacity to do so, something which unsurprisingly proved to be a considerable hindrance in the concurrent 'Uruguay Round' of GATT negotiations (*Opinion 1/94*). The Court's ruling, that such agreements could be 'mixed' and that the Community could share competence, has since been affirmed in a newly drafted fifth paragraph to article 133, added in the Amsterdam Treaty and refined once again in the Nice Treaty (Bourgeois, 2000; Herrmann, 2002).

The latter Opinion clearly involved both the 'internal' aspect, of the relationship between the Community and its member states, and the 'external' aspect of its CCP, its relationship with international organisations. It is in the case law regarding this latter, 'external', aspect that the Court has perhaps gone furthest in the drafting of a CCP jurisprudence, and in so doing, transposing principles of international law into Community law. For example, the Court has repeatedly recognised the extent to which it, and the Community, is bound by the ordinary principles of international law, both statutory and customary. In *Poulsen* the Court famously confirmed that the 'Community must respect international law in the exercise of its powers' (*Poulsen*, 1992). This is particularly so with regard to the international agreements to which the Community is a contracting party. As the Court affirmed in *Kupferberg*, such agreements are 'an integral part of the Community legal system' (*Kupferberg*, 1982).

The Court has confirmed this position in relation to various international agreements and commitments. In two leading cases relating to the GATT, *Fediol* and *Nakajima*, the Court acknowledged that it was, for example, broadly bound by the principles articulated in the Vienna Convention on the Law of Treaties (*Fediol*, 1989; *Nakajima*, 1993). It has further repeated this acknowledgment in cases which resulted from the translation of UN sanctions against Yugoslavia, *Bosphorus*, to which we shall return in due course, and *Ebony Maritime* (*Bosphorus*, 1996; *Ebony Maritime*, 1997). Furthermore, in the recent *Hermes* case, the Court confirmed that it expects national courts to be just as firmly bound, and to exercise consistency in the interpretation of international agreements (*Hermes*, 1998; Cremona, 1999, pp 246–247). Similarly, if a member state, or its courts, fails to uphold Union commitments in international law, the Court has affirmed that the Commission can institute legal actions for enforcement (*Commission v Germany*, 1996). The Court has been just as ready to admit that the Community is bound by the ordinary principles of international convention. In the *Opel Austria* case, the Court of First Instance held that, in codifying the customary principle of good faith in international law, the Vienna Convention reinforced its accepted status in Community law (*Opel Austria*, 1997; Lenaerts and de Smijter, 1999, pp 124–125).

The case law through which the Court of Justice has developed a Community law of external commercial relations is, therefore, considerable, whilst its broad acceptance of the founding principles of international law is striking. But this, of course, opens up a series of collateral questions. One relates to the possible direct effect of the provisions articulated in various international agreements. Its resolution has proved to be just as vexed in the Community's 'external' commercial law as it has in its 'internal' equivalent. The Court's hesitant response has been to countenance direct effect, but only under the strictest of conditions, most importantly those relating to the perceived 'spirit' and 'scheme' of the agreement or commitment (*International Fruit*, 1972; *Racke*, 1998; Eeckhout, 1997, pp 24–48; Bourgeois, 2000, pp 113–123).

A second question relates to an equally familiar principle, supremacy. It is clear that the Community and now the Union, in acceding to these various international agreements, has remitted at least part of its sovereign authority. There is a very obvious irony here. Just as individual member states have agonised about how to reconcile the 'supremacy' of Community law with residual notions of legal and political sovereignty, so too does the Union find itself faced with precisely the same dilemma in its external commercial relations. The extent to which the Court expressly recognised the nature of this dilemma, whilst still recognising the supremacy of international law, was seen in the *International Fruit* case as early as 1972, and was revisited and reaffirmed in the equally famous *Kupferberg* case a decade later (*International Fruit*, 1972; *Kupferberg*, 1982; Lenaerts and de Smijter, 1999, pp 106–107). In its *Opinion 1/91*, the Court suggested that the 'capacity to conclude international agreements necessarily entails the power to submit to the decisions of a court which is created or designated by such an agreement as regards interpretation and application of its provisions'. In doing so, the Court echoed a rationale to which a generation of tortured UK judges have eventually staggered.

A more recent example of the supremacy of international obligations, but one which further reveals the difficulties that can be encountered in the instance of rival and conflicting obligations, is provided by the 'bananas' litigation. Here it was the dispute settlement panel of the WTO which ruled that the Union was in breach of its inherent obligations by engaging in a preferential trading regime for bananas under the Lomé Convention.[2] The litigation has drifted on for a decade or more, with the Union receiving rulings which it has then tried to ameliorate, if not negate, and then being challenged once again by the United States, and various other fellow members of the WTO, and being further subjected to retaliatory sanctions. Whilst the Union has tried to evade the rigours of its commitments to the

---

[2]   The Lomé Convention offers special trading concessions to African, Caribbean and Pacific states.

WTO, it has still recognised its subjection to them, and to the deci-sions of its dispute settlement panel. Accordingly, regardless of the seemingly endless legal technicalities which pervade the 'bananas' lit-igation, one conclusion is unavoidable. Even as it engages in the 'Millennium Round' of WTO negotiations, and indeed a revision of the Lomé Convention, the Community does not need its own Court to confirm that it is bound by the international agreements to which it is a party, regardless of the strength of any notional principles of supremacy or sovereignty (Smith, 2000).

The rotten heart of Europe

If globalisation underpins the emergence of a 'new world order', there is something rather more particular that colours the European per-ception of it. The 'new' European order is, of course, inextricable from the wider experiences of globalisation.

As he visited a rapidly disintegrating Balkans in 1991, the Luxembourg Prime Minister, Jacques Poos, was able to announce that 'The hour of Europe has dawned' (Garton Ash, 2000, p 211). Pictures of the Berlin Wall being torn down, of crowds milling in Wenceslas Square, of the Ceausescus being placed before a wall in Bucharest and shot – all contributed to the thrill. Commentators aligned events with the prophetic 'end' of history and the triumph of liberal democracy. The fate of the former Eastern 'bloc' could be said to be a semiotic for the conjoined fates of the 'new' Europe and the 'new' world order.

But the European experience was rather different still. For whilst the 'end of history' theorists could chatter about the triumph of liberal-ism, the European Union peered anxiously across its south-eastern border, and watched in horror as its neighbours set about slaughter-ing one another. This was not supposed to happen. The whole purpose behind the original inception of the Community was to make sure that such horrors would never again be inflicted on the conti-nent. The horror was even greater, as William Wallace wrily observes, because so many of us had been on holiday to the Dalmatian coast, and had been skiing on the hills around Sarajevo (Wallace, 2000, pp 279–280). And the Croats and Bosnians had seemed to be such nice people; just like us indeed.

With the end of the Cold War, it suddenly became apparent that, rather than being safer, the world, and particularly the European bit of it, had suddenly become an altogether more dangerous place, and an altogether less pleasant one. Such a thesis found a famous expression in William Huntingdon's suggestion that 'new' world order would ultimately descend into a 'tribal conflict on a global scale' (Huntingdon, 1997, pp 281–291).[3] Alain Finkielraut refined the suggestion, arguing that with the end of the Cold War 'the great confrontation of world systems has been reduced to bitter little wars, to disagreements over borders, to a ridiculous hotch-potch of squabbles' (Finkielraut, 2001, p 97).

In addition, the specifically European implications were spelled out by John Mearsheimer who, writing in 1990, prophesied that 'the prospects for major crises and war in Europe are likely to increase markedly' following the end of the Cold War. According to Mearsheimer, the root of this danger lay in the necessary emergence of a 'multipolar' rather than 'bipolar' system. And with a particular prescience, he further argued that the real problems would almost certainly continue to recur along the Union's eastern boundaries, more often than not the result of resurgent 'nationalism'. The Union, in holding out the half-hearted offer of long-term accession, had failed to understand that the 'desire to achieve prosperity' was not a primary political motivation amongst the newly 'liberated' former Soviet satellites, and it was certainly far less compelling than the baser instincts that attach to national and ethnic identity (Mearsheimer, 1990, pp 6–7, 33–35, 44–51).

The savagery of the Balkan wars, which drifted on for most of the 1990s, reaching their sad apogees first in Bosnia and then more latterly in Kosovo, seemed to prove the pessimists right, brutally erasing the illusion that the 'new' Europe had somehow evolved beyond the bestialities that characterised the 'old' (Borinski, 1997, pp 143–149). The International Criminal Tribunal for Yugoslavia, subsequently established under the auspices of the UN, received harrowing testimony, of which the following, describing life in the Omarska detention camp, was merely one example:

---

[3] Huntingdon went a further, implying that this conflict would be engaged between east and west, Christian and Muslim. The resultant controversy which flowed from this suggestion has been unsurprisingly fierce.

Prisoners were often forced to excrete and urinate in their rooms. There were no effective washing facilities, and men and their clothes quickly became filthy and skin diseases were prevalent, as were cases of diarrhoea and dysentery . . . Women who were held at Omarksa were routinely called out of their rooms and raped. One witness testified that she was taken out five times and raped and after each rape she was beaten . . . The white house was a place of particular horror. One room in it was reserved for brutal assaults on prisoners, who were often stripped, beaten and kicked and otherwise abused. Many died as a result of these repeated assaults on them. Prisoners who were forced to clean up after these beatings reported finding blood, teeth and skin of victims on the floor. Dead bodies of prisoners, lying in heaps on grass near the white house, were not an infrequent sight. (Akhaven, 1998, p 789.)

Something was, indeed, very rotten at the heart of Europe. Testaments of such horror abounded, the numbers almost defying comprehension: 8,000 led away to fields outside Srebrinica and executed by Bosnian Serb troops, the single most shuddering example of inhumanity in Europe since 1945; the European Union estimates there were around 20,000 rape victims, the Bosnian Ministry of the Interior suggests at least 50,000 Muslim women alone (Niarchos, 1995, pp 654–659; Salzman, 1998, pp 348–366; MacKinnon, 1994a).

In all, it is estimated that 250,000 men disappeared during the Balkan wars. According to the UN Commission on Refugees, approximately 3.5 million more were 'ethnically cleansed' (Stiglmayer, 1994, pp 16–22). The UN indictment issued against the former Serbian President, Slobodan Milosevic, in 1999, related solely to Kosovo, and cited the deportation of 740,000 and the deaths of 340 identified Albanians. The indictment suggested that Milosevic had 'planned, committed or otherwise aided and abetted in a campaign of terror and violence directed at Kosovo Albanian civilians'. And Milosevic only appeared at the International Tribunal in The Hague because he had lost the war.[4] Croat and Bosnian hands were just as bloody, over 100,000 being 'ethnically cleansed' from Kosovo with the aid of NATO military intervention. According to a UN report, the damage

[4]   Also because the allies paid the former Yugoslavia $1.3bn for him, what Chancellor Schroeder of Germany passed off as the 'dividend of democracy'.

caused by NATO aircraft in the former Yugoslavia was not merely excessive, but 'near apocalyptic' (Falk, 1995, p 23).[5]

So much for the 'new' Europe, and its allies. It did indeed seem that there was precious little new about either the world order or the European bit of it. The Balkan wars had been devised and fought as crusades, their battle lines regional and ethnic, the struggle brutalised as only religious wars can be (Akhaven, 1998, pp 758–765). No quarter was given. No laws of international conflict seemed to apply. As Misha Glenny observes, it was a particular tragedy that the 'confessional detritus' of three empires, the Catholic, the Eastern Orthodox and the Islamic, should have 'collided' in Bosnia, at the 'heart' of Europe (Glenny, 1992, pp 1–30). It did not take long for regional skirmishes to escalate into a full-blown inter-civilizational religious war. Tony Blair termed it a war 'between good and evil; between civilization and barbarity' (Rawnsley, 2000, p 263). All the usual suspects lined up behind the scenes. Whilst Russia expressed its support for fellow members of the Orthodox church, the Muslim diaspora donated billions of dollars, and thousands of zealots, to Islamic Bosnia.

Europe, however, dithered. Or at least the European Community dithered. Various European states merrily started shouting from the terraces. Germany led the way aligning with the Catholic Slovenes and Croats, and doing some tidy business selling the latter some ageing fighter aircraft. As events started to run apace, the Pope declared that Croatia was the 'rampart of Christianity', and whispered the call for a new crusade. Goaded by Germany, the new European Union recklessly recognised the territorial integrity of Slovenia and Croatia, a gesture which made the dismemberment of Yugoslavia not only inevitable, but inevitably disordered (Glenny, 1992, pp 62–65, 98–112, 178–180; Woodward, 2000, pp 227–232, 249–250). Nothing the Union or its member states did seemed to help, and when, belatedly, it got involved, it just seemed to make matters worse.

Over a quarter of a million died in a European war that the European Union was clearly unable to do much about. As Timothy Garton Ash observes, looking back to 1992, the Union 'fiddled at Maastricht whilst Sarajevo began to burn' (Garton Ash, 2000, pp 22–27,

---

[5]   And also very probably unlawful in international law (Sofaer, 2000, pp 2–8).

180–189, 327). The result, as Romano Prodi admits, is that the Union now faces a 'credibility' problem in south-eastern Europe. Redressing it will be the 'acid test' of its foreign policy over the next decade. The commitment will be 'long and costly', but a failure to commit will condemn the rhetoric of enlargement to a justifiable contempt (Prodi, 2000). We shall revisit the 'rhetoric' of enlargement shortly.

Prodi admits that the 'credibility' problem was borne of series of mixed emotions, fear and horror being the predominant, together with obvious structural failings in the nascent area of Union 'foreign and security' policy. For a long time, far too long indeed, the Union hovered like a flustered neighbour as the obviously deranged folk next door indulged in a seemingly endless bout of domestic violence. Then, when the failure to act became so embarrassing, the Union made a series of hideous mistakes. Of course, the Union was not alone in making mistakes, but there were few to which it was not a contributor. In the end, when the going got tough, devoid of any effective military capability, incapable of influencing events through diplomatic media, the Union just faded away, leaving NATO to pick up the pieces (Bonvicini, 1998, pp 69–70). A tragic example was provided by the misguided attempt to establish 'safe-havens' within Bosnia, such as Bihac, Tuzla and Srebrenica. In the end it was clear that neither the EU, nor indeed NATO or the UN, had the effective capacity to ensure anybody's safety anywhere in Bosnia (Garry, 2002, p 178).

In large part, of course, 'safe-havens' were devised in order to minimise the potential 'threat' of migration to the west. As we shall shortly see, the Union has a particular paranoia regarding migration, and how to prevent it. It was only after much pleading that, in 1995, the UN High Commissioner for Refugees (UNHCR) was able to persuade the Union to accept refugees on a temporary basis. Thereafter everyone bid to take as few refugees as possible, whilst the Commission talked rather uncharitably of the need to ensure an equitable 'burden-sharing'. When the Kosovo crisis reached its pitch in 1999, in the wake of NATO bombing, the UNHCR pleaded with the Union to keep its 'borders open' for fleeing Kosovars. The EU remained silent, its borders firmly shut (Marshall, 2000, pp 421–424). It was all something of a mess, and not a particularly good advertisement for a united, or indeed a compassionate,

Europe (Bonvicini, 1998, pp 65–67). Something, it was generally agreed, would have to be done. The time had come for the 'new' Europe to assume its place in the 'new world order', or at least assume a responsibility for its own continent.

Building fortress Europe

It would be too simplistic to assert that the establishment of the European Union, in 1992, was solely a response to the Balkan wars. Europe's response to the Iraqi invasion of Kuwait was no less incoherent. Moreover, the idea that, following the completion of the market, the next stage should be a political union carried its own momentum. At the same time, however, it is undoubtedly true that the events taking place in the former Yugoslavia had a significant impact (Howorth, 2001, p 767). The absence of a coherent foreign policy competence, together with the inevitable fears regarding migration, set the backdrop for the Maastricht Council. As Stanley Hoffmann suggests, the idea of a 'common foreign and security policy' became 'not only tempting, but necessary' (Hoffmann, 2000, p 191).

Accordingly, in the Preamble to the Union Treaty could be found the statement that the Union was 'resolved' to implement a 'common foreign and security policy' that would reinforce 'European identity and its independence in order to promote peace, security and progress in Europe and the world'. Article 2 (ex B) then fleshed out the aspiration rather further, listing amongst the Union's wider aims, two immediately pertinent objectives. In its present form, the first is :

> to assert its identity on the international scene, in particular through the implementation of a common foreign and security policy including the progressive framing of a common defence policy, which might lead to a common defence.

The second, in turn, is:

> to maintain and develop the Union as an area of freedom, security and justice, in which the free movement of persons is assured in conjunction with appropriate measures with respect to external border controls, asylum, immigration and the prevention and combating of crimes.

The common denominator here is 'security'. This was, and is, the primary concern, and the primary responsibility, of the new Union. As we noted in the second chapter, the framework of the new Union was described in terms of three 'pillars': the Community 'pillar', a 'pillar' describing a 'Common Foreign and Security Policy', and a 'pillar' which was originally entitled 'Justice and Home Affairs', but which has now been refined into a more specific 'pillar' on 'Police and Judicial Co-operation in Judicial Matters'. The latter two pillars were designed to pursue these two related 'security' objectives. And so, given the nature of the objective, it is perhaps unsurprising that both of these pillars should remain firmly intergovernmental, the playthings, in effect, of the Council and the member states. Article 3 (ex D) TEU confirms that the responsibility for ensuring 'consistency' in matters of 'external relations' and 'security' is limited to the Council, and the Commission.

However it is the Council that really matters, and this is particularly so with regard to Title V of the Union Treaty which relates to the 'Provisions on a Common Foreign and Security Policy' (CFSP).[6] The specific jurisdiction of the Council here is explicitly affirmed in article 13 (ex J3), and it is aired once more, in a rather more oblique fashion, in article 18 (ex J8) which states that 'The Presidency shall represent the Union in matters coming within the common foreign and security policy'. The only institutional concessions are given in article 21 (ex J11), which requires the Presidency to 'consult' with the Parliament. The idea of using the Presidency as a focus for Union foreign policy is rooted in the sense that Europe needs a head, someone to answer Henry Kissinger's famous query; 'when I want to speak to Europe, whom do I call?' (Bonvicini, 1998, p 67; Manners and Whitman, 1998, pp 236–238).

Article 11 (ex J1) presents the mission-statement of Title V, stating that, amongst various objectives, the CFSP is designed to 'safeguard the common values' of the Union in 'conformity with principles of the United Nations', to 'strengthen the security of the Union in all ways', to 'preserve peace and strengthen international security' and to 'promote international cooperation'. Article 12 (ex J2) then goes on to list means by which these objectives might be promoted, including

---

[6]   The equivalent acronym in German is GASP, which some might think is rather more appropriate.

the adoption of 'common strategies', 'joint actions' and 'common positions'.[7] The distinction between these categories is not always clear, though 'joint actions', as the title suggests, tend to be more proactive, whilst 'common positions' are often reactive. Examples of the latter have included embargos on arms sales to Sudan, the restriction of trade with Haiti, and various sanctions in relation to Yugoslavia, whilst examples of the former include the passage of humanitarian aid to Bosnia, the implementation of the Bosnian peace plan and the Union's administration of Mostar (McGoldrick, 1997, pp 152–153). It is worth noting, in passing, how many of these specific 'actions' and 'positions' relate to the Balkans.

One of the more awkward matters that the Union encountered in devising Title V lay in reconciling the clear need, post-1989, for a credible foreign policy and defence structure with the pre-existence of various pan-European defence bodies, including the Western European Union (WEU) and, of course, on a rather grander scale, NATO. Article 17 (ex J7) relates more precisely to the development of a 'common defence policy'. It further gives specific recognition to the 'integral' role of the WEU in the 'development of the Union', and undertook to ensure that the Union and the WEU should work together more closely than ever. It also affirms that the CFSP 'shall not prejudice' any individual member state undertakings with regard to NATO. As we shall see shortly, this particular reassurance may have been compromised by the recent establishment of a new European 'defence policy' at the Nice Council. The second part of article 17 then goes on to identify the kind of 'defence' activities with which the Union might become engaged. The ensuing list, 'humanitarian and rescue tasks, peacekeeping tasks and tasks of combat forces in crisis management, including peacemaking', encapsulates what are generally known as the Petersburg 'tasks'.

Whilst the provisions of Title V, though amended in both 1997 and 2002, have remained reasonably consistent, the nature of the third pillar, originally entitled 'Justice and Home Affairs' has changed significantly, with the transference of a number of provisions on immigration and asylum to the Community 'pillar' in 1997. We have already encountered these provisions in the previous chapter, and we

---

[7]   The latter mechanism, 'common positions', is given further explicit authority in article 15 (ex J5).

shall do so again shortly, when we take a closer look at immigration. The remaining features of Title VI are just as heavily couched in terms of security. Article 29 (ex K1) opens by refining the Union's 'objective' to that of providing citizens 'with a high level of safety within an area of freedom, security and justice'. It further enumerates a list of particular concerns, namely 'terrorism, trafficking in persons and offences against children, illicit drug trafficking and illicit arms trafficking, corruption and fraud'. These concerns, article 30 (ex K2) goes on to say, will be addressed by 'common action in the field of police cooperation'. In practice, such actions cover extradition proceedings, exchange of information, and the reinforcement of Europol.

Both these Titles have attracted considerable criticism, not the least of which relates to their lack of democratic accountability and transparency. We shall take a closer look at the evolution of the CFSP in due course, but suffice to say that most commentators have duly noted that there is far greater concern with internal 'security' than there is with the rather grander aim of promoting 'peace' and 'progress' around the world (Wessel, 2000, p 1138). The sense that the two intergovernmental 'pillars' are predominantly insular in tone is obviously enhanced by the provisions contained in Title V. Indeed, it is hard to argue against the conclusion that the two 'pillars', rather than being distinct, are actually indistinguishable, at least in their purpose, and in their predominant concern with 'security' (Wessel, 2000, pp 1145–1149).

The politics of exclusion

In its original form, immigration policy fell under the remit of Title V. Much of it has subsequently been transferred to the Community 'pillar'. However, the spirit of exclusion remains. Council and Commission documents continue to talk of immigration in terms of a security 'problem', and it remains indelibly wedded in the psyche of the Union with regard to the collateral matters of foreign, defence and security policy. As John Roper has observed, whilst Union 'foreign policy' might be couched in terms of 'humanitarian motives', it is really geared by a visceral 'aversion to refugees' (Roper, 2000, p 22). Despite the nominal transfer of immigration matters to the Community 'pillar' in the Amsterdam Treaty, in practice immigration remains a firmly intergovernmental concern. The tone of the Union's aversion to immigrants resonates with its comparable aversion to internal migrants. In essence, immigration policy merely describes a slightly more fevered symptom of the same underlying neurosis, a fear of 'others'.

Of course, when labour was needed, the Community could not get enough immigrants. Now that it cannot find employment for its own citizens, the Union has set up a series of draconian regulations and procedures to keep out those who most want to enter. Ironically, given the demographic context of consistent depopulation, the reality is that Europe needs immigrants. But fear overcomes reason, and so hysteria sets in. Events in the Balkans led the Commission to start talking of an immigration 'problem' during the early 1990s. Between 1988 and 1991, the number of asylum-seekers in the Union more than doubled, from 170,000 to 420,000 (Bell, 2002, p 66; Joly, 1999, pp 341–343). Hysteria gave way to inhumanity. Thousands of Albanians were deported from Italy in the dead of night, in blatant contravention of any judicial procedures demanded by international law. Internment camps were set up to 'deal' with thousands more fleeing the conflict (Nascimbene, 1992, pp 719–720; Garry, 2002, p 164). There were, the Commission sagely warned, 'floods' of immigrants on the way, threatening to 'swamp' the Community with lots of poor people. Populist xenophobia is one thing. Populist hysteria whipped up by people who should know better is something else again (Spencer, 1995, pp 109–110; Huysmans, 2000, pp 754–756).

As the perceived fear of mass immigration mounted, Union immigration ministers drew up a series of measures in 1990 which were intended to harmonise asylum application procedures, including the immediate rejection without appeal of all that could be deemed 'manifestly unfounded', and the concomitant responsibility to return such failed applicants immediately. Moreover, in contravention of the European Convention, the Dublin Convention, as it was called, confirmed that member states should enjoy the 'power in appropriate circumstances to restrict the personal liberty of people liable to expulsion'. The pervasive neurosis was further reinforced by a series of complementary provisions, such as the tightening of carrier sanctions and the 'one application only' procedures for asylum-seekers (Spencer, 1995, pp 91–94; Garry, 2002, p 167).[8]

[8] Which means that asylum-seekers can only make one application to one member state.

The creation of the Union's three 'pillar' structure was, then, in large part an immediate expression of this neurosis. Immigration policy was consigned to the jurisprudential twilight world of the non-justiciable third pillar, 'Justice and Home Affairs'. And, accordingly, at the heart of the Union Treaty, in the new article K could be found a whole raft of measures of dubious legality in international human rights law. As with the plight of Europe's internal 'others', it might be thought that the fate of immigrants would be alleviated following the creation of Title IV at the Amsterdam Treaty. Article 61 (ex 73i) introduced the broad areas of 'asylum and immigration' into the Community Treaty, whilst article 63 (ex 73k) further confirmed the Union's commitment to the principles of the Geneva Convention. However, it was notable that the measures denoted in article 61 were recast as 'flanking measures', which meant, in effect, measures for tightening external borders as a counterweight to the putative 'opening' of internal borders. Moreover, the article 68 limitation on the jurisdiction of the Court of Justice in matters relating to the 'maintenance of law and order and the safeguarding of internal security', applied, unsurprisingly, to the condition of immigrants as well as third-country nationals.

It is for this reason that Union policy regarding the treatment of immigrants has been condemned as virulently after Amsterdam as it was before. Given the presence of article 68, it is doubtful whether Community competence in the area of immigration has actually increased at all. Furthermore, a number of provisions from the Dublin Convention which appear to breach article 14 of the UN Declaration regarding the rights of asylum-seekers, can now be found nestling in Title IV (Hailbronner, 1998, pp 1055–1065; Guild, 1999, pp 318–322; Lavanex, 2001, pp 865–866; Garry, 2002, pp 173–178). The mere fact that the Dublin and Schengen Conventions have finally arrived in the Community Treaty does not detract from the fact that such limitations continue to exist. The situation of the asylum-seeker is no less 'grim', as Elspeth Guild puts it, after Amsterdam than it was before (Guild, 1999, p 335).

Indeed, as Theodora Kostakopoulou has pointed out, the presence of the Schengen *acquis* in the Community, with its judicial limitations, actually opens 'the way for the installation of the logic of exclusion' within the 'system of Community law'. It also reinforces the dominant 'security paradigm', as well as tending to criminalise asylum and

immigration matters, despite the effective absence of judicial competence. The fact that immigration matters have now been detached
from the rump of 'provisions on police and judicial cooperation'
which remain in Title VI of the Union Treaty, does not entirely
remove the stigma of their original alignment pre-1997
(Kostakopoulou, 2000, pp 499, 514–515; Huysmans, 2000, pp
756–762; Garry, 2002, pp 175, 182–183).[9] The peculiar status of Title
IV EC, apparently part of the Community *acquis*, but residing in a
non-justiciable twilight zone, vividly testifies to the Union's continuing fear of the 'others', whether they be inside or out.

As far as its member states are concerned, Union immigration
remains a problem of 'security', its sole purpose being to contain,
and reduce, migration (Guild, 2000, pp 169–190; Huysmans, 2000, pp
756–758). The redefinition of asylum-seekers, to exclude 'economic
refugees', is merely the most obvious mechanism by which to tighten
exclusion. The need to eat is not, it seems, sufficient an excuse to seek
entry to the 'new' Europe. The statistics, as ever, are telling. In 1980,
65 per cent of asylum-seekers were granted access to the Community.
By 1990, that figure had declined to just 10 per cent, and it has continued to decline ever since. Less than 5 per cent of the 350,000
asylum-seekers are currently granted residence in Union member
states (Baldwin-Edwards, 1991, p 200; de Jong, 1999, pp 369–373;
Garry, 2002, p 164). And yet, even though it hovers at such a minimal
level, the former French Interior Minister, Charles Pasqua, can still
seek to curry popular support with a promise of 'zero immigration'.
So far, the 'new' Europe has, in all, provided sanctuary for less than 10
per cent of the estimated 25 million refugees and 26 million displaced
persons who remain abroad in the world (Spencer, 1995, p 76;
Lavanex, 2001, pp 358–364; Joly, 1999, p 354).

Then, if all else fails, there is always money. Countries can be paid to
take back their fleeing refugees, or, as the Commission prefers to
term it, there can be incentives paid for 'stimulating and facilitating'
their return (O'Keeffe, 1995, p 31). This latter idea has become very
popular, with various member states happily dispatching large
cheques to all kinds of dubious regimes in return for their accepting

---

[9]   The alignment of immigration with various criminal activities can be traced back
to the reports of the Trevi Group in the early 1980s. Much of the Trevi 'proposals' found their way into the Dublin and Schengen Conventions.

back thousands of those who risked their lives to escape in the first place. It has been termed migration policy by 'remote control' (Giraudon, 2000, p 259). Germany, in particular, has signed 're-admission agreements' with an array of eastern European countries, along, rather incongruously, with Vietnam and Sri Lanka. Italy agreed to invest $150m in Tunisia in return for the repatriation of putative immigrants. The rump state of Yugoslavia has received considerable financial support in return for receiving back thousands of its former residents displaced during the wars. One of the most expensive of such ventures has proved to be the funding of refugee camps in Turkey, in order to detain Iraqi Kurds (Marshall, 2000, p 416; Giraudon, 2000, p 266; Joly, 1999, pp 351–353). Union immigration policy would be far better described as deportation policy (Baldwin-Edwards, 1997, pp 513–514).

The Union's treatment of the 'others' outside, like indeed its treatment of those inside, is more than merely regrettable. It speaks to the continued crises of identity that besets the 'new' Europe. Worse still, it fosters the conditions within which populist xenophobia prospers. Meeting at the Seville Council in summer 2002, the Union's leaders could conclude that mass immigration remains one of the most pressing 'problems' that must be faced, alongside the collateral need to 'restore public confidence' in this area. The rhetoric is absurd. And it is certainly not the tone in which European political debate should be conducted. It is hard to argue against David Cesarini's conclusion, that the 'new' Europe is beset by a 'new racism', much of it the product of the Community's own law and policy (Cesarini, 1996, p 69; Ruzza, 2000). It is equally hard to deny Carole Lyon's similar resolution, that the 'integrative process' as a whole remains xenophobic and divisive, characterised by 'exclusionary trends' of 'marginalisation, identity manipulation, member state domination and a lack of a moral dimension' (Lyons, 1998, p 171; Geddes, 1995, pp 205–215). The fact that the Commission seems to be unconcerned by the migration of the wealthy is striking. It is poor people that the 'new' Europe would prefer not to admit (O'Keeffe, 1991, p 195).

The kind of rhetoric articulated at Seville echoes the same primal expressions of xenophobic nationalism that the 'new' Europe was supposed to be leaving behind. As yet, however, it seems to be unable, or unwilling, to make this step forward. As Joseph Weiler comments:

Nationality as a referent for interpersonal relations, and the human alienating effect of *Us* and *Them* are brought back again, simply transferred from their previous intra-Community context to the new inter-Community one. We may have made little progress if the *Us* becomes European (instead of German or French or British) and the *Them* becomes those outside the Community or those inside who do not enjoy the privileges of citizenship. (Weiler, 1991b, p 436.)

So long as forms of discrimination based on nationality or race continue to exist in the 'new' Europe, it can make no credible claim to possessing a human rights foundation, still less talk the language of liberty, democracy, the rule of law, or even common decency. So long as individual member states are encouraged to herd asylum-seekers into detention camps, the image of 'otherness', as well as the stigma of criminality, is unlikely to be dissipated (Joly, 1999, pp 345–347).[10]

The need to integrate the various 'peoples' of Europe is, arguably, the Union's primary responsibility. So long as it fails to apply the most basic principles of humanity to the treatment of putative immigrants, it cannot claim to be taking this responsibility seriously. As Juergen Habermas asserts, the 'new' Europe was not designed so that its constituent nation states could 'draw their wagons around themselves and their chauvinism of prosperity, hoping to ignore the pressures of those hoping to immigrate or seek asylum'. The desire to 'preserve one's own political culture' must not become an excuse to exclude others from a 'common political culture'. The way in which the Union treats its immigrant supplicants, Habermas suggests, can be taken as a weather-vane for its own sense of humanity (Habermas, 1992, p 17). It is a challenging, if also troubling, thought.

The principled case is unarguable. But so too is the practical. The Union's borders are porous. They will always be porous, and tens of thousands of illegal immigrants enter the Union every year. Only,

---

10   The extent to which such policies descend to the incongruous as well as the inhumane is evidenced by varying policies regarding education in detention camps. In Denmark, for example, internees and their children are only educated in their native tongue, as if learning Danish might somehow make them a greater threat to all the other Danes. In the UK, meanwhile, government policy is to insist that asylum applicants should only learn English. Presumably they might then be persuaded to forget that they ever came from anywhere else, at least until they are returned.

because they enter 'illegally', no one has any means of seeking to integrate them into the Union, any means of using their skills, or their labour potential. Meanwhile, because immigrant entry remains shrouded in this half-light, all the mythologies that surround the millions of apparently indigent, malevolent, and invariably black, 'others' who seek entry in order to rape, pillage and draw social security, actually gain some kind of popular credibility. Eurobarometer figures, taken at the end of the century, revealed that a third of European citizens were happy to be described as 'quite racist' or 'very racist'. Commission President Santer was moved to admit that it was rather 'worrying' (Elman, 2000, p 730; Huysmans, 2000, pp 764–770). But not so moved that he demanded significant reforms in Union immigration policy.

Back in 1992, the UN High Commissioner for Refugees commented:

> As we move into the nineties there is no doubt that Europe is at a crossroads. Will Europe turn its back on those who are forced to move, or will it strengthen its long tradition of safeguarding the rights of the oppressed and the uprooted? Will Europe build new walls, knowing that walls did not stop those who were fleeing totalitarian persecution in the past? Or will Europe help to bridge the abyss which now separates East from West and North from South? Will Europe and the rest of the industrialised world have the courage to commit themselves politically and economically to attack severe poverty, underdevelopment and social injustice which leads to oppression, violence and displacement? The path we follow will create the kind of world we bestow on future generations. (Spencer, 1995, pp 98–99.)

The challenge is, again, both compelling and troubling. As yet, the Union has still to take it up (Monar, 1998, p 335).

A greater Europe?

The Union's response to immigration, and indeed to the plight of third-country nationals, cannot be extricated from the overwhelming question of enlargement, the idea of a 'Greater' Europe. The end of the Cold War catapulted enlargement onto the political map. It was clear that the Union could not shirk a very particular responsibility to the rest of the continent, a responsibility that became ever more exacting as the Balkan wars took hold. For much of the 1990s, the question of enlargement has haunted the Union (Ginsberg, 1999, p 436). As we have already noted, the Nice Treaty was devoted to the question of enlargement, whilst the Commission and its President remain obsessed by it. According to Prodi, 'the noble task of reuniting Europe' is carried along with the 'tide of history' (White et al, 2002, p 136).

The excitement, and the concern, is justified. This fourth enlargement will be quite unlike any previous one, and not just in scale. The Union is about to enlarge itself by approximately a third, and that third will be noticeably weaker in terms of economic capability, and vastly different in terms of social, cultural and ethnic composition (Pentland, 2000). The Commission has warned of the 'unique challenge' which would be posed by integrating the 'wealth of different histories and cultures' that come along with 105 million more Union citizens. Of course, it is not really the wealth of cultures that matters, but a rather different sort of wealth, the altogether more prosaic wealth of money. Whilst the Agenda 2000 programme has given rise to a certain cautious optimism, it remains wedded to the need for a visible economic 'track record' first established at the 1993 Copenhagen IGC.

The Copenhagen 'criteria' addressed various criteria. On the one hand, aspiring members would have to accept the *acquis communautaire*, in other words the entire body of law and principles which govern the Union. The Madrid Council, in 1995, further confirmed that aspirants would also have to put in place the necessary administrative and judicial structures. And by the time of the Helsinki Council in 1999, the spirit of article 6 TEU had been confirmed: putative members would also need to evidence their commitment to the 'values and objectives' of the Union as 'set out in the Treaties'. The need for applicants to fulfil specific civil and human rights criteria has been welcomed, though not without a certain ironic aside to its own shortcomings in the area. The ultimate refusal to accept the Turkish application, together with clear signals of doubts regarding the efficacy of human rights provisions in Estonia and Romania, reinforces the sense that the Union is taking human rights seriously, at least outside its borders (Williams, 2000).

Above all, however, aspiring members of the Union need to be rich enough, or at least show a sufficient enthusiasm for becoming rich. The Copenhagen 'criteria' require evidence of 'the irreversible, sustained and verifiable implementation of reforms and policies for a long enough period to allow for a permanent change in the expectations and behaviour of economic agents and for judging that achievements will be lasting'. In October 2000, Tony Blair told the assembled bankers and businessmen of Poland, the only audience that seemed to be worth addressing, that the Union's 'greatest opportunity' is an 'economic one'; an odd inversion of the received wisdom that the Union should add a political, perhaps even ethical, dimension to the completed market of the Community. 'Nobody', he cheered himself, 'who considers the role that open markets have played in generating wealth and prosperity in the European Union can doubt the benefits of creating a market of half a billion consumers'. But there was still much to be done, for economic 'reform', he sternly reminded his hosts, 'is the only entry ticket' (Blair, 2000).

In order to assist in their preparation, applicant states have been invited to sign ten-year bilateral Partnership and Co-operation Agreements, which have since become known as 'Europe' Agreements. Virtually all eastern European states have done so, along with a number of rather more distant former Soviet states, including, not just Russia, but Ukraine, Moldova and Belarus. Whilst the latter's prospects of quick accession are remote, there are still political and economic benefits in tightening their associations with the rest of 'Europe'. Various other more specific agreements are also in place with a number of aspirant states, many such as the Poland and Hungary Assistance for Economic Restructuring Programme (PHARE) geared to providing shorter-term technical, humanitarian and economic assistance. These agreements invariably bring with them various measures for Union scrutiny (Monar, 2000, pp 318–324; Kahl, 1997, pp 167–179, 174–175; Evans, 1997).

Of course, it does rather open up the question of where 'Europe' is. President de Gaulle famously, if not very precisely, declared that it stretched 'from the Atlantic to the Urals'. At much the same time, in 1963, US President Kennedy prophesied a grand 'Atlantic Community' that would encompass both Europe and North America. The latter assertion was, of course, bound up with the Cold War rhetoric and rationale of NATO. Current US support for the parallel enlargement of both the Union and NATO is driven by the same vision that enthused Kennedy. According to former Deputy Secretary of State, Strobe Talbott, European 'enlargement' will strengthen the foundations of a 'broader, deeper transatlantic community' (Walker, 2000, pp 459, 466–473).

The geopolitical idea of Europe has never settled. As Martin Walker has observed, the 'geography' is as 'variable' as the 'geometry' (Walker, 2000, p 465). The Europe defined in turn by the Community and the Union has always been challenged by other 'Europes', not least the Europe which has been encompassed by the European Free Trade Association, and its more recent manifestation, the European Economic Area; to which a number of applicant states, together with those that have declined to join the Union, such as Norway, Iceland and Switzerland, have been associated. Geography alone provides a rather idiosyncratic measure. One current applicant, Cyprus, for example, is barely 200 kilometres from the coast of Lebanon, is further south than Tunis and further east than Kiev. Yet, somehow, the idea of Cyprus joining the Union seems that bit more credible than Tunisia or the Ukraine.

The 'centre' of Europe, moreover, seems to be a particular subject of contestation. According to the prominent Czech novelist, Milan Kundera, the true geographical 'centre' of Europe lies in his home-land (Wallace, 2000, p 478). The 'centre' of Europe that Prime Minister Blair hopes that the United Kingdom will occupy is pre-sumably rather different. Everyone, it seems, would like to be at the centre of Europe. President Putin has repeatedly confirmed his hope that Russia could be at the 'centre' of a 'Greater Europe', though the extent to which his compatriots share that vision is dubious. Recent Eurobarometer surveys suggest that less than 20 per cent of Russians see themselves as being European. Less than 10 per cent of Moldovans and Ukrainians do (White et al, 2002, p 141). At the same time, of course, the figures amongst citizens of many of the existing member states would barely look any more positive. But Putin's vision of a 'Greater Europe', and the mere geographical extension of a prospective Union so far to the east does raise serious questions of European identity.

The King of Morocco's recent comment that his country would like to renew its application to join the Union, together with the continuing embarrassment that is the Turkish application, adds a further, rather awkward, frisson of concern. For whilst the Union would hesitate to openly admit the fact, it has always been assumed that the 'new' Europe is a Christian Europe, or at least it is not a Muslim one. As far as Chancellor Kohl was concerned, Europe was 'a Christian club' (Walker, 2000, p 462). However, as the King suggested, this 'taboo' is no longer credible in the 'new' ethnically diverse Europe (Wallace, 2000, p 477). Of course, he is right, or at least he should be. But that does not make the truth any easier to swallow. The kind of 'values' reinforced at the Helsinki Council, and which find expression in article 6 TEU and the notional Charter of Fundamental Rights are assumed to be derived from a distinctive 'western' tradition of political morality. The fear of the 'other' militates against the thought that the boundaries of a European Union might stretch as far as Fez or Marrakesh. The thought is little more appealing than the notion that Brussels officials might one day have to embark on the Trans-Siberian Express in order to find out what is happening at the further reaches of 'Greater Europe'.

The fear of the 'other' cannot be laid. And as we noted above, the question of enlargement cannot readily be distinguished from the Union's paranoia regarding mass migration (Monar, 2000). The Tampere Council, in late 1999, spoke of the need for 'more efficient management of migration flows at all their stages'. In effect, this means the establishment of a system of 'concentric circles', with the Union buffered by various applicant states to east, as well as suppliant, and easily bribed, states in North Africa. These barriers are supposed to provide 'Fortress Europe' with a series of outer defences against the barbarian 'other' (Kostakopoulou, 2000, pp 511–512; Marshall, 2000, pp 419–420).[11] The ability to police their eastern borders is one of the most important attributes of any prospective applicant. The suggestion that they might need financial assistance in order to do this is also one of the surest ways of attracting large cheques from Brussels, or more often indeed, from Berlin. The German government, anxious to avoid any further migratory flows has spent hundreds of millions of ECU funding border controls in Poland, Belarus, and the Czech and Slovak republics (Marshall, 2000, pp 416–417). All in all, as Catherine Phuong has suggested, the

[11]   The idea of 'concentric circles' emerged most forcefully in a document produced by the Austrian government, during their Presidency of the Council in 1998.

removal of one Iron Curtain in 1989, has simply led, a decade or so later, to the establishment of another a little further to the east (Phuong, 2003).

Towards the end of the 1990s, the Union undertook a 'screening' process to ensure that the Copenhagen 'criteria' had been met, and to provide some kind of legitimacy to the selection of who it might wish finally to admit (Smith, 2000). Then at another Copenhagen Council, a decade on, in late 2002, it was confirmed that ten applicants have fulfilled the 'criteria' for accession, ranging from the larger former Warsaw Pact states such as Poland, the Czech Republic, Slovakia and Hungary, through smaller Baltic satellites, including Estonia, Latvia and Lithuania, to the very much smaller Mediterranean islands of Malta and Cyprus. The capacity of the latter to accede remains clouded by the Greek–Turkish partition, and Turkey's willingness to be helpful has not been encouraged by the Union refusal to countenance its application for membership. The remaining applicant is Slovenia, a state on the edge of the Balkans that has long enjoyed the rather nostalgic support of a Germany that has tended to regard it as part of a greater German diaspora.[12] A range of other countries, including Bulgaria and Romania, were given a gentle pat on the back, and encouraged to keep trying and to become a little wealthier. As ever, Turkey was given a barely disguised poke in the eye, and told to sort out its human rights record and be nicer to its ethnic minorities, the Luxembourg Prime Minister having earlier commented that he did not 'with to sit at the table with a bunch of torturers', at least not Turkish ones (Walker, 2000, p 462).

Europe's leaders talk of 'locking in' peace and stability across the continent. The question of who is going to bankroll the estimated 275bn ECU that will be need to provide immediate 'structural' support remains unresolved. Squabbles concerning the extent of necessary reform to the CAP continue to rumble on. Politicians and commentators alike ponder the prospects of a 'wider but weaker' Europe, one that might devolve, perhaps into an inner core of original members, perhaps into a series of 'regions', the Western, the Danubian, the Hanseatic, the Baltic (Pentland, 2000, pp 278, 284–285; Wallace, 2000, pp 491–493). Meanwhile those applicants fortunate enough to

---

[12]   It was, of course, Germany's precipitate recognition of Slovenian independence that did much to hasten the cataclysmic break-up of the former Yugoslavia.

receive the Union's blessing await the 'swift and purposeful measures' which, the Commission has insisted, will be necessary in order to make their respective economies competitive in the Greater Europe.

The evolution of a 'European' foreign policy

The arrival of the CFSP in 1992 represented a significant change of pace, one demanded not least by the prospects of enlargement. There had been earlier, looser arrangements designed to cover foreign and defence arrangements, most obviously the system of European Political Cooperation (EPC), which was inaugurated in 1970, and then confirmed in the Single European Act. Its general aim was to ensure periodic meetings of Foreign Ministers, at which 'common policies' might be drawn up as necessary (Bonvicini, 1998, pp 62–63; Smith, 2001, 86–89). The CFSP was altogether tighter, for reasons to which we have already alluded, allowing for both a foreign and a defence policy directed under the dominant control of the Council, and replete with all kinds of mechanisms and strategy objectives. And yet, as ever, whilst the rhetoric might have been impressive, the actual working of the CFSP during much of the 1990s proved to be both 'painful and problematic' (Ginsberg, 1999, p 431).

To a certain extent, the problems were rooted in the original structure of the Union, and related more immediately to the irreducible problem of competence. Since its inception in 1992, it has become ever more obvious that the CFSP cannot always be cleanly distinguished from either the 'area of freedom, security and justice', or indeed the Community 'pillar'. A common example of this latter overlap relates to the administration of sanctions, measures that speak to both foreign policy concerns and to the economics of the market. The overlap has a further, and important, jurisprudential implication, for in cases such as the 1998 *Commission v Council* action concerning transit visas, the Court has confirmed its own competence to adjudge the Community implications of sanctions and similar proceedings (*Commission v Council*, 1998).

A similar, and famous, example is the *Bosphorus* case, in which the Irish government grounded a Yugoslav aircraft in line with Union Regulation 990/93 which transposed a UN Security Council Resolution on sanctions. The initial actions had been quashed by an

Irish Court on the basis that the plane was managed by a Turkish rather than a Yugoslav company, and so its grounding infringed Community law. This decision was reversed by the Court of Justice, on the familiar ground that, in matters of international law, it, and member state courts, should look to the 'purpose' and the 'context' of the Regulation. The 'purpose' of the Regulation, as the Advocate General affirmed, had to be 'interpreted in such a way as to make the sanctions fully effective' (*Bosphorus*, 1996).[13] The Court's decision was, thus, both politically expedient, as well as being in line with its own jurisprudence, even if it was never clear how the grounding of a plane that did not fly to Yugoslavia, or provide any profits to Yugoslav nationals, actually advanced the 'purpose' of the sanctions themselves (Canor, 1998). Above all, however, the *Bosphorus* case revealed the collateral competence of the Court in matters that might otherwise have been thought to fall within the intergovernmental remit of the CFSP.

These sanctions cases, then, emphasise the extent to which the interests of the Union and the Community cannot readily be distinguished. And as such they lend support to those who argue that the Union 'pillars' should be rationalised further, possibly merged, possibly even made justiciable. As Commissioner Chris Patten observed, if the Balkan wars, and the Union's muddled attempt to ameliorate them, have taught Europeans anything, it is that the Union's policy spheres can never be kept in 'neatly separated boxes' (Howorth, 2001, pp 775–777). The concerns of the Community and the Union are common, just as the nature of internal and external 'security' is inexorably linked.

Moreover, the related sense that the intergovernmental nature of the CFSP might be counter-productive was further reinforced by the experience of its operation during the later 1990s. Despite the presence of a Union foreign policy, it was clear that various member states, most obviously the United Kingdom, France and Germany, continued to operate outwith the Union, most obviously under the auspices of NATO. Moreover, NATO was keen that they should. There is perhaps no better example of the tensions that continue to

---

[13] Something that is required by article 31.3 of the Vienna Convention on the Law of Treaties. Although the Union is not a signatory to the Convention, the Court of Justice has always recognised its persuasive authority.

exist between the alternative supranational and intergovernmental impulses in the 'new' Europe than the fate of the CFSP during the 1990s. It suggests both unity and differentiation at the same time. The arrival of the CFSP had created expectations of the Union, expectations that, as the following six years revealed, were rather grander than its capabilities (Hill, 1998).

Recognising the debilitating effect of this tension, the Council has attempted to tighten the nature of the CFSP. A key event here was the Anglo–French summit at St Malo in late 1998, at which the United Kingdom finally signalled its acceptance that an 'autonomous' Union defence policy was desirable. The acknowledgment was made in the immediate context of the renewal of hostilities in Kosovo, and could be interpreted as an admission that, on this occasion, the Union must not be found wanting once again (Roper, pp 7–10). This spirit of renewed co-operation was taken on to the Helsinki and Cologne Councils held during the following year. The Cologne Declaration affirmed that:

> The Union must have the capacity for autonomous action, backed up by credible military forces, the means to decide to use them, and a readiness to do so, in order to respond to international crises without prejudice to actions by NATO. (Roper, 2000, 12.)

It represented, the Declaration affirmed, 'a new step in the construction of the European Union'. The appointment of the Secretary General of NATO as the Union's new High Representative, or 'Mr CFSP', provided a further signal of intent. According to Stanley Hoffmann, these events signalled a significant 'shift from NATO predominance to a potentially autonomous European security policy' (Hoffmann, 2000, pp 193–195; Howorth, 2001, pp 769–771).

The desire not to 'prejudice' the actions of NATO acknowledges an especial tension. Whilst NATO's Secretary General seeks to assure everyone that relations between his organisation and the European Union have never been better, and whilst the likes of Strobe Talbott can resurrect the dream of a 'transatlantic community', the presence of very real tensions cannot be denied (Robertson, 2001). It was vividly displayed in the tortuous rhetoric of the Helsinki Declaration, which stated that the Union must 'develop an autonomous capacity to take decisions and, where NATO is not as a whole engaged, to launch and conduct EU-led military operations in response to international crises', whilst at the same time trying to reassure everyone that such a 'determination' would 'not imply the creation of a European army' that might somehow be perceived as providing an alternative to NATO. The tension can be reduced to two particular, and perhaps countervailing, concerns, both articulated most commonly by the United States. The first concerns the funding of NATO operations in Europe, whilst the second relates to the inevitable shift in power and influence that will result from what the St Malo Summit gnomically alluded to as a 'modernised Atlantic Alliance' (Roper, 2000, pp 12–16; Howorth, 2001, pp 782–783).

The inauguration of a new 'common European security and defence policy', in articles 17 and 25 of the Nice Treaty in 2000 provides further evidence that an autonomous defence capability might finally be realised. 'Security', as ever, is the watchword, though it has been rightly noted that it is not entirely clear what the 'new' Europe is supposed to be defending itself against. It has been suggested that the emergence of this refined policy is a final recognition that the Union is prepared to accept its responsibilities in trying to maintain peace and stability across the so-called 'arc of crisis' that stretches from the Baltic to northern Africa. The institution of a European Rapid Reaction Force is intended to reinforce this sense of responsibility. Of course, whether the Nice reforms will actually make the Union any more effective in the foreign policy field remains to be seen. At present, the remit of the Reaction Force is limited to the Petersberg 'tasks', as well as notional 'defence' of the Union. However, should there be further warfare in the Balkans, it is clearly intended that the Union would now have a capability to match its expectations (Howorth, 2001, pp 766–781).

Above all, however, it must noted that, whilst the Union might indeed finally be speaking in 'one voice' in matters of foreign policy and security, it continues to do so at the behest of its constituent nation states (Dashwood, 1999, pp 214–215, 221–223). Events at Amsterdam and then Nice have not detracted from this hard reality. The matter of 'security' remains firmly beyond the reach of democracy or accountability, and it is very much 'security' that matters. It continues to bind internal and foreign policy concerns. As the Tampere Council concluded at the end of 1999, 'the challenge' of the future lay in the achievement of 'conditions of security and justice'.

The complementarity is striking. But is clear which of the two concepts really matters in what the Cologne Council recognised as the new 'new' Europe.

Europe and the new world order

We noted above the statistics that trace globalisation, the reality that we are all rather more dependent upon another than we may have previously believed, and the related presumption that some of us at least are all the richer and happier for it. The statistics that chart the downside of this process are just as striking. The 1999 UN Human Development Report stated that around one-fifth of the highest income countries control 82 per cent of the world export markets, 86 per cent of world gross domestic product, 68 per cent of foreign direct investments and 74 per cent of world telephone lines. The bottom one-fifth controls barely 1 per cent of any of these. The wealthiest one-fifth consume 45 per cent of all the meat and fish that is eaten. The poorest one-fifth consumes less than 5 per cent. The UNICEF Report, *Development Goals and Strategies*, noted that over 45 per cent of children in developing countries suffer 'critical poverty', whilst 250,000 die every week of malnutrition. 'Death on this scale', the Report concluded, 'is simply no longer necessary; it is therefore no longer acceptable'. In its 1993 Report *The State of the World's Children*, it noted that $25m per year would suffice to eradicate such death rates. Each year, it was noted, European Union citizens spend far more than this on buying wine. Robert Falk refers to an environment of 'global apartheid' and 'inhumanity' (Falk, 1995, pp 49–48, 190; Friedman, 2000, pp 9, 319–320).

The statistics warrant our attention, because the European Union has a responsibility for them. Indeed, as an emergent economic 'superpower' of undoubted global muscle, the Union's responsibility becomes daily the greater (McGoldrick, 1999, p 267). It is not an exclusive responsibility, of course, but the nature of globalisation means that no one, certainly not the wealthiest and most powerful, can exclude themselves from the economic fate of everyone else (Soros, 2000, pp xii–xiii). To a certain extent, the Union has taken on this responsibility. The fact that the Union is the largest contributor of humanitarian aid and development is one of its proudest claims (McGoldrick, 1999, pp 262–263). But it is also one of the most incompetent, its programmes taking years and years to process, millions of ECU stalled in various Union bank accounts whilst bureaucrats fiddle around worrying about the potential disruption to trade flows.

Moreover, immediate financial support is only one aspect of the Union's greater responsibility. There is, perhaps unsurprisingly given the above statistics, and the generally disorientating effect of globalisation, a mood of despondency abroad. Robert Falk projects 'a new world disorder', one in which 'strife, extremism, despair abound' (Falk, 1995, p 25). According to John Gray, the 'era' of 'hallucinatory vistas' and imagined 'new world orders' is over. Instead, we peer anxiously over a precipice, dimly perceiving before us a 'tragic epoch' of 'deepening international anarchy'. The 'inherent instability of global markets', he further prophecies, will ultimately crush a soporific, politically disengaged, humanity (Gray, 1998, pp 3, 22–24, 72–74, 205–208). As George Soros admits, the realm of politics, particularly democratic politics, has been severely 'distorted' by globalisation (Soros, 2000, 167–168). And the malaise, and the potential threat, reaches into the heart of Europe and its citizens. As much was admitted by the Commission in its *Agenda 2000* document which noted that 'the process of globalisation, from which the Union has benefited so much, also exposes it to both economic and political risks in this international arena'.

According to Ulrich Beck, Europeans, like everyone else, 'struggle to live their own lives in a world that increasingly and more evidently escapes their grasp, one that is irrevocably and globally networked'. So now we are expected to live 'our lives with the most diverse and contradictory transnational and personal identities and risks'. Our received identities have been undermined. We are not comfortable with the 'multi-local transnationality' that has been foisted upon us; any more than we are happy reflecting upon the possibility of multiple identities, multiple *demoi*, or 'multi-layered democracy'. The lack of a clear identity may seem to be a primarily cultural misfortune, but is has very definite political implications; for we have lost our ability to access a 'public realm'. Life is no longer a question of 'solidarity or obligation but of conflictual coexistence' (Beck, 2000, pp 168–173). The need to reinvest this 'realm' is a popular complaint. According to Will Hutton, the capacity for social and participatory democracy described by the social contractarian tradition defines the 'new'

Europe. It is indeed, the 'golden thread' of European 'civilization'. But it is, as yet, despite the passages of centuries, still to be fully realised (Hutton, 2002, pp 51–54, 73, 277–279, 288–290).[14]

The root of our present despondency, then, lies in a failure of governance. It is for this reason that the European experience is so pertinent. We have already encountered, on more than one occasion, the perceived failings of governance in Europe. At the same time, we must also recognise that the 'new' Europe represents the flagship of the 'new world order'. If such an 'order' is to succeed, then surely it must succeed in Europe, rapidly becoming, not merely the wealthiest, but the most liberal, political community in the world. The 'new' Europe certainly has its faults, not least of which is its treatment of those who are deemed not to be 'European'. But it can also lay justifiable claim to being the most progressive and the most exciting experiment in post-modern governance in the world. Whilst being consistently critical of much of the European experience, Philip Allott can still express his enthusiasm for the 'possibility of reconstituting' a global 'society', and with it 'the international society of the whole human race, the society of all societies' (Allott, 1992, p 223).

For those who advise the need for a new form of global governance which can lend some legitimacy to the 'new world order', the example of Europe is not merely exciting. It is critical. Even as committed a free-marketeer as Charles Fried has argued that something must be done with regard to the legitimacy 'gap' in the 'new world order' in order to deflect the less desirable effects of 'tyrant capitalism' (Fried, 2000). John Gray similarly argues that a 'regime of global governance is needed in which world markets are managed so as to promote the cohesion of societies and the integrity of states'. The future of humanity depends upon such a construction, for 'only a framework of global regulation' can 'enable the creativity of the world economy to be harnessed in the service of human needs' (Gray, 1998, p 199). The European common market, despite its protestations regarding free trade and competition, represents a model for just how such markets might still be regulated. The irony is, of course, striking.

Advocates of global governance, such as Antony Giddens, often seek recourse to the European project. For Giddens it provides a model of reinvigorated transnational 'regulation', one that will 'build up a

---

[14]   We shall revisit the idea of participatory democracy in the next chapter.

global civil society and a framework of law' and which will encourage us to think 'about possible forms of transnational democracy' (Giddens and Hutton, 2000, pp 23, 38–39, 45). Such ideas have also attracted David Held, who argues that the 'circumstances' of globalisation 'present significant opportunities for the establishment of an international order based upon the principles of constitutionality and democracy' (Held, 1995, pp ix, 22–23, 236, 267, 270–278). This relation, between democratic legitimacy and the law, is inextricable. A post-modern system of governance must be founded on a post-modern understanding of law. The dynamics of globalisation have crushed the pretences of classical public international law (Baxi, 1998, pp 163–164). Harold Koh has readily acknowledged that there has been an 'epochal transformation of international law', with the emergence of a 'transnational legal process' that locates 'reasons for compliance' at a 'transactional level', one of 'interaction, interpretation, and internalization of international norms into domestic structures' (Koh, 1997, pp 2604, 2630–2631, 2648–2649, 2655–2659).

Perhaps the most compelling account of such an understanding of law can be found in William Twining's suggestion that there must be a 're-mapping' of law, one that will better enable us to accommodate the 'complexities' of our present existence. What we need, according to Twining, is a map that properly 'emphasises the complexities and elusiveness of reality, the difficulties of grasping it, and the value of imagination and multiple perspectives in facing these difficulties' (Twining, 2000, pp 140, 152, 172–174, 243). We shall return to the more immediately jurisprudential implications in the next chapter. But for now we can certainly admit that if the European experience has taught jurists anything, it is that classical notions of 'positive' law, attached to the various collateral mythologies of 'sovereignty', have been rendered virtually meaningless.

In all, the 'new' Europe can lay justifiable claim to being the pioneer for the 'new world order'. It has set about re-mapping law and governance. It has certainly made mistakes, and it remains riven by tensions, consumed indeed by self-doubt. But such tensions and such doubts are the lot of pioneers. The world, as Will Hutton has advised, 'needs an order that is more subtle and more sophisticated', and Europe, where notions of equality, democracy and fairness are 'more deeply embedded', presents itself as the only credible champion of democratic transnational governance. 'If America championed a liberal order in the twentieth century', Hutton suggests, 'Europe will have to sustain that vision in the twenty-first', for unlike the United States, Europe has actually embraced the 'new world order' and all its various collateral implications. In providing the 'exemplar of what a peaceful multilateral system of governance can achieve', the 'new' Europe is 'trail-blazing for the globe' (Hutton, 2002, pp 10–12, 17–18, 48, 312, 365).

Robert Falk deploys the resonant phrase 'citizen pilgrim', to describe someone who is committed to 'an imagined community of the future that embodies non-violence, social justice, ecological balance and participatory democracy in all arenas of policy and decision' (Falk, 1995, p 95). His conclusion is compelling:

> Only by reconstructing intimate relations on a humane basis can the world move toward the wider public and collective realities of human community. This reconstruction, starting at home, is a critical precondition for the emergence of the sort of global polity that could inspire trust and have a reasonable prospect of providing humane governance for a democratically constituted global civil society. (Falk, 1995, p 69.)

This is the rhetoric of cosmopolitan humanism, and we will revisit the subject in the next chapter. The case for democratic global governance, regardless of the extent to which it is founded on cosmopolitan or international precepts, is unarguable. If the much-vaunted 'new world order' is not to continue to disappoint, then the ideal will have to become reality. If the 'new' Europe has a destiny, at least an inspiring one, it is this: to provide a compelling example of how the ideal of democratic governance can become a reality in the 'new' world order. But if it is to do so, it will need to revisit the 'challenge' identified by the Tampere Council at the end of 1999, and strive to make just as much of 'justice' as it does of 'security'. It is an enormous challenge, but one that cannot, and should not, be resisted. As George Soros has suggested, along with the 'future of Europe' lies the 'validity of the concept of open society' (Soros, 2000, p 329).

Chapter 8

In search of a public philosophy

The last decade has seen a burgeoning theoretical interest in the European 'project', not so much along traditional jurisprudential lines perhaps, but certainly in the broader area of public philosophy. In this final chapter, we will take a closer look at four such approaches: the liberal, the social democratic, the post-modern and the cosmopolitan. Such an interest has clearly been generated, at least to some degree, by the tangible sense that the process of European integration has come unstuck, that it suffers from a legitimacy crisis that has continued to debilitate public support. To a certain extent, it can be reasonably suggested that the European 'project' is in crisis. The resolution of a coherent, even inspiring, public philosophy offers itself as the most convincing means by which this crisis might be assuaged. And what has become ever more apparent is the realisation that the institution of more and more laws provides no credible substitute for such a philosophy.

The limits of legalism

In his *Memoirs*, Jean Monnet wrote that the 'Community we have created is not an end in itself. It is a process of change'. He continued:

> It is impossible to foresee today the decisions that could be taken in a new context of tomorrow. The essential thing is to hold fast to the few fixed principles that have guided us since the

beginning: gradually to create among Europeans the broadest common interest, served by common democratic institutions to which the necessary sovereignty has been delegated. This is the dynamic that has never ceased to operate.

And he concluded with the following, even more revealing, admission:

I have never doubted that one day this process will lead us to the United States of Europe; but I see no point in trying to imagine today what political form it will take. (Monnet, 1978, pp 522–523.)

A similar sentiment was voiced by Robert Schuman, who declared that 'Europe will not be built in a day, or in a single construction: it will be built by practical actions' (Devuyst, 1999, p 111). To a certain extent this sentiment chimed with the iconoclastic postwar attitude towards grand ideologies. As texts such as Friedrich Hayek's *The Road to Serfdom* and Karl Popper's *The Open Society and its Enemies* advised, such ideologies, most recently National Socialism and Communism, had visited horror after horror upon Europe.

Instead of ideology, the 'new' Europe had what is commonly termed a 'method', something which amounts to little more than bare incrementalism, the assumption that the Community, and in due course Union, will evolve in the form of chain-novel, with each fresh generation adding another chapter, but with no one really knowing what the conclusion might be, or whether there will even be one. Martin Westlake has recently likened this to the Darwinian idea of the 'blind watchmaker' (Westlake, 1998).[1] And yet, ideology can never be thoroughly exorcised. Political models are never atheoretical. Any political community is underpinned by some kind of theoretical rationale, one that, invariably, seeks to provide a measure of collateral political, even moral, legitimacy.

[1] The idea of the 'blind watchmaker' was famously deployed by Richard Dawkins, to describe the process of evolution as something which gains its drive from the process itself, rather than by any prescribed end. In *The Blind Watchmaker*, he describes it thus: 'A true watchmaker has foresight: he designs his cogs and springs, and plans their interconnections, with a future purpose in his mind's eye. Natural selection, the blind, unconscious, automatic process which Darwin discovered, and which we now know is the explanation for the existence and apparently purposeful form of all life, has no purpose in mind. It has no mind and no mind's eye. It does not plan for the future. It has no vision, no foresight, no sight at all. If it can be said to play the role of watchmaker in nature, it is the blind watchmaker' (Dawkins, 1986, p 5).

As we have already noted, from its very inception, the lack of a clear political blueprint invited a distinctive reliance on law, on the idea that law would provide the cement that could keep the edifice of the European Community from crashing to the ground. European integration would be institutional in the broader sense, and legal in the particular. Unsurprisingly, therefore, some of the first attempts to locate a 'European' public philosophy tended to be narrow and legalistic. Moreover, these earliest approaches were invariably either normative or comparative, and in both cases preferred to describe rather prescribe, and to do so in the light of received intellectual wisdom. Rather than looking at the 'new' Europe as indeed new, such approaches presumed that this Europe could be described by recourse to established theoretical models and strategies.

The normative approach, most commonly adopted by legal theorists, relied heavily upon the received tenets of classical legal positivism. The legal positivist, following the tradition of John Austin and Herbert Hart, understands law to be a series of rules, primary and secondary.[2] The primary rule, the ultimate source of legitimate law, at least in the Austinian tradition, is located in the sovereign body. Dicey cast the British constitution in exclusive honour of Austin's idol, and generations of jurists and their students have paid dutiful obeisance at the same shrine.

One of the most interesting of these early attempts to make normative sense of European legal integration was Frank Dowrick's *A Model of the European Communities' Legal System*. Dowrick took the ideas of Hart, along with those of the Austrian jurist Hans Kelsen, and tried to make them work in the 'new' Europe. It was clear that they did not, for the simple reason that there is no ultimate sovereign body, at least not in the uncompromising Austinian tradition. Such a jurisprudence, he commented, nothing more than a 'collection of norms', plainly

---

[2] John Austin's *The Province of Jurisprudence Determined*, published in 1832, is generally regarded as the definitive statement of classical legal positivism. It was extensively revised by Herbert Hart's *The Concept of Law*, published in 1961. Austin concentrated on the capacity of an identifiable sovereign body to issue and enforce 'commands'. Hart adopted much of Austin's thesis, but deployed the ideas of 'primary' and 'secondary' rules in order to address more precisely the question of legitimacy. A legitimate sovereign must be identified by a 'rule of recognition', such a rule being an ultimate source of law (Ward, 1998, pp 101–104).

'ignores the dynamics' of the Community 'system', the various 'economic, political, moral and social values that animate it'. 'Without a clear appreciation of these', he concluded, a positivist 'legal system is neither intelligible nor workable' (Dowrick, 1983, p 168). In its place, Dowrick recommended a jurisprudence that could be more readily termed Kantian, one perhaps that bore some resemblance to that currently articulated by Ronald Dworkin. Such a jurisprudence, which demands that legal rules must be legitimated in terms of a deeper 'political morality', might be better equipped to meet the demands of the 'new' Europe (Dowrick, 1983, pp 205–237). The insight was telling, and we shall return to the Kantian alternative in due course.

The gauntlet thrown down by Dowrick was taken up in at least a couple of notable instances. The first such instance was Joxerramon Bengoetxea's attempt to flesh out the Dworkinian analysis in his *The Legal Reasoning of the European Court of Justice*. Here Bengoetxea attempted to apply Dworkin's 'integrity' thesis to the European Community, and more precisely to its Court of Justice. According to Dworkin, any legitimate court reasons with 'integrity', meaning with regard to the surrounding moral and political context. In simple terms, as well as applying legal rules, such courts apply what they perceive to be those rules of 'political morality' which also govern the community. To a certain extent such an analysis can provide a striking justification for the experience of legal integration, and more precisely, perhaps, for the often criticised instances of judicial activism, such as the development of principles of supremacy and direct effect (Bengoetxea, 1993, pp vi, 8–9, 34–37, 75–79). At the same time, however, such an analysis, as Bengoetxea admits, does not take us much nearer to establishing what such a 'political morality' should look like in the 'new' Europe (Bengoetxea, 1993, pp 270–274).

A second instance was presented in Neil MacCormick's essay *Beyond the Sovereign State*. As the title of the essay implies, the recognition that the age of the integral nation state has passed necessarily suggests that the age of sovereignty-based jurisprudence has passed too. The idea that the age of the integral nation state has 'ended' was explored in the last chapter. Even if the claim is perhaps slightly overstated, there can be no doubt that the 'new world order', of which the 'new' Europe is a singular example, has cast traditional conceptions of national integrity into considerable doubt. No state in western

Europe, MacCormick rightly asserts, is 'any longer' a 'sovereign state' (MacCormick, 1993, pp 5–10, 16). Taking a similar approach to Dowrick, MacCormick suggested that a more pluralistic conception of sovereignty can be excavated from Austin and Hart. Such a suggestion chimes to a certain degree with the admission, made in countless UK courts during the previous thirty years, that sovereignty is now 'dual'. At the same time, of course, 'plural' means rather more than 'dual'. Most of all, however, a post-sovereignty jurisprudence, according to MacCormick, should be liberating: 'To escape from the idea that all law must originate in a single power source, like a sovereign, is thus to discover the possibility of taking a broader, more diffuse, view of law' (MacCormick, 1993, p 8). The observation is compelling, and we shall return to MacCormick in due course.

The comparative approach was as recidivist as the positivist. It assumed that the 'new' Europe could be understood in comparison with similar polities, both past and present. We have already noted that the Court of Justice has tended to take a comparative approach at times, most obviously in its development of principles of human rights and of a 'common' administrative law. At the same time, of course, it has also shown great inventiveness in creating entirely fresh principles of law, such as direct effect. Such comparative inclinations in the Court, however, inspired certain commentators to recommend such a strategy as the surest way to progress the project of European integration (Jolowicz, 1978; Koopmans, 1991).

On the grander scale, most comparative analyses of European law and politics tend to end up with some kind of federal comparator. To a certain extent there is a measure of wish fulfilment in such a recommendation. The idea of a 'United States of Europe' has been around for some time, articulated variously by the likes of Churchill and Monnet at the very inception of the Community. It is often suggested that the idea of a European 'Union' only makes clinical sense if that union resembles the other United States across the Atlantic. Perhaps the most striking example of this kind of analysis, both descriptive in tone and prescriptive in sentiment, is Ernest Wistrich's *The United States of Europe*. According to Wistrich, federation is Europe's destiny (Wistrich, 1994). A similar approach, if a rather different prescription, can be found in Cappelletti, Seccombe and Weiler's *Integration Though Law*, which provided an extensive survey of possible compativist models and influences, but which also concluded that comparativism can only discover so much. It certainly cannot dispense with the reality that the European political 'Community' still needs a deeper public philosophy (Cappelletti et al, 1985).

The overriding problem, of course, with comparative approaches, particularly those like Wistrich's which rely on the US example, is that the 'new' Europe does not really fit the federal model, either in political or legal terms. It is, as Simon Hix has rightly concluded, quite 'different' from any familiar polity (Hix, 1994).The division of competences in Europe, between the central institutions and the nation states, is very different from that which exists between federal and state authorities in the United States. Moreover there is no clear division in Union government between legislative and executive functions, something that is dear to the heart of the classical federalist, and particularly to those who cherish the US model. Indeed, neither the Council nor the Commission bear any immediate comparison with any institution either in the United States or elsewhere. And the same is, of course, true of the Court of Justice. The Court of Justice is a court of reference, to which individuals cannot apply for redress, and whilst it may have taken on a constitutionalising role, this is still very different from the ambit of the Supreme Court, with its power to select cases, and its assumed primary responsibility for protecting individual rights enshrined in the US Constitution (Jacobs and Klarst, 1985). Following the debacle surrounding the mooted Charter of rights at the Nice Council, the comparison between the Court of Justice and the Supreme Court becomes ever less viable.

The conclusion is undeniable. It is increasingly obvious that received traditions of jurisprudence cannot account for the 'new' Europe. Still less can they provide a broader and coherent public philosophy for it (Bankowski and Christodoulidis, 2000, p 17). Comparativism, meanwhile, though it might have its uses, is equally limited, both in conception and in aspiration. There is no obvious comparison with the 'new' Europe, any more than there is an obviously workable tradition in classical jurisprudence. In simple terms, there has to be something more, something fresher, something that can, indeed, not merely better account for Europe, but also provide the substance of a genuine and inspiring public philosophy.

In search of a public philosophy

Responses to this predicament, to the obvious shortcomings of the normative and comparative approaches, are various. For some, it merely reinforces a residual scepticism of the whole European project. For others, it leads to the inevitable conclusion that the 'new' Europe is very much more obviously intergovernmental than supranational. There is, in this view, no European public philosophy because the 'new' Europe is, in truth, nothing more than a collection of nation states joined together by an overblown customs union. The supranational institutions are merely feints, which seek to provide some kind of illusory European-ness, but which barely mask the reality that the 'new' Europe, like the old, dances exclusively to the tune of its, often bickering, nation states (Wallace, 1982; Hoffmann, 1995). For still others, however, it is equally plain that the 'new' Europe has become something more than its constituent nation states, and that something more is dangerously bureaucratic and managerial in tone, and undemocratic in practice. Either way, scepticism about European integration is no longer a minority interest. As the 1990s have progressed, the whole idea of a European 'project' has become ever more doubtful, whilst Europe's citizens have become ever more doubting (Hansen and Williams, 1999).

A strong sense of this kind of scepticism can be found in Philip Allott's critique of the 'managerial absolutism' of the Community, written in 1991:

> The absence of a transcendent social framework for the Community power-system has generated a cascade of consequences in the constitutional development of the EC over the last forty years. It has meant that the EC system, a particular political and legal system, reminiscent of national state systems, has come to be equated with the idea of 'Europe' for many people. It has meant that the EC has seemed to have no reason for existing other than the continued willing of the state systems of the states that formed it. Above all, it has meant that the EC communal interest has come to be perceived as an aggregated interest, aggregated from separate national interests . . . This in turn means that there is a sense of retrograde motion in the development of democracy in Western Europe, as politicians and civil servants take over the

negotiation of new laws as if they were negotiating treaties. (Allott, 1991, pp 2498–2499.)

The 'people of Europe', he concludes, 'have watched patiently as one gang after another has strutted across the stage of European history'. The present 'so-called European Community is merely the latest in a long line' (Allott, 1991, p 2499).

In articulating such a caustic dismissal of the European 'project', Allott is making both a sceptical, and also a constructive, statement. Euroscepticism is often dismissed as somehow anti-European. Such easy insults deny the deeper the truth, that progress can only be founded on scepticism, on the willingness to recognise weaknesses and to work to resolve them. It is for this reason that Allott emphasises that the 'true' community can only arise from the ashes of the Community. This seemingly cataclysmic conclusion is deceptive. For what Allott really means is that a 'true' Europe, one that is founded upon shared moral as well as political values, can only emerge once the legalistic mindset, the assumption that the institution of laws themselves are enough, has been once and for all banished. It will require, not merely the appreciation that political philosophy is a 'phenomenology' rather than a 'science', but also the more particular recognition that there must be a 'revolutionary change in the Community's consciousness of itself' (Allott, 1991, pp 2485–2488). In simple terms, if Europe is to have a healthy future it must replace its present 'managerial absolutism' with a genuinely democratic embrace.

Such a conclusion lends itself to the more positive search for a credible public philosophy. The need for such a philosophy has been articulated with increasing urgency during the previous decade. As Peter Sutherland noted back in 1992, the experience of legal integration in particular has made plain the fact that the 'limits of debate' have been 'pushed out' to 'horizons far beyond those contemplated by more pragmatic politicians concerned with day to day realities' (Sutherland, 1992, pp 11–17). The sentiment was echoed by the former President of the French National Assembly, Laurent Fabius, who urged Europe to 'move beyond the traditional forms of community'. In doing so, he rightly suggested, it 'appears to foreshadow a more general movement' across the globe. His conclusion was equally pertinent: 'Where our nations are concerned, states are increasingly integrated into wider structures, while nation states are at the same time showing a growing trend toward devolution' (Ladrech, 1993, pp 66–67). The idea that the 'new' Europe might be in the vanguard of a new global movement seeking the reinvestment of broader principles of liberal public philosophy has gained an increasing number of adherents. Michael Sandel, writing more immediately in the context of the apparent 'discontent' in American public philosophy, cites the 'new' Europe as symbolic of the kind of emergent polity that has 'so far failed to cultivate' a necessary political and moral 'identity' (Sandel, 1996, p 339).

Some of the most recent, and perhaps most compelling, statements in this vein have been articulated by the Czech President, Vaclav Havel. Speaking within the European context, Havel has repeatedly suggested that the 'best laws will not in themselves guarantee legality or freedom or human rights' unless they are 'underpinned by certain human and social values', by a 'real moral awareness'. The time has come, therefore, for Europe's political elite to recognise that 'a legal relationship or legal order must be preceded by a connection to an order from the realm of morality, because only a moral commitment imbues the legal arrangements with meaning and makes them truly valid' (Havel, 1992, pp 12–20; Havel, 1998, pp 247–248).

Havel has gone on to describe a critical 'discrepency' in today's Europe, between an obsession with 'quotas, tariffs and rebates', and an apparent disinterest, or perhaps disinclination, to provide the 'framework of a broad civil society':

> To put it more succinctly, Europe today lacks an ethos; it lacks imagination, it lacks generosity, it lacks the ability to see beyond the horizon of its own particular interests, be they partisan or otherwise, and to resist pressure from various lobbying groups. It lacks a genuine identification with the meaning and purpose of integration. Europe appears not to have achieved a genuine and profound sense of responsibility for itself or as a whole, and thus for the future of all those who live in it. (Havel, 1998, pp 129–130.)

The post-modern critique

There is a very real consonance between the kind of sentiments articulated by the likes of Allott and Havel, and the identifiably post-modern critiques of the kind most famously articulated by the controversial French philosopher Jacques Derrida. Derrida's notoriety has come from his theory of deconstruction. Deconstruction provides a specifically textual form of post-modernism, asserting the argument that the indeterminacy of language renders all meaning variable, and because of this all philosophical and political conceptions indeterminate too (Balkin, 1987; Cornell, 1985). It denies what fellow post-modernist, Jean-Francois Lyotard, famously termed 'meta-narratives', statements of supposed absolute truths (Lyotard, 1984). To a certain extent this approach enjoys an affinity with the more prosaic post-war arguments that sought to dismiss all ideology.

It also enjoys an affinity with those who are sceptical of the role of law, seeing it as an expression of power, the ultimate mouthpiece, indeed, of ideology. It is for this reason that the post-modern jurist tends to concentrate rather more on the promotion of justice, than on the institutions of law, frequently suggesting that there is a necessary tension between the two. This is certainly Derrida's approach, as he explained in his essay *The Force of Law*. Here Derrida contrasted the 'differential force' of law, an expression of power relations, with the ethics of a justice, which he understood to be an expression of human relations. Such a conception of justice recognises the reality of particular relations over abstract metaphysical concepts. It becomes a matter of mediating 'self' and 'other'. Accordingly, it also embraces contingency, recognising that liberty comes through the capacity to assert oneself against social and moral norms. Above all, justice denies homogeneity, the assumption, for whatever reason, that all our political and moral aspirations are the same (Derrida, 1990).

Derrida has taken this deconstructive technique, as well as this particular idea of justice, and applied it to the specifically European context in his essay *The Other Heading: Reflections on Today's Europe*. Europe, Derrida argues, is a symbol. This kind of statement has been made before. Andre Malraux famously observed that 'There is no Europe. There never was one'. There are instead merely ideas of 'what Asia is not' (Fitzpatrick, 1998, pp 31–33). And Derrida, likewise, intimates that it is impossible to ascertain precisely what Europe 'is'. Instead, history throws up assumptions of what it might be. There is no such thing as Europe, merely discourses about Europe, and it is in these discourses that the locus of power can be excavated (Derrida, 1992, pp x–xi, xlii–xliii).

Derrida stresses that the 'critical' tradition in European discourse has always been aware of this power, and more particularly of those who are disempowered, those who are 'other'. To this extent the Europe of 'yesterday' has always been critically self-determinative. It has presented itself as a 'universal' that is defined by its constituent 'differentness' as something, indeed, that was exemplary in its intellectual and political pluralism, heterogeneous not homogenous (Derrida, 1992, pp xvii–xxxiii). 'Today', however, there is 'something unique afoot in Europe'. Europe is trying to redefine itself, but is doing so by trying to ignore its own cultural history. It is trying to forget this 'differentness'. Derrida's use of the word 'today' is important, not just because it conveys a sense of indeterminate temporality, but because it also distinguishes the past from the present. The overriding theme of *The Other Heading*, is the suggestion that the Europe of 'today' is in danger of forgetting the 'other'. In failing to remember the temporality of 'today', it is no longer able to distinguish itself from, or determine itself through, its past (Derrida, 1992, pp 3–5, 12, 24–25).

The politics of contemporary Europe, then, is a 'crisis' of 'memory' (Derrida, 1992, pp 29–32). This crisis has two particular roots, which Derrida explores by the classic deconstructionist methodology of uncovering linguistic ambiguity. This ambiguity surrounds the words *capitale* and *capital*. *Capitale* denotes cultural dominion, whilst *capital* denotes economic dominion. With regard to the former conception, of *capitale*, Europe must promote once again the essential 'differentness' of its culture, and develop a discourse that is appropriate to 'today', a discourse of pluralism (Derrida, 1992, pp 11–12). At present this discourse, however, is homogenous; a discourse of *capital* that threatens to create an *ethos* of *capital* (Derrida, 1992, pp 47–55). Taken together, *capitale* and *capital* combine to present a universalism which pretends to extinguish difference, and with it justice.

The term 'other heading' is itself ambiguous, suggesting both an alternative direction, and a recognition of the ever-presence of the 'other'. The alternative direction must be taken from a place, from 'today' and thus from yesterday (Derrida, 1992, p 27). To rectify Europe's present pretence to ahistoricism, Derrida suggests that we must search for a new 'identity', one that is founded on a respect for universal values as well as for 'differentness'. Only a truly pluralist discourse can do this, because it alone can subvert the kind of ends-oriented politics which today's Europe champions. To define itself in terms of substantive ethical universal values is to represent the traditional determination of Europe, but to recognise the ever-presence of 'difference' is to appreciate the contingency and historicity of the particular (Derrida, 1992, pp 22–26, 29).[3]

Such a discourse must also be reconstructive. It must construct an ethics from within, by empowering the creative moral self.[4] According to Derrida, the critical duty:

> dictates assuming the European, and uniquely European, heritage of an idea of democracy, while also recognizing that this idea, like that of international law, is never simply given, that its status is not even that of a regulative idea in the Kantian sense, but rather something that remains to be thought and to come . . . the memory of that which carries the future, the to-come, here and now. (Derrida, 1992, p 78.)

Derrida goes on to articulate a series of particular ethical values, drawn from the Enlightenment traditions that found the 'new' Europe. These include such things as minority rights and religious liberties. The most important philosophical construct is 'responsibility', something that must be taken up by all those who enjoy a privileged role in the creation of a European discourse; not just politicians, but intellectuals, writers, teachers (Derrida, 1992, pp l–lii). The Europe of 'today', Derrida repeats, is trying to deny pluralism by overcoming the critical discourse, by denying the past. This will, ultimately, prove to be futile. Irreducibly it 'resembles', becoming a self-determinative process which in seeking itself to be 'different', demands comparison with that which it tries to deny. The time to renounce this futility has come (Derrida, 1992, pp lviii–iv).

---

[3]   In his introduction to Derrida's *The Other Heading*, Michael Naas emphasises the importance of embracing this apparent ambiguity, suggesting that 'Derrida argues for the necessity of working with and from the Enlightenment values of liberal democracy while at the same time recalling that these values are never enough to ensure respect for the other'. In doing so, 'Derrida thus seeks a redefinition of European identity that includes respect for both universal values and difference – since one without the other will simply repeat without submitting to critique the politics of the example' (Derrida, 1992, p xlvi).

[4]   Something which Derrida recognises to be specifically Kantian in aspiration. For Kant, the ultimate foundation of any moral and legal philosophy lay in the 'autonomy' of the 'moral self'.

In his *Specters of Marx*, Derrida has subsequently revisited the European question, suggesting that it's very 'existence' is haunted by various intellectual 'specters', most immediately the Kantian and the Marxist. And as it struggles to exorcise these 'specters', the 'very essence of humanity' is at stake. As he suggested in *The Other Heading*, Europe is at the vanguard of an intellectual struggle between the past, the present and the future. Unfortunately, it remains trapped by its dual fascination, with laws and with markets, wedded to the belief that liberty lies in the gifting of rights and constitutions. The alternative, once again, is to cherish the mutually constitutive ideas of justice and humanity (Derrida, 1994, pp 4–5, 45–46, 59–61, 135–137, 147–158). In his more recent writings, most notably his essay *On Cosmopolitanism*, Derrida has sought to flesh out his idea of justice further, relating it more immediately to Aristotelian and 'humanist' conceptions of 'public friendship' (Derrida, 1997, pp 198–199). It is an intriguing thesis, to which we shall return in due course, not least because it might be that some kind of resurrected humanism can offer itself as the most attractive foundation for a distinctive European public philosophy.

The specifically European pertinence of Derrida's thesis is obvious, and the post-modern critique has gained in voice during the 1990s. James Bergeron articulates the classic post-modernist distrust of a legal and political order that 'teems with mythic creativity', rightly citing the Court of Justice as merely the most stunning example of this ultimately illegitimate mysticism (Bergeron, 1998a, pp 8–11). A similar distrust is expressed in Peter Fitzpatrick's misgivings surrounding what he perceives to be the 'new' Europe's attempt to 'replicate' the same 'forms and dynamics' which underpinned the old (Fitzpatrick, 1998, pp 27, 38). At root, both Bergeron and Fitzpatrick share Derrida's suspicion that the European 'project' is a giant delusion, a vast political pretence masking a primordial and visceral form of overwrought consumer fetishism (Bergeron, 1998b, pp 67–89).

Concentrating on the related issues of identity and difference, Gerard Delanty has suggested that Europe remains 'an idea as much as a reality', a 'fantasy homeland that goes hand in hand with a retrospective invention of history', arguing further that the 'new' Europe is presently beset by a 'crisis of identity', one that is exacerbated by the increasing popular xenophobia which has swept across the Union during the 1990s (Delanty, 1995, pp 1, 8, 130–163). Carole Lyons reaches a similar conclusion, commenting that the various 'exclusionary trends in the integrative process', most obviously those that afflict immigrants and third country nationals, the Derridean 'other', are 'marginalization, identity manipulation, member state domination and lack of moral dimension' (Lyons, 1998, p 171).

Clearly, then, the post-modern critique enjoys a certain immediate pertinence for European studies. The reason, perhaps, for this acceptance of the post-modern critique, at least in part, is the apparent consonance between the reality of fragmentation and the present vogue for 'flexibility' championed by Europe's political elite during the later 1990s. Whilst post-modernism is often decried for its utopianism, as well as its superficial nihilism, the experience of the first ten years of European 'union' has seemed to make aspects of its critique rather more compelling. Settling into the mood, Deirdre Curtin has recently written of the need for a fundamental 're-imagining' of democratic politics in today's Europe, one that can conceive of a politics that is 'fragmented and fluid'. Such a reconciliation, she avers, will confirm the 'new' Europe as the first truly 'post-national', even 'postmodern', polity in the new world order (Curtin, 1997, p 16).

The liberal critique

Whilst it might be the most strident, the post-modern is certainly not the only critical voice to have emerged during the past decade. Two alternative critiques, both rather more reformist than revolutionary, warrant our immediate attention. Importantly, both these critiques, the liberal and the social democratic, retain a faith in the potential of law to legitimate the political process, as well as sharing the same aspiration, to promote a more genuine democracy and a deeper sense of affinity through a meaningful conception of citizenship.

One of the leading advocates of the liberal critique has been Joseph Weiler. In the preface to his recent *The Constitution of Europe*, Weiler acknowledges the critical disjuncture in '*fin-de-siècle*' Europe, between the 'empowerment' of the consumer and the 'disempowerment' of the 'political citizen'. This thesis had been advanced as early as 1991, in his essay *The Transformation of Europe*, which traced the relative march of negative market rights against the apparent retreat of positive civic rights. It is here, in this experience of disempowerment that Weiler cites the cause of Europe's much-debated 'democratic deficit'. And it is here too that we can distinguish the root of the debilitating popular apathy that presently afflicts the very idea of European integration. Indeed, Weiler goes further still, suggesting that this apathy translates into a more specifically jurisprudential 'rebellion against the image of constitutionalism' (Weiler, 1999a, pp xi, 77–84, 233–234, 259–260).

This 'rebellion' has a still deeper importance, for it reveals a fundamental 'crisis of ideals', the ideals of Enlightenment liberalism to which Europe is 'heir'. It 'is a totally serious, and possibly longer-lasting enterprise', Weiler observes, 'to try to define European integration in terms of its ideals and not only in terms of its structural, processual and material components'. As such the ideals that the 'new' Europe has tended to pronounce must somehow be elevated from the rhetoric of 'prosperity' and 'solidarity' to those of 'humanity' itself. In other words, the rhetoric of article 6 TEU must come to surmount that of article 2 TEU. Otherwise, the new Union will be unable to assuage the growing and 'disconcerting realization' that 'Europe has become an end in itself' and 'no longer a means for higher human ends' (Weiler, 1999a, pp 238–245, 250–252, 259–262).

It is the reality of the 'democratic deficit' and the related 'crisis of ideals' that leads Weiler to place so much emphasis upon a revived notion of *demos*. Democracy must be revitalised. If representative forms of democracy were ever deemed to be truly adequate in the context of national politics, they clearly are not in the kind of supranational polity described by the European Union. The European Parliament, Weiler confirms, remains shamefully 'debilitated', both by 'its formal absence of powers' and by its 'structural remoteness' from the 'peoples' it claims to represent (Weiler, 1999a, p 266). The need for institutional reform in the Union is, therefore, critical. And it must be a tectonic reform, one that is sufficiently sizeable that it can shift the current plates of institutional imbalance.

At the same time, the resurrection of the classical idea of *demos* demands more than merely institutional reform. It speaks to a deeper understanding of democracy as the free exercise of free will across a myriad of social and political situations, an understanding of empowerment which is inextricably linked with civic freedoms and political participation. It is here that democracy aligns with citizenship. An active, as opposed to purely passive, conception of citizenship is the critical component in the 'formation' of *demos* (Weiler, 1999a, p 262). It is for this reason that Weiler is so caustic in his dismissal of the 'trite, banal phrase' which was enacted in article 17 (ex 8) in order to enact Union citizenship. As Weiler argues, the muddled conception of citizenship found in article 17 can only exacerbate the critical problems of identity and affinity that presently beset the Union. The 'importance of European citizenship', he avers, 'is a lot more than a device for placating an alienated populace'. It 'goes right to the very foundations of political legitimacy' (Weiler, 1999a, pp 324, 336).

The absence of a credible conception of citizenship lies at the 'root of European angst and alienation'. Along with democracy, citizenship is the essential expression of a vital *demos*. And conversely, as Weiler points out, 'if there is no *demos*, there can be no democracy', nor, indeed, any genuinely empowering conception of citizenship (Weiler, 1999a, pp 337, 343). It is for this reason that Weiler advances the idea of 'multiple *demoi*', of various sites of civil empowerment that might be scattered throughout the Union, and to which various citizens might feel a sense of affinity. Such an idea of multiplicity not only accounts for the reality of a Europe that does indeed seem to be multifaceted, but is also able to promote an ethic of liberality and 'tolerance' amongst the various 'peoples' of Europe (Weiler, 1999a, pp 343–347).

The invocation of 'multiple *demoi*' bears some similarity, at least in conceptual terms, with John Rawls' later 'political liberalism', at the heart of which can be found his influential idea of an 'overlapping consensus'. According to Rawls, the purpose of this 'overlapping consensus of reasonable comprehensive doctrines' is to provide a degree of unity and stability, whilst also acknowledging the reality that we live in a world of 'reasonable' pluralism. Such a 'consensus' is, of course, essentially instrumental, something that is dependent upon the provision of a myriad 'public spaces' in which alternative moral and political visions can be articulated, but in which persuasion, rather than compulsion, is the preferred recourse (Rawls, 1993a, pp 133–172). In his essay *The Law of Peoples*, Rawls advocated this model as a means to achieving consensus, not just between people, but between peoples (Rawls, 1993b).

In many ways Rawls's idea of an 'overlapping consensus' offers itself as a compelling model for a new European public philosophy. But there is a problem in that it is essentially instrumental, providing a rationale for liberal government whilst eschewing questions of moral substance. And, in reality, public philosophies cannot really evade such issues, as other leading liberal philosophers such as Ronald Dworkin recognise (Dworkin, 1993; Dworkin, 1996). This does not mean that a liberal public philosophy must lay claim to some 'comprehensive' moral vision, still less that it must be intolerant. But it does require it to allow for, perhaps even promote, shared values, what Dworkin terms a 'political morality'. If it fails to do this, to embrace the reality of a world in which communities do indeed define themselves in ethical terms, then it will leave itself open to the same criticism that ultimately afflicts the post-modern critique, that of naivety.

It is perhaps with this thought in mind that Larry Siedentop has recently presented a liberal constitutionalist critique of the 'new' Europe that seeks to provide a rather thicker public philosophy. According to Siedentop the very idea of 'democratic legitimacy' in Europe is presently 'at risk' (Siedentop, 2000, p 1). In his suggestion that Europe's 'crisis' can be traced to the rise of 'economism', and in liberalism's supplication before the idol of 'consumerism', there is much in Siedentop's thesis that bears comparison with those of Weiler and indeed Derrida. So too does the demand that, in order to ameliorate overbearing consumer fetishism, Europe must reinvest the idea of 'democratic society' alongside that of 'democratic governance' (Siedentop, 2000, pp 32–35, 40, 51–52). It is in his description of what such a society might look like that Siedentop ventures rather further into the realms of prescriptive political morality.

More particularly, Siedentop invokes the kind of democratic idyll described in Alexis de Tocqueville's *Democracy in America*. At the heart of this idyll was the idea of a federalism which encourages citizens to recognise 'different layers of association', and with them different layers of rights and responsibilities (Siedentop, 2000, pp 54–63). Of course, the presence of a proper European constitution, or at least a coherent Charter of rights, will be a necessary prerequisite for such a reinvigorated liberal community. But, above all, rather that worrying about arguments surrounding the 'location of sovereignty', Siedentop advises that a 'truly self-governing Europe must be our goal' (Siedentop, 2000, pp 25–28). This is, of course, a political, even instrumental, aspiration.

However, it is also a moral one, at least in terms of civic morality. It is here that the communitarian drift in Siedentop's thesis becomes most obviously apparent. The decentralisation of power, which is the hallmark of the communitarian idea of democracy, is not merely political. Such a 'dispersal', as Siedentop affirms, is 'fundamental to the development of human character'. It 'breeds emulation, self-reliance and humility', as opposed to the 'fear, sycophancy and resentment' that characterise the 'bureaucratic' forms of statism, the forms, indeed, into which it is all too obvious that the 'new' Europe is in 'danger' of falling (Siedentop, 2000, pp 22–23). In articulating these sentiments, Siedentop is gesturing towards the kind of humanism that is, as we shall shortly see, currently gaining ground in European and international studies. And in arguing the case for a radically decentralised form of democracy as a means to re-empowering communities, he is also treading on ground well worn, not least by the social democratic critic.

The social democratic critique

The social democratic critique shares, not only the aspiration, but many of the conceptual tools articulated by liberals such as Weiler, Rawls and Siedentop. The need to provide for revitalised forms of citizenship and democracy are shared concerns. The distinction lies more immediately in the balance between the individual and the community in which they live. Whereas the classical liberal concentrates more particularly on the idea of autonomous rights, and defines citizenship in these terms, the social democrat focuses upon ideas of community and 'solidarity'. It is for this reason that social democratic ideas of both citizenship and democracy, in the abstract and in the specifically European context, can take a very different shape.

The definitive statement of contemporary social democracy is to be found in Juergen Habermas' *Between Fact and Norms*, published in 1992. Its influence across Europe has been immense, not least in the specific area of European Union studies. Before addressing Habermas' particular critique of the European 'project', it is first necessary to flesh out a little further the central tenets of his thesis. At its heart is the overriding desire to reform western conceptions of democracy, in order to reinvigorate contemporary faith in the principles of equality and justice. Such reform is demanded by our position in what Habermas has termed our 'post-metaphysical world' (Habermas, 1990; Habermas, 1995).

According to Habermas, the most striking feature of our current politics is the rise of the 'administrative State', of the executive, a rise that has necessarily been at the expense of the 'constitutional State', of the state governed by laws instituted by its citizens. The re-establishment of the 'constitutional State' will depend upon realising 'new forms of participation and arenas for deliberation in the decision making process' (Habermas, 1996a, pp 430–452). The critical concept here, which Habermas derives ultimately from the Aristotelian tradition, is that of 'public space'. Genuine democracy demands the provision of such spaces, as media through which individuals can participate in the government of their own communities and their own lives. The 'public' spaces can be sharply contrasted with the 'private' rights that underpin liberal philosophy (Habermas, 1996a, pp 44–52). They encourage the participation of the active 'social citizen', as opposed to the passive, autonomous and purely rights-bearing citizen championed by classical liberalism.

The 'success' of what Habermas terms a 'deliberative politics' depends on the 'institutionalisation of corresponding procedures and conditions of communication, as well as the interplay of institutionalised deliberative processes with informally developed public opinions' (Habermas, 1996a, p 298). A 'participatory' democracy is thus a 'deliberative' democracy, one in which citizens not only vote, but they also speak, and are listened to. In this way, participatory democracy is a form of democracy that can become embedded in political reality, in what Habermas terms 'lifeworld contexts' (Habermas, 1996a, p 25). In providing this facility, a social democratic polity does more than restore the principle of democracy. It also reinforces the bonds of 'social solidarity', of affinity with the wider community. People feel that they belong to their polity, because it is one in which they feel that they have a say. In practical terms, Habermasian democracy demands the radical decentralisation of power to all kinds of 'lifeworlds', from the town hall to the workplace to the family.

Significantly, Habermas places great stress on the role of law. Whereas the 'post-modern' might rail against our fetish for the law, Habermas argues that the law, more particularly the principle of the rule of law, is pivotal in the restoration of public faith in contemporary politics. The law should be a bastion against the excesses of the 'administrative State', as well as a guardian, not just of individual rights, but of access to 'public spaces'. In this sense, law and politics are 'mutually constitutive'. The law is the

> medium through which the structures of mutual recognition already familiar from simple interactions and quasi-natural solidarities can be transmitted, in an abstract but binding form, to the complex and increasingly anonymous spheres of a functionally differentiated society. (Habermas, 1996a, p 318.)

The essential function of the law, in short, is to provide 'legitimacy'. 'One cannot', according to Habermas, 'adequately describe the operation of a constitutionally organised political system, even at an empirical level, without referring to the validity dimension of law and the legitimating force of the democratic genesis of law' (Habermas, 1996a, pp 196–288). In making this assertion, of course, Habermas is following liberals such as Rawls, who refuse to countenance the idea that any particular moral vision might be sufficient to legitimate political activity.

In the final analysis, *Between Facts and Norms* seeks to present a revitalised idea of law and social justice as a means to reinvigorating the present debilitated conceptions of citizenship and democracy. As Habermas concludes, political community, and its legal and political order:

> can be preserved as legitimate only if enfranchised citizens switch from the role of private legal subjects and take the perspective of participants who are engaged in the process of reaching understanding about the rules for their life in common. (Habermas, 1996a, p 461.)

But what does the Habermasian critique mean for the 'new' Europe? At first blush there do seem to be certain resonances. The European Union does indeed seem to bear many of the characteristic features of an 'administrative State', and there is equally little doubt that it is in urgent need of some measure of democratic reform. Moreover, the 'legitimacy crisis' that rumbles across much of European politics has its epicentre in Brussels.

Famously, Habermas has referred to a 'melancholic mood' that pervades turn of the century Europe (Habermas, 1996a, p xlii). The agonies of European integration, he suggests, provide a semiotic for the greater global contest between 'democracy and capitalism', between the rule of law and the anarchy of the markets. Whilst, at the same time, the 'technocratic shape' of this Europe 'reinforces doubts as to whether the normative expectations one associates with the role of the democratic citizen have not actually always been mere illusion'. The specific 'crisis of legitimacy' presently experienced in Europe is, thus, less about the 'claims to sovereignty', and more about the failure of 'democratic processes' that remained trapped within the boundaries of decaying nation states (Habermas, 1992, pp 8–9; Habermas, 1996b, pp 135–137).

Moreover, so long as the 'new' Europe continues to shy away from the demands of genuine democracy, then it will be impossible to make any sense of such a thing as European 'citizenship'. Without democracy, without rights even, it is unreasonable to expect Europe's 'citizens' to feel the sense of 'social solidarity' which is necessary to any genuine sense of citizenship or belonging (Habermas, 1992, pp 9–13; Habermas, 1996b, pp 131–133). The only solution to this 'crisis' is to institute new 'communication networks of European-wide public spaces', networks that can reach deep into the various communities and 'life-worlds' of the European citizens, whilst also tapping into the larger institutions of government, at regional, national and supranational levels of governance. If Europe is to move beyond the destructive affinities of raw nationalism, its Union must provide for a 'democratic citizenship' that is more than 'just a legal status', but which can 'become the focus of a shared political culture'. This kind of affinity, which Habermas terms 'constitutional patriotism', will be attached to civic institutions rather than to cultural mythologies (Habermas, 1996b, pp 132–133).

In his more recent writings, such as his essay *The Postnational Constellation*, Habermas has reiterated his argument that the experience of European integration should be seen as a semiotic for the wider challenges of globalisation, challenges that 'could potentially degrade the capacity for democratic self-steering within a national society' (Habermas, 2001, pp 6, 67). These challenges have already produced 'growing social inequities' in Europe, along with a corrosive popular indifference, even resentment. It is for this reason that the need to invest a sense of 'social solidarity' is so important:

If Europe is to be able to act on the basis of an integrated, multilevel policy, then European citizens, who are initially
characterized as such only by their common passports, will have
to learn to mutually recognize one another as members of a
common political existence beyond national borders.
(Habermas, 2001, p 99.)

Also, if we are to move beyond a state of 'barbaric nationalism', the
nexus between citizenship and the right of democratic participation is,
once again, irreducible (Habermas, 2001, pp 76–77, 103). Not only
will Europe's citizens have to recognise their identifiably European
political existence, but so too must they be properly equipped to participate in it. And for this to be true, Habermas concludes, the future
structure of a genuinely democratic Europe cannot be other than
federal; an 'effective European Union, constituted along federal lines'
is the 'only normatively satisfactory alternative' (Habermas, 2001, p
xix). Anything less will remain essentially defenceless against the justifiable accusation of 'democratic deficit'.

Whilst it is the most compelling, the Habermasian approach is not
the only form of social democracy on offer. For much of the 1990s,
the European academy was tantalised by a so-called 'Third Way', a
public philosophy which, according to one of its leading advocates,
Antony Giddens, described the 'future' of a 'social democratic politics' that lies between the 'discredited' alternatives of neo-liberalism
and classical socialism. We encountered aspects of the 'Third Way',
and its mooted influences on UK politics, and more specifically its
new Human Rights Act 1998, in chapter 4. According to Giddens, the
'Third Way' is about a 'life politics' that is distinctive from the 'eman-
cipatory politics' of classical liberalism, a politics that is not simply
about securing autonomous rights, but about facilitating the individual capacity to interact with society (Giddens, 1998, pp vii, 44, 80–81).
In doing this it certainly talks the language of Habermasian social
democracy, even if Habermas himself is caustic of such a vacuous and
'naïve' politics (Habermas, 2001, p xviii).

The apparent affinity between the 'Third Way' and alternative forms
of social democracy, the rhetoric of solidarity rights, of stakeholding,
of social justice, has also been noted by Paul Spicker who suggests
that it is indeed a pan-European aspiration (Spicker, 2000). At a rather
grander level, it has also been suggested that a variant of the social

democratic critique might represent the best way forward in the search for a European public philosophy. For Ulrich Beck, the 'hopes of a Europe of the Third Way' coincide with the revival of social democratic politics in a number of member states, most obviously Germany. Such a politics, he maintains, encompassing the reinvigoration of 'democratic families, local communities, cosmopolitan nations', will 'allow people and economy to creatively renew themselves' (Beck, 2000, pp 177–181).

Citizens

For the first 35 years, the Community was happy to deal in terms of workers and consumers. In 1992, however, to the sound of much trumpeting, the Community Treaty introduced another type of European 'person', the 'citizen' of the Union. The arrival of the citizenship 'chapter' in the Maastricht Treaty was intended to provide a political 'face', to complement the economic and social faces already in existence. It was supposed, indeed, to provide the first step towards an inspiring public philosophy. Article 17 (ex 8) of the Community thus declares that:

> Citizenship of the Union is hereby established. Every person holding the nationality of a Member State shall be a citizen of the Union. Citizenship of the Union shall complement and not replace national citizenship.

There then follows an array of articles which seek to define what rights the newly ennobled Union citizen enjoys. Article 18 (ex 8a) articulates the 'right to move and reside freely', whilst article 19 (ex 8b) provides for a right to vote and stand for municipal election in the member state within which a Union citizen resides, and also the right to vote and stand for election to the European Parliament. Article 20 (ex 8c), then adds a right to diplomatic or consular protection, whilst article 21 (ex 8d) provides for a right to petition the European Parliament. In other words, the remainder of the citizenship 'Chapter' provides a list of civil rights of marginal value. If they have a greater value it is undoubtedly symbolic.

The more pressing question, perhaps, is that of entitlement. Not everybody who resides and works in the Union can be a citizen. Most obviously, Union citizenship is restricted to those who are citizens of member states. As Carlos Closa observed, the presence of this sub-clause speaks volumes for the power-relation between the Union and its constituent nation states. More prosaically it testifies to the 'subordination of the Union to its Member-States' (Closa, 1994, p 118). The tone of article 17 testifies to the member states' lack of enthusiasm for the idea of citizenship. The ability to vest citizenship is a cherished possession of the modern nation state. Without it, the very idea of a nation state becomes questionable. For this reason, Union citizenship could never be seen to challenge the countervailing idea of national citizenship.

In order to dispense with any lingering doubts, a declaration at the ensuing Edinburgh Summit emphasised that Union citizenship merely accorded 'additional rights', and did not 'in any way take the place of national citizenship'. The tortuous balance between the lure of Union citizenship and the jealousy of member states regarding the preservation of national citizenship is further evidenced by the fact that article 1 (ex A) TEU relates to a union 'between the peoples of Europe'. There is no question, it seems, of creating a European people. And yet, it is clear that the one thing that might address the current state of popular apathy would be the forging of some kind of common European political identity. There needs to be a European 'people' if European political 'union' is to have any meaning.

In the meantime, the anomalies are various, exacerbated by the fact that a number of those who are denied Union citizenship can still be deemed to be 'market citizens', those who work in the common market, and who live their working lives by its rules and regulations. As Michelle Everson notes, the 'political citizen' is clearly intended to be something quite distinct from the existing 'market citizen' idolised by the neo-liberal economist and the Community Treaty alike (Everson, 1995, p 73). The 'political citizen' possesses the array of civil rights listed in articles 18–21, whilst the 'market citizen' possesses those defined by the economic and social law of the Community. In practical terms, rather than providing a means to unite Europe, to provide it with a mechanism for crafting Community 'solidarity', the idea of Union citizenship merely opens up an absurd array of different categories of European 'person'; such that today's Europe is populated by citizens who are workers, by citizens who are not workers, by workers who are not citizens, and by some who are neither citizens nor workers. And there is a very real paradox at play here:

citizenship could matter to those denied it, whilst for the rest it means little or nothing.

Unsurprisingly, article 17 has not been well received. Joseph Weiler is contemptuous in his dismissal of such a 'trite, banal phrase'. Union citizenship, he rightly opines, should be a 'lot more than a device for placating an alienated populace', whilst Elspeth Guild is similarly suspicious of 'some fancy words on a piece of paper' (Weiler, 1999a, pp 324, 336; Guild, 1996, p 30). Sionaidh Douglas-Scott, meanwhile, regretted such a 'fragmented' and 'uncentred notion of citizenship', and like Olivia O'Leary, wondered why a Union that was, in certain instances, so keen to chatter about its support of fundamental rights, should be so conspicuously silent on the subject when ascribing for itself a notion of political citizenship (Douglas-Scott, 1998, pp 35, 64; O'Leary, 1995, pp 519–521). David O'Keeffe similarly 'regretted' the conspicuous lack of a 'human rights component' (O'Keeffe, 1994, p 103). Perhaps the greatest condemnation was voiced by those who expressed a particular concern for those excluded from Union citizenship (Garcia, 1993, pp 25–26; O'Keeffe, 1994, pp 104–106).

More immediately, there are two particular problems that require resolution. The first relates to those who are vested with Union citizenship, but who are clearly either bewildered or indifferent, or most probably both. One solution would be to make Union citizenship actually mean something; this something being more than the scattered array of political entitlements catalogued earlier. But this would require a significant intellectual shift, away from the dominant liberal paradigm of citizenship and towards an alternative classical or social democratic model (Shaw, 1997, pp 571–572).

The contrast between these two models lies at the heart of modern political philosophy, and has been more recently explored by Charles Taylor (Taylor, 1989, p 178). The roots of the classical model, as Taylor explains, can be traced back to Aristotle's *Ethics*. It 'defines participation in self-rule as of the essence of freedom', and thus an 'essential component of citizen capacity'. Those who currently argue the case for a social democratic Europe, such as Juergen Habermas, urge a more participatory kind of citizenship wedded to a more participatory kind of democracy (Habermas, 1992; Habermas, 1996a). However, it is questionable whether the 'new' Europe is democratic at all, still less that it nourishes a vigorous, active kind of democracy.

The alternative liberal idea of citizenship is indelibly associated with the idea of 'individual rights and equal treatment'. Citizens are those in whom certain civil rights are vested. Critically, this particular idea enjoys an immediate historical consonance with the emergence of the modern nation state (Kristeva, 1993, pp 25–37). The liberal citizen is a passive receiver of rights, bound by no greater duty than that of not infringing the rights of others.[5]

At present Union citizenship is clearly founded on the liberal model of citizenship, even though, perhaps paradoxically, the 'new' Europe is supposed to represent something rather different from the modern nation state (de Lange, 1995, pp 97, 109–112). Moreover, the present mood of the 'new' Europe, of 'flexibility' and subsidiarity, of a reinvestment of political powers in constituent nation states, militates against any radical recasting of Union citizenship, still less any sudden democratisation of European governance. The liberal paradigm is likely to remain dominant, not least because it seems to be the least intrusive. The fact that it does not seem to fit in the 'new' Europe, still less actually empower anybody, will be quietly ignored, and in the meantime, Europeans will be left to muddle on as best they can.

The second problem relates to those excluded from citizenship. The obvious solution here must be to disentangle Union citizenship from national citizenship. The obvious solution, however, is the solution that is least palatable to those who ultimately decide Treaty amendments, the member states who govern the Council. An alternative would be somehow to harmonise citizenship entitlements within member states. But that would be little more appealing to nation states whose very rationale is founded on the presumption that they alone can confirm pretended political affinities by the vesting of citizenship. A third possibility would be for the Court of Justice to construct some kind of de facto European citizenship. A sense of this responsibility can be gleaned from the Advocate General's comments in *Boukhalfa*, that it is for the Court to 'ensure' that the 'full scope' of Union citizenship is 'attained' (*Boukhalfa*, 1996). The judgment in *Martinez Sala* (*Martinez Sala*, 1998) adds some further encouragement.

---

[5]   This idea was most famously articulated by John Stuart Mill who postulated his 'harm principle' in his 1859 essay *On Liberty*. According to this principle, individuals should be free to act as they wish except and insofar as their actions might harm others.

But it would be better still if Europe's political leaders could actually summon up the moral dignity to revise article 17 so that it respected the common humanity of all those who live in the 'new' Europe.

This latter thought leads us to another conception of citizenship, one that can resolve both the confusion and the exclusion which is presently described by article 17, as well as furnishing it with some necessary moral fibre. This model founds citizenship on fundamental human rights. It presumes that everyone who lives or works in a political community is entitled to a full range of legal and political rights, including rights to participate in the various forms of governance that pertain, by virtue of being human. In this vein, Joseph Weiler has also argued the case for a Kantian conception of citizenship, one based on the integrity of the 'moral' self. Such a conception would, of course, be liberal, but it would also be progressive and inclusive, for it would recognise the reality of a 'cosmopolitan' Europe (Weiler, 1999a, pp 342–348).

The idea has perhaps been most forcefully argued by Olivia O'Leary, who has rightly noted that such a conception of citizenship would be derived 'from the inherent dignity of the human person, regardless of his or her state of membership'. The 'establishment of a connection between the Community's commitment to fundamental rights and Community citizenship', she continues, 'could promote the protection of individual rights as one of the central objectives of Community law and might help to displace nationality as the single most important condition for the full enjoyment of Community citizenship'. It would, furthermore, assist in the 'formation of some sort of identity based on shared values and expectations' (O'Leary, 1995, pp 541–543, 553). In more prosaic terms, it would give, not only the idea of Union citizenship some kind of meaning, but also the very idea of a European Union some tangible purpose. We can only hope.

Multiplicity

It is perhaps worth recalling the words of Albert Camus, written in 1957, at the very dawn of the European Community:

> Unity and diversity, and never one without the other – isn't that the very secret of our Europe? Europe has lived on its contradictions, flourished on its differences, and, constantly

transcending itself thereby, has created a civilization on which the whole world depends even when rejecting it. This is why I do not believe in a Europe unified under the weight of an ideology or of a technocracy that would overlook these differences. Any more than I believe in a Europe left to its differences alone – in other words, left to an anarchy of enemy nationalisms. (Camus, 1974, pp 234–235.)

Writing in the same post-war mindset, Hannah Arendt likewise advised that a future European 'community' would have to define itself in opposition to those who seek to enforce a 'universalistic world view' (Arendt, 1977, pp 173–196). This idea of a universality of differences has, of course, received Derrida's more recent approbation. But the acceptance that a European public philosophy, and a European legal theory, must make sense of this seeming paradox, of universality and difference, has become ever more apparent across all intellectual boundaries. We have already encountered Joseph Weiler's idea of 'multiple *demoi*', and it is implicit in Habermas' radically decentred conceptions of 'post-metaphysical' democracy.

It finds a further and compelling statement in Zenon Bankowski and Emilios Christodoulidis's description of an 'essentially contested' Europe, one that is defined by a 'fluid' politics of 'interlocking normative spheres'. Such a 'system', they advise, must be seen 'as a continuous process of negotiation and renegotiation; one that does not have to have one single reference point to make it either a stable state system or one that is approaching that end'. The fluidity, the contestation and the pluralism run together. Indeed, it defines 'what we can call Europe'; a conclusion that chimes very obviously with Derrida's suggestion that the Europe of 'yesterday' was defined by its accommodation of difference (Bankowski and Christodoulidis, 2000, pp 18, 24).

According to Neil Walker, the 'new' Europe is a testing ground for a new kind of 'constitutional pluralism' (Walker, 2002). Ingolf Pernice similarly refers to a 'multilevel constitutionalism' as a process of integration that can be better seen as a 'dynamic process of constitution-making' rather than 'a sequence of international treaties which establish and develop an organization of international cooperation'. In this vision, constitutional integration describes a 'divided power system', with governance conducted at various differentiated levels, at Union level, at national level, and at regional level. Such a model would place a proactive idea of subsidiarity at its heart (Pernice, 1999). In pretty much the same vein, Kenneth Armstrong deploys an idea of 'multi-level governance' as the only sensible way of describing the regulation of the single market. Today's market, he argues, can only be described in terms of a myriad of 'complex, multi-level, interacting governance regimes populated by an array of actors utilizing a reservoir of policy goals, policy ideas, and policy instruments' (Armstrong, 1999, pp 746, 785–786). The clear resonance in these various theories of multi-level governance and plural constitutionalism can be found in the Rawlsian 'overlapping consensus'. According to Massimo La Torre, the evolution of such a consensus, even if it's 'stability' remains questionable, has defined European integration during the 1990s (La Torre, 2000, pp 133–135).

Along with invocations of pluralism and multiplicity comes the prefix 'post'. The rhetoric of post-modernism and the 'post-metaphysical' has been pillaged by European commentators, many of whom might still recoil from its more deconstructionist implications. One who does seem to be prepared to accept the post-modern embrace, as we have already noted, is Deirdre Curtin who has hazarded the thought that the 'new' Europe might represent the first 'post-modern' polity in the new world order (Curtin, 1997, p 16). Jo Shaw's description of an evolving 'post-national constitutionalism', the strength of which is gauged by the vigour of its 'continuing conversation', can be interpreted in the same vein (Shaw, 2000b, pp 19–24).

Post-national constitutionalism attaches to similar ideas of post-national citizenship (Shaw, 2000b, pp 30–31). As we have just noted, the ambiguity surrounding the relation of Union and national citizenship, speaks volumes for a Union that seems to be conceptually paralysed by a chronic lack of confidence. The entitlement to Union citizenship has been made entirely conditional upon a prior receipt of nation state citizenship; thereby making it a conception that confuses as many millions as it excludes. As we also noted, various alternative visions of citizenship have been suggested. The Habermasian alternative, of social citizenship, has attracted support (Shaw, 1997, pp 571–572). Some have talked of 'market' or 'economic' citizenship, whilst others have pressed the case for citizenship founded on fundamental human rights. Alongside these possibilities, Ulrich Preuss, for example, has advocated a conception of 'multiple citizenship' in terms of providing citizens with the opportunity to engage in 'manifold economic, social, cultural, scholarly, and even political activities irrespective of the traditional territorial boundaries of the European nation states', opening up the potential for everyone to enjoin a 'multiplicity of associative relations' (Preuss, 1995, p 280)

A 'multiple' citizen will not merely be a citizen of different polities, such as the Union or a nation state or a region, but will also be a political citizen entitled to certain civic rights, a social citizen entitled to certain social rights, and an economic citizen entitled to certain market rights. He or she will also develop a series of interlocking cultural and political affinities. Someone who lives in Edinburgh, for example, will feel liberated by a series of political and social affinities, with Scotland, with the United Kingdom, with the Union, and, of course, with Edinburgh. Someone who lives in Barcelona will feel a similar sense of affinities with Catalans, Spaniards, Europeans, and fellow residents of Barcelona. Bewilderment, it is fondly hoped, will then give way to an overwhelming sense of gratitude and joy.

It is certainly true that the problem of citizenship is inextricably tied to that of 'identity' and affinity, the kind of problem which underpins the post-modern critique advanced by Derrida. And the resolution of these related issues will take considerable effort; far more, indeed, than the 'new' Europe has invested so far. Making people think of themselves as 'multiple' citizens will not be easy. But it will be necessary. The stakes could not be higher. If the 'new' Europe cannot properly address the question of affinity, then it has, quite simply, no future. It is for this reason that the related ideas of multiplicity and multiple citizenship are so tempting, if also so elusive.

Cosmopolitanism and the new humanism

The growing consolidation of contemporary European legal theory around the idea of pluralism or multiplicity, taps into a related set of ideas which enjoy a considerable intellectual provenance, and which can be loosely termed cosmopolitan. One of the most compelling defences of this idea, as we noted in the first chapter, was articulated by one of the great prophets of European integration, Immanuel Kant. In his essay *Perpetual Peace*, written in 1795, Kant suggested that:

The peoples of the earth have thus entered in varying degrees into a universal community, and it has developed to a point where a violation of rights in one part of the world is felt everywhere. The idea of a cosmopolitan right is therefore not fantastic and overstrained; it is a necessary complement to an unwritten code of political and international right, transforming it into a universal right of humanity. Only under this condition can we flatter ourselves that we are continually advancing towards perpetual peace. (Kant, 1991, pp 107–108.)

History was to make something of a mockery of the aspiration. But it remains a noble one. Indeed, in historical terms at least, the defining aspiration of *Perpetual Peace*, for a Europe in which the principle of 'universal hospitality' was paramount, is the ultimate reason for the very existence of the 'new' Europe.

The idea of a cosmopolitan Europe has attracted a number of rather more recent adherents. We have already witnessed Juergen Habermas' embrace of a 'federalist' Union that can point the way to 'a future cosmopolitan order sensitive both to difference and to social equality' (Habermas, 2001, p xix). In similar terms, Antony Giddens opines that the establishment of the European Union 'is the most important and promising experiment in transnational governance going on', a critical example of the kind of 'cosmopolitan democracy' which might ultimately emerge at global level (Giddens, 1998, pp 141–147; Giddens and Hutton, 2000, p 51).

It is, furthermore, no coincidence that Derrida's most recent writings have addressed the idea of cosmopolitanism in greater detail. Opening his essay *On Cosmopolitanism* with the sobering, but undoubtedly valid, observation that 'we are still a long way from the idea of cosmopolitanism as defined in Kant's famous text as the right to universal hospitality', Derrida revisits an idea he had advanced in his earlier *Politics of Friendship*, of a 'politics of friendship', a politics which 'amounts to creating (to producing, to making etc) the most friendship possible' (Derrida, 1997, p 8; Derrida, 2001, p 11). It is also no coincidence that Derrida alights upon the European Union as the signal example of inhospitality in the contemporary world, the one polity that seems, more than any other, to fear the 'other', to deny the one universal truth that underpins cosmopolitanism, that 'Hospitality is culture in itself and not simply one ethic amongst others' (Derrida, 2001, p 16).

There is a well-established provenance aligning the cosmopolitan ideal with the tradition of the 'commonwealth' or *respublica*. It finds a more modern expression in Michael Sandel's observation that the 'cosmopolitan ideal rightly emphasises the humanity we share and directs our attention to the moral consequences that flow from it' (Sandel, 1996, p 341). Just as compelling is Robert Falk's injunction:

> Only by reconstructing intimate relations on a humane basis can the world move toward the wider public and collective realities of human community. This reconstruction, starting at home, is a critical precondition for the emergence of the sort of global polity that could inspire trust and have a reasonable prospect of providing humane governance for a democratically constituted global civil society. (Falk, 1995, p 69.)

Perhaps the most substantive defence of a humanitarian cosmopolitanism in the geopolitical context of the 'new' world order is William Twining's *Globalisation and Legal Theory*. According to Twining, in our increasingly cosmopolitan world, in which political identities remain 'elusive', the limits of classical legalism are all too apparent. In their place, we must embrace once again the idea of a *ius humanitatis*, a conception of law and justice that is able to 'transcend jurisdictions and cultures, so far as that is feasible and appropriate, and which can address issues about law from a global and transnational perspective (Twining, 2000, pp 49, 198, 243).

This alignment of the cosmopolitan ideal with that of *humanitas* has found an equally compelling expression in Neil MacCormick's resurrection of early Enlightenment conceptions of 'commonwealth'. Rightly noting that the European Union invites a 'new form of legal and political order', MacCormick observes:

> The particular point of what we can call a 'commonwealth' is that is should comprise a group of people to whom can reasonably be imputed some consciousness that they have a 'common weal', something which really is a common good, and who are able to envisage themselves or their political representatives and governing authorities realizing this or striving after it through some form of organized political structure, embodied in some common constitutional arrangements. In this sense, both member states and the Union are commonwealths, one more intensive and localized, more strongly rooted in a sense of

tradition and of personal identity and loyalty, the other more extensive and broadly inclusive. Here in Europe we have something which is a constituted order, which does have however imperfectly a legal constitution, whose members have certain vital interests in peace and prosperity that they can best pursue as common interests through policies oriented towards this common good. Commonwealth seems a natural term here to use. (MacCormick, 1999, p 143.)

Ultimately, MacCormick describes a cosmopolitan Europe that is perhaps best described as a commonwealth of commonwealths. And, as he also points out, the constitutionalisation of subsidiarity already infers a measure of cosmopolitan sentiment, as does the more recent rhetoric of 'flexibility' and 'variable geometry' (MacCormick, 1999, pp 193–194).

Similar invocations of commonwealth and *humanitas* can be found elsewhere. Enthused by the idea of a Europe of 'local communities' and 'cosmopolitan nations', Ulrich Beck suggests that the 'alternative' public philosophy that today's Europe 'needs', will be described by 'citizen work combined with citizen income as condition *sine qua non* for a political republic of individuals who create a sense of compassion and cohesion through public commitment' (Beck, 2000, pp 77–81). Rather more explicitly, Massimo La Torre has linked the idea of constitutional pluralism with the cosmopolitan idea of a 'mixed commonwealth' of constituent commonwealths (La Torre, 2000, p 138).

However the most striking recent defence of a commonwealth *humanitas* is undoubtedly that presented by Larry Siedentop. Building on his assertion that democracy is constitutive, not just of good citizens, but of good 'character', Siedentop suggests that liberal constitutionalism is a 'surrogate for religion', and, as such, the 'latest frontier of European Christianity' (Siedentop, 2000, p 101). It was, he continues, within the European *respublica Christiana* that the first seeds of democracy were planted. Christianity 'provided the moral foundations of modern democracy', furnishing it with a public philosophy of 'universal' autonomy and difference, of a model of 'human society' composed, not of tribes or peoples even, but of 'individuals'. In doing this, the idea of the *respublica* or 'commonwealth' provides not merely a moral or political philosophy, but the 'original constitution of Europe' (Siedentop, 2000, pp 190–195, 200–201).

There is a tangible sense here of a Europe that must go back to the future. Just as the cosmopolitan model still finds its definitive statement in Kant's essay written two centuries ago, so too the kind of *humanitas* recommended by Siedentop and MacCormick and La Torre can readily be traced back to its early Enlightenment roots, and then again further back to the medieval scholastic sequestration of classical Greek conceptions of the 'good society'. A classic early Enlightenment defence of *humanitas* and the *respublica* can be found in Gottfried Wilhelm Leibniz's political writings, most obviously perhaps in his *Meditation on the Common Concept of Justice*.[6] Writing in 1679, Liebniz suggested that the 'universal jurisprudence' that defines the European *respublica* is founded on a 'universal benevolence', a 'habit of loving' that equips the 'wise man' to pursue the 'greatest good' (Leibniz, 1988, pp 98–99; Ward, 2001, pp 32–40).

Three centuries later, Pierre Bourdieu can likewise recommend the very idea of Europe as being definitively 'humanist' in precisely these terms (Bourdieu, 1998, pp 9, 40–41). And Vaclav Havel can comment, with some passion, that the 'salvation of this human world lies nowhere else than in the human heart, in the human power to reflect, in human modesty, and in human responsibility' (Havel, 1998, pp 18–19). The promotion of the 'idea of humanity', and of the politics that such a philosophy demands, of 'civic coexistence, solidarity, and participation', is, he repeatedly avers, Europe's destiny (Havel, 1998, pp 147–148).

This same sentiment, that the idea of a revitalised humanism might be definitive of the very idea of Europe has, finally, found a contemporary echo in the words of the current President of the European Commission, Romano Prodi. First, in a speech to the European Parliament in February 2000:

> Europe needs a sense of meaning and purpose. We Europeans are the heirs of a civilisation deeply rooted in religious and civic values. Our civilisation today is being enriched by its openness to other cultures. What we need now is a humanist perspective. Daily and systematically, our economic and social system must

---

[6]   It is not, of course, the only one. MacCormick makes much of David Hume's similar idea of 'commonwealth'. Whilst Hume eschewed Leibniz's more explicitly theological rhetoric, they both shared the same Aristotelian foundation in the idea of the 'good society'.

recognise the primacy of human dignity. It must ensure that all our citizens have genuine access to liberty, inter-personal communication, culture and spiritual life. (Prodi, 2000.)

And, again, in a speech given a year later in Poland, in which he spoke of Europe's 'humanist tradition of tolerance and intellectual openness', he concluded with the following observation:

Let us enrich Europe through its great diversity. After all, Europe has always been about diverse peoples with varied cultures and religions learning to live together because they share a common destiny. In doing so, we discover shared values, a shared sense of identity and European citizenship. (Prodi, 2001).

The rhetoric, as ever, is strong. The reality, as always, appears to lie in the future. The final word should, perhaps, rest with Havel's pressing and pertinent observation: 'We shall never build a better Europe, if we cannot dream of a better Europe' (Havel, 1998, p 46).

Bibliography

Ackers, L (1994) 'Women, Citizenship and European Community Law: The Gender Implications of the Free Movement of Persons' *Journal of Social Welfare and Family* 391

Ackrill, M (1995) 'The Common Agricultural Policy: Its Operation and Reform' in Healey, N (ed) *The Economics of the New Europe* London, Routledge

Adnett, N (2001) 'Modernizing the European Social Model: Developing the Guidelines' 39 *Journal of Common Market Studies* 353

Akhaven, P (1998) 'Justice in the Hague, Peace in the Former Yugoslavia? A Commentary on the United Nations War Crimes Tribunal' 20 *Human Rights Quarterly* 758

Aldcroft, D (1993) *The European Economy 1914–1990* London, Routledge

Allan, T (1983) 'Parliamentary Sovereignty: Lord Denning's Dexterous Revolution' 3 *Oxford Journal of Legal Studies* 22

Allan, T (1985) 'The Limits of Parliamentary Sovereignty' *Public Law* 614

Allan, T (1988) 'Pragmatism and Theory in Public Law' 104 *Law Quarterly Review* 422

Allott, P (1991) 'The European Community is Not the True European Community' 100 *Yale Law Journal* 2485

Allott, P (1992) 'Reconstituting Humanity – New International Law' 3 *European Journal of International Law* 219

Alter, K (1998) 'Who Are the "Masters of the Treaty"?: European Governments and the European Court of Justice' 52 *International Organization* 121

Alter, K, and Meunier-Aitsahalta, S (1994) 'Judicial Politics in the European Community: European Integration and the Pathbreaking *Cassis de Dijon* decision' 26 *Comparative Political Studies* 535

Amos, M (2001) 'Extending the Liability of the State in Damages' 21 *Legal Studies* 1

Anav, G (1989) 'Parliamentary Sovereignty: An Anachronism?' 27 *Columbia Journal of Transnational Law* 631

Arendt, H (1977) *Between Past and Future* London, Penguin

Armstrong, H (1995) 'The Regional Policy of the European Union' in Healey, N (ed) *The Economics of the New Europe* London, Routledge

Armstrong, K (1999) 'Governance and the Single European Market', in Craig, P, and de Burca, G (eds), *The Evolution of EU Law* Oxford, Oxford University Press

Arnull, A (1985) 'Reflections on Judicial Attitudes at the European Court' 34 *International and Comparative Law Quarterly* 168

Arnull, A (1989) 'The Use and Abuse of Article 177 EEC' 52 *Modern Law Review* 622

Arnull, A (1991) 'What Shall We Do on Sunday?' 16 *European Law Review* 112

Arnull, A (1996) 'The European Court and Judicial Objectivity: A Reply to Professor Hartley' 112 *Law Quarterly Review* 411

Artis, M (1992) 'The Maastricht Road to Monetary Union' 30 *Journal of Common Market Studies* 299

Baker, D, Gamble, A, and Ludlam, S (1993) 'Whips or Scorpions? The Maastricht Vote and the Conservative Party' 46 *Parliamentary Affairs* 151

Balanya, B, et al (2000) *Europe Inc: Regional and Global Restructuring and the Rise of Corporate Power* London, Pluto

Baldwin-Edwards, M (1991) 'Immigration After 1992' 19 *Policy and Politics* 199

Baldwin-Edwards, M (1997) 'The Emerging European Immigration Regime: Some Reflections on Implications for Southern Europe' 35 *Journal of Common Market Studies* 497

Balkin, J (1987) 'Deconstructive Practice and Legal Theory' 96 *Yale Law Journal* 743

Bamforth, N (2000) 'Sexual Orientation Discrimination After *Grant v South-West Trains*' 63 *Modern Law Review* 694

Bankowski, Z, and Christodoulidis, E (2000) 'The European Union as an Essentially Contested Project', in Bankowski, Z, and Scott, A (eds) *The European Union and its Order: The Legal Theory of European Integration* Oxford, Blackwell

Banks, K (1992) 'Constitutional Implications of Community Sex Equality Law' in Curtin, D, and O'Keeffe, D (eds) *Constitutional Adjudication in European Community Law and National Law* Dublin, Butterworths

Barber, B (1992) 'Jihad v McWorld' *The Atlantic* 53

Barber, B (2000) 'Can Democracy Survive Globalization?' 35 *Government and Opposition* 275

Barnard, C (1994) 'Sunday Trading: A Drama in Five Acts' 57 *Modern Law Review* 449

Barnard, C (1999) 'EC Social Policy' in Craig, P, and de Burca, G (eds) *The Evolution of EU Law* Oxford, Oxford University Press

Barnard, C (2001) 'Fitting the Remaining Pieces into the Goods and Persons Jigsaw?' 26 *European Law Review* 35

Barnard, C, and Sharpston, E (1997) 'The Changing Face of Article 177 References' 34 *Common Market Law Review* 1113

Basedow, J (1996) 'A Common Contract Law for the Common Market' 33 *Common Market Law Review* 1169

Basedow, J (1998) 'The Renascence of Uniform Law: European Contract Law and its Components' 18 *Legal Studies* 121

Baxi, U (1998) 'Voices of Suffering and the Future of Human Rights' 8 *Transnational Law and Contemporary Problems* 125

Bebr, G (1983) 'The Rambling Ghost of Cohn-Bendit: Acte Clair and the Court of Justice' 20 *Common Market Law Review* 439

Bebr, G (1988) 'The Reinforcement of the Constitutional Review of Community Acts under Article 177 EEC Treaty' 25 *Common Market Law Review* 667

Beck, U (2000) 'Living Your Own Life in a Runaway World: Individualisation, Globalisation and Politics' in Hutton, W, and Giddens, A (eds) *On the Edge: Living with Global Capitalism* London, Jonathan Cape

Bell, M (1999) 'Shifting Conceptions of Sexual Discrimination at the Court of Justice: from *P v S* to *Grant v SWT*' 5 *European Law Journal* 63

Bell, M (2002) *Anti-Discrimination Law in the European Union* Oxford, Oxford University Press

Bengoetxea, J (1993) The *Legal Reasoning of the European Court of Justice: Towards a European Jurisprudence* Oxford, Clarendon

Bercusson, B (1990) 'The European Community's Charter of Fundamental Social Rights of Workers' 53 *Modern Law Review* 624

Bercusson, B (1994) 'The Dynamic of European Law Labour Law After Maastricht' 23 *Industrial Law Journal* 1

Bergeron, J (1998a) 'An Ever Whiter Myth: The Colonization of Modernity in European Community Law' in Fitzpatrick, P, and Bergeron, J (eds) *Europe's Other: European Law Between Modernity and Postmodernity* Aldershot, Ashgate

Bergeron, J (1998b) 'Europe's Emprise: Symbolic Economy and the Postmodern Condition' in Fitpatrick, P, and Bergeron, J (eds), *Europe's Other: European Law Between Modernity and Postmodernity* Aldershot, Ashgate

Bermann, G (1989) 'The Single European Act: A New Constitution for the Community?' 27 *Columbia Journal of Transnational Law* 529

Beveridge, F, et al (2000) 'Mainstreaming and the Engendering of Policy-making: A Means to an End?' 7 *Journal of European Public Policy* 385

Beyleveld, D (1995) 'The Concept of a Human Right and Incorporation of the European Convention on Human Rights' *Public Law* 577

Bibas, S (1992) 'The European Court of Justice and the US Supreme Court: Parallels in Fundamental Rights Jurisprudence' 15 *Hastings International and Comparative Law Review* 253

Bieber, R, et al (1986) 'Implications of the Single Act for the European Parliament' 23 *Common Market Law Review* 767

Bingham, T (1993) 'The European Convention on Human Rights: Time to Incorporate' 109 *Law Quarterly Review* 390

Blair, T (2000) 'Speech to the Polish Stock Exchange' http://www.number-10.uk/news

Bonner, D, and Graham, C (2002) 'The Human Rights Act 1998: The Story So Far' 8 *European Public Law* 177

Bonvicini, G (1998) 'Making European Foreign Policy Work', in Westlake, M (ed) *The European Union Beyond Amsterdam: New Concepts of European Integration* London, Routledge

Bordieu, P (1998) *Acts of Resistance: Against the Tyranny of the Market* London, Pluto Press

Borinski, P (1997) 'Realism and the Analysis of European Security' 20 *Journal of European Integration* 131

Bourgeois, J (2000) 'The European Court of Justice and the WTO: Problems and Challenges', in Weiler, J (ed) *The EU, the WTO and the NAFTA* Oxford, Oxford University Press

Boyron, S (1992) 'Proportionality in English Administrative Law: A Faulty Translation?' 12 *Oxford Journal of Legal Studies* 237

Bradley, K (1987) 'Maintaining the Balance: The Role of the Court of Justice in Defining the Institutional Position in the European Parliament' 24 *Common Market Law Review* 41

Bradley, K (1988) 'The Variable Evolution of the Standing of the European Parliament in Proceedings Before the Court of Justice' 8 *Yearbook of European Law* 27

Bradley, K (1991) 'Sense and Sensibility – Parliament v Council Continued' 16 *European Law Review* 245

Bradley, K (1994) '"Better Rusty Than Missin"?: Institutional Reforms of the Maastricht Treaty and the European Parliament' in O'Keeffe, D, and Twomey, P (eds) *Legal Issues of the Maastricht Treaty* London, Chancery

Bradley, K (2001) 'Institutional Design in the Treaty of Nice' 38 *Common Market Law Review* 1095

Bretherton, C (2001) 'Gender Mainstreaming and EU Enlargement; Swimming Against the Tide?' 8 *Journal of European Public Policy* 62

Burgess, M (1986) 'Altiero Spinelli, Federalism and the EUT' in Lodge, J (ed) *European Union: The European Community in Search of a Future* New York, St Martins

Burgess, M (1989) *Federalism and European Union: Political Ideas, Influences and Strategies in the European Community* 1972–1978 London, Routledge

Butler, F (1993) 'The EC's Common Agricultural Policy (CAP)' in Lodge, J (ed) *The European Community and the Challenge of the Future* London, Pinter

Bzdera, A (1992) 'The Court of Justice of the European Community and the Politics of Institutional Reform' 15 *West European Politics* 122

Campbell, J, et al (1990) 'Implementing the Internal Market' in Crouch, C, and Marquand, D (eds) *The Politics of 1992: Beyond the Single European Market* Oxford, Blackwell

Camus, A (1974) *Resistance, Rebellion and Death* London, Vintage

Canor, I (1998) 'Can Two Walk Together, Except They Be Agreed? The Relationship Between International Law and European Law: The Incorporation of United Nation Sanctions Against Yugoslavia into European Community Law Through the Perspective of the European Court of Justice' 35 *Common Market Law Review* 137

Cappelletti, M (1987) 'Is the European Court of Justice "Running Wild"?' 12 *European Law Review* 3

Cappelletti, M, et al (1985) 'Integration Through Law: Europe and the American Federal Experience' in Cappelletti, M, et al (eds) *Integration Through Law* Berlin, de Gruyter

Caranta, R (1993) 'Governmental Liability After *Francovich*' 52 *Cambridge Law Journal* 272

Cardozo, R, and Corbett, R (1986) 'The Crocodile Initiative' in Lodge, J (ed) *European Union: The European Community in Search of a Future* New York, St Martins

Cesarini, D (1996) 'The Changing Character of Citizenship and Nationality in Britain', in Cesarini, D, and Fulbrook, M (eds) *Citzenship, Nationality and Migration in Europe*, London, Routledge

Chalmers, D (1994) 'Repackaging the Internet Market – The Ramifications of the *Keck* Judgment' 19 *European Law Review* 385

Chalmers, D (2000) 'The Application of Community Law in the United Kingdom,1994–1998' 37 *Common Market Law Review* 83

Churchill, R, and Foster, N (1987) 'Double Standards in Human Rights? The Treatment of Spanish Fishermen by the European Community' 12 *European Law Review* 430

Clapham, A (1990) 'A Human Rights Policy for the European Community' 10 *Yearbook of European Law* 309

Closa, C (1994) 'Citizenship of the Union and Nationality of Member States' in O'Keeffe, D, and Twomey, P (eds) *Legal Issues of the Maastricht Treaty* London, Chancery

Cockfield, Lord (1990) 'The Real Significance of 1992' in Crouch, C, and Marquand, D (eds) *The Politics of 1992: Beyond the Single European Market* Oxford, Blackwell

Cockfield, Lord (1994) *The European Union: Creating the Single Market* London, Wiley Chancery Law

Colman, D, and Roberts, D (1994) 'The Common Agricultural Policy' in Artis, M, and Lee, N (eds) *The Economics of the European Union* Oxford, Oxford University Press

Constantinesco, V (1991) 'Who's Afraid of Subsidiarity?' 11 *Yearbook of European Law* 33

Coppel, J (1993) 'Edinburgh Subsidiarity' 44 *Northern Ireland Legal Quarterly* 179

Coppel, J, and O'Neill, A (1992) 'The European Court of Justice: Taking Rights Seriously?' 12 *Legal Studies* 271

Corbett, R (1992) 'The Intergovernmental Conference on Political Union' 30 *Journal of Common Market Studies* 271

Cornell, D (1985) 'Toward a Modern/Postmodern Reconstruction of Ethics' 133 *University of Pennsylvania Law Review* 291

Craig, P (1991) 'Sovereignty of the United Kingdom Parliament After *Factortame*' 11 *Yearbook of European Law* 221

Craig, P (1992) 'Once Upon a Time in the West: Direct Effect and the Federalization of EEC Law' 12 *Oxford Journal of Legal Studies* 453

Cremona, M (1999) 'External Economic Relations and the Amsterdam Treaty', in O'Keeffe, D, and Twomey, P (eds) *Legal Issues of the Amsterdam Treaty*, Oxford, Hart

Cullen, H (1994) 'The Subsidiary Women' *Journal of Social Welfare and Family Law* 407

Curtin, D (1990a) 'The Province of Government: Delimiting the Direct Effect of Directives in the Common Law Context' 15 *European Law Review* 195

Curtin, D (1990b) 'Directives: The Effectiveness of Judicial Protection of Individual Rights' 27 *Common Market Law Review* 709

Curtin, D (1992a) 'The Decentralized Enforcement of Community Law Rights: Judicial Snakes and Ladders' in Curtin, D, and O'Keeffe, D (eds) *Constitutional Adjudication in European Community and National Law* Dublin, Butterworths

Curtin, D (1992b) 'Constitutionalism in the European Community: The Right to Fair Procedures in Administrative Law' in O'Reilly, J (ed) *Human Rights and Constitutional Law: Essays in Honour of Brian Walsh* Dublin, Round Hall

Curtin, D (1993) 'The Constitutional Structure of the Union: A Europe of Bits and Pieces' 30 *Common Market Law Review* 17

Curtin, D (1997) *Postnational Democracy: The European Union in Search of a Public Philosophy* Dordrecht, Kluwer

Curtin, D (1999) 'The Fundamental Principle of Open Decision-making and EU (Political) Citizenship' in O'Keeffe, D, and Twomey, P (eds) *Legal Issues of the Amsterdam Treaty* London, Hart

Curtin, D, and Meijers, H (1995) 'The Principle of Open Government in Schengen and the European Union: Democratic Retrogression?' 32 *Common Market Law Review* 391

Curwen, P (1995) 'The Economics of Social Responsibility in the European Union' in Healey, N (ed) *The Economics of the New Europe* London, Routledge

Dallen, R (1990) 'An Overview of European Community Protection of Human Rights, with some special references to the UK' 27 *Common Market Law Review* 761

Dankert, P (1982) 'The European Community – Past, Present and Future' 21 *Journal of Common Market Studies* 3

Dashwood, A (1998) 'States in the European Union' 23 *European Law Review* 201

Dashwood, A (1999) 'External Relations Provisions of the Amsterdam Treaty', in O'Keeffe, D, and Twomey, P (eds) *Legal Issues of the Amsterdam Treaty*, Oxford, Hart

Daugbjerg, C (1999) 'Reforming the CAP: Policy Networks and Broader Institutional Structures' 37 *Journal of Common Market Studies* 407

Dawkins, R (1986) *The Blind Watchmaker* Harlow, Longman

de Burca, G (1992) 'Giving Effect to European Community Directives' 55 *Modern Law Review* 215

de Burca, G (1998) 'The Principle of Subsidiarity and the Court of Justice as an Institutional Actor' 36 *Journal of Common Market Studies* 217

de Lange, R (1995) 'Paradoxes of European Citizenship' in Fitzpatrick, P (ed) *Nationalism, Racism and the Rule of Law* Aldershot, Dartmouth

Dehousse, R (1988) '1992 and Beyond: The Institutional Dimension of the Internal Market Programme' *Legal Issues of European Integration* 109

Delanty, G (1995) *Inventing Europe: Idea, Identity, Reality* London, Macmillan

Demaret, P (1994) 'The Treaty Framework' in O'Keeffe, D, and Twomey, P (eds) *Legal Issues of the Maastricht Treaty* London, Chancery

Derrida, J (1990) 'The Force of Law: The Mystical Foundations of Authority' 11 *Cardozo Law Review* 921

Derrida, J (1992) *The Other Heading: Reflections on Today's Europe* Bloomington, Indiana University Press

Derrida, J (1994) *Specters of Marx* London, Routledge

Derrida, J (1997) *Politics of Friendship* London, Routledge

Derrida, J (2001) *On Cosmopolitanism and Friendship* London, Routledge

Devuyst, Y (1999) 'The Community-Method After Amsterdam' 37 *Journal of Common Market Studies* 109

Diamond, P (1991) 'Dishonourable Defences: The Use of Injunctions and the EEC Treaty – A Case Study of the Shops Act 1950' 54 *Modern Law Review* 71

Dickinson, H (1976) 'The Eighteenth-Century Debate on the Sovereignty of Parliament' 26 *Transactions of the Royal Historical Society* 5th ser 189

Docksey, C (1991) 'The Principle of Equality Between Women and Men as a Fundamental Right Under Community Law' 20 *Industrial Law Journal* 258

D'Oliveira, H (1994) 'Expanding External and Shrinking Internal Borders: Europe's Defence Mechanism in the Areas of Free Movement, Immigration and Asylum' in O'Keeffe, D, and Twomey, P (eds) *Legal Issues of the Maastricht Treaty* London, Chancery

Dougan, M (2000) 'The "Disguised" Vertical Direct Effect of Directives?' 59 *Cambridge Law Journal* 586

Douglas-Scott, S (1998) 'In Search of Union Citizenship' 18 *Yearbook of European Law* 29

Douglas-Scott, S (2002) *Constitutional Law of the European Union* London, Longman

Downes, T (1997) 'Trawling for a Remedy: State Liability under Community Law' 17 *Legal Studies* 286

Downes, T, and MacDougall, D (1994) 'Significantly Impending Effective Competition: Substantive Appraisal under the Merger Regulation' 19 *European Law Review* 286

Dowrick, F (1983) 'A Model of the European Communities' Legal System' 3 *Yearbook of European Law* 169

Duff, A (1998) 'Britain and Europe: The Different Relationship' in Westlake, M (ed) *The European Union Beyond Amsterdam: New Concepts of European Integration* London, Routledge

Dunkley, G (2000) *The Free Trade Adventure: The WTO, the Uruguay Round and Globalism* New York, Zed Books

Dunnett, D (1994) 'Legal and Constitutional Issues affecting Economic and Monetary Union' in O'Keeffe, D, and Twomey, P (eds) *Legal Issues of the Maastricht Treaty* London, Chancery

Dworkin, R (1993) *Life's Dominion: An Argument about Abortion and Euthanasia* London, HarperCollins

Dworkin, R (1996) *Freedom's Law: The Moral Reading of the American Constitution* Oxford, Oxford University Press.

Edward, D (1987) 'The Impact of the Single Act on the Institutions' 24 *Common Market Law Review* 19

Eeckhout, P (1997) 'The Domestic Legal Status of the WTO Agreement: Interconnecting Legal Systems' 34 *Common Market Law Review* 11

Ehlermann, C (1990) 'The "1990 Project": Strategies, Structures, Results and Prospects' 11 Michigan Journal of International Law 1097

Ehlermann, C (2000) 'The Modernization of EC Antitrust Policy: A Legal and Cultural Revolution' 37 *Common Market Law Review* 537

Eicke, T (2000) 'The European Charter of Fundamental Rights – Unique Opportunity or Unwelcome Distraction' 3 *European Human Rights Law Review* 280

Eksteins, M (1989) *The Rites of Spring* Toronto, Lester and Orpen Dennys

Eleftheriadis, P (1996) 'Aspects of European Constitutionalism' 21 *European Law Review* 32

Eleftheriadis, P (1998) 'Begging the Constitutional Question' 36 *Journal of Common Market Studies* 255

Ellis, E (1991a) *European Community Sex Equality Law* Oxford, Clarendon

Ellis, E (1991b) 'Discrimination on the Grounds of Pregnancy in EEC Law' *Public Law* 159

Ellis, E (1994a) 'Recent Case Law of the Court of Justice on the Equal Treatment of Women and Men' 31 *Common Market Law Review* 43

Ellis, E (1994b) 'The Definition of Discrimination in European Community Sex Equality Law' 19 *European Law Review* 653

Elman, A (2000) 'The Limits of Citizenship: Migration, Sex Discrimination and Same-Sex Partners in EU Law' 38 *Journal of Common Market Studies* 729

Emiliou, N (1996) 'State Liability under Community Law' 21 *European Law Review* 399

Engel, C (2001) 'The European Charter of Fundamental Rights: A Changed Political Opportunity Structure and its Normative Consequences' 7 *European Law Journal* 151

Evans, A (1997) 'Voluntary Harmonisation in Integration Between the European Community and Eastern Europe' 22 *European Law Review* 201

Everling, U (1992) 'Reflections on the Structure of the European Union' 29 *Common Market Law Review* 1053

Everson, M (1995) 'The Legacy of the Market Citizen', in Shaw, J, and More, G (eds) *New Legal Dynamics of European Union* Oxford, Oxford University Press

Ewing, K (1999) 'The Human Rights Act and Parliamentary Democracy' 62 *Modern Law Review* 79

Falk, R (1995) *On Humane Governance: Toward a New Global Politics* Cambridge, Polity Press

Feld, W, and Mahant, E (1986) 'New Efforts for European Union: Hopes, Progress, and Disappointments' 10 *Journal of European Integration* 39

Feldman, D (1999) 'The Human Rights Act 1998 and Constitutional Principles' 19 *Legal Studies* 665

Fenwick, H, and Hervey, T (1995) 'Sex Equality in the Single Market: New Directions for the European Court of Justice' 32 *Common Market Law Review* 443

Finkielraut, A (2001) *In the Name of Humanity: Reflections on the Twentieth Century* London, Pimlico

Fitzpatrick, P (1998) 'New Europe and Old Stories: Mythology and Legality in the European Union' in Fitzpatrick, P, and Bergeron, J (eds) *Europe's Other; European Law Between Modernity and Postmodernity* Aldershot, Ashgate

Flynn, L (1999) 'The Implications of Article 13 EC – After Amsterdam will Some Forms of Discrimination be more Equal than Others?' 36 *Common Market Law Review* 1127

Fredman, S (1992) 'European Community Discrimination Law: A Critique' 21 *Industrial Law Journal* 119

Freestone, D, and Davison, S (1986) 'The EUT: Legal Problems' in Lodge, J (ed) *European Union: The European Community in Search of a Future* New York, St Martins

Fried, C (2000) 'Markets, Law and Democracy' 11 *Journal of Democracy* 5

Friedman, T (2000) *The Lexus and the Olive Tree* New York, Anchor Books

Fukuyama, F (1992) *The End of History and the Last Man* London, Penguin

Gaja, G (1998) 'How Flexible is Flexibility under the Amsterdam Treaty?' 35 *Common Market Law Review* 855

Galbraith, J (1987) *The Affluent Society* London, Penguin

Galbraith, J (1991) *A History of Economics: The Past as the Present* London, Penguin

Galbraith, J (1996) *The Good Society: The Humane Agenda* London, Sinclair Stevenson

Garcia, S (1993) 'Europe's Fragmented Identities and the Frontiers of Citizenship' in Garcia, S (ed) *European Identity and the Search for Legitimacy* London, Pinter

Gardner, B (1987) 'The Common Agricultural Policy: The Political Obstacle to Reform' 58 *Political Quarterly* 167

Garry, H (2002) 'Harmonisation of Asylum Law and Policy within the European Union: A Human Rights Perspective' 20 *Netherlands Quarterly of Human Rights* 163

Garton Ash, T (2000) *History of the Present: Essays, Sketches and Despatches from Europe in the 1990s* London, Penguin

Gearty, C (1999) 'The Human Rights Act 1998 and the Role of the Strasbourg Organs: Some Preliminary Reflections' in Anderson, G (ed) *Rights and Democracy: Essays in UK–Canadian Constitutionalism* London, Blackstone

Geddes, A (1995) 'Immigrant and Ethnic Minorities and the EU's "Democratic Deficit"' 33 *Journal of Common Market Studies* 197

Geertz, C (1973) *The Interpretation of Cultures* London, Fontana

George, S (1990) *An Awkward Partner: Britain in the European Community* Oxford, Oxford University Press

George, S (1991) *Politics and Policy in the European Community* Oxford, Oxford University Press

Giddens, A (1998) *The Third Way: The Renewal of Social Democracy* Cambridge, Polity

Giddens, A, and Hutton, W (2000) 'In Conversation', in Hutton, W, and Giddens, A (eds) *On the Edge: Living with Global Capitalism* London, Jonathan Cape

Gill, S (1995) 'Globalisation, Market Civilization and Disciplinary Neo-Liberalism' 24 *Millennium* 399

Gilpin, R (1987) *The Political Economy of International Relations*, Princeton, Princeton University Press

Ginsberg, R (1999) 'Conceptualizing the European Union as an International Actor: Narrowing the Theoretical Capability–Expectations Gap' 37 *Journal of Common Market Studies* 429

Giraudon, V (2000) 'European Integration and Migration Policy: Vertical Policy-Making as Venue Shopping' 38 *Journal of Common Market Studies* 251

Glenny, M (1992) *The Fall of Yugoslavia: The Third Balkan War* London, Penguin

Goldsmith, Lord (2001) 'A Charter of Rights, Freedoms and Principles' 38 *Common Market Law Review* 1201

Goodrich, P (1992) 'Critical Legal Studies in England: Prospective Histories' 12 *Oxford Journal of Legal Studies* 195

Gould, M (1989) 'The European Social Charter and Community Law – A Comment' 14 *European Law Review* 223

Gray, J (1998) *False Dawn: The Delusions of Global Capitalism* London, Granta

Greenwood, S (1992) *Britain and European Cooperation Since 1945* Oxford, Blackwell

Guild, E (1996) 'The Legal Framework of Citizenship of the European Union' in Cesarini, D, and Fulbrook, M (eds) *Citizenship, Nationality and Migration in Europe*, London, Routledge

Guild, E (1999) 'The Impetus to Harmonise: Asylum P.olicy in the European Union' in Nicholson, F, and Twomey, P (eds) *Refugee Rights and Realities: Evolving International Concepts and Regimes* Cambridge, Cambridge University Press

Guild, E (2000) 'Between Persecution and Protection: Refugees and the New European Asylum Policy' 3 *Cambridge Yearbook of European Legal Studies* 169

Habermas, J (1990) *The Philosophical Discourse of Modernity* Cambridge, Polity

Habermas, J (1992) 'Citizenship and National Identity: Some Reflections on the Future of Europe' 12 *Praxis International* 1

Habermas, J (1995) *Postmetaphysical Thinking* Cambridge, Polity

Habermas, J (1996a) *Between Facts and Norms: Contributions to a Discourse Theory of Law and Democracy* Cambridge, Polity

Habermas, J (1996b) 'The European Nation State. Its Achievements and Its Limitations. On the Past and Future of Sovereignty and Citizenship' 9 *Ratio Juris* 125

Habermas, J (2001) *The Postnational Constellation* Cambridge, Polity

Hailbronner, K (1998) 'European Immigration and Asylum Law under the Amsterdam Treaty' 35 *Common Market Law Review* 1047

Hall, S (1991) 'The European Convention on Human Rights and the Public Policy Exceptions to the Free Movement of Workers under the EEC Treaty' 16 *European Law Review* 466

Hansen, L, and Williams, M (1999) 'The Myth of Europe: Legitimacy, Community and the Crisis of the EU' 37 *Journal of Common Market Studies* 233

Hansen, R (1998) 'A European Citizenship or a Europe of Citizens? Third Country Nationals in the EU' 24 *Journal of Ethnic and Migration Studies* 751

Hartley, T (1993) 'Constitutional and Institutional Aspects of the Maastricht Treaty' 42 *International and Comparative Law Quarterly* 213

Hartley, T (1996) 'The European Court, Judicial Objectivity and the Constitution of the European Union' 112 *Law Quarterly Review* 95

Hartley, T (1999) *Constitutional Problems of the European Union* Oxford, Hart

Harvie, C (1994) *The Rise of Regional Europe* London, Routledge

Hattersley, R (1997) *Fifty Years On: A Prejudiced History of Britain Since the War* London, Little, Brown

Havel, V (1992) *Summer Meditations: On Politics, Morality in Practice* New York, Fromm International

Hayek, F (1962) *The Road to Serfdom* London, Routledge

Hayek, F (1992) *Law, Legislation and Liberty: Liberal Principles of Justice and Political Economy* London, Routledge

Heater, D (1992) *The Idea of European Unity* Leicester, Leicester University

Heath, E (1988) 'European Unity Over the Next Ten Years: From Community to Union' 64 *International Affairs* 199

Hedemann-Robinson, M (1996) 'Third-Country Nationals, European Citizenship, and Free Movement of Persons: A Time for Bridges rather than Divisions' 16 *Yearbook of European Law* 321

Held, D (1995) *Democracy and Global Order: From the Modern State to Cosmopolitan Governance* Cambridge, Polity Press

Hennis, M (2001) 'Europeanization and Globalization: The Missing Link' 39 *Journal of Common Market Studies* 829

Hepple, B, and Byre, A (1989) 'EEC Labour Law in the United Kingdom – A New Approach' 18 *Industrial Law Journal* 129

Herdergen, M (1994) 'Maastricht and the German Constitutional Court: Constitutional Restraints for an "Ever Closer Union"' 31 *Common Market Law Review* 235

Herringa, A (2000) 'Towards an EU Charter of Fundamental Rights?' 7 *Maastricht Journal of European and Comparative Law* 111

Herrmann, C (2002) 'Common Commercial Policy After Nice: Sisyphus Would Have Done a Better Job' 39 *Common Market Law Review* 7

Hervey, T (1999) 'Putting Europe's House in Order: Racism, Race Discrimination and Xenophobia After the Treaty of Amsterdam' in O'Keeffe, D, and Twomey, P (eds) *Legal Issues of the Amsterdam Treaty* Oxford, Hart

Hiljemark, L (1997) 'Enforcement of EC Competition Law in National Courts – The Perspective of Judicial Protection' 17 *Yearbook of European Law* 83

Hill, C (1998) 'Closing the Capabilities–Expectation Gap', in Peterson, J, and Sjursen, H (eds) *A Common Foreign Policy for Europe?* London, Routledge

Hix, S (1994) 'The Study of the European Community: The Challenge to Comparative Politics' 17 *West European Politics* 1

Hoezler, H (1990) 'Merger Control' in Montagnon, P (ed) *European Competition Policy* London, Pinter

Hoffmann, S (1995) 'Reflections on the Nation-State in Europe Today' in Hoffmann, S (ed) *The European Sisyphus: Essays on Europe 1964–1994* Boulder, Westview

Hoffmann, S (2000) 'Towards a Common European Foreign and Security Policy?' 38 *Journal of Common Market Studies* 189

Holland, M (1994) *European Integration: From Community to Union* London, Pinter

Holland, S (1980) *The UnCommon Market* London, Macmillan

Holland, S (1993) *The European Imperative: Economic and Social Cohesion in the 1990s* London, Spokesman

Howe, G (1995) 'Sovereignty, Democracy and Human Rights' 66 *Political Quarterly* 127

Howe, P (1995) 'A Community of Europeans: The Requisite Underpinnings' 33 *Journal of Common Market Studies* 27

Howorth, J (2001) 'European Defence and the Changing Politics of the European Union: Hanging Together or Hanging Separately?' 39 *Journal of Common Market Studies* 765

Hunt, M (1999) 'The Human Rights Act and Legal Culture: The Judiciary and the Legal Profession' 26 *Journal of Law and Society* 423

Huntingdon, W (1997) *The Clash of Civilizations and the Remaking of World Order* New York, Simon & Schuster

Hutton, W (2002) *The World We're In* London, Little, Brown

Huysmans, J (2000) 'The European Union and the Securitazation of Migration' 38 *Journal of Common Market Studies* 751

Jacobi, O (1990) 'Elements of a European Community of the Future: A Trade Union View' in Crouch, C, and Marquand, D (eds) The Politics of 1992: *Beyond the Single European Market* Oxford, Blackwell

Jacobs, F (1992) 'Preparing English Lawyers for Europe' 17 *European Law Review* 232

Jacobs, F (1999) 'Public Law – The Impact of Europe' *Public Law* 232

Jacobs, F, and Klarst, K (1985) 'The "Federal" Legal Order: The USA and Europe Compared – A Juridical Perspective' in Cappelletti, M, et al (eds) *Integration Through Law* Berlin, de Gruyter

Joerges, C (2002) 'The Commission's White Paper on Governance in the EU – A Symptom of Crisis?' 39 *Common Market Law Review* 441

Jolowicz, J (1978) 'New Perspectives of a Common Law of Europe: Some Practical Aspects and the Case for Applied Comparative Law' in Cappelleti, M (ed) *New Perspectives for a Common Law of Europe* Florence, European University Institute

Joly, D (1999) 'A New Asylum Regime in Europe', in Nicholson, F, and Twomey, P (eds) *Refugee Rights and Realities: Evolving International Concepts and Regimes*, Cambridge, Cambridge University Press

Kahl, M (1997) 'European Integration, European Security, and the

Transformation of Central and Eastern Europe' 20 *Journal of European Integration* 153

Kant, I (1991) *The Metaphysics of Morals* Cambridge, Cambridge University Press

Kastendiek, H (1990) 'Convergence or a Persistent Diversity of National Politics' in Crouch, C, and Marquand, D (eds) *The Politics of 1992: Beyond the Single European Market* Oxford, Blackwell

Kay, J (1989) *1992: Myths and Realities* London, London Business School

Kemp, M, and Wan, H (1976) 'An Elementary Proposition Concerning the Formation of Customs Unions' 6 *Journal of International Economics* 95

Kitschelt, H (1995) 'A Silent Revolution in Europe?' in Hayward, J, and Page, E (eds) *Governing the New Europe* Cambridge, Polity

Klug, F (2000) *Values for a Godless Age: The Story of the United Kingdom's New Bill of Rights* London, Penguin

Koh, H (1997) 'Why Do Nations Obey International Law?' 106 *Yale Law Journal* 2599

Koopmans, T (1986) 'The Role of Law in the Next Stage of European Integration' 35 *International and Comparative Law Quarterly* 925

Koopmans, T (1991) 'The Birth of European Law at the Crossroads of Legal Traditions' 39 *American Journal of Comparative Law* 493

Kostakopoulou, T (1998) 'European Citizenship and Immigration After Amsterdam: Openings, Silences, Paradoxes' 24 *Journal of Ethnic and Migration Studies* 639

Kostakopoulou, T (2000) 'The Protective Union: Change and Continuity in Migration Law and Policy in Post-Amsterdam Europe' 38 *Journal of Common Market Studies* 497

Kristeva, J (1993) *Nations Without Nationalism* New York, Columbia

Lackhoff, K, and Nyssens, H (1998) 'Direct Effect of Directives in Triangular Situations' 23 *European Law Review* 397

Ladrech, R (1993) 'Parliamentary Democracy and Political Discourse in EC Institutional Change' 17 *Journal of European Integration* 53

Lange, D, and Sandage, J (1989) 'The *Woodpulp* Decision and its Implications for the Scope of EC Competition Law' 26 *Common Market Law Review* 137

Langrish, S (1998) 'The Treaty of Amsterdam: Selected Highlights' 23 *European Law Review* 3

Lasok,D, and Bridge, J (1994) *Law and Institutions of the European Communities* London, Butterworths

La Torre, M (2000) 'Legal Pluralism as an Evolutionary Achievement of European Community Law' in Snyder, F (ed) *The Europeanisation of Law: The Legal Effects of European Integration* Oxford, Hart

Laurent, P (1989) 'Historical Perspectives on Early European Integration' 12 *Journal of European Integration* 89

Lavenex, S (2001) 'The Europeanization of Refugee Policies: Normative Challenges and Institutional Legacies' 39 *Journal of Common Market Studies* 851

Lavigne, M (1995) 'Market Economics as Project and Practice' in Hayward, J, and Page, E (eds) *Governing the New Europe* Cambridge, Polity

Laws, J (1996) 'The Constitution: Morals and Rights' *Public Law* 622

Leibniz, G (1988) *Political Writings* Cambridge, Cambridge University Press

Lenaerts, K (1991) 'Fundamental Rights to be Included in a Community Catalogue' 16 *European Law Review* 367

Lenaerts, K (2000) 'Fundamental Rights in the European Union' 25 *European Law Review* 575

Lenaerts, K, and de Smijter, E (1999) 'The European Union as an Actor under International Law' 19 *Yearbook of European Law* 95

Lenz, C (1989) 'The Court of Justice of the European Communities' 14 *European Law Review* 127

Lenz, M, Tynes, D, and Young, L (2000) 'Horizontal What? Back to Basics' 25 *European Law Review* 509

Lewis, C, and Moore, S (1993) 'Duties, Directives and Damages in European Community Law' *Public Law* 151

Liisberg, J (2001) 'Does the EU Charter of Fundamental Rights Threaten the Supremacy of Community Law?' 38 *Common Market Law Review* 1171

Lipschutz, R (1992) 'Reconstructing World Politics: The Emergence of Global Civil Society' 21 *Millennium* 389

Lodge, J (1984) 'European Union and the First Elected European Parliament: The Spinelli Initiative' 22 *Journal of Common Market Studies* 337

Lodge, J (1986a) 'Institutional Provisions: Towards a Parliamentary Democracy' in Lodge, J (ed) *European Union: The European Community in Search of a Future* New York, St Martins

Lodge, J (1986b) 'The Single European Act: Towards a New Euro-Dynamism?' 24 *Journal of Common Market Studies* 203

Lodge, J (1990) 'Social Europe' 13 *Journal of European Integration* 135

Lodge, J (1993a) 'EC Policymaking: Institutional Dynamics' in Lodge, J (ed) *The European Community and the Challenge of the Future* London, Pinter

Lodge, J (1993b) 'Towards a Political Union?' in Lodge, J (ed) *The European Community and the Challenge of the Future* London, Pinter

Loughlin, M (1992) *Public Law and Political Theory* Oxford, Oxford University Press

Luckhaus, L (1990) 'Changing Rules, Enduring Structures' 53 *Modern Law Review* 655

Lyons, C (1998) 'The Politics of Alterity and Exclusion in the European Union' in Fitzpatrick, P, and Bergeron, J (eds), *Europe's Other: European Law Between Modernity and Postmodernity* Aldershot, Ashgate

Lyotard, J (1984) *The Postmodern Condition: A Report on Knowledge* Manchester, Manchester University Press

MacCormick, N (1993) 'Beyond the Sovereign State' 56 *Modern Law Review* 1

MacCormick, N (1999) *Questioning Sovereignty: Law, State and Nation in the European Commonwealth* Oxford, Oxford University Press

McDonald, F (1995) 'Completing the Internal Market in the European Union' in Healey, N (ed) *The Economics of the New Europe* London, Routledge

McGlynn, C (1995a) '*Webb v EMO*: A Hope for the Future?' 46 *Northern Ireland Legal Quarterly* 50

McGlynn, C (1995b) 'European Works Councils: Towards Industrial Democracy?' 14 *Industrial Law Journal* 78

McGlynn, C (2000a) 'A Family Law for the European Union?' in Shaw, J (ed) *Social Law and Policy in the European Union*, Oxford, Hart

McGlynn, C (2000b) 'Ideologies of Motherhood in European Community Sex Equality Law' 6 *European Law Journal* 29

McGlynn, C (2001a) 'Reclaiming a Feminist Vision: The Reconciliation of Paid Work and Family Life in European Union Law and Policy' 7 *Columbia Journal of European Law* 241

McGlynn C (2001b) 'Families and the European Charter of Fundamental Rights: Progressive Change of Entrenching the Status Quo?' 26 *European Law Review* 582

McGoldrick, D (1997) *International Relations Law of the European Union* London, Longman

McGoldrick, D (1999) 'The European Union After Amsterdam: An Organisation with General Human Rights Competence?', in O'Keeffe, D, and Twomey, P (eds) *Legal Issues of the Amsterdam Treaty*, Oxford, Hart

Mackenzie Stuart, Lord (1987) 'Problems of the European Community – Transatlantic Parallels' 36 *International and Comparative Law Quarterly* 183

Mackenzie Stuart, Lord (1992) 'Subsidiarity – A Busted Flush?' in Curtin, D, and O'Keeffe, D (eds) *Constitutional Adjudication in European Community Law and National Law* Dublin, Butterworths

MacKinnon, C (1994) 'Turning Rape into Pornography: Postmodern Genocide' in Stiglmayer, A (ed) *Mass Rape: The War Against Women in Bosnia–Herzegovina* Lincoln, Nebraska University Press

McMahon, J (2002) 'The Common Agricultural Policy: From Quantity to Quality' 53 *Northern Ireland Legal Quarterly* 9

MacShane, D (1995) 'Europe's Next Challenge to British Politics' 66 *Political Quarterly* 23

Maganza, G, and Piris, J (1999) 'The Amsterdam Treaty: Overview and Institutional Aspects' 22 *Fordham International Law Journal* 32

Maher, I (1996) 'Alignment of Competition Laws in the European Community' 16 *Yearbook of European Law* 223

Major, J (1999) *The Autobiography* London, HarperCollins

Mancini, F (1989) 'The Making of a Constitution for Europe' 26 *Common Market Law Review* 595

Mancini, F (1991) 'The Making of a Constitution for Europe' in Keohane, R, and Hoffmann, S (eds) *The New European Community: Decisionmaking and Institutional Change* Boulder, Westview

Mancini, F (1992) 'The Free Movement of Workers in the Case-Law of the European Court of Justice' in Curtin, D, and O'Keeffe, D (eds) *Constitutional Adjudication in European Community Law and National Law* Dublin, Butterworths

Mancini, F (1999) *Democracy and Constitutionalism in the European Union* Oxford, Hart

Mancini, F, and Keeling, D (1991) 'From *CILFIT* to *ERT*: the Constitutional Challenge facing the European Court' 11 *Yearbook of European Law* 1

Mancini, F, and Keeling, D (1994) 'Democracy and the European Court of Justice' 57 *Modern Law Review* 175

Manners, I, and Whitman, G (1998) 'Towards Identifying the International Identity of the European Union: A Framework for Analysis of the EU's Network of Relationships', 21 *European Integration* 231

Marin, R, and O'Connell, R (1999) 'The European Convention and the Relative Rights of Resident Aliens' 5 *European Law Journal* 4

Marshall, B (2000) 'Closer Integration or Re-nationalization? Recent Trends in EU Migration and Asylum Policies: the Case of Germany' 22 *Journal of European Integration* 409

Martin, C (1994) 'Furthering the Effectiveness of EC Directives and the Judicial Protection of Individual Rights Thereunder' 43 *International and Comparative Law Quarterly* 6

Marx, K (1975) *Capital* London, Lawrence & Wishart

Mayne, R (1966) 'The Role of Jean Monnet' 2 *Government and Opposition* 349

Mazey, S (1988) 'European Community Action on Behalf of Women: The Limits of Legislation' 27 *Journal of Common Market Studies* 63

Mearsheimer, J (1990) 'Back to the Future: Instability in Europe After the Cold War' 15 *International Security* 5

Meehan, E (1990) 'Sex Equality Policies in the European Community' 13 *Journal of European Integration* 185

Mill, J (1989) *Autobiography* London, Penguin

Mill, J (1994) *Principles of Political Economy* Oxford, Oxford University Press

Millett, Lord (2002) 'The Right to Good Administration in European Law' *Public Law* 309

Milward, A (1992) *The European Rescue of the Nation State* London, Routledge

Milward, A (1993) 'Conclusions: The Value of History' in Milward, A, et al (eds) *The Frontier of National Sovereignty* London, Routledge

Milward, A, and Soerensen, V (1993) 'Interdependence or Integration? A National Choice' in Milward, A, et al (eds) *The*

Frontier of National Sovereignty London, Routledge

Moebius, I, and Szyszczak, E (1998) 'Of Raising Pigs and Children' 18 *Yearbook of European Law* 125

Monar, J (1998) 'Justice and Home Affairs in the Treaty of Amsterdam: Reform at the Price of Fragmentation' 23 *European Law Review* 320.

Monar, J (2000) 'Enlarging the Area of Freedom, Security and Justice: Problems of Diversity and EU Instruments and Strategies' 3 *Cambridge Yearbook of European Legal Studies* 301

Monnet, J (1978) *Memoirs* London, Doubleday

Montagnon, P (1990) 'Introduction' in Montagnon, P (ed) *European Competition Policy* London, Pinter

More, G (1992) 'Reflections on Pregnancy Discrimination Under European Community Law' *Journal of Social Welfare and Family Law* 48

More, G (1999) 'The Principle of Equal Treatment: From Market Unifier to Fundamental Right?' in Craig, P, and de Burca, G (eds) *The Evolution of EU Law* Oxford, Oxford University Press

Mortelmans, K (1998) 'The Common Market, the Internal Market and the Single Market: What's in a Market?' 35 *Common Market Law Review* 101

Moxon-Browne, E (1993) 'Social Europe' in Lodge, J (ed) *The European Community and the Challenge of the Future* London, Pinter

Mullender, R (2000) 'Theorizing the Third Way: Qualified Consequentialism, the Proportionality Principle, and the New Social Democracy' 27 *Journal of Law and Society* 493

Murphy, P (1980) 'The Briand Memorandum and the Quest for European Unity 1929–1932' 4 *Contemporary French Civilization* 319

Nascimbene, B (1992) 'The Albanians in Italy: The Right of Asylum under Attack?' 3 *International Journal of Refugee Law* 714

Niarchos, C (1995) 'Women, War and Rape: Challenges Facing the International Tribunal for the Former Yugoslavia' 17 *Human Rights Quarterly* 649

Nicoll, W (1984a) 'The Luxembourg Compromise' 23 *Journal of Common Market Studies* 35

Nicoll, W (1984b) 'Paths to European Unity' 23 *Journal of Common Market Studies* 199

Noel, E (1989) 'The Single European Act' 24 *Government and Opposition* 3

Nussbaum, M (2000) *Women and Human Development: The Capabilities Approach* Cambridge, Cambridge University Press

Ohmae, K (1996) *The End of the Nation State and the Rise of Global Economics* London, HarperCollins

O'Keeffe, D (1991) 'The Schengen Convention: A Suitable Model for European Integration?' 11 *Yearbook of European Law* 185

O'Keeffe, D (1992a) 'Judicial Interpretation of the Public Policy Exception to the Free Movement of Workers' in Curtin, D, and O'Keeffe, D (eds) *Constitutional Adjudication in the European Community Law and National Law* Dublin, Butterworths

O'Keeffe, D (1992b) 'The Free Movement of Persons and the Single Market' 17 *European Law Review* 3

O'Keeffe, D (1994) 'Union Citizenship' in O'Keeffe, D, and Twomey, P (eds) *Legal Issues of the Maastricht Treaty* London, Chancery

O'Keeffe, D (1995) 'The Emergence of a European Immigration Policy' 20 *European Law Review* 20

O'Leary, O (1990) 'The Free Movement of Persons and Services', in Craig, P, and de Burca, G (eds) *The Evolution of EU Law* Oxford, Oxford University Press

O'Leary, S (1995) 'The Relationship Between Community Citizenship and the Protection of Fundamental Rights in Community Law' 32 *Common Market Law Review* 519

O'Leary, S (1999) 'The Free Movement of Persons and Services' in Craig, P, and de Burca, G (eds) *The Evolution of EU Law* Oxford, Oxford University Press

Oliver, D (1991) 'Fishing on the Incoming Tide' 54 *Modern Law Review* 442

Oliver, P (1994) 'The French Constitution and the Treaty of Maastricht' 43 *International and Comparative Law Quarterly* 1

Oliver, P (1999) 'Some Further Reflections on the Scope of Articles 28–30 (ex 30–36)' 36 *Common Market Law Review* 783

Paine, T (1985) *The Rights of Man* London, Penguin

Papandreou, V (1990) 'Free Movement of Qualified Labour: A Commissioner's Perspective' 13 *Journal of European Integration* 197

Peers, S (1996) 'Toward Equality: Actual and Potential Rights of

Third-Country Nationals in the European Union' 33 *Common Market Law Review* 7

Peers, S (1998) 'Building Fortress Europe: The Development of EU Migration Law' 35 *Common Market Law Review* 1235

Pentland, C (2000) 'Westphalian Europe and the EU's Last Enlargement' 22 *European Integration* 271

Pernice, I (1999) 'Multilevel Constitutionalism and the Treaty of Amsterdam: European Constitution-Making Revisited?' 36 *Common Market Law Review* 703

Pescatore, P (1983) 'The Doctrine of Direct Effect: An Infant Disease of the Community' 8 *European Law Review* 155

Pescatore, P (1987) 'Some Critical Remarks on the Single European Act' 24 *Common Market Law Review* 9

Pescatore, P (2001) 'Nice – Aftermath' 38 *Common Market Law Review* 265

Phelan, D (1992) 'Right to Life of the Unborn v Promotion of Trade in Services: The European Court of Justice and the Normative Shaping of the European Union' 55 *Modern Law Review* 670

Phillipart, E, and Edwards, G (1999) 'The Provisions on Closer Co-operation in the Treaty of Amsterdam: The Politics of Flexibility in the European Union' 37 *Journal of Common Market Studies* 87

Phuong, C (2003) 'Enlarging Fortress Europe: The Impact of EU Accession on Asylum and Immigration Laws and Policies in Candidate Countries' 53 *International and Comparative Law Quarterly* forthcoming

Pinder, J (1991) 'The European Community, the Rule of Law and Representative Government: The Significance of the Inter-governmental Conference' 26 *Government and Opposition* 199

Pinder, J (1993) 'The Single Market: A Step towards Union' in Lodge, J (ed) *The European Community and the Challenge of the Future* London, Pinter

Piris, J, (2000) 'The Treaty of Nice: An Imperfect Treaty but a Decisive Step Towards Enlargement' 3 *Cambridge Yearbook of European Law* 15

Pollack, M, and Hafner-Burton, E (2000) 'Mainstreaming Gender in the European Union' 7 *Journal of European Public Policy* 432

Posner, R (1986) *Economic Analysis of Law* Boston, Little Brown

Prechal, S (2000) 'Does Direct Effect Still Matter?' 37 *Common Market Law Review* 1047

Preuss, U (1995) 'Problems of a Concept of European Citizenship' 1 *European Law Journal* 267

Prodi, R (2000) *Shaping the New Europe* 15/2/2000 www.europa.eu.int

Prodi, R (2001) *Poland and Europe: Building on the Past, Shaping the Future* 10/3/2001 http://www.europa.eu.int

Pugliese, E (1995) 'New International Migrations and the European Fortress', in Hadjimichalis, C, and Sadler, D (eds) *Europe at the Margins: New Mosaics of Inequality* London, Chancery

Ransome, P (1991) *Towards the United States of Europe* London, Lothian Foundation

Rasmussen, H (1984) 'The European Court's *Acte Clair* Strategy in *CILFIT*' 9 *European Law Review* 242

Rasmussen, H (1986) *On Law and Policy in the European Court of Justice: A Comparative Study in Judicial Policy Making* Dordrecht, Nijhoff

Rawlings, R (1993) 'The Eurolaw Game: Some Deductions from a Saga' 10 *Journal of Law and Society* 309

Rawlings, R (1994a) 'Legal Politics: The United Kingdom and Ratification of the Treaty on European Union' *Public Law* 254

Rawlings, R (1994b) 'Legal Politics: The United Kingdom and Ratification of the Treaty on European Union' *Public Law* 367

Rawls, J (1993a) *Political Liberalism* New York, Columbia University Press

Rawls, J (1993b) 'The Law of Peoples' in Shute, S, and Hurley, S (eds) *On Human Rights: The Oxford Amnesty Lectures 1993* New York, Basic Books

Rawnsley, A (2000) *Servants of the People: The Inside Story of New Labour* London, Hamish Hamilton

Raworth, P (1994) 'A Timid Step Forwards: Maastricht and the Democratisation of the European Community' 19 *European Law Review* 16

Reiss, H (1991) *Kant's Political Writings* Cambridge, Cambridge University Press

Rhode, D (1990) 'Feminist Critical Theories' 42 *Stanford Law Review* 617

Riley, A (1989) 'The European Social Charter and Community Law' 14 *European Law Review* 80

Riley, P (1996) *Leibniz; Universal Jurisprudence: Justice as the Charity of the Wise* Cambridge, Mass, Harvard University Press

Robertson, A (1993) 'Effective Remedies in EEC Law Before the House of Lords?' 109 *Law Quarterly Review* 27

Robertson, Lord (2001) 'European Defence: Challenges and Prospects' 39 *Journal of Common Market Studies* 791

Roper, John (2000) 'Two Cheers for Mr Blair?: The Political Realities of European Defence Co-operation' 38 *Journal of Common Market Studies* 7

Rose, R (1995) 'Dynamics of Democratic Regimes' in Hayward, J, and Page, E (eds) *Governing the New Europe* Cambridge, Polity

Rosow, S (2000) 'Globalisation as Democratic Theory' 29 *Millennium* 27

Ross, G (1995) *Jacques Delors and European Integration* Cambridge, Polity

Ross, I (1995) *The Life of Adam Smith* Oxford, Oxford University Press

Ruzza, C (2000) 'Anti-Racism and EU Institutions' 22 *Journal of European Integration* 145

Salzman, T (1998) 'Rape Camps as a Means of Ethnic Cleansing: Religious, Cultural and Ethical Responses to Rape Victims in the Former Yugoslavia' 20 *Human Rights Quarterly* 348

Sandel, M (1996) *Democracy's Discontent: America in Search of a Public Philosophy* Cambridge, Mass, Harvard University Press

Santos, B (1995) *Towards a New Common Sense: Law, Science and Politics in Paradigmatic Transition* London, Routledge

Scheiwe, K (1994) 'EC Law's Unequal Treatment of the Family: The Case Law of the European Court of Justice on Rules Prohibiting Discrimination on Grounds of Sex and Nationality' 3 *Social and Legal Studies* 243

Schermers, H (1989) 'Is there a Fundamental Human Right to Strike?' 9 *Yearbook of European Law* 225

Schermers, H (1990) 'The Scales in the Balance: National Constitutional Court v Court of Justice' 27 *Common Market Law Review* 97

Schwarze, J (1986) 'The Administrative Law of the Community and the Protection of Human Rights' 23 *Common Market Law Review* 401

Schwarze, J (1991) 'Tendencies Towards a Common Administrative Law in Europe' 16 *European Law Review* 3

Schwarze, J (1992) *European Administrative Law* London, Sweet & Maxwell

Schwarze, J (2000) 'The Convergence of the Administrative Laws of the EU Member States', in Snyder, F (ed) *The Europeanisation of Law: The Legal Effects of European Integration* Oxford, Hart

Schwarze, J (2002) 'Constitutional Perspectives of the European Union with Regard to the Next Intergovernmental Conference in 2004' 8 *European Public Law* 241

Sciarra, S (1999) 'The Employment Title in the Amsterdam Treaty: A Multi-language Legal Discourse' in O'Keeffe, D, and Twomey, P (eds) *Legal Issues of the Amsterdam Treaty* Oxford, Hart

Scott, J (1995) *Development Dilemmas in the European Community: Rethinking Regional Development Policy* Buckingham, Open University

Sedley, S (1995) 'Human Rights: A Twenty-first Century Agenda' *Public Law* 386

Sen, A (1987) *On Ethics and Economics* Oxford, Blackwell

Shackleton, M (1985) 'The Politics of Fishing in Britain and France: Some Lessons for Community Integration' 9 *Journal of European Integration* 29

Shapiro, M (1999) 'The European Court of Justice', in Craig, P, and de Burca, G (eds) *The Evolution of EU Law* Oxford, Oxford University Press

Shaw, J (1993) *European Community Law* London, Macmillan

Shaw, J (1994) 'Twin-track Social Europe – the Inside Track' in O'Keeffe, D, and Twomey, P (eds) *Legal Issues of the Maastricht Treaty* London, Chancery

Shaw, J (1995) 'Decentralization and Law Enforcement in EC Competition law' 15 Legal Studies 128

Shaw, J (1997) 'The Many Pasts and Futures of Citizenship in the European Union' 22 *European Law Review* 554

Shaw, J (1998) 'The Treaty of Amsterdam: Challenges of Flexibility and Legitimacy' 4 *European Law Journal* 63

Shaw, J (2000a) 'Importing Gender: The Challenge of Feminism and the Analysis of the EU Legal Order' 7 *Journal of European Public Policy* 406

Shaw, J (2000b) 'Process and Constitutional Discourse in the European Union' 27 *Journal of Law and Society* 4

Shaw, J (2001) 'The Treaty of Nice: Legal and Constitutional Implications' 7 *European Public Law* 1195

Siedentop, L (2000) *Democracy in Europe* London, Penguin

Siune, K (1993) 'The Danes said No to the Maastricht Treaty: The

Danish EC Referendum of June 1992' 16 *Scandinavian Political Studies* 93

Slater, M (1982) 'Political Elites, Popular Indifferences and Community Building' 21 *Journal of Common Market Studies* 69

Slynn, G (1987) 'But in England there is no' in Fuerst, E (ed) *Festschrift fuer Wolfgang Zeilder* Berlin, de Gruyter

Smith, A (1976) *An Inquiry into the Nature and Causes of the Wealth of Nations* Oxford, Oxford University Press

Smith, A (1992) 'National Identity and the Idea of European Unity' 68 *International Affairs* 55

Smith, A (1994) 'Post-Modern Politics and the Case for Constitutional Renewal' 65 *Political Quarterly* 128

Smith, F (2000) 'Renegotiating Lomé: The Impact of the World Trade Organisation on the European Community's Development Policy After the *Bananas* Conflict' 25 *European Law Review* 247

Smith, J (2000) 'Enlarging Europe' 38 *Journal of Common Market Studies* 121

Smith, M (2001) 'Diplomacy by Degree: The Legalization of EU Foreign Policy' 39 *Journal of Common Market Studies* 79

Snyder, F (1985) *The Law of the Common Agricultural Policy* London, Sweet & Maxwell

Snyder, F (1990) *New Directions in European Community Law* London, Weidenfeld & Nicholson

Snyder, F (1999) 'EMU Revisited: Are We Making a Constitution? What Constitution Are We Making?' in Craig, P, and de Burca, G (eds) *The Evolution of EU Law* Oxford, Oxford University Press

Snyder, F (2000) 'Europeanisation and Globalisation as Friends and Rivals: European Union Law in Global Economic Networks', in Snyder, G (ed) *The Europeanisation of Law* Oxford, Hart

Sofaer (2000) 'International Law and Kosovo' 36 *Stanford Journal of International Law* 1

Sohrab, J (1994) 'Women and Social Security: The Limits of EEC Equality Law' *Journal of Social Welfare and Family Law* 5

Sorensen, V (1993) 'Between Interdependence and Integration: Denmark's Shifting Strategies' in Milward, A, et al *The Frontier of National Sovereignty: History and Theory 1945–1992* London, Routledge

Soros, G (2000) *Open Society: Reforming Global Capitalism* London, Little, Brown

Spencer, M (1995) *States of Injustice: A Guide to Human Rights and Civil Liberties in the European Union* London, Pluto

Spicker, P (2000) 'A Third Way?' 5 *European Legacy* 229

Stein, E (1983) 'The European Community in 1983: A Less Perfect Union?' 10 *Common Market Law Review* 641

Stiglmayer (1994) 'The War in Former Yugoslavia' in Stiglmayer, A (ed) *Mass Rape: The War Against Women in Bosnia–Herzegovina* Lincoln, Nebraska University Press

Story, J (1990) 'Europe's Future: Western Union or Common Home?' in Crouch, C, and Marquand, D (eds) *The Politics of 1992: Beyond the Single European Market* Oxford, Blackwell

Story, J (1990) 'Social Europe: Ariadne's Thread' 13 *Journal of European Integration* 151

Strange, S (1998) 'Who are EU? Ambiguities in the Concept of Competitiveness' 36 *Journal of Common Market Studies* 101

Stuyck, J (2000) 'European Consumer Law After the Treaty of Amsterdam: Consumer Policy in or Beyond the Internal Market?' 37 *Common Market Law Review* 367

Sutherland, P (1992) 'Joining the Threads: The Influences Creating a European Union' in Curtin, D, and O'Keeffe, D (eds) *Constitutional Adjudication in European Community Law and National Law* Dublin, Butterworths

Swann, D (1992) 'The Single Market and Beyond – an Overview' in Swann, D (ed) *The Single European Market and Beyond* London, Routledge

Swinbank, A (1989) 'The Common Agricultural Policy and the Politics of European Decision Making' 27 *Journal of Common Market Studies* 303

Szyszczak, E (1992) '1992 and the Working Environment' *Journal of Social Welfare and Family Law* 3

Szyszczak, E (1994) 'Social Policy: A Happy Ending or a Reworking of the Fairy Tale?' in O'Keeffe, D, and Twomey, P (eds) *Legal Issues of the Maastricht Treaty* London, Chancery

Szyszczak, E (1996) 'Making Europe More Relevant to its Citizens: Effective Judicial Process' 21 *European Law Review* 351

Szyszczak, E (2001) 'A New Paradigm for Social Policy: A Virtuous Circle?' 38 *Common Market Law Review* 1125

Tartwijk-Novey, L (1995) *The European House of Cards* London, Macmillan

Taylor, C (1989) 'The Liberal-Communitarian Debate' in Rosenblum, N (ed) *Liberalism and the Moral Life* Cambridge, Mass, Harvard University Press

Teague, P (1989) *The European Community: The Social Dimension* London, Kogan Page

Teague, P (1993) 'Coordination or Decentralization? EC Social Policy and Industrial Relations' in Lodge, J (ed) *The European Community and the Challenge of the Future* London, Pinter

Teasdale, A (1993) 'Subsidiarity in Post-Maastricht Europe' 64 *Political Quarterly* 187

Thatcher, M (1993) *The Downing Street Years* London, HarperCollins

Therborn, G (1995) *European Modernity and Beyond: The Trajectory of European Societies 1945–2000* London, Sage

Timmermans, C (1997) 'Community Directives Revisited' 17 *Yearbook of European Law* 1

Timmermans, C (1999) 'The EU and Public International Law' 4 *European Foreign Affairs Review* 181

Tomkins, A (1999) 'Transparency and the Emergence of a European Administrative Law' 19 *Yearbook of European Law* 217

Tovias, A (1994) 'A Survey of the Theory of Economic Integration' in Michelmann, H, and Soldatos, P (eds) *European Integration: Theories and Approaches* Lanham, University Press of America

Tridimas, T (1996) 'The Court of Justice and Judicial Activism' 21 *European Law Review* 199

Tsoukalis, L (1991) *The New European Economy: The Politics and Economics of Integration* Oxford, Oxford University

Twining, W (2000) *Globalization and Legal Theory* London, Butterworths

Twomey, P (1994) 'The European Union: Three Pillars without a Human Rights Foundation' in O'Keeffe, D, and Twomey, P (eds) *Legal Issues of the Maastricht Treaty* London, Chancery

Unger, R (1983) *The Critical Legal Studies Movement* Cambridge, Mass, Harvard University Press

Urwin, D (1995) *The Community of Europe: A History of European Integration since 1945* London, Longman

Usher, J (2000) 'Flexibility – the Experience So Far' 3 *Yearbook of European Legal Studies* 479

Van Gerven, W (2002) 'Codifying European private law? Yes, if..!' 27 *European Law Review* 156

Verhoeven, A (1998) 'How Democratic Need European Union Members Be? Some Thoughts After Amsterdam' 23 *European Law Review* 217

Volcansek, M (1992) 'The European Court of Justice: Supranational Policy-Making' 15 *West European Politics* 109

Von Bogdandy (2000a) 'The European Union as a Supranational Federation: A Conceptual Attempt in the Light of the Amsterdam Treaty' 6 *Columbia Journal of European Law* 27

Von Bogdandy (2000b) 'The European Union as a Human Rights Organization? Human Rights and the Core of the European Union' 37 *Common Market Law Review* 1307

Waddington, L, and Bell, M (2001) 'More Equal Than Others: Distinguishing European Union Equality Directives' 38 *Common Market Law Review* 587

Wade, W (1991a) 'What has Happened to the Sovereignty of Parliament?' 107 *Law Quarterly Review* 1

Wade, W (1991b) 'Injunctive Relief Against the Crown and Ministers' 107 *Law Quarterly Review* 4

Walker, M (2000) 'Variable Geography: America's Mental Maps of a Greater Europe' 76 *International Affairs* 459

Walker, N (2002) 'The Idea of Constitutional Pluralism' 65 *Modern Law Review* 317

Wallace, H (1994) 'European Governance in Turbulent Times' in Bulmer, S, and Scott, A (eds) *Economic and Political Integration in Europe: Internal Dynamics and Global Context* Oxford, Blackwell

Wallace, W (1982) 'Europe as a Confederation: The Community and the Nation-State' 21 *Journal of Common Market Studies* 57

Wallace, W (2000) 'From the Atlantic to the Bug, from the Arctic to the Tigris? The Transformation of the EU and NATO' 76 *International Affairs* 475

Walters, A (1992) 'The Brussels Leviathan' in Minford, P (ed) *The Cost of Europe* Manchester, Manchester University Press

Ward, I (1994) 'The Story of M: A Cautionary Tale from the United Kingdom' 6 *International Journal of Refugee Law* 194

Ward, I (1998) *An Introduction to Critical Legal Theory* London, Cavendish.

Ward, I (2001) 'Beyond Constitutionalism: The Search for a European Political Imagination' 7 *European Law Journal* 24

Ward, I (2003) *Justice, Humanity and the New World Order* Aldershot, Ashgate

Watson, P (1991) 'The Community Social Charter' 28 *Common Market Law Review* 37

Weatherill, S (1996) 'After *Keck*: Some Thoughts on how to Clarify the Clarification' 33 *Common Market Law Review* 885

Weatherill, S (1999) 'Recent Case Law Concerning the Free Movement of Goods: Mapping the Frontiers of Market Deregulation' 36 *Common Market Law Review* 51

Wedderburn, Lord (1991) 'The Social Charter in Britain: Labour Law and Labour Courts' 54 *Modern Law Review* 1

Weigall, D, and Stirk, P (1992) *The Origins and Development of the European Community* Leicester, Leicester University Press

Weiler, J (1986) 'Eurocracy and Distrust: Some Questions Concerning the Role of the European Court of Justice in the Protection of Fundamental Rights within the Legal Order of the European Communities' 61 *Washington Law Review* 1103

Weiler, J (1989) 'Pride and Prejudice – Parliament v Council' 14 *European Law Review* 334

Weiler, J (1991a) 'The Transformation of Europe' 100 *Yale Law Journal* 2403

Weiler, J (1991b) 'Problems of Legitimacy in Post 1992 Europe' 46 *Aussenwissenschraft* 411

Weiler, J (1992) '"Thou Shalt Not Oppress a Stranger": On the Judicial Protection of the Human Rights of Non-EC Nationals – A Critique' 3 *European Journal of International Law* 65

Weiler, J (1998) 'Bread and Circus: The State of European Union' 4 *Columbia Journal of European Law* 223

Weiler, J (1999a) *The Constitution of Europe* Cambridge, Cambridge University Press

Weiler, J (1999b) 'Prologue: Amsterdam and the Quest for Constitutional Democracy' in O'Keeffe, D, and Twomey, P (eds) *Legal Issues of the Amsterdam Treaty* London, Hart

Wessel, R (2000) 'The Inside Looking Out: Consistency and Delimitation in EU External Relations' 37 *Common Market Law Review* 1135

Wesseling, R (1997) 'Subsidiarity in Community Antitrust Law: Setting the Right Agenda' 22 *European Law Review* 35

Wessels, W (1991) 'The EC Council: The Community's Decisionmaking Centre' in Keohane, R, and Hoffmann, S (eds) *The New European Community: Decisionmaking and Industrial Change* Boulder, Westview

Wessels, W (2001) 'Nice Results: The Millennium IGC in the EU's Evolution' 39 *Journal of Common Market Studies* 197

Westlake, M (1998) 'The European Union's "Blind Watchmakers": The Process of Constitutional Change' in Westlake, M (ed) *The European Union Beyond Amsterdam: New Concepts of European Integration* London, Routledge

White, S, et al (2002) 'Enlargement and the New Outsiders' 40 *Journal of Common Market Studies* 135

Whiteford, E (1993) 'Social Policy After Maastricht' 18 *European Law Review* 202

Whynes, D (1995) 'After 1992: The Political Economy of the Single European Act' in Healey, N (ed) *The Economics of the New Europe* London, Routledge

Williams, A (1991) *The European Community* Oxford, Blackwell

Williams, A (2000) 'Enlargement of the Union and Human Rights Conditionality: A Policy of Distinction?' 25 *European Law Review* 601

Williams, P (1991) *The Alchemy of Race and Rights* Cambridge, Mass, Harvard University Press

Williams, S (1991) 'Sovereignty and Accountability in the European Community' in Keohane, E, and Hoffmann, S (eds) *The New European Community: Decisionmaking and Industrial Change* Boulder, Westview

Williams, S (1995) 'Britain in the European Union: A Way Forward' 66 *Political Quarterly* 5

Wincott, D (1995) 'The Role of Law or the Rule of Law in the ECJ?' 2 *Journal of European Public Policy* 583

Wincott, D (2001) 'Looking Forward or Harking Back? The Commission and the Reform of Governance in the European Union' 39 *Journal of Common Market Studies* 897

Wise, M, and Gibb, R (1993) *Single Market to Social Europe: The European Community in the 1990s* London, Longman

Wistrich, E (1994) *The United States of Europe* London, Routledge

Woodward, S (2000) 'War: Building States from Nations' in Tariq Ali (ed) *Masters of the Universe? NATO's Balkan Crusade* London, Verso

Woolf, Lord (1995) 'Droit Public – English Style' *Public Law* 57

Wyatt, D (1988) 'The Direct Effect of Community Social Law – Not Forgetting Directives' 8 European Law Review 241

Wyatt, D (1989) 'Enforcing EEC Social Rights in the United Kingdom' 18 *Industrial Law Journal* 197

Wyatt, D, and Dashwood, A (1993) *European Community Law* London, Sweet & Maxwell

Yataganas, X (2001) 'The Treaty of Nice: The Sharing of Power and the Institutional Balance of the European Union – a Continental Perspective' 7 *European Law Journal* 242

Young, D, and Metcalfe, S (1994) 'Competition Policy' in Artis, M, and Lee, N (eds) *The Economics of the European Union* Oxford, Oxford University Press

Young, H (1998) *This Blessed Plot: Britain and Europe from Churchill to Blair* London, Macmillan

Young, J (1993) *Britain and European Unity 1945–1992* London, Macmillan

Young, J (1999) 'The Politics of the Human Rights Act' 26 *Journal of Law and Society* 27

Zuern, M (2000) 'Democratic Governance Beyond the Nation-State: The EU and other International Institutions' 6 *European Journal of International Relations* 183

Index

Introduction. The index covers Chapters 1 to 8. Index entries are to page numbers. Alphabetical arrangement is word-by-word, where a group of letters followed by a space is filed before the same group of letters followed by a letter, eg 'Equal work' will appear before 'Equality'.